Michael Meredith

SOCIETY
AND THE
HOLY
IN LATE
ANTIQUITY

SOCIETY AND THE holy IN LATE ANTIQUITY

PETER BROWN

faber and faber

First published in 1982
by Faber and Faber Limited
3 Queen Square London WC1N 3AU
Printed in the United States of America
by Vail-Ballou Press, Binghamton, New York

British Library Cataloguing in Publication Data

Brown, Peter, 1935–
    Society and the holy in late antiquity.
    1. Sociology, Christian—Addresses, essays, lectures.
    I. Title.
    261.1   BT738

ISBN 0-571-11686-8

CONTENTS

v

CONTENTS

PREFACE

I have brought together these articles, the fruit of a decade of work since the appearance of my *Religion and Society in the Age of Saint Augustine*, in the hope that to have them collected in one volume would be both convenient and even, perhaps, instructive to the reader. I have, therefore, added between square brackets those works which have since become available to me, that appear to me to add to the argument of those articles which already carried footnotes; and I have added some footnotes, in much the same spirit, to articles and reviews which either appeared without footnotes or which appear to me now to carry insufficient documentation.

I trust that the reader will find in these additions some indication of the heartening progress of Late Antique studies in so many directions in one single decade. The reader must also be warned that I also, I trust, have learned much from this progress, and should, therefore, pay especial attention to those articles to which I refer as having modified or criticized my opinions on many topics, in such a way that I would certainly treat these topics in a very different manner were I to write on them at the present time.

Peter Brown
Department of Classics
University of California
Berkeley
December, 1979

PART I
APPROACHES

Learning and Imagination[†]

I T IS ONLY TOO EASY TO PRESENT THE STUDY OF history in a modern university system as if it were a discipline for the mind alone, and so to ignore the slow and erratic processes which go to the enrichment of the imagination. Yet it is precisely this imaginative curiosity about the past that is a unique feature of western civilization. Since the eighteenth century, we westerners have taken pleasure, and even thought to derive wisdom, from a persistent attempt to project ourselves into the thoughts and feelings of men and women whose claim to our respect was precisely that they were sensed to be profoundly different from ourselves. This unique respect for the otherness of the past and of other societies did not begin in archives; nor was it placed in the centre of European culture by antiquarians. It began among dreamers and men of well-stocked imagination. The taproots of the western historical tradition go deep into the rich and far from antiseptic soil of the Romantic movement. By the standards of a well-run History Department, the Grand Old Men of the historical tribe were wild and woolly. Giam-

[†]An Inaugural Lecture delivered at Royal Holloway College on 26 May 1977. I have appended references only to citations and to some principal authors: the themes I touch on are dealt with more fully both in the articles collected here and in my Haskell Lectures at the University of Chicago, *The Cult of the Saints: Its Rise and Function in Latin Christianity* (Chicago: University of Chicago Press; London: SCM Press, 1981).

battista Vico, author of the *Scienza Nuova*, abandoned law in his youth to write poetry—and emerged a better historian for it. 'For at this age,' he wrote, 'the mind should be given free rein to keep the fiery spirit of youth from being numbed and dried up, lest from too great severity of judgement, proper to maturity but too early acquired, they should later scarcely dare to attempt anything.'[1]

In the middle of an exacting history course, it takes a high degree of moral courage to resist one's own conscience: to take time off; to let the imagination run; to give serious attention to reading books that widen our sympathies, that train us to imagine with greater precision what it is like to be human in situations very different from our own.

It is essential to take that risk. For a history course to be content to turn out well-trained minds when it could also encourage widened hearts and deeper sympathies would be a mutilation of the intellectual inheritance of our own discipline. It would lead to the inhibition, in our own culture, of an element of imaginative curiosity about others whose removal may be more deleterious than we would like to think to the subtle and ever-precarious ecology on which a liberal western tradition of respect for others is based.

In warm and lucid pages, my teacher, Arnaldo Momigliano, a man who can both represent and embrace in his own writings the full richness of the western tradition of historical learning, has warned us ever more frequently that the grip of the study of history on the face of a great culture can be a mere finger-hold. Greeks, Romans and Jews slid with disquieting ease from the frustrations of the study of the past to take their rest in the eternal verities of science and religion. They readily preferred what was, or could claim to be, a 'discipline for the mind', abstract, rigorous and certain, to a study of ambiguous status that involved the clash of critical opinion on issues that intimately affected their estimate of

1. *The Autobiography of Giambattista Vico*, trans. M. H. Fisch and T. G. Bergin (Ithaca, 1944), p. 118.

4

their fellows, that exposed them to the strains of travel and political experience, and that might even commit the articulate and intelligent man to the tiresome labour of learning foreign languages.[2]

Pro nobis fabula narratur. If the capacity for imaginative curiosity is part of our handhold on the culture of our age, then it becomes all the more urgent to insist that we train this imagination; that we ask ourselves whether the imaginative models that we bring to the study of history are sufficiently precise and differentiated, whether they embrace enough of what we sense to be what it is to be human, to enable us to understand and to communicate to others the sheer challenge of the past.

As an historian of Late Antiquity, I have been brought up against this issue in an abrupt form. I have been forced to understand nothing less than the dynamics of a religious revolution. Faced by such a challenge, the historian has to take time off for a moment: he has to allow his imagination to be chastened and refined. He has to examine the imaginative models, handed down to him from within his own tradition of learning, that affect his views on a subject as profound as the nature and workings of the religious sentiment in society.

What I had wished to understand is an aspect of the religious revolution of Late Antiquity that has left a permanent mark on the life, even on the landscape, of western Europe— the rise of the cult of saints and of their relics. What I found was that interpretation of this phenomenon is a cross-roads at which the conflicting imaginative models that we bring to the understanding of Late Antiquity as a whole can be seen to converge.

Let me begin by sketching out the phenomenon, as it appears in its most concrete form: the genius of Late Antique men lay in their ability to map out, to localize and to render magnificently palpable by every device of art, ceremonial,

2. See, most recently, A. D. Momigliano, *Alien Wisdom: The Limits of Hellenisation* (Cambridge, 1975).

religious practice and literature those few, clearly-delineated points at which the visible and the invisible worlds met on earth.

As Professor Hussey wrote of a Byzantine entering a church: 'as he entered the narthex or stood in the nave, the participant in the services did not simply learn something about the great truths of Christian teaching, but he could realise that he himself was actually present in both seen and unseen worlds.'[3]

The peculiar feature of the rise of Christianity was that these points of joining coincided to an ever-increasing degree with human beings. A Late Antique landscape was dotted with human figures, each of whom was held to be a point where heaven and earth were joined. They were the living dead: ascetic holy men, whose life-style involved them in prolonged and clearly visible rituals of self-mortification and 'death' to society. Then there were the dead who lay in their tombs. Because they had made themselves 'dead' to the world when alive, all that was most alive in this world—healing, vision and justice—could be seen to spring from the dust of their bodies, to show how fully they now lived in the other world.

By the sixth century, a network of shrines containing complete tombs or fragments of dead bodies covered the Mediterranean. These would often be called, quite simply, ὁ τόπος: 'The Place'. In 600 A.D., an enterprising gang of burglars could move from the 'place' of St Colluthos near Antinoe, in Egypt, walk a few miles upstream to the 'place' of St Victor Stratelates, cross over the Nile to the 'place' of St Timothy, and head downstream again to the 'place' of St Claudius, reaping, in a good night's work, a heavy swag of silver ornaments and *ex voto* offerings.

At such a 'place', the iron laws of the grave were suspended. In a relic, the anonymity of human remains could be

3. J. M. Hussey, 'The Byzantine Empire in the Eleventh Century: Some Different Interpretations', *Transactions of the Royal Historical Society*, 4 s., XXXII (1950): 79.

thought to be still heavy with the fullness of a beloved person. As Gregory of Nyssa said: 'Those who behold them embrace, as it were, the living body in full flower, they bring eye, mouth, ear, all the senses into play, and there, shedding tears of reverence and passion, they address the martyr their prayers of intercession as though he were present.'[4]

Such places, therefore, were created to pinpoint relations with invisible human beings. The sensibilities of Late Antique men came increasingly to be moulded by a need to achieve *closeness* to a specific category of fellow-humans—the saints. Hence the highly concrete manner in which the striving for closeness was mapped out on the ground in terms of physical distance. The pilgrim covers long and arduous distances to his shrine. But the pilgrim is only a special case. Every believer has to put himself out to make a visit; and in Late Antiquity this visit would usually have taken him away from the classical centre of his city to its peripheral cemetery areas. This is what the senator Pinianus did in early fifth-century Rome, when his wife was facing a miscarriage: he ran out to the graveyard shrine of St Lawrence, and spent the night stretched in prayer before the tomb—*ad Dominum Laurentium*, 'at the Lord Lawrence's'.

The best occasion is when the invisible person visits you: hence the high drama, in all Late Antique and early medieval literature, that surrounds the discovery, the translation and the arrival of relics. The dialectic of closeness is highlighted in the festivals of the saints: crowds 'swarm like bees' around the tomb; and the saint himself makes his presence felt all the more strongly by a ceremonial closely modelled on the *adventus*, the 'arrival in state', of a Late Roman emperor.

After death, to lie close to the grave of the saint is a privilege reserved for the few. The western practice of *depositio ad sanctos* provided each community with a clear map of the ranking-order of its departed members, in the patchwork of mosaic plaques that clustered around the holy grave: 'Pro-

4. Gregory of Nyssa, *Encomium on Saint Theodore*, P.G. XLVI, 740B.

bilianus . . . for Hilaritas, a woman whose chastity and good nature was known to all the neighbours. . . . She remained chaste for eight years in my absence, and for this reason she lies in this holy place.'[5]

I have spent some time sketching the immediate visible effects of the Late Antique cult of saints. The rise to power in Western Europe of the Catholic Church was intimately connected with this localization of the holy. It was by orchestrating and controlling the religious life of the great urban shrines of the western Mediterranean, from Rome to Mérida, and from Tours to Carthage and Tebessa, that the bishops of the early medieval West gained their unique position in society. The development itself is so clear a feature of the ecclesiastical history of the Middle Ages that the revolution on which it is based has very largely been taken for granted. I would suggest that this is so because our curiosity for the subject has been blocked by an imaginative model that is not sufficiently sensitive to help us enter into the thought-processes and the needs that went into the rapid creation and expansion of the cult of saints in the Late Antique period.

The religious history of Late Antiquity and the early Middle Ages still owes more than we realize to attitudes summed up so persuasively in the 1750s by David Hume in his essay, *The Natural History of Religion*. For Hume faced squarely the problems of the origins of religious sentiment and presented these origins in terms of the way that men habitually think about their environment. Men, he insisted, were not natural monotheists who, through sin, had lost the original simplicity of vision of Adam and the Jewish patriarchs. Theism remains an ideal, but it is a precarious ideal. The reason for this lies no longer in human sinfulness, but rather in the intellectual, and, by implication, the cultural and social preconditions for attaining a theistic view of the world. Theism depended on achieving a coherent and rational view of the universe from which the enlightened mind might then deduce

5. E. Diehl, *Inscriptiones latinae christianae veteres* I (Berlin, 1925), 2157.

the existence of a Supreme Being. Hence the extreme rarity of monotheism in human history. For 'the vulgar, that is all mankind, a few excepted,' have always lived in an intellectual and cultural milieu that tended to fragment those experiences of order on which a coherent view of the universe might be based. The average man was unable to abstract general principles from his immediate environment; and, in any case, in most ages this limitation was compounded by the fears and anxieties of day-to-day existence.

The history of mankind, therefore, is not a simple history of decline from an original theism: it is marked by a constant tension between theistic and polytheistic ways of thinking. 'It is remarkable that the principles of religion have had a flux and reflux in the human mind, and that men have a natural tendency to rise from idolatry to theism and to sink again from theism to idolatry.'[6] Hume's short essay owes its cogency to the concrete manner in which he enabled his Christian readers to enter with some degree of understanding into the minds of men for whom polytheism had been the norm. In so doing he provided historians with an imaginative model whose influence has remained all the more pervasive for having entered so imperceptibly into the tradition of historical learning.

For Hume's characteristically sad and measured assessment of the concrete circumstances of human thinking provided him with a model of the social and cultural preconditions for the evolution of religious thought. The idea of a 'flux and reflux in the human mind' could be given a historical dimension. The respective rise and fall of theism and idolatry could be assessed in terms of the relative balance of the rational and the irrational elements in a society. That balance could be given a clear social *locus* by assessing the distribution and relative influence of 'the vulgar' in relation to the potentially enlightened few; and change could be ac-

6. David Hume, *The Natural History of Religion* VIII, in *Essays, Moral, Political and Literary* II (London, 1875), 334.

counted for by assessing shifts in the balance between the two and in the degree of anxiety and disruption, hence the increase of fears that bring about that 'reflux in the human mind', which Hume associated with the polytheistic manner of conceiving the world.

This is hardly a model calculated to see the best in the springing up around the Late Antique Mediterranean world of impenitently concretized *loci* of the holy, drawing great crowds, in the wake of the spread of Christianity, the theistic system *par excellence*.

Yet, if anything, it was the religious revival of the nineteenth century that hardened the outlines of Hume's model, and that has made it an integral part of our interpretation of early medieval Christianity. Milman's *History of Latin Christianity* shows how this could happen. He could present the spread of the cult of saints in Dark Age Europe in a manner touched with Romantic enthusiasm. But Hume's model was part of Milman's mental furniture. For he identified the theism of the enlightened few with the elevated message of the leaders of the Christian Church; and the barbarian settlers of Europe, though their mental processes might be deemed by Milman, the post-Romantic, as 'poetic' (not, as Gibbon had said more bluntly, 'fierce and illiterate'), nevertheless retained to the full the qualities of Hume's 'vulgar'. They represented modes of thinking that fell far below those of the more enlightened leaders of the Catholic Church. Thus the balance between the few and the masses remains at the centre of Milman's picture. As Duncan Forbes has seen so clearly in his *Liberal Anglican Idea of History*: 'The relation, then, between Christianity and the course of history is one of condescension.'[7] 'Now had commenced', Milman wrote, 'what may be called, neither unreasonably nor unwarrantably, the mythic age of Christianity. As Christianity worked downwards into the lower classes of society, as it received the crude and igno-

7. Duncan Forbes, *The Liberal Anglican Idea of History* (Cambridge, 1952), p. 79.

rant barbarians within its pale, the general effect could not but be, that the age would drag down the religion to its level, rather than the religion elevate the age to its own lofty standard.'[8]

Paradoxically, the renewed loyalty of sensitive and learned minds to the religious traditions of the past, in Anglicanism and Catholicism alike, heightened the lack of sympathy for the thought-processes of the average man. Many thinkers, though prepared as Hume had never been to accept the dogmas handed down to them from the past, had entered sufficiently deeply into the world of early medieval Catholicism to know that, by their standards, the river of Christian doctrine has flowed along strange and muddy banks: 'The religion of the multitude is ever vulgar and abnormal; it will ever be the tinctured with fanaticism and superstition, while men are what they are. A people's religion is ever a corrupt religion.'[9] Not Hume this time . . . but John Henry, Cardinal Newman.

It is by these stages that Hume's model came insensibly to permeate the great tradition of liberal Anglican and Catholic scholarship that has fostered so much of the learning on which the ecclesiastical history of the Late Antique and medieval world is based.

The most enduring feature in that tradition is Hume's 'two-tier' model for the development of religious sentiments in any society. In this model, the views of the potentially enlightened few are subjected to continuous upward pressure from the habitual thought-processes of the 'vulgar'. Pessimistic though he was about the few—far more pessimistic than those robust and upright Victorians we have just described—Hume had few doubts about who constituted the 'vulgar': they included, for instance, all women: 'What age or period of life is most addicted to superstition? The weakest and the most timid. What sex? The same answer must be

8. H. Milman, *A History of Latin Christianity*, III (New York, 1903), 417.
9. J. H. Newman, *Difficulties of Anglicans*, II (London, 1891), 80–81.

given. *The leaders of every kind of superstition*, says Strabo, *are the women. These excite men to devotion and supplications, and the observance of religious days.*' [10]

Applied to the study of the religious history of Late Antiquity, the 'two-tier' model encourages the historian to assume that any change in the piety of Late Antique men must have been the result of the intrusion into the élites of the Christian Church of modes of thought current among the masses; and that these changes coincided with massive external events, such as fear and anxiety caused by the barbarian invasions or disorientation caused by mass-conversions to Christianity. Such religious phenomena are deemed to belong to the category of 'popular religion'. The category of 'popular religion' is, by definition, timeless and faceless, because it exhibits modes of thinking that are unintelligible except in terms of failure to be something else—failure through the pressures of anxiety, failure through the absence of the cultural and social preconditions of rational thought, failure through that hard fate that has condemned half of the population of any age, through the accident of gender, to being members of 'that timorous and pious sex'.

Hence the relief with which the historian turns from his own learned tradition to other strands in the culture of his own age. The prevalent model of a split between the rational few and the irrational many cannot long survive a reading of Evans-Pritchard's patient laying-bare of the intricate inner logic of a seemingly fearsome and irrational system of beliefs, in his *Witchcraft, Oracles and Magic among the Azande*. A respect for the checks and balances with which small communities can be acutely observed to live, twenty-four hours of the day, with the facts of the blood feud or the localized presence of the supernatural in their midst, demonstrated by Max Gluckman's *Custom and Conflict in Modern Africa* and in Ernest Gellner's penetrating *Saints of the Atlas*, goes no small way to answer a tradition of explanation that gives pride of place to physical insecurity and to unmodified fear of invisi-

10. David Hume, *The Natural History of Religion*, III, *Essays*, 319.

ble forces in its rhetoric of explanation, when presenting the religious changes of the early medieval world. The rigorous artistry with which Mary Douglas, in her *Purity and Danger* and her *Natural Symbols*, has proposed a method of seizing, in all beliefs and rituals, a code by which a society can present itself and thus tacitly delimit and define what it is to hope to be human within it, overcomes brilliantly that cramping dualism inherent in so much ecclesiastical history, between high thoughts and low practices, elevating doctrines and sad social realities. Those books, to which I wish to pay a debt of personal gratitude—for they have been part of my attempt to take time off to feed the imagination—are now as much part of the English tradition of culture as are Hume, Milman and Newman. To read and to encourage others to read them is nothing as pretentious or as transient as striking up an alliance with another discipline. They are simply part of a common attempt, as cultivated western men, to give back to the alien, whether this is in the present, outside Europe, or in a European past remote from our present, some of the full stature of its humanity.

Let us return then to the cult of the saints. It seems to me that the growth of the cult of the saints in Late Antiquity has little to do with an upsurge of 'popular religion' in the manner in which such an upsurge has been presented. But it has a lot to do with a theme that preoccupied late Roman men increasingly: it was about people, and about the types of relationships that can be established between people. The relic is a person in a place; and, in that place, all that Late Antique men could value in unalloyed relations of friendship, protection and mercy in their society can come to be played out with liberating precision.

Late Antique men had inherited a continuum of Mediterranean sensibility that longed for invisible and ideal companions. As Bishop Synesius of Cyrene wrote of his guardian angel: 'and give me a companion, O King, a partner, a sacred messenger of sacred power, a messenger of prayer illumined by the divine light, a friend, a dispenser of noble gifts, a guard of my soul, a guard of my life, a guard over prayers, a guard over deeds.'[11]

Yet by the late fourth century, the guardian angel tends to recede into the background: his position as an invisible friend and protector is taken over by the human figure of the saint. In a late third-century catacomb fresco, the lady Vibia is shown being led through the gate of Paradise by her Good Angel; in 396, the lady Veneranda is shown, flanked by another, elegant Late Roman woman—the martyr saint Petronilla, daughter of St Peter: a suitable protectress for Veneranda, a good 'daughter of the Roman church'.[12]

Because either relationship would fall equally into the suspect category of 'popular beliefs', the decisive nuance separating the two scenes is blurred. We are dealing with a comparatively recent determination to find the well-known face of a fellow human being where previous generations had wished to seek, in the guardian angel, the shimmering presence of a bodiless power, whose function identified it with the vast and tranquil hierarchy of the universe.

The idea of replication has been invoked fruitfully to explain this aspect of the cult of the saints. For it has shifted attention from the questions we had been accustomed to ask of the cult—was it superstitious, did it represent a survival of paganism?—to the more hard-headed and useful questions that Late Antique men would ask: what types of relationship have I entered into? How can we both act in it? What can I expect from it? Yet the idea of replication should not be used to trivialize the phenomenon. We are not dealing with a mirror in Heaven that reflects, in rosy tints, the hard facts of patronage and *prepotenza* on the late Roman earth.

The language of patronage was chosen because it was the idiom with which to conduct an obscure but urgent debate on the nature of power in Late Antique society and the relation of power to mercy and justice.

11. Synesius of Cyrene, *Hymn* IV, 264, trans. A. Fitzgerald, in *The Essays and Hymns of Synesius of Cyrene*, II (Oxford, 1930), 386.
12. P. Styger, *Römische Märtyrergrüfte* I (Berlin, 1935), 168.

Late Roman and early medieval men appear to be drawing a network of invisible fellow human beings ever closer around themselves. They work out a series of intense relationships with these, that are modelled with zest on what they consider to be good relationships in their ordinary life.

The poems of Paulinus of Nola enable us to see a late Roman aristocrat for whom the cult of saints had tapped a new well-spring of articulateness. Here is a poet for whom all that love and warmth of which classical Mediterranean men were so capable shifts from one beloved figure to another—from his elder friend and teacher, Ausonius, to a new, invisible, friend, St Felix at Nola:

> videbo corde, mente complectar pia
> ubique praesentem mihi.[13]

To speak of a man such as Paulinus as if he had merely replaced the worship of the old gods by the worship of St Felix is to use too inert a model for the change. Men of the late Roman aristocracy, such as Paulinus or Paulinus' friend Sulpicius Severus—who would dream of his recently-dead hero, Martin, 'dressed in a white toga, his face alight, with glowing eyes and shimmering hair . . . He smiled at me, and handed me the little book that I had just written . . .' (none other than the classic of western historiography, the *Vita Martini*)[14]—obliterated their past because they could add something new: the warm blood of late Roman senatorial *amicitia* and the intensities of late Roman relationships with beloved teachers could flow freely into a newly-forged style of relationships with the other world.

Amicitia, for a late Roman man, also meant protection and power. The saint was the *patronus*, the protector, with whom it was desirable to enter into a client relationship. Early medieval relics are often called, quite simply, *patrocinia*: portable tokens of the patronage of the saints. There was no need to teach late Roman men, and there is no need to teach

13. Paulinus, *Carmen* XI, 55.
14. Sulpicius Severus, *Ep.* 2, *P.L.* 20, 178/9.

the late Roman social historians of today, about the hard facts of the systems of patronage and dependence that hardened throughout the early medieval West.

Yet, once again, we should not underestimate the speed and the certainty of touch with which Christians of the late fourth century created a system of idealized relationships of dependence with invisible human beings.

> And, as imagination bodies forth
> The forms of things unknown, the poet's pen
> Turns them to shapes, and gives to airy nothing
> A local habitation and a name.[15]

The shape that late Roman men decided, in no uncertain terms, to give to their saints was that of the *patronus*.

The idea that the just man could intercede for the sins of his fellows was part of a long continuum of Jewish, Christian, even pagan, belief. But the belief had remained faceless: only a century of late imperial art could enable the late-fourth-century painter of the *Coemeterium Maius* to convey so vividly what it was like to kneel for protection on either side of the still, upright figure of the martyr—the *patronus* and *dominus*.[16]

For the arrival of a relic and its installation in a church was the arrival of a *sublimis potestas*, a person wielding absolute power in the community. But the relic was a very particular sort of person. He or she was a martyr: that is, a fellow-human who had suffered death from an unjust power. As Victricius of Rouen was careful to stress in his great panegyric, *In Praise of the Saints*, behind the altar on which the relic case now glittered, surrounded by the pomp of an Imperial arrival, there still lurked the dark memory of an unjust execution: the 'clean' power of the martyr was shadowed by the memory of an act of 'dirty' power.

The debate on the nature of power and its exercise in the

15. W. Shakespeare, *Midsummer's Night Dream*, act V, scene 1, line 14.
16. E. Josi, "Il 'coemeterium maius'", *Rivista di archeologia cristiana* X (1933): 11–13.

world derived much of its energy from the tension generated by these juxtaposed images. For at every festival, the *Passio* of the martyr would be read aloud. This was the tale of his condemnation and execution. The reading was the climax of the ceremony. At that moment, the invisible presence was given a full human face; and it was a moment when 'clean' and 'dirty' power were brought abruptly together. Becco, the Frankish count of Brioude and of its harsh and freedom-loving transhumant hinterland, was a hard man. Surrounded by his armed retinue, he took up his place at the head of the congregation at the festival of St Julian. The moment the reader took up the book of the *Passio*, and the opening word *Julianus* rang out across the basilica, Becco fell to the floor in a fit. It was the sort of miracle that late Roman men had put themselves out to remember.

Other miracles follow a similar rhythm. If we treat them merely as manifestations of 'popular religion', their interest to us is exhausted once we have noted the degree of credulity or excitability that they betray. To say, as one writer has said recently, that these and related phenomena belong not to the sphere of religious history, but of crowd psychology, is to give up prematurely. The historian can dare to go a little further. The studies of Natalie Davis, for instance, on the Charivari festivals of the sixteenth century or on the Rites of Violence accompanying the massacres of the French Wars of Religion have shown how apparently uncontrolled manifestations of crowd behaviour, at their most exuberant or their most brutal, nevertheless betray a system of restraints, and unfold according to rhythms, that are all the more controlling for being unconsciously lodged in the tacit expectations of the participants in a small community. The historian has to strain the ear to catch an alien music in what had first sounded a cacophony.[17]

Late Roman shrines were places where good, 'clean'

17. Natalie Zemon Davis, *Society and Culture in Early Modern France* (Stanford, 1975), pp. 95–123 and 152–188.

power could be shown to exist on earth by being played out in the form of miracles. Of such miracles, the most puzzling to modern men, but the one most valued by Late Antique observers, was the miracle of healing by the exorcism of the possessed.

Let us look carefully at the rhythms of the cure of the possessed at a shrine.

We are seldom dealing with isolated, disturbed individuals. Along with the beggars, the possessed were a recognized category grouped round the shrine. They would be given their meals, were blessed once a day—and set to scrubbing the paving of the church. In many cases one can guess that they had not come to the shrine in a state of acute possession; they had come so as to become possessed—so that the tensions of their life could be worked through and resolved in a single public drama. This drama followed through a pattern that was intelligible to everyone present. For the possessed are not themselves. They are dissociated. It is the demons who speak through them. Often the demons speak out about the latent anxieties and resentments of the community: the imminence of a barbarian raid on the city; the sins of a king; the acts of hard dealing through which the suffering human had lost his identity to the demonic. The heavy shouting of the possessed is the audible side of an interrogation by the invisible *dominus*, the saint. For the demons in the possessed are in the presence of 'clean' power. Thus the horrors of a late Roman courtroom are re-enacted, but without the grim accompaniments of judicial torture; and it is not the human who is judged, but the invisible criminal who disrupts the human.

The dénouement, therefore, is not punishment. It is the re-integration of a human being into the community. For the great Late Antique formulae of exorcism emphasize not only the punishment and expulsion of the demon, they re-iterate the re-establishment of that tranquil integrity of body, soul and nature which Adam had first enjoyed in God's Paradise. A great basilica, where the light of day was trapped in the

shimmering apse and the translucent marble of the colon-
nades, where, as in the words of an inscription 'darkness and
chaos are fled way', stood in a rough world as a model of the
untroubled order of the morning of God's creation: it was the
right place for disrupted integrity to be restored, and for a human being, who, while possessed by the demonic, had flailed
between heaven and earth and, in his cries, had even broken
the boundaries that separated man from animal, to be replaced
in his rightful category.

The rhythm of re-integration made the miracle of exorcism at a shrine the paradigm of Late Antique miracles of the
saints. For in a shrine, the hard laws of the world were suspended, and the harsh boundaries of the human community
were relaxed. A different justice was meted out, all the more
satisfying for having taken the words of its *libretto* from the
normal relationships of the late Roman world. A miracle was
always conceived of as an act of justice and amnesty. Those
who had been placed outside the human group by their sins
or by their hard dealings, or who had been broken by the
injustice of others, might, through the rhythm of a cure
played out in public, find their way back to that small face-
to-face world which is the basic unit of Late Antique and
early medieval religion.

It is on such themes that our imagination could linger.
The way that Mediterranean men of the Late Antique period found a language for themselves to use in order to work
through, at the shrines of their saints, the lasting, urgent problems of any civilized community—friendship and protection,
justice, power and mercy—may repay study as close as that
which we are prepared to lavish on the more abstract and
seemingly more elevated authors who form the high road of
ecclesiastical history. In straining his imagination to catch the
meaning of such situations as we have described, the historian may still have something to add even to the culture of his
own times.

So we have arrived where we began. The unrelieved tension of learning and imagination is the mainspring of the

work of the historian. No one knew that better than the greatest English historian, Edward Gibbon. Gibbon was a man of awesome learning and unbending criteria as to what was worth his while to understand in the past. In deciding to be a 'philosophical historian' and not a mere antiquarian, he had decided to draw on the full range of the culture of his age in order to understand the great themes he had proposed himself. Few modern history libraries known to me have yet flanked their collection of historical sources with those shelves upon shelves of works on human geography, of travellers' accounts, of ethnographic monographs on distant tribes and regions which Gibbon mobilized in the footnotes that support the deceptively untroubled flow of his narrative. We can see him at work in his notebooks. Faced by a problem of the origins of feudalism in France: 'Je combine l'expérience avec le raisonnement,' (as you see, then as now, this sort of history is best written in French) 'J'ouvre les codes de ces peuples qui renversoient l'empire. . . . J'ouvre leur annales. . . . Tel est l'esprit qui s'est répandu du nord au midi, depuis les frontières de la Chine jusqu'au fond de l'Afrique.'[18] And yet he also knew how to begin as an historian. Meeting, for the first time in his narrative, the history of the circus factions in sixth-century Constantinople—a topic which, until recently, had been rendered anaemic with knowingness by modern scholars—he begins with a simple footnote, *Read and feel*: 'Read and feel the twenty-second book of the Iliad, a living picture of the manners, passions and the whole form and spirit of the chariot race.'[19]

Now Gibbon was one of the last late classical men. He must have known that this had been the advice which, fourteen hundred years previously, the young Julian the Apostate

18. 'I combine experience with reasoning. I open the law-codes of those peoples who overturned the empire . . . I open their chronicles . . . This is the style of [barbarian] society as it exists in a wide sweep from north to south, from the frontiers of China to the depths of Africa.' Edward Gibbon, *Collected Works* III, 189.

19. Edward Gibbon, *History of the Decline and Fall of the Roman Empire*, ed. J. B. Bury (London, 1929), chap. 50, n. 41.

had received from his wise tutor, the Gothic eunuch Mardonius: 'Have you a passion for horseraces? There is one in Homer, very clearly described. Take the book and study it.'[20] Julian was a lonely boy, growing up in perilous seclusion. The reveries of lonely children, reading and feeling about things they might never do or see . . . this is the beginning of the growth of the historical imagination in so many of us. It was plainly good enough for Gibbon.

But the imagination itself must go to school. To recapture the fullness of human life in the past—or, indeed, anywhere at any time—harder qualities are called for. They are summed up in the proud intention of one of the founders of modern thought—who, at the same time, was the heir to all that was best in a millennium of Greco-Roman, Islamic and Jewish rationalism—Benedict Spinoza, when he wrote, in his *Tractatus Politicus: sedulo curavi humanas actiones non ridere non lugere neque detestari, sed intellegere*. 'I have laboured carefully, when faced with human actions, not to mock, not to lament, not to execrate, but to understand.'[21]

20. Julian, *Misopogon*, 351D.
21. Spinoza, *Tractatus Politicus*, Introduction, section 4.

Gibbon's Views on Culture and Society in the Fifth and Sixth Centuries[†]

To EXAMINE GIBBON'S IDEAS ON CULTURE and society in the fifth and sixth centuries after Christ, I must begin the *Decline and Fall* at a point where Horace Walpole had already begun to chafe: 'Then having both the Eastern and Western Empires in his hands at once, and nobody but *imbéciles* and their eunuchs at the head, one is confused with two subjects, that are quite alike, though quite distinct; and in the midst of this distraction enters a deluge of Alans, Huns, Goths, Ostrogoths and Visigoths, who with the same features and characters are to be described in different terms, without any substantial variety, and he is to bring you acquainted with them when you wish them all at the bottom of the Red Sea.'[1]

Yet, to follow Gibbon through the centuries after he had brought the Roman monarchy to an end in Western Europe is to appreciate in him far more than a majestic narrator who can span the centuries. For we can seize in those chapters a perspective that made Gibbon's work the peak of a century of scholarship conducted in the belief that the study of the de-

[†] *Daedalus* CV (1976): 73–88; *Edward Gibbon and the Decline and Fall of the Roman Empire*, ed. G. W. Bowersock, J. Clive, and S. R. Graubard (Cambridge, Mass., 1977), pp. 37–52. All references in this chapter to the *History of the Decline and Fall of the Roman Empire (DF)* are to chapter and page of the seven-volume Bury edition (London, 1914; 2nd ed., 1929)

1. *The Letters of Horace Walpole*, ed. P. Toynbee (Oxford, 1934), pp. 408–409. Walpole to the Reverend William Mason, March 3, 1781.

clining Roman Empire was also the study of the origins of modern Europe. Exclusive preoccupation by classical scholars with the initial sections of the *Decline and Fall* seriously restricts the range and the relevance to present-day scholarship of Gibbon's concerns. Gibbon was very much the heir of Pietro Giannone. As a young student in Naples, Giannone had already realized that the 'immense and boring' work that lay before him on the legal writings of the later Roman Empire, as he set to work in 1702 on studies that would culminate in his *Istoria civile del Regno di Napoli* of 1723, '. . . non l'avea come fine, ma l'indirizzava come efficaci mezzi per intendere le origini ed i cangiamenti dell' Impero romano e come, poi ruinato, fossero surti tanti nuovi domini, tante nuove leggi, nuovi costumi e nuovi regni e repubbliche in Europa.'[2]

It is not only the range of Gibbon's work and the preoccupations that lie behind such a range that have to concern us: Gibbon's criteria of what is relevant to the study of Late Antiquity and the early Middle Ages are also laid bare in his treatment of this period. These would repay attention. The modern specialist who is invited to offer an opinion on the merits and possible relevance to modern studies of the *Decline and Fall* tends to register, with varying degrees of self-satisfaction, those points on which our information and, to an even greater extent, our historical sensibility have gone beyond Gibbon. Yet, such a treatment obtains only partial results and is liable to obscure the extent of Gibbon's relevance to modern research. We are, indeed, better informed than Gibbon; and, at first sight, our sympathies appear to be wider. We are more capable of that whole-hearted empathy for Late Antique men which, in our generation at least, has been held to be the touchstone of historical skill. But in lay-

2. Pietro Giannone, *Vita scritta da lui medesimo*, ed. S. Bertelli (Milan, 1960). 'These the author [Giannone speaks of himself] did not treat as ends in themselves, but directed them to be the effective means by which he should understand the origins and transformations of the Roman Empire, and the manner in which, once that Empire lay in ruins, so many new lordships, so many new laws, new customs and new kingdoms and republics sprang up in Europe' (p. 14).

ing bare Gibbon's limitations, we often fail to allow the exercise to provoke us to scrutinize our own. Put bluntly: we may differ from Gibbon largely in the degree of our unclarity on what is relevant to the study of Late Antiquity.

If Gibbon seems, at first reading, to be different from ourselves, it is because he embarked upon his enterprise with a deeply premeditated criterion of relevance. The iron discipline which enabled him to carry through so great a work was based upon this criterion. It was built up by innumerable acts of renunciation. Volumes could be filled with what Gibbon was in a position to put into the *Decline and Fall* and yet decided to leave out: Basnage 'might have added from the canons of the Spanish councils and the laws of the Visigoths many curious circumstances, essential to his subject, though foreign to mine.'[3] We first meet Gibbon in Italy, quietly absorbing the artistic and archaeological evidence which modern scholars now use for the cultural history of Late Antiquity. Only very seldom is it the stereotype of the eighteenth-century gentleman who stands before a statue, as in the Villa Ludovisi: 'He stabs himself with spirit but a good deal too high, . . . she sinks down with a most beautiful faintness. I think the story is taken a moment too late.'[4]

But in the galleries of Turin and Florence, it is an eye as alert as that of any modern scholar which lights up: an *ossuarium*, *'c'est bien là qu'on prend une idée de la domus exilis Plutonis'*;[5] conclusions for social history are drawn from a collection of *missiones honestae*;[6] two inscriptions detrimental to the reputation of a mother-in-law;[7] syncretism on a medal of Sarapis—'Je pense que les Egyptiens (qui commençoient à raffiner sur le paganisme pour le fortifier contre les attaques des chrétiens) . . .';[8] a coin of the Palaeologi—'La gravure ne ressemble qu'à la première et la plus ancienne sculpture. Tel

3. *DF*, chap. 37, p. 104, n. 143.
4. *Gibbon's Journey from Geneva to Rome*, ed. G. A. Bonnard (London, 1961), p. 247.
5. Ibid., p. 24.   6. Ibid., pp. 148–51.   7. Ibid., p. 156.
8. Ibid., p. 200.

est le cercle des arts';[9] the Velleia Tablet is diligently copied out: 'C'est un travail sec et ingrat, mais quand on construit un Édifice il faut en creuser les fondements. L'on est obligé de faire le rôle de maçon aussi bien qui celui d'Architecte. J'espère pouvoir tirer quelque chose de cette espèce de recensement.'[10]

Gibbon, therefore, possessed a visual sensitivity to precisely those material objects the interpretation of which by archaeologists and art historians has been regarded as a unique achievement of modern late Roman scholarship. Yet little or nothing of his awareness of that particular aspect of Late Antique culture survives into the pages of the *Decline and Fall*. Thus, much of what we value as central to our access to the cultural and social life of Late Antiquity was appreciated by Gibbon, and yet it was regarded as irrelevant to the theme of the *Decline and Fall*. It may well be that it is in those aspects which make Gibbon appear to be most alien to the sympathies of modern scholars that he has remained most relevant: for behind his dismissal of much of the evidence and many of the phenomena that have come to interest us, there lies a theory of the relation between the ideas and society of a large empire which still merits our careful attention.

In the first place, even to cut Gibbon's history into periods and areas may be unwise. Few writers illustrate so magnificently the ideal of the universal historian. Gibbon was convinced that societies widely scattered in space and time were comparable and that their rhythms of growth and decay and the patterns of the exercise of power within them followed a roughly similar course. When he deals with the crisis of the Roman Empire in the third century, he writes that

9. Ibid., p. 202.
10. Ibid., p. 129. 'It is dry and ungrateful work, but when one constructs a building the foundations have to be dug. One has to turn mason as well as architect. I hope to derive some information from this kind of survey.' This was done—and very well—in 1974; see Ramsay MacMullen, *Roman Social Relations* (New Haven, 1974), p. 98, fig. 2.

'though he [the historian] ought never to place his conjectures in the rank of facts, yet the knowledge of human nature, and of the sure operation of its fierce and unrestrained passions, might, on some occasions, supply the want of historical materials.'[11] This meant more for Gibbon than the imaginative reconstruction of certain incidents in the past: 'the knowledge of human nature' demanded a knowledge of societies from the whole breadth of the Eurasian landmass. Such knowledge nourished and attuned Gibbon's awareness of the decline and fall of the Roman Empire. He was always prepared to see in the Roman Empire a paradigm of the universal dilemma of empires. Gibbon, 'the historian of the Roman empire', frequently emerges as something more. He is a sociologist of empire; and we must be prepared to meet him and learn from him on that high level.

Gibbon is at his best when he is analysing the accumulation and manifestation of despotic power over an extended geographical area. Readers of the *Decline and Fall* will relish the brilliant dissection of the Augustan constitution. The contrast between the canny veiling of absolutism by Augustus and the equally premeditated ostentation of Diocletian marks a turning point in the narrative and recurs like a musical 'subject,' at widely differing stages of the decline of the Empire. Yet Gibbon appears to have come to this problem from a period and an area far removed from the Roman world. A comparison of the Achaemenid Empire of the sixth century B.C. with the rise of Tamerlane in the fourteenth century A.D. enabled him to perceive a similar pattern in the rise to power of Cyrus. Getting behind the flat picture of Cyrus presented in the *Cyropaedia* of Xenophon, Gibbon is able to conjure up a three-dimensional picture of the creation of an absolute monarchy. The resultant portrait of Cyrus in the *Essai sur la monarchie des Mèdes*[12] is a triumph of binocular vision. It was the fruit of an intimate knowledge of two millennia of empire-building in the Near East. We are dealing,

11. *DF*, chap. 10, p. 256.
12. E. Gibbon, 'Essai sur la monarchie des Mèdes', *Collected Works*, III, 132ff.

therefore, with a historian who treads with certainty and clear eyes on any ground where any empire has risen and declined in the Eurasian landmass.

To take a small example from the period under discussion: Gibbon was impatient of a purely diplomatic and military narrative of Byzantine-Sassanian relations in the late sixth century: 'Lamenting the barren superfluity of materials, I have studied to compress the narrative of these uninteresting transactions, but the just Nushirvan is still applauded as the model of oriental kings, and the ambition of his grandson prepared the revolution of the East.'[13] We know that we are due for yet another majestic unfolding of the decline of the Empire. 'By the fatal vicissitude of human affairs, the same scenes were renewed at Ctesiphon, which had been exhibited in Rome after the death of Marcus Aurelius.'[14] Just as a changing position of the monarch in the delicate weave of Roman society provided Gibbon with the leitmotiv for his account of the third-century crisis of the Roman Empire, so a spasm of despotism tore apart the society of late-sixth-century Iran: '. . . the intermediate powers between the throne and the people were abolished: and the childish vanity of Hormouz, who affected the daily use of the tiara, was fond of declaring that he alone would be the judge as well as the master of his kingdom.'[15] A great empire, subject to the same tensions as Rome, Iran is viewed with an impartial curiosity, unclouded by any romantic sense of the exotic. We meet the legendary vizier Buzurg Mihr: 'Buzurg Mihr may be considered, in his character and station, as the Seneca of the East: but his virtues, and perhaps his faults, are less known than those of the Roman, who appears to have been much more loquacious.'[16]

13. DF, chap. 46, p. 43.   14. Ibid., p. 46.

15. Ibid., p. 47. Whether Gibbon's picture of Hormizd IV is correct is another matter. What struck him, in Roman terms, as 'childish vanity' was a manifestation of the 'personalization of power' peculiar to Sasanian Iran that is not strictly comparable to Roman practice; see P. Brown, 'The Sasanian Empire in the Near East,' *Iran* (forthcoming).

16. DF, chap. 46, p. 46, n. 11.

In one of his implacable square brackets, Professor Bury adds: 'Buzurg Mihr is a favourite figure in rhetorical literature, but is unknown to strict history. Cp. Nöldeke, *Tabari* p. 251'—a saddening victory of nineteenth-century criticism and Europocentrism.

Faced with the phenomenon of such effortless universality, we must attempt to analyse not so much Gibbon's account of the culture and society of the Roman Empire and barbarian Western Europe in the fifth and sixth centuries as that firm constellation of insights on culture and society in general that enabled Gibbon to write about it as he did.

It would be best to start with culture. Here, we come up against a sternly maintained barrier of relevance. A vast amount of what men have shown themselves capable of thinking and dreaming, and hence of what survives in their writings, has no relevance whatsoever. For such thoughts and dreams find no outlet in the society around them. Large tracts of Christian dogmatic history are irrelevant to the historian: 'The oriental philosophy of the Gnostics, the dark abyss of predestination and grace, and the strange transformations of the Eucharist from the sign to the substance of Christ's body, I have purposely abandoned to the curiosity of speculative divines.'[17] The reason Gibbon offers for so strict a delimitation is misleadingly trenchant: 'I have reviewed, with diligence and pleasure, the objects of ecclesiastical history, by which the decline and fall of the Roman empire were materially affected. . . .'[18]

What lay at the root of his approach is a firm distinction between the 'real' and the 'unreal'—between what was concrete and useful and what he would often call 'folly'. At a given moment in the development of a society, an 'unreal' force—a body of religious ideas or a train of metaphysical speculation—might become active. At other times, 'folly' was effectively excluded or kept within narrow bounds. For Gibbon, the study of society and culture was very largely the study of the meeting point of a 'real' texture of society with

17. *DF*, chap. 49, p. 261.   18. Ibid.

the forces of 'folly' in its various manifestations—human vanity, passion, and superstition. Some topics belonged too much to the world of the 'unreal' to admit a meeting point. His tone can be *cassant* with such intruders: 'The Church of St. Autonomous (whom I have not the honour to know)';[19] the monk Antiochus, 'whose one hundred and twenty homilies are still extant, if what no one reads may be said to be extant.'[20] History viewed by Gibbon is punctuated by exuberant outbursts of unreality. What angers him, for instance, about the Middle Ages is less that it was an Age of Ignorance, than that it became an Age of Folly. The Arabs had 'bewildered themselves very ingeniously in the maze of metaphysics'; but they had, at least, 'improved the more useful sciences of physic, astronomy and the mathematics.'[21] In the twelfth century, however, 'with the Liberty of Europe its genius awoke; but the first efforts of its growing strength were consumed in vain and fruitless pursuits. Ignorance was succeeded by error.'[22] 'Universities arose in every part of Europe, and thousands of students employed their lives upon these grave follies. The love songs of the Troubadours, or Provençal bards, were follies of a more pleasing nature. . . .'[23] Gibbon's insistence on what was relevant to his own history of society and culture, therefore, was the product of a sense of the unbounded capacity of human beings for irrelevance.[24]

Behind such an attitude lay a century of philosophical skepticism and empiricism; these had already been allied, in the case of Pietro Giannone and the historians of the Scottish Enlightenment (whose relevance to Gibbon has been lucidly demonstrated by Professor Giarrizzo), with a direct concern

19. *DF*, chap. 46, p. 66, n. 55.   20. Ibid., p. 75, n. 73.
21. E. Gibbon, 'Outlines of the History of the World', *Collected Works* III, 4.
22. Ibid., p. 19.   23. Ibid., p. 29.
24. Gibbon's attitude is admirably summed up by Professor Giarrizzo: 'La giustificazione consapevole di questi limite è dato dalla convinzione che essi non toccherebbero la decadenza e caduta dell'impero. La realtà è che essi non toccano soprattutto a Gibbon: laddove non gli riesce di sentire, dietro un pronunciamento teologico o una formula dommatica l'interesse 'politico' che traduce la credenza superstitziosa in un pregiudizio per farne trama del tessuto connettivo della società' (G. Giarrizzo, *Edward Gibbon e la cultura europea del settecento* [Naples, 1954], p. 302).

for the study of the past in terms of the problems raised by the impact of the 'unreal' on the 'real'. As a result of this attitude, a more modern dichotomy of social and cultural forces in a society is alien to Gibbon. For Gibbon transcends this dichotomy. 'Ideas' and 'society' do not exist over against each other, still less are they to be studied separately—as has happened far too often in the course of recent late Roman scholarship—for the simple reason that most ideas do not exist: they are fine-spun cobwebs brushing against the solid tissue of society. Yet, once these ideas harden into 'prejudices' they take on weight and interest for Gibbon.

It is, therefore, the society and its behaviour that give flesh and blood to the wraiths of fantasy and metaphysics. This is as true of religion as of any other aspect of society. In the mid-fourth century, Roman society could still make the gods live: 'Our familiar knowledge of their names and characters, their forms and attributes, *seems* to bestow on these airy beings a real and substantial existence. . . . In the age of Julian, every circumstance contributed to prolong and fortify the illusion: the magnificent temples of Greece and Asia, the works of those artists which had expressed, in painting and in sculptures, the divine conceptions of the poet; the pomp of festivals and sacrifices; the successful art of divination; the popular traditions of oracles and prodigies; and the ancient practise of two thousand years.'[25]

Gibbon was the last man to dismiss 'airy beings', once belief in them was woven into society in so solid and intricate a manner. Merciless on Christian metaphysical folly, he is more tolerant than we might think of Christian ceremonial: 'Experience had shewn him [Pope Gregory the Great] the efficacy of these solemn and pompous rites, to soothe the distress, to confirm the faith, to mitigate the fierceness, and to dispel the dark enthusiasm, of the vulgar. . .'[26] For what was visible and concrete, even if it was superstitious, could be controlled and modified. It was the 'folly' that welled up from the isolated intellect that both disgusted and frightened

25. *DF*, chap. 23, p. 460.   26. *DF*, chap. 45, p. 38.

him. The anxieties of the first pagan observers of Christianity were his own: '. . . they supposed that any popular mode of faith and worship which presumed to disclaim the assistance of the senses would, in proportion as it receded from superstition, find itself incapable of restraining the wanderings of the fancy and the vision of fanaticism. The careless glance which men of wit and learning condescended to cast on the Christian served only to confirm their hasty opinion, and to persuade them that the principle, which they might have revered of the Divine Unity, was defaced by the wild enthusiasm, and annihilated by the airy speculations of the new sectaries.'[27]

'Inside every fat man', Cyril Connolly once remarked, 'there is a thin man crying to be let out.' In the young Gibbon, the thin man had cried ever louder. It was possible to credit him with the following exchange with his beloved Aunt Catherine: 'Once, it was said (but Gibbon declined to confirm the story), he proposed to kill her. "You see," he explained, "you are perfectly good now, so if you die you will go to heaven. If you live you may become wicked and go to hell." "But where do you expect to go if you kill me?" "That," he replied, "my godfather will answer for. I have not been confirmed. . . ,"'[28] nor 'had the elastic spring been totally broken by the weight of the Atmosphere of Oxford. The blind activity of idleness encouraged me to advance without armour into the dangerous maze of controversy.'[29] He arrived in Lausanne: 'a thin little figure with a large head, disputing and urging, with the greatest ability, all the best arguments that had ever been used in favour of popery.' The slow reweaving of the web of reality around the angular young Gibbon by Pavilliard, a man 'rational because he was moderate', is a microcosm of the concern of Gibbon's life-work. Seldom has a historian watched with such close atten-

27. *DF*, chap. 16, p. 82, n. 11.
28. G. M. Young, *Gibbon* (2nd ed., London, 1948), p. 12.
29. *The Autobiography of Edward Gibbon*, ed. John Murray (London, 1896), p. 84 f.

tion in the distant past the tragic working out of forces which had once strained so dangerously on the leash within himself. His history of the society and culture of Late Antiquity is a study of how the hard bones of speculative 'folly' came to push through the wasted flesh of the Empire.

More is involved in this, however, than Gibbon's attitude toward Christian controversy and Christian otherworldliness. For these were merely paradigms of the more general tension between reality and 'folly' in society as a whole. To be effective, in Gibbon's view, institutions and legal systems had to be firmly swaddled in an integument of 'prejudices' and values. This integument kept them in touch with reality and exposed them to the modifying influence of human contact. Cut it, and the enduring human propensity for 'folly'—for vanity, for cruelty, for fanaticism—will be released. Thus, religious and institutional experiences can be congruent: in both a religious and a political system, decline and breakdown take the form of a kind of 'folly', whether this is speculative theology or tyrannical vanity, bursting out of the net of controls in which it had been held. The imperial court, once it had burst its way out of the delicate restraints of the Augustan settlement, came to exist in as great an isolation from the modifying influences of humane society as did any Christian hermit.

Though the tearing of the web of reality may often be brutal and dramatic, as with the emergence of the monks, this tearing is preceded by a long and insidious process. This process might be seen as a 'leakage of reality': what is natural and spontaneous insensibly passes to the artificial, and the artificial in turn gives way to 'folly'. The process is at no time irreversible: it admits no sudden, catastrophic breaks; and a frequent reweaving of the broken web of restraints on 'folly' occurs, if often, in this period, at a more primitive level. Individuals and institutions are allowed by Gibbon to tremble for generations on a knife edge between artifice and unreality. Hence a sense of tension and movement runs through the *Decline and Fall*.

Let us examine aspects of Gibbon's attitude to the irruption of 'folly' in the fifth- and sixth-century Roman world in terms of this 'leakage of reality'. First, let us consider the religious evolution of the period. In this, Gibbon is the heir of a long tradition. We still share his problem. The rise of the Christian Church is the story of the rise to great power in this world of an institution whose basis was a claim to be interested only in the other world. By Gibbon's time, however, the problem had changed. What to later medieval and Reformation thinkers had appeared as a religious and moral incongruity had become a problem strictly of religious and cultural history. For not only could the Christian Church be said to have abandoned its otherworldly vocation, it had actually risen to greater and greater power by inflating belief in the other world. With Pietro Giannone, for instance, we already have a man wrestling with the problem of the religious psychology of the Late Antique world. How had the mercifully pedestrian attitudes of the ancient Hebrews to the afterlife, joined by the reverential simplicity of the authors of the Gospels, blossomed into the rank growth of fantasy on which the Christian Church had built its power in society?[30]

It is from this standpoint that we can best appreciate Gibbon's contribution. Where Giannone had looked with fascinated horror at the growth of the plant, Gibbon, not in any way surprised to find such a weed in the human mind, looked to the remissness of the gardeners. His thought on the role of religion in society draws its nuances from a deep pessimism. Superstition and the vanity of metaphysicians being an ineradicable part of the human condition, what mattered was the system of social constraints that ensured that these did not get out of hand and that might yet, *per impossibile*, channel them into useful functions. Hence his attitude to the paganism of the Roman world. He was untouched by romantic regret for the pagan past. Paganism was a system of belief mercifully deprived, by its incoherence, of the power

30. P. Giannone, *Vita*, pp. 199–210. [Carlo Gentile, *Pietro Giannone, Edward Gibbon ed il Triregno* (Livorno, 1976).]

to build up those strong imaginative and speculative structures beneath whose pressure the tissue of society might yield: it was a world of 'faint and imperfect impressions'.[31]

In any case, these impressions would have met their match in the system of social restraints that characterized the social and religious establishment of the Roman Empire. Writers whose works keep modern experts in *Religionsgeschichte* busy for a lifetime on the second century after Christ are dismissed in one curt footnote: 'I do not pretend to assert that, in this irreligious age, the natural terrors of superstition, dreams, omens, apparitions, &c. had lost their efficacy.'[32] They existed, but they did not impinge.

Religious phenomena which the modern historian might regard in isolation as symptoms of irreversible changes in mentality are held by Gibbon in a network of checks and balances. If anything, the irrational rises to the surface less rapidly in Gibbon's narrative than in many modern treatments of the religious world of Late Antiquity. In his highly differentiated account of the Emperor Julian, for instance, Gibbon gives us something far more satisfying than the usual balance sheet of 'superstitious' and 'public-spirited': his portrait has the fascination of allowing us to see the tissue of reality giving and springing back under pressure from a world of dreams and visions, and so allows us to appreciate all the more fully how much of it had already given way among Julian's contemporaries: 'These sleeping or waking visions, the ordinary effects of abstinence and fasting, would almost degrade the Emperor to the level of an Egyptian monk. But the useless lives of Anthony or Pachomius were consumed in these vain occupations. Julian could break from the dream of superstition to arm himself for battle.'[33]

Hence the horror of the ascetic movement for Gibbon and the consequent change of tone when he described the Christological controversies and those Christian groupings that were increasingly presided over by monks in the fifth

31. *DF*, chap. 15, p. 59.   32. *DF*, chap. 2, p. 34, n. 8.
33. *DF*, chap. 23, p. 466.

and sixth centuries. For, with the appearance of the monks, the restrained irony with which Gibbon traces the rise of the Christian Church breaks down. The irony had reflected a tension in Gibbon's own thought. The rise of an institution within an institution still held out the remote promise of weaving, if from the coarse thread of Christian belief, yet another web of social control. Gibbon's attitude to the Church in the early centuries has retained its fertility because it was developed under a perpetual question mark. Despite a heavy indictment, the Christian bishops were let out on parole: 'Yet party-spirit, however pernicious or absurd, is a principle of union as well as of dissension. The bishops, from eighteen hundred pulpits, inculcated the duty of passive obedience to a lawful and orthodox sovereign; their frequent assemblies, and perpetual correspondence, maintained the communion of distant churches, and the benevolent temper of the gospel was strengthened, though confined, by the spiritual alliance of the Catholics.'[34]

With the monks, however, Gibbon is confronted by men who had finally destroyed the knife-edge balance between superstition and the social constraints which the Christian Church might have woven from its own institutions. The monk ceased to be a man because he had burst free from the merciful integument of society.

After all, superstition is not the only disruptive and potentially brutalizing component of the human mind. Sexuality, if unmellowed by society, can have similar effects. The Emperor Heliogabalus was not only debauched: he was debauched in a particular way. 'A rational voluptuary', however, 'adheres with invariable respect to the temperate dictates of nature and improves the gratification of the senses by social intercourse, enduring commitments and the soft coloring of taste and imagination.'[35] The monk was a Heliogabalus of the spirit: 'The lives of the primitive monks were consumed in penance and solitude, undisturbed by the various occupations which fill the time, and exercise the faculties, of

34. *DF*, chap. 38, p. 175.   35. *DF*, chap. 6, p. 159.

35

reasonable, active, and social beings.'[36] A culture of monks was a culture of non-men: 'glorious was the *man* (I abuse that name). . . .'[37] It is the sharpest phrase in the *Decline and Fall*.

The rise of the ascetic movement, therefore, represents a nadir of depletion. The tissues that had held even the Christian bishops in a web still woven with the firm ironies of social existence had snapped. The point is driven home by a magisterial juxtaposition. The same chapter in which Gibbon describes the unravelling of the web of civilized life at the hands of the monks ends with a warm appreciation of how the Christian Gothic Bishop Ulfilas and the later Catholic bishops of the West patiently took up again those tattered shreds to weave, albeit unconsciously, yet another web of civilized living around the barbarians of the north: 'while they studied the divine truth, their minds were insensibly enlarged by the distant view of history, of nature, of the arts, and of society.'[38] Seldom does Gibbon's irony stretch to such a courageous assertion of the silent craftsmanship of civilization.

This brings us to the social dimensions of the 'leakage of reality' in the Roman world. For if the monks are depleted men, it is not merely because of their ideas: it is because they are paradigms of the change that had insensibly made the Roman Empire a depleted society. We return, by this roundabout route, to Gibbon the sociologist of empire. For the 'leakage of reality' that had loosened the web of social restraint around the individual fantasy was mirrored in Rome, as in every great empire, by the dissolution of those tissues that had once held the Empire together as a balanced commonwealth.

Gibbon transferred the new awareness of the texture of society, exemplified in the work of Montesquieu, from the study of small and organic units, to a gigantic empire. Furthermore, he treated the Roman Empire as only one in a wide typology of empires. In so doing, he gained the sense of scale and analytic skill that enabled him to write the *Decline and*

36. *DF*, chap. 37, p. 76.   37. Ibid., p. 79.   38. Ibid., pp. 85–86.

Fall. Early on, Gibbon appears to have realized the quantita-
tive differences that the sheer size of the Empire would im-
pose on the interpretative tools available to him. The vast
geographical erudition of Gibbon is in itself evidence for his
sense of the problem of scale in empires. It is an alertness that
he carried with him on his journeys: the style of a cameo, he
observed, betrays a fifty-year time-lag in the spread of taste
to the frontiers of the Empire.[39] When he arrived in Rome, it
is far from certain what actually passed through his mind as
he viewed its ruins. I suspect that it was not only a sad appreciation of the beauties of classical architecture. Our 'philosophic historian' was already thinking of the problems of
empire made manifest in building. As he wrote of the ruins
of Persepolis: these could only have been erected at the ap-
ogee of the Achaemenid Empire, not earlier, as Caylus had
suggested: '. . . je ne sais s'il a assez réfléchi sur la combinai-
son de la puissance despotique avec la grandeur, les trésors, et
la résolution de triompher sur tous les obstacles. J'ai encore
devant les yeux les restes augustes de l'amphithéâtre de Ves-
pasien, des bains de Tibère, de la colonne de Trajane.'[40]

Yet it is precisely in his sociology of empire that Gibbon's
subtlety tends to elude us. For in his 'General Observations
on the Fall of the Empire in the West' he dangerously simplified his own perspective: 'The rise of a city, which swelled
into an Empire, may deserve, as a singular prodigy, the reflection of a philosophic mind. But the decline of Rome was
the natural and inevitable effect of immoderate greatness.
Prosperity ripened the principle of decay; the causes of destruction multiplied with the extent of conquest; and, as soon
as time or accident had removed the artificial supports, the
stupendous fabric yielded to the pressure of its own weight.

39. *Gibbon's Journey*, p. 194.
40. 'I do not know if he has reflected sufficiently on the combined effects of
despotic power and a sense of grandeur, treasures and the resolve to triumph over all
obstacles. I have still before my eyes the image of the august ruins of the amphitheatre of Vespasian, the baths of Titus, the column of Trajan.' 'Sur la monarchie des
Mèdes', *Collected Works*, III, 132 ff.

The story of its ruin is simple and obvious; and, instead of inquiring why the Roman empire was destroyed, we should rather be surprised that it had subsisted so long.'[41]

This statement has been used by modern historians as carte blanche for reducing the problem of the decline of the Roman Empire to manageable proportions. It has enabled them to direct attention to those developments in late Roman society that can be documented with reassuring precision—the increasing weight of taxation and the rapid expansion, in the fourth century, of the governmental and ecclesiastical superstructure of the Empire. Yet, I suspect that Gibbon's attitude has been subtly simplified by such appeals to his authority. The remarks of the 'General Observations' derive their deceptive simplicity from having been framed in terms of a comparison between the Roman Empire and the Europe of Gibbon's own day. The emphasis on the 'immoderate greatness' of the Roman Empire is made in terms of qualities that this Empire did not have in common with the more realistically based states of modern Europe. But just because one trait is highlighted by comparison with other societies, it does not follow that this is a privileged cause of the weakness of that society. In his narrative, the size of the Empire alone does not seem to have satisfied Gibbon as an explanation, and the growth, in the late third and fourth centuries, of the relative size of its superstructure—which happened as a comparatively late development in terms of the problems which, in Gibbon's view, had faced the Empire since the reign of Augustus—seems to have satisfied him even less.

For what concerned Gibbon was not the size of the Empire as such, but its cohesion. The relative weight of its superstructure concerned him less than the extent to which this superstructure threatened to detach itself from the web of social relations whose tenacity and differentiation, in the age of Augustus and even of the Antonines, had distinguished the Roman Empire from all other despotisms. With this we

41. *DF*, chap. 38, pp. 173–74.

return to the leitmotiv of the 'leakage of reality.' The declining Roman Empire is marked by a slow and largely irreversible process of the weakening of the tissue of prejudices and interests which, in Gibbon's view, had enabled the already unlimited power of Augustus to be exercised decorously and, as a result, both effectively and in a civilized manner.

This is as much a cultural as an institutional problem. For the 'prejudices' which made for cohesion were expressed and carried by cultural, quite as much as by institutional, means. Our starting point is Gibbon's view of the small society. In such a society, artifice, the thin end of the wedge of 'folly', has only limited freedom of play: strong 'impressions' fit closely to manageable institutions. We find this best expressed in a remarkable note by Gibbon on the religious beliefs of the Germanic tribes at the time of their settlement in the Mediterranean world, written as a comment on Mallet's *History of Denmark.* The German conquerors of the Roman provinces did not, in his opinion, convert to Christianity in order to fit more easily into the social system of the conquered. Rather, Gibbon preferred to trace the process of acculturation that followed the migrants to their loss of local spontaneous roots. A North African scene, with the Vandals helplessly exposed to a zealous Catholic community 'tout jusqu'à leur maîtresses qui meloient les caresses et la controverse',[42] is a straightforward enough Gibbonian tableau. Less accustomed, but more revealing of Gibbon, is the brief analysis of the local nature of Scandinavian religion: 'Toutes les religions sont locales, jusqu'à un certain point. . . . Mais chez les nations savantes, les livres et la réflexion et chez les peuples de l'Orient une Imagination échauffée suppléent à la presence actuelle des objets. . . . Les idées ou les images étoient trop subtiles pour ne pas échapper à la dureté tranquille et phlegmatique des Scandinaves. . . . Ce temple d'Upsal où ils avoient acheté la faveur d'Odin par des milliers de victimes humains, ces rochers que les anciens Scaldes avoient couvert de carac-

42. *Gibbon's Journey,* p. 164.

39

tères Runiques . . . tous ces objets frappoient son Esprit parce qu'ils avoient frappé les sens.'[43]

The problem of empire is at the opposite end of the scale from this state of quasi-physical immediacy. In an empire, the spontaneous is attenuated and replaced by artifice. Yet Gibbon was not a man to reject artifice. Part of the conviction that Gibbon's account of the Roman Empire in the age of Antonines carries derives from his sober sense of the necessity of artifice and of its viability in an extended society. In his opinion, no large society is doomed merely because it has lost the virtues appropriate to a small community. The classical Roman Empire functioned well enough on an ersatz for public spirit: the decline from artifice to unreality was slow and complex.

Play-acting, we should remember, struck Gibbon as a necessary social discipline. For some people to wear a mask did no harm. The portrait of Augustus owes its three-dimensional quality to this assumption. Many other figures in Gibbon's narrative learned to act their parts on the stage of Roman life: Maximin Thrax 'displayed on every occasion a valour equal to his strength; and his native fierceness was soon tempered or disguised by the knowledge of the world.'[44] When Gibbon uses the imagery of the the theatre, as he often does, he uses it with a full-blooded sense of the necessity of role-playing in a complex society. Without it, for instance, the religious establishment of the pagan world would not have functioned the way it did; 'sometimes condescending to act a part in the theatre of superstition, they concealed the sentiments of an Atheist under the sacerdotal robes.'[45] Some ac-

---

43. 'All religions depend to some degree on local circumstances . . . Among learned nations reading and reflection, and among the nations of the East, a natural warmth of fancy, supply, in some measure, the real presence of objects . . . But mental representations are too subtle to make an impression on the phlegmatic insensibility of the Scandinavians . . . The temple of Upsal in which they had purchased the favour of Odin by thousands of human victims, those rocks which the ancient Scalds had covered with Runic characters . . . all the objects kept possession of their minds, because they were continually striking their senses.' Ibid., p. 163.
44. *DF*, chap. 7, p. 183.   45. *DF*, chap. 2, p. 34.

tors acted in better plays than others: 'Like the modesty affected by Augustus, the state maintained by Diocletian was a
theatrical representation; but it must be confessed that, of the
two comedies, the former was of a more liberal and manly
character than the latter. It was the aim of the one to disguise,
and the object of the other to display, the unbounded power
which the emperors possessed over the Roman world.'[46]

Once again, the studied ambiguity of Gibbon's attitude
to the tissue of society enabled Gibbon to place the new court
life of the age, as he placed the Christian Church, on parole.
It was not inevitable that the balance should tilt irreversibly
toward the mere show against the substance of power. Hence
the vital importance for Gibbon of Constantine. In the *Decline and Fall*, it is not Constantine the convert of the Milvian
Bridge who holds the centre of the stage, it is Constantine
the victorious autocrat of the period after 324. The reign of
Constantine emerges as of crucial significance in the history
of the formation of late Roman absolutism: for with Constantine the balance shifted from role-playing to fantasy.
This, and not his relations with the Christian Church, is
what gives Constantine his place in the *Decline and Fall*. 'Diocletian was a man of sense, who, in the course of private as
well as public life, had formed a just estimate both of himself
and of mankind: nor is it easy to conceive that, in substitut-
ing the manners of Persia to those of Rome, he was seriously
actuated by so mean a principle as that of vanity.'[47] 'Constantine, however, was spun into the illusion which his great
predecessor had manipulated: 'The Asiatic pomp, which had
been adopted by the pride of Diocletian, assumed an air of
soft effeminacy in the person of Constantine.'[48] 'In the life of
Augustus, we behold the tyrant of the republic converted,
almost by imperceptible degrees, into the father of his country and of humankind. In that of Constantine, we may contemplate a hero, who had long inspired his subjects with love

46. *DF*, chap. 13, p. 413.   47. Ibid., p. 412.
48. *DF*, chap. 18, p. 217.

and his enemies with terror, degenerating into a cruel and dissolute monarch, corrupted by his fortune or raised by conquest above the necessity of dissimulation.'[49]

From that time onward, Gibbon's eyes remain on the court. This is not because he was interested solely in politicians, nor because he regarded the court and its demands as the main cause of the decline of the Empire. Rather, the rise of a court, for Gibbon, was the paradigm of the weakening of the tissues of Roman society. This is shown by the differentiated quality of his attitude toward courts and court ceremonial. The phenomenon fascinated and repelled him. He met his first and most impressive one in Turin: 'Une cour est à la fois pour moi un objet de curiosité et de dégout. La servilité des courtisans me révolte et je vois avec horreur la Magnificence des palais qui sont cimentés du sang du peuple. . . . Dans chaque chambre dorée je crois voir un village de Savoyards prêts à périr de faim, de froid et de misère.'[50]

Yet his moral outrage does not blind him to the subtler ramifications of a court society: 'The architecture and government of Turin presented the same aspect of tame and tiresome uniformity.'[51] Such an observation prepares us for the dying fall in his summary of the age of the Antonines: 'This long peace, and the uniform government of the Romans, introduced a slow and secret poison into the vitals of the Empire.'[52] The ceremonial of a court itself is a measure of its increasing isolation from reality. 'The most brilliant shows in courts, the carousals of Lewis XIV or the festivities of the Dukes of Wurtemberg attested the wealth, and sometimes the taste, of princes'; this contrasts with the more cohesive society of the Roman Republic: 'In the triumph, every circumstance was great and interesting. To receive its full im-

49. Ibid., p. 216.
50. 'A court is for me at one and the same time an object of curiosity and distaste. The servility of courtiers repells me, and I see with horror the magnificence of palaces cemented with the blood of the people . . . In each gilded chamber I think I see a village of Savoyards near to dying of hunger, cold and poverty.' *Gibbon's Journey*, p. 23.
51. *Autobiography*, p. 266 C.   52. *DF*, chap. 2, p. 62.

pression, it was enough to be a man and a Roman. With the eyes of citizens, the spectators saw the image, or rather the reality of the public glory.'[53]

Byzantine society is repugnant to Gibbon less through any reputed limitation in his sympathies and knowledge than precisely because he saw with singular clarity the most obtrusive feature of that society as it was faithfully reflected in the historical sources available to him. It was the Byzantine historiographical tradition itself, often the work of courtiers or of writers who purveyed court slander, that betrayed Byzantium to this regular and critical attendant at the stage play of autocracy. Byzantium, a society of monks and courtiers, represented the final weakening, on both the religious and the institutional plane, of the merciful restraints of civilized society. The development of the Holy Roman Empire, by contrast, poignantly illustrated the other aspect of this process of depletion. The 'leakage of reality' reaches its height at the imperial court of Charles IV of Bohemia: 'If we annihilate the interval of time and space between Augustus and Charles, strong will be the contrast between the two Caesars: the Bohemian, who concealed his weakness under the mask of ostentation, and the Roman, who disguised his strength under the semblance of modesty.'[54]

Gibbon's attitude is best illustrated by the manner in which two young scholars of our time have corrected it. The resilience of the provincial aristocracies of the Western Empire has recently been studied by John Matthews. His book leaves little room for Gibbon's picture of the social structure of the later Empire: this was not, in fact, a society reduced to uniformity beneath an all-powerful court.[55] The pioneering studies by Sabine MacCormack of the relation between imperial art, ceremonial, and panegyric show a court culture that was far less concerned than Gibbon had thought merely

53. Gibbon, 'On the Triumphal Shows of the Romans', *Collected Works*, IV, 394–95.

54. *DF*, chap. 49, p. 330.

55. John Matthews, *Western Aristocracies and Imperial Court, A.D. 364–425* (Oxford, 1975).

with the display of the unlimited power of the Emperor: far from it—what emerges from such differentiated studies is a picture of an imperial autocracy, still subject to a continuous, discreet pressure from below, whose panegyrics could be used to stress the traditional limitations of the imperial office and whose ceremonies were very often ceremonies that left room for a large measure of consensus and popular participation.[56]

These works show that to go beyond Gibbon in his views on the weakening of the traditional texture of Roman society and the consequent loosening of traditional restraints on the court may be the more fruitful manner of meeting his views on the causes of the decline and fall of the Roman Empire. Merely to appeal to the authority of Gibbon's 'General Observations' in emphasizing the oppressive weight of the governmental superstructure of the Empire gets us less far than we might think. The deeper problem remains: by what means and with what success were local groupings and particular vested interests within the Empire induced for so many centuries—deep into the Late Antique period, in fact—to lend their support to the 'stupendous fabric'?

To turn to the barbarian states of Western Europe is to have this impression confirmed. Here, Gibbon saw a society which, though primitive, was somehow less exposed to a 'leakage of reality' than the Empire had been. 'Folly' was not so strong a thread in the fabric of social life. The Latin Church had always been protected 'by propitious ignorance'[57] from the metaphysical rigors of the East. Even in the fourth century, 'the inhabitants of the West were of a less inquisitive spirit; their passions were not forcibly moved by invisible objects.'[58] In such a society the Christian Church could exer-

56. Sabine G. MacCormack, 'Change and Continuity in Late Antiquity: The Ceremony of *Adventus*', *Historia* XXXI (1972): 721–52; 'Latin Prose Panegyric', *Empire and Aftermath* (*Silver Latin*, II, ed. T. A. Dorey [London, 1975]), pp. 143–205; 'Latin Prose Panegyrics: Tradition and Discontinuity in the Later Roman Empire', *Revue des études augustiniennes* XXII (1976): 29–77; and *Art and Ceremony in Late Antiquity* (Berkeley and Los Angeles, 1981).

57. *DF*, chap. 37, p. 103.   58. *DF*, chap. 21, p. 374.

cise the cohesive role which Gibbon had always been prepared to allot it. For 'the Franks and the Visigoths were dis-
posed to embrace, with equal submission, the inherent evils,
and the accidental benefits, of superstition.'[59] 'The bishops of
Spain respected themselves and were respected by the public;
their indissoluble union disguised their vices and confirmed
their authority; and the regular discipline of the Church introduced peace, order and stability into the government of
the state.'[60]

In a similar manner, the 'leakage of reality' was avoided
by the barbarian societies which occupied the former provinces of the Empire. Here, we find Gibbon at his most differentiated, because at his most pragmatic. Any system that
did violence to the observed quality of human nature in a
given society repelled him. In an essay on the origins of the
feudal system in France, he declared his methods: 'Je combine l'expérience avec le raisonnement. J'ouvre les codes de
ces peuples qui renversoient l'empire. . . . J'ouvre leurs annales. . . . Enfin j'aperçois l'aurore de la nouvelle institution.' Again, this is conducted with Gibbon's breathtaking
sense of scale; the whole quality of barbarian society is involved: 'Tel est l'esprit qui s'est répandu du nord au midi,
depuis les frontières de la Chine jusqu'au fond de l'Afrique.'[61]

The method brings unexpected warmth and texture to
his treatment of the barbarian societies of the West. To take
one example, that of the Lombards in Italy: Giannone and,
before him, Grotius had stressed the essentially secular, non-
clerical nature of the legislation of the Lombards. This, wrote
Giannone, was sufficient merit in itself; it proved the independence of the laws of the original Italian states from the
law of the Church. Gibbon follows Giannone, and yet he

59. DF, chap. 38, p. 152.   60. Ibid., p. 153.
61. 'I combine experience with reasoning. I open the law-codes of those peoples who overturned the empire . . . I open their chronicles . . . At last I perceive the
dawn of a new institution. This is the style of [barbarian] society as it exists in a wide
sweep from north to south, from the frontiers of China to the depths of Africa.'
Gibbon, 'Du Governement féodal surtout en France', Collected Works, III, 189.

draws a subtly different conclusion. The absence of bishops meant the absence of Romans. Not being clericalized, the Lombards were not Romanized, and so their laws reflected the essential spirit of their society: they were "the genuine fruits of the reason of the barbarians.'[62] Faithful to his methods, Gibbon brings alive this 'reason of the barbarians'. Hence his preference for Paul the Deacon: 'His pictures of national manners, though rudely sketched are more lively and faithful than those of Bede or Gregory of Tours.'[63] And so we are treated, as an *apéritif* to the laws, to a story from Paul: 'the adventurous gallantry of Autharis, which breathes the true spirit of chivalry and romance.'[64]

Yet Gibbon was no Romantic. He could react with seismographic sensitivity to the slightest tremor of Romanticism in Montesquieu. When Montesquieu 'condescended to explain and excuse *la manière de penser de nos pères* on the subject of judicial combats . . . , the philosopher is sometimes lost in the antiquarian.'[65] Gibbon regarded romantic empathy as a shortcut. When it came to understanding the irrational elements in barbarian law, Gibbon was firm: rationality was a long, hard road, and no amount of special pleading could excuse a Frank of the sixth century from having to travel it, nor make him travel any faster than his general level of culture and manners could allow him: 'the fierce and illiterate chieftain was seldom qualified to discharge the duties of a judge, which require all the faculties of a philosophic mind, laboriously cultivated by experience and study.'[66]

What impressed Gibbon, therefore, about barbarian society was less any exotic or Romantic qualities it might have possessed than the manner in which its institutions avoided the 'leakage of reality' that weakened the structure of extended empires. The comparison of Western Europe with the sixth-century Byzantine state makes this plain: 'In the Salic laws and the Pandects of Justinian we may compare the first

62. *DF*, chap. 45, p. 32. 63. Ibid., p. 6, n. 10. 64. Ibid., p. 29.
65. *DF*, chap. 38, p. 137, n. 86. 66. Ibid., p. 136.

rudiments and the full maturity of civil wisdom; and, whatever prejudices may be suggested in favour of Barbarism, our calmer reflections will ascribe to the Romans the superior advantages, not only of science and reason, but of humanity and justice. Yet the laws of the Barbarians were adapted to their wants and desires, their occupations, and their capacity; and they all contributed to preserve the peace, and promote the improvements, of the society for whose use they were originally established.'[67]

'The *Decline and Fall* is probably the most majestic work of history ever written.'[68] But its author was a down-to-earth man. The intricate craftsmanship with which men can be observed to weave the web of civilized society concerned him more deeply than systems. We have followed him through the period in the history of Europe when the web seemed to be in tatters. Only a few strands of what had once been so rich a weave are being replaited by unskilled hands. Yet how much of his web has actually been broken? Gibbon's sense of civilization and of its resilience goes far deeper than the mere study of courts and churches: 'Private genius and public industry may be extirpated: but these hardy plants survive the tempest, and strike an everlasting root into the most unfavorable soil. The splendid days of Augustus and Trajan were eclipsed by a cloud of ignorance; and the Barbarians subverted the laws and palaces of Rome. But the scythe, the invention or emblem of Saturn, still continued annually to mow the harvests of Italy; and the human feasts of the Laestrygons have never been renewed on the coast of Campania.'[69]

If the modern historiography of Late Antiquity can regain some of Gibbon's anxious alertness to the weaving and reweaving of the restraining web of society, can reintroduce

67. Ibid., p. 132.
68. H. Trevor-Roper, *Gibbon: The Great Histories* (New York and London, 1966), p. xxi. This fine introduction is the distillation of a knowledge of Gibbon and the historiography of the Enlightenment, from which I have frequently benefitted in personal conversation and to which I wish to acknowledge a debt of gratitude.
69. *DF*, chap. 38, p. 181.

into its analysis of the social structure of the later Roman Empire and of the role of religion in this structure something of Gibbon's sense of the irony of a complex society, and, when faced with the overwhelming mass of material for the religious and cultural history of the age, be prepared to follow Gibbon in his many acts of silent renunciation, then we may move yet again from an age of erudition to an age of 'philosophic' history.

In Gibbon's Shade[†]

BOOKS ON THE ROMAN EMPIRE AND ON THE RISE of Christianity coming before a reviewer in 1976 brought author and reviewer alike into the disturbing presence of a mighty shade. Two centuries previously, in 1776, Edward Gibbon published the first volume of his *Decline and Fall*. It was twelve years before that, in 1764, 'as I sat musing amidst the ruins of the Capitol, while the barefooted friars were singing Vespers in the Temple of Jupiter, that the idea of writing the decline and fall of the city first started to my mind.'[1]

In January 1976, with pardonable hubris, the participants of a congress on Edward Gibbon and his *Decline and Fall* organized by the American Academy of Arts and Sciences, posed for a group photograph on that spot. The summer 1976 issue of *Daedalus* ranged widely and deeply in the immediate intellectual background of Gibbon, and presented a picture less of Gibbon's relevance to modern scholarship in ancient and medieval history than of the deep roots of Gibbon's thought and erudition in the religious and social preoccupations of post-Renaissance Europe.[2]

[†] *New York Review of Books* XXIII (1976): 14–18.

1. Edward Gibbon, *Memoirs of My Life*, ed. G. A. Bonnard (London, 1966), p. 136.

2. *Edward Gibbon and the Decline and Fall of the Roman Empire*, *Daedalus* CV (Summer 1976); and *Edward Gibbon and the Decline and Fall of the Roman Empire*, ed. G. W. Bowersock, J. Clive and S. R. Graubard (Cambridge, Mass., 1977).

In this review, a group of authors on the period of history that Gibbon himself covered is presented to the shade. An excellent short survey of *Roman Social Relations* by Professor Ramsay MacMullen, a short work of characteristic intellectual distinction on *Christianity in the Roman World* by Professor Robert Markus; a sensitive and pioneering study—the most specialized and the most original in our group—of the religious language of a Christian community that stretched from the Roman shore of the eastern Mediterranean deep into Asia, *Symbols of Church and Kingdom: A Study in Early Syriac Tradition*, by Robert Murray; and *The Fall of the Roman Empire: A Reappraisal*, skilfully written by Professor Michael Grant, and magnificently illustrated.[3]

The shade would have inspected this group with some curiosity, and would have inspired no little trepidation. For Gibbon's range was awesome. Within twenty years he had covered the history of a millennium, and in so doing he had scanned almost every society in the Eurasian landmass. What is even more disturbing: before he set pen to paper, he had amassed vast knowledge which he did not even consider worth his while to put into the *Decline and Fall*, so great was his sense of relevance and of the overriding importance of his main themes. On page 98 of his book, Professor MacMullen presents us with a diagram illustrating the distribution of wealth in an Italian region in the reign of the Emperor Trajan: the salient features of Roman society—its 'verticality' and the accumulation of wealth and status in the hands of a tiny few—spring to the eye. This is a characteristically felicitous exploitation of data from an inscription—the Veleia tablet. It is the way history is done, and done well, in the 1970s. But Gibbon had seen the Veleia tablet in 1764. He had copied it out: '*C'est un travail sec et ingrat, mais quand on construit un Édifice il faut en creuser les fondements. L'on est obligé de faire le rôle de*

3. Ramsay MacMullen, *Roman Social Relations, 50 B.C. to A.D. 284* (New Haven, Conn., 1974); R. A. Markus, *Christianity in the Roman World* (London, 1974); Robert Murray, *Symbols of Church and Kingdom: A Study in the Early Syriac Tradition* (Cambridge, 1975); Michael Grant, *The Fall of the Roman Empire: A Reappraisal* (Annenberg School Press, 1976).

maçon aussi bien que celui d'Architecte. J'espère pouvoir tirer quelque chose de cette espèce de recensement' [4]. . . and then decided that it was not worth using in the *Decline and Fall.*

Gibbon would have passed by Professor MacMullen's book. This was because he had come to believe that the social development of the classical Empire could be of little relevance to his theme if it did not explain to him the main feature of the period of decline and fall—that is, the rapid and unprecedented accumulation of social and political power in the hands of new religious leaders, the Christian bishops and monks. But then Gibbon did not have the opportunity to be persuaded by a reading of Professor MacMullen's *Roman Social Relations,* or by the author's previous works, *Soldier and Civilian in the Later Roman Empire* and *Enemies of the Roman Order: Treason, Unrest and Alienation in the Empire.*[5] For Gibbon would have met in MacMullen the one author in the English language whose highly distinctive view of what the social history of the ancient world was about (a view pursued with Gibbonian tenacity and erudition, and with more than a touch of Gibbonian empiricism) has enabled him to write convincingly of just those religious and cultural developments that so preoccupied Gibbon in the *Decline and Fall.*

Professor Markus's book would have brought Gibbon to a halt. This book is directly relevant to his own concerns. It is a clear-headed exposition of intellectual history, yet concerned throughout to grasp the meaning of ideas by way of the attitudes they encouraged groups to take toward their cultural and social environment—a central concern of Gibbon. Professor Markus calls his little book 'a history of Christian self-awareness in the Roman world.'[6] It is just that,

4. 'It is dry and ungrateful work, but when one constructs a building the foundations have to be dug. One has to turn mason as well as architect. I hope to derive some information from this kind of survey.' *Gibbon's Journey from Geneva to Rome,* ed. G. A. Bonnard (London, 1961), p. 129; see above, p. 25.

5. *Soldier and Civilian in the Later Roman Empire* (Cambridge, Mass., 1963); *Enemies of the Roman Order: Treason, Unrest and Alienation in the Empire* (Cambridge, Mass., 1966); see now *Roman Government's Response to Crisis,* A.D. 235–337 (New Haven, Conn., 1976).

6. Markus, *Christianity in the Roman World,* p. 9.

and the best short account now available, giving the inside of a development which Gibbon had watched, from the outside, with fascinated curiosity.

It is precisely because it is a history from the inside that the book differs so markedly from Gibbon's. It displays, in a nutshell, where modern scholarship has changed, indeed advanced, in its handling of the problems set out by the *Decline and Fall*. For Gibbon was a theologian *manqué*. As a young man in Magdalen College, Oxford, he had been projected for a moment into Catholicism by the 'elastic spring' of metaphysical controversy. A few generations later, he might have been a pillar of the Oxford Movement—a 'perpendicular prig of Puseyism'. In his later life, the spring was weighted down safely by rational and humane considerations. But never for a moment did he lose his sense of its dangerous powers in others, or of the havoc it could wreak when, in the hands of fanatics, such as Christian monks and theologians, it flicked loose. For Gibbon, therefore, the 'history of Christian self-awareness' was a history of deadly certainties. The hard bones of metaphysical cerebration and clerical ambition press ineluctably through the wasting flesh of the Empire.[7]

Professor Markus writes in an age where the spring is safely broken. The finest passages of his own masterly exposition of the thought of St Augustine, *Saeculum: History and Society in the Theology of Saint Augustine*,[8] are those in which he shows Augustine's subtle and hard mind learning to live with uncertainty, and explains how relevant such uncertainty can be to a modern Christian. Gibbon and Gibbon's *bêtes noires* alike thought in straight lines and right angles. Markus's early Christians, by contrast, are left to fumble. Whatever 'fanaticism' they might have had was tempered by a humane inability to breathe any other air than that of the Roman world and to see with any other eyes than those in-

7. Above, pp. 31–32.
8. *Saeculum: History and Society in the Theology of Saint Augustine* (Cambridge, 1970).

herited from a long classical past. Professor Markus's history of the early Christian Church is the history of a 'subculture': the angular figures of Gibbon give way to men groping obscurely 'in their confrontation with what they came to recognize as non-Christian only in the moments of dawning self-definition.'[9]

Not surprisingly, this is an amply and skilfully illustrated book. It is typical of the gap between Gibbon and ourselves that the scholars to whom Professor Markus acknowledges a debt should be one Platonic metaphysician (Professor Hilary Armstrong) and two interpreters of late Roman art (Gervase Mathew and Sabine MacCormack). Gibbon's *Decline and Fall* is unillustrable. The excellent set of pictures provided in J. B. Bury's edition of 1908 almost invariably remind us of what is *not* in the text. For Gibbon's text describes what early Christian art could not show—men whose minds were bemazed by the deadly clarities of speculative theology. Such certainties speak most clearly only in cold print. Markus's Christians come alive in their uncertainties; and the sheer weight of these uncertainties can be seen in so many of his illustrations. Christian themes struggle with a millennium of pagan craftsmanship to take on a profile of their own. The polished marble holds them back, imposes a classical reticence on them, and blurs each new face with a disturbing sense of *déjà vu* from an ancient past.

To Gibbon's discredit, he might have found Robert Murray's book unworthy of consideration. To bring alive the rich religious language of a Near Eastern province of the later Roman Empire was not a service likely to commend itself to him. He had a brusque way with representatives of the 'Syriac tradition', and especially, as was generally the case, if they were monks: the monk Antiochus was only one such—'whose one hundred and twenty nine homilies are still extant, if what no one reads may be said to be extant'.[10]

9. Markus, *Christianity in the Roman World*, p. 10.

10. E. Gibbon, *The History of the Decline and Fall of the Roman Empire*, ed. J. B. Bury (London, 1929), chap. 46, n. 73.

He might have missed the point of Murray's beautiful and patient evocation of an early Christian religious language. For just as the tentativeness of Markus's Christians differs *toto caelo* from the fanatical clarities of Gibbon's princes of the Church, so Murray's concern to explore the basic, mystery-laden 'Symbols of Church and Kingdom' used by Syriac religious poets takes us far away from the arid world of the theologians, down to the roots of Christian piety in the Near East. Indeed, the deeper we sink into the inner dimensions of the 'history of Christian self-awareness in the Roman world', the less we smell the acrid smoke of theological battle which Gibbon managed, for all his distaste, to breathe with such gusto.

Murray's Syrians knew Gibbon's theologians, and did not like them. Ephraim, in his long, passionate songs, called them 'the Questioners'. They were the self-confident heirs of Aristotelian logic, whose scholastic method sought to strip from the Godhead the rustling, shimmering, shot-silk veils of symbols. In the fourth century, these men were the Arian heretics in Edessa. A long tradition of scholastic thought in Western Christianity has made their like, until quite recently, the official spokesmen of orthodoxy. *Symbols of Church and Kingdom* is a scrupulous book, with unfailing historical sense and aliveness to the language of late Roman men. But it has serious theological implications; it lays bare with rare sympathy the way in which the Christians of the Syriac-speaking provinces spoke of the Church. It is a subtle and mellow voice from the past that has been too long drowned by the articulate and rigid certainties of Western churchmen. Gibbon can have his speculative divines. Father Murray, I suspect, is happiest with his poet-monks: 'He was a fine sight as he stood among the sisters, singing a melody of praise.'[11]

Professor Grant's book would have surprised Gibbon. It is written with the elegance and talent for making the evidence speak that we have come to expect in Professor Grant's

11. Murray, *Symbols*, p. 30, n. 1; see now his 'Der Dichter als Exeget', *Zeitschrift für katholische Theologie* C (1978): 484–494.

work. Clearly laid out, well signposted with maps and ta-
bles, the thirteen causes of the fall of the Roman Empire are
made crystal clear in 314 pages. What would astonish Gibbon, though, is that of these thirteen causes, every one, Professor Grant points out at every turn, is also apparent and
active in contemporary American and Western European society. The Roman Empire in its last hundred years is brought
briskly up to the twentieth century. The effect is like seeing a
near-by object through a telescope of high resolution: the
sudden abolition of distance and the close-up detail is baffling
and unnecessary.

Gibbon would not have done that. He had weightier concerns. The 'awful revolution' he described was about the deep
change in the whole quality of an ancient civilization, and
about the slow recovery of that civilization many centuries
later. So deep a concern was not to be 'blown up' by preaching and alarms. In any case, Gibbon felt that his own age had,
if but recently, recovered from the fall of the Roman Empire,
even from the rise of Christianity. Like many eighteenth-century Europeans, he felt that the 'more polished nations of
Europe', at least, had come out on a plateau. The plateau
might not have been very high, but it was safer than that of
the Roman Empire at the time of its greatest prosperity and
apparent security; and they would stay on it. When Gibbon
writes with fascinated horror of the developments that he saw
in the distant past, it is with the chill of a man who looks back
over the precipice that his civilization has scaled successfully—
che nel pensier rinnuova la paura. Grant's book would have it
that the civilization of America and Europe had rolled back
and was clinging again to the edge of that precipice.

One would be content to leave to Mr. Gibbon the decision whether Professor Grant's opinions are correct. One
thing, however, is plain: this is a slight and basically a trivial
book. Facing the problem of the possible decline and fall of a
civilization, Professor Grant has none of Gibbon's sense of
scale and gives little evidence of commitments as deep and
complex as Gibbon's.

Gibbon began his narrative and close analysis of the de-cline of the Roman Empire with Augustus; he came to wish that he had started even earlier. Grant begins with the reign of Valentinian I in 364 A.D. Gibbon's deep concern with the quality of western civilization as such led him to follow the themes that obsessed him far beyond the conventional date of the fall of the Roman Empire. Grant ends his book in 476. Gibbon was aware not only of the military importance of the barbarian invasions but of the need to explain the nature of that great Third World that pressed in on Rome, finally ac-cepted its religion, and passed on its culture. He learned to scrutinize the records of the early Middle Ages and to train his historical insight with a knowledge of primitive societies as far apart as those of China and Africa: in Florence he sits reading Mallet's *History of Denmark* and speculates on what it was like for a Nordic pagan to live among rocks scratched by the Scaldic bards with dread, incomprehensible runic signs. Apart from a few portraits, some artifacts, and an elegant pair of trousers and shirt rescued from Thorsberger Moor, Grant leaves this world outside his scope. The 'disastrous disunities' of his own western society hold his attention entirely.

It is merely a fruit of comparatively modern classical prejudice that we concentrate almost exclusively on the ear-lier part of Gibbon's majestic narrative. Like all great books, the *Decline and Fall of the Roman Empire* raises themes that stretch far deeper and far wider than a conventional inter-pretation of its title would lead us to expect. Gibbon and his contemporaries had a far larger historical vision than ours, products as we are of the specialized disciplines of a modern university system. For Gibbon the history of the decline and fall of the Roman Empire was meaningful only as the prelude to the rise of modern Europe.

Thus after the deceptively trenchant 'General Observa-tions' on the fall of the Empire in the West, Gibbon resumed his unhurrying pace. There were more interesting things to explain than merely the collapse of the Roman Empire: barbarian Europe had to be Christianized and sent on Crusade; the papacy and the Holy Roman Empire had to rise out of the ruins of Dark Age Italy; the 'Revolution of the East', the rise of Islam and the Arab and Turkish conquests, had to be played out until its fateful climax in the fall of Constantinople in 1453.

Then, as now, conventional gentlemen, reared on the classics, chafed and tried to cry 'Halt.' Walpole, having fluted praise to Gibbon in 1776 over the Age of the Antonines—'that Elysian era'—predictably lost interest even by the early fifth century: too many tribes by far, 'who with the same features and characters are to be described in different terms, without any substantial variety, and he is to bring you acquainted with them when you wish them all at the bottom of the Red Sea.'[12] More robust souls stood the pace for a few more centuries: in 1781 Lord Hardwick still wanted a little more, 'at least till the irruption of the Arabs, after Mahomet. From that period the History of the East is not very interesting and often disgusting.'[13] Undeterred, magnificently un-Europocentric, Gibbon strode on until the job was done. As a result, the 'historian of the Roman Empire' wrote some of his best chapters as a medievalist and as a connoisseur of Asiatic empire-building.

Furthermore, throughout the *Decline and Fall*, Gibbon's sense of the causes of the 'awful revolution' is marked by a sober respect for weighty and complex processes: the word 'insensibly', the image of 'poison' convey this sense throughout the narrative.[14] By contrast, Grant's causes are clear-cut and flimsy. To take one example: the rise of monasticism and of the ascetic movement is briskly brought into relation with modern 'drop out' movements, and then the effect of the whole development is summed up as having weakened the

12. *The Letters of Horace Walpole*, ed. P. Toynbee (Oxford, 1934), pp. 408–409.
13. Lord Hardwick to Gibbon, Sept. 20, 1781. Edward Gibbon, *Miscellaneous Works* II, CXXXV (Dublin, 1796), 87.
14. G. W. Bowersock, 'Gibbon on Civil War and Rebellion in Rome', *Daedalus* CV (1976): 66–67; *Edward Gibbon*, pp. 30–31.

Empire by diminishing the birth rate—too much chastity! In the same way, the careers of bishops and theologians are regretted: 'men of superior brains and character who in earlier times would have been public servants.'[15] There is an element of bathos in such pinpointing of the causes of the decline of the Empire that is only too common in modern scholarship.

Gibbon mentioned these issues and then passed on: they disquieted him far less than did the deeper changes in men's relation to civilized living. He hated monks; but he hated them for weighty reasons, and not because of a sudden onset of charismatic contraception. He hated them because he detected a sloughing off of the merciful restraints of humanity in these men, and feared it for its consequences of fanaticism, inhumanity, and violence.

How to understand the movement toward a radical rejection of the bonds of society that swept the Near East remains one of the major unsolved problems of late Roman history. We come closer to understanding it, and with far greater sympathy, in Murray's patient study. Even if a book such as *Symbols of Church and Kingdom* shows that Gibbon misunderstood some of the deeper drives and the latent social function of these strange men, at least Gibbon had a sense of the size of the phenomenon he was grappling with, both in the past and in his own age. Grant's account is that of a man who would encourage us to understand neither St Anthony nor the Beat generation.

We need only turn to Professor MacMullen's *Roman Social Relations* to see the weakness of Grant's approach. Grant's last Romans appear to move in a weight-free environment, taking choices and performing antics that arouse the disquiet of westerners of liberal temper. The fact that they were grappling with the eternal problems of Mediterranean empires is hardly apparent.

MacMullen's short book makes such a view of the causes of the decline and fall of the Roman Empire untenable, and does so all the more cogently for never mentioning it. Let us first praise the book's learning, which is like one of the fig-

15. Grant, *Fall of the Roman Empire*, pp. 232–48.

ures he describes so well—'exuberantly formidable'.[16] Text-book stereotypes and popular illusions alike are quietly and ineluctably buried forever beneath a shifting dune of minute grains of erudition. It is a book that is all the more persuasive for being utterly undogmatic, the product of humble patient craftsmanship, which is rare in modern writings on ancient economic history. MacMullen's emphasis on the paramount importance of non-economic factors in Roman life—on concern for status, on the role of sheer brute force in the relations of rich and poor and in the accumulation of wealth—these subjects on which misconception long rested in respectable circles, and around which, at long last, controversy now rages, are silently and firmly put in their place.[17]

For just as Gibbon became learned because he was convinced that a particular type of history was possible, so, I suspect, did MacMullen. This short book illustrates a break-through in classical scholarship. For classical scholars, tied as they have been to their texts and tied yet more firmly to the elitist prejudices of these texts and of their own peculiar academic environment, have never been noted for their optimism about the amount of evidence available for the writing of ancient social history. In fact, they condemn themselves to this impression by sheer snobbishness. One scholar in a distinguished university was heard to remark that, in his opinion, the Acts of the Apostles were not history; they were only footnotes to history.

But, then, what is ancient 'history'? Professor MacMullen throws open the windows in that narrow room. The whole landscape lies at our feet, in whatever language, from whatever region—*Roman Social Relations* embraces and skilfully uses it. MacMullen makes plain that he is up against the problems posed by the consciousness of the type of society he is describing. A society so rigidly 'vertical' in its structure can hardly be expected to show interest for the average man, or for men who, though far from average, did not share in

16. MacMullen, *Roman Social Relations*, p. 12.
17. Ibid., pp. 88–120, on the vexed issue of 'class' and its relation to sources of wealth in the Roman world.

their narrow horizons—the Jewish rabbis, for instance, whose remarks in the Talmud provide MacMullen with some astonishingly vivid views of the Roman world. 'The senatorial stratum amounted to something like two-thousandths of one percent (a figure that Tacitus would have found deeply gratifying).'[18] Unfortunately, it is to Tacitus and his modern exponents that the student is first directed in his study of the 'history' of the ancient world. Professor MacMullen will have nothing of this, and he makes his reasons abundantly plain. We have a choice: 'Ammianus Marcellinus [who said]: "Not everything deserves narration that goes on among the lower orders." In contrast, Marc Bloch: "I can hardly be persuaded that it is perfectly legitimate to describe a state, without having first tried to analyse the society on which it rests." Two views, ancient and modern. Which shall we follow?'[19]

Roman Social Relations is a portrait of the Roman Empire as it existed in its fullness. It stretches beyond the awareness of its governing classes, embracing the whole of provincial society. MacMullen writes tartly that 'the accident of source-survival has pushed Italy forward as equivalent to "Roman civilization"';[20] and characteristically he goes on to redress the accident, by bringing in the eastern shores of the Mediterranean, where, in the Jewish literature of the time, we see a world viewed without illusions, and betrayed right down to the names used for its main social categories—the rich are 'the Haughty Ones', and their agents 'the Men of the Arm'.[21]

Professor MacMullen's classical Roman Empire of the first and second centuries—a society where wealth has already drained into the hands of the few, whose countryside was ravaged by endemic violence, whose population lived on the brink of famine—is not the sort of empire to have a straightforward 'Decline and Fall'. For it could hardly have declined much further. The only difference between the Roman Empire of the Age of the Antonines and the later Roman Empire may well be that we know far more about the

18. Ibid., pp. 88–89.   19. Ibid., pp. 127.   20. Ibid., p. 189, n. 35.
21. Ibid., p. 195, n. 68.

later Empire: a social structure glimpsed with a taper is suddenly lit up under an arc lamp. We know more because its rulers and articulate groups within it—the Christian bishops —set themselves to know more about it.

In the Age of the Antonines, 'the one sure maxim of extended empire, a wise and salutary neglect', held good throughout the Roman world. The Roman Empire, whose professional administrative class numbered a little less than one thousand, gave a free hand to the local oligarchies to do the business of government. Comparatively little was demanded by way of taxes, and no questions were asked how that little was extorted from the peasantry. It is a type of 'soft' government on which many a colonial empire has rested in recent times, and on which the economic empires of many developed western nations still do rest. The later Roman Empire could not afford to blind itself so thoroughly. The emperors had to get in the taxes and the recruits in order to meet the strain of constant war. They had to lift ancient and respectable stones. It is hardly surprising that some unpleasant creatures were found to be crawling beneath them; but Professor MacMullen has the good sense to realize that they had been there a long time; the oppressive relations of landowner and peasant, for instance, were 'only the further development of predatory arrogance long latent in the *pax romana*.'[22]

Nor was public opinion so blind. By the beginning of the fifth century, congregations flocked to hear a preacher like John Chrysostom denouncing the exploitation of seasonal labourers, and Asterius of Amaseia (a small-town bishop) would describe in vivid detail the poor of the city, pressing up against the warm sides of the public bathhouse for a little bit of comfort against the icy winter of Anatolia. Such themes would not have drawn an audience for the polished rhetoricians of the Antonine age.

At the risk of a paradox, one might almost say that the 'fall' of the Roman Empire—that is, the collapse of its political superstructure in its western provinces—happened because,

22. Ibid., pp. 7–8.

in a few desperate generations, the Roman emperors of the fourth century, their servants and advisers, decided that the time had come to reverse the trend of its 'decline'—a decline too long masked behind a façade of classical dignity.

Gibbon's problem, therefore, remains. It was not why the Roman Empire fell, but why it lasted so long, and why its culture and social infrastructure long survived the collapse of the imperial administration in the western Mediterranean. This, and not the facile blame-pinning of a modern commentator, remains the unsolved mystery of late Roman studies.

It is not a mystery in which the inhabitants of the western world have a monopoly of interest. The problem of the decline and fall of the Roman Empire may not be relevant to a western man's image of himself and his society. Gibbon could write as he did about the Roman Empire because the society of pre-industrial Western Europe was still close enough to that of the Roman world for him to understand that world, and to observe that the Europe of his own days had done better with similar materials. We have moved on into more dangerous times, to which the Roman Empire and its dilemmas are irrelevant. But the problems of how great traditional societies, in Asia, Africa, and the Andes, grapple today with unprecedented political and ideological change— these are the problems which might more fruitfully engage the sympathy and the understanding of western readers of the *Decline and Fall*.

It would take a society even more complacent and more inward-looking than the later Empire, as Grant imagines it to have been, to be satisfied that its own ills could be diagnosed so briskly and to believe that the fate of a long-past Mediterranean empire could be marshalled so peremptorily to give answers only to its own needs and anxieties. However much we scholars may disagree with him, Gibbon gave us a Roman Empire that was bigger, stranger, richer, and more resilient than the pocket-mirror image of modern discontents that emerges from Grant's *Reappraisal*.

Mohammed and Charlemagne
by Henri Pirenne[†]

ahomet et Charlemagne APPEARED POST-humously in 1937.[1] Pirenne had formulated its central thesis as early as 1916 and put it forward from 1922 onwards with a rigour of proof to which the book itself adds little other than a wealth of supporting evidence.[2] *Mahomet et Charlemagne*, therefore, was hailed less as a novelty than as the 'historical testament' of the foremost interpreter of the social and economic development of medieval Europe. To reconsider it as a 'historical testament' may help the future reader and the past connoisseur of this succinct and brilliant monograph to seize through its pages the outline of modern attitudes toward the history of the end of the ancient world and the beginning of the Middle Ages.

It is important to treat *Mahomet et Charlemagne* as a historical testament. From the outset, it was vigorously contested by Pirenne's intellectual next of kin, and, as a result, the argument of *Mahomet et Charlemagne* has entered circulation in the academic world as the 'Pirenne thesis'. Debates for

[†] *Daedalus* CIII (1974): 25–33.
1. Henri Pirenne, *Mohammed and Charlemagne*, trans. B. Miall (New York, 1939); see now B. Lyon, *Henri Pirenne: A Biographical and Intellectual Study* (Ghent, 1974).
2. H. Pirenne, 'Mahomet et Charlemagne', *Revue belge de philologie et d'histoire* I (1922): 77–86; and 'Un contraste économique: Mérovingiens et Carolingiens', ibid., II (1922): 223–35.

and against this thesis have provided historians of the later
Roman Empire, Byzantium, early medieval Islam and western Europe, not to mention numismatists, with material for a
respectable academic light industry, one whose products
have, on the whole, proved ingenious and serviceable. That
the terms of reference in the debate should stretch from the
ceramic industry of third-century A.D. Gaul to the relations
between Scandinavia and Central Asia in the tenth century is
no small tribute to the issues compressed into 285 pages in
the English translation.[3]

As with many a 'classic', it is even possible for the specialist today to do without *Mahomet et Charlemagne*. Histories
of the social and economic development of western Europe
after the fall of the Roman Empire can be written both with a
greater range of detail and with a more sober sense of the
human possibilities of an underdeveloped economy than was
shown by Pirenne in his *Mahomet et Charlemagne*; they need
contain only a passing reference to the dazzling paradoxes of
Pirenne's exposition.[4] Happy tillers of the ever-richer delta of

3. The most important of these articles, and the two articles of Pirenne cited
above, are collected in their original languages in *Bedeutung und Rolle des Islam beim
Übergang vom Altertum zum Mittelalter*, ed. P. E. Hübinger, Wege der Forschung
CCII (Darmstadt, 1968).

4. For a stern warning, see Renée Doehaerd, *Le Haut Moyen Âge occidental*,
Nouvelle Clio XIV (Paris, 1971), p. 350. What is under criticism among modern
scholars is Pirenne's robust conviction that fluctuations of trade and the resultant
quality of urban life were the privileged causes of change in the economy of the
Middle Ages. The trend in modern scholarship of both the ancient and the medieval
worlds is to emphasize the overwhelming importance of the agrarian base of these
societies and to stress the consequent 'primitivism', or 'non-modernity', of their
economies: M. I. Finley, *The Ancient Economy* (London, 1973) and Ramsay Mac-
Mullen, *Roman Social Relations* (New Haven, Conn., 1974), pp. 88–120. The
tendency to look at an agrarian base capable of little change and so to see the non-
mercantile factor of structures of interpersonal relations as determining the distribution of wealth in early medieval society owes much to the influence of the social
anthropologists: J. LeGoff, *Pour un autre Moyen-âge* (Paris, 1977): 'D'où, grâce au
regard ethnologique, une ruralisation de l'histoire. Après le Moyen-âge urbain et
bourgeois que l'histoire du xixe. siècle a imposé d'Augustin Thierry à Henri Pirenne, voici, qui nous semble plus vrai, le Moyen-âge rural . . . .' (p. 339). For
thought-provoking and learned discussion of the period in general: Philip Jones, 'La
storia economica. Dalla caduta dell'Impero romano al secolo xiv', *Storia d'Italia* II
(Einaudi, Turin, 1974): 1469–1810.

Late Antique and early medieval studies can now get on with the job giving little thought to the headwaters of that Nile which once swept so great a mass of alluvium down to their respective fields.

The 'Pirenne thesis' can be succinctly summarized: for centuries after the political collapse of the Roman Empire in the West, the economic and social life of western Europe still moved exclusively to the rhythms of the ancient world. *Romania*, a robust 'functional Romanity' (whose resources were too easily overlooked by strict classical scholars), survived intact from the so-called 'Germanic Invasions' of the fifth century A.D. Shabby but irreplaceable, much as the slipshod cursive script of a Merovingian document is an unmistakeable descendant of the ancient Roman hand, worn down by uninterrupted use, the civilization of *Romania* long outlived the Roman Empire. It survived because the economic life based on the Mediterranean had continued unscathed. It was only with the Arab conquests of the eastern and southern Mediterranean in the seventh century A.D. that this Mediterranean-wide economy was disrupted. Islam marks a breach in the continuum of ancient civilization incomparably deeper than that of the Germanic Invasions. For the first time, half of the known world took on an alien face. The Arab war fleets of the late seventh century closed the Mediterranean to shipping: the fall of Carthage in 698 sealed the fate of Marseille and with it the fate of *Romania* in Gaul. Deprived of its Mediterranean-wide horizons, the civilization of western Europe closed in on itself, and the under-Romanized world of northern Gaul and Germany suddenly gained a prominence inconceivable in earlier generations. The southern-oriented *Romania* was replaced by a western Europe dominated by a northern Frankish aristocracy. It was a society where wealth was restricted to land; its ruler, lacking the gold currency that taxation could have drawn from the economy had trade remained vigorous, was forced to reward his followers by grants of land, and feudalism was born. Its Church no longer included a laity bathed in the living slipshod Latinity of the south, but was dominated by a clerical élite whose very handwriting 'ploughed' into parchment made from the hides of their northern flocks, whereas that of earlier clerics and laymen had slipped easily over sheets of Egyptian papyrus shipped direct from pre-Islamic Alexandria to the quays of Marseille. Clothes and diet lost all hint of the 'Roman' elegance which had been based on continued commerce in the spices and silk products of the eastern Mediterranean. In short, the Empire of Charlemagne, a northern Germanic empire unimaginable in any previous century, marks the true beginning of the Middle Ages; all that had preceded it was the autumn of the ancient Mediterranean culture. The change happened, Pirenne insisted, not through any slow entropy of *Romania* in the south, nor through any discrete rise in the economic and human potential of the Germanic north. Rather, by breaking the unity of the Mediterranean, the Arab war fleets had twisted a tourniquet around the artery by which the warm blood of ancient civilization in its last Romano–Byzantine form had continued to pulse into western Europe. 'It is therefore strictly correct to say that without Mohammed, Charlemagne would have been inconceivable.'[5]

So much for the 'Pirenne thesis'. Modern readers who are grappling with the implications of our own shift from an 'Atlantic' to a 'Pacific' civilization will find the verve and deep historical empathy with which Pirenne entered into a world whose people considered any alternative to the Mediterranean basin unthinkable particularly thrilling. *Mahomet et Charlemagne* is history written in terms of human horizons that suddenly close and tumble upside-down.

This thrill alone has carried historians of all periods through this book. Yet the historian of the end of the ancient world may well look beyond *Mahomet et Charlemagne* for a moment. The 'Pirenne thesis' is a spark, brilliant but frail, between solid electrical points, patiently constructed and manoeuvred into position by Pirenne and the scholars of his

5. Pirenne, *Mohammed and Charlemagne*, p. 234.

generation. We can see their outline clearly in the light of the spark they generate. In order to read *Mahomet et Charlemagne* with an eye for present and future development in early medieval studies, it is as well to inquire how these electrical points came to be set up as they were, whether they can now stand where they did, and what new leap of current might yet pass between them.

The first and most lasting impression of Henri Pirenne's work as a whole is the one to which the readers of *Mahomet et Charlemagne* constantly return. Pirenne was the master of his age in expounding the social and economic basis of medieval civilization. It is as a series of chapters in the history of western civilization and its transformations that *Mahomet et Charlemagne* remains an irreplaceable book.

Discussion of the separate facets of the 'Pirenne thesis' can divert attention from the stature of the book much as a charged cloud disintegrates into a discharge of discrete hailstones. Nevertheless, let us examine in passing some of the facets of Pirenne with which it is now possible to disagree. First, economically, the commercial role of the Mediterranean in the fifth and sixth centuries was not such as to support the continuity of ancient civilization that Pirenne posited;[6] determined, as we shall see, to cut the Germanic Invasions of the fifth century down to size, Pirenne, as scholars of the late Roman Empire were quick to point out, underrated the slow dislocation of western Roman society from the third century A.D. onwards.[7] One might add that the hushed generations following the great visitation of the plague after 543, which saw the saddened old age of Jus-

6. J. Rougé, *Recherches sur l'organisation de commerce maritime en Méditerranée sous l'empire romain* (Paris, 1966) and F. Braudel, *The Mediterranean and the Mediterranean World in the Age of Philip II*, trans. S. Reynolds (London, 1962), pp. 103–37, 168–230. Though full of admiration for Pirenne's capacity to synthesize and aware of the importance of long-distance trade, Braudel's study stresses the diversity of the Mediterranean and the great complexity of its economic relations with its northern European hinterland.

7. A. Riising, 'The Fate of Henri Pirenne's Thesis on the Consequences of the Islamic Expansion', *Classica et Medievalia* XII (1951): 87–130, collected in *Bedeutung und Rolle des Islam*, esp. pp. 180–89.

tinian, the maturity of Pope Gregory I, and the youth of Mohammed, might repay more close consideration as a possible turning point in the history of the Mediterranean.[8]

Second, to have introduced Islam into a debate previously restricted to western Europe was a master stroke of integration, the brightest 'leap' of current of all between two hitherto separate poles. The pages in which Pirenne describes the ease with which the Muslim conquerors changed the civilization of populations that had remained untouched by the Germanic settlers are the most profound in the book.[9] Yet early Islam trembled on the brink of becoming (like its nominal ancestors—Judaism and Christianity) a Mediterranean civilization. Shimmering on the surface of medieval Islamic civilization, like the path of a moonbeam over water, are reminders of *Romania*—in Islam's spread of Mediterranean legends as far as Indonesia, in its revival of Greek philosophy,[10] in its preservation of gestures of ancient Mediterranean Christian worship so long forgotten in western Europe that today they stand for all that is alien and 'oriental' in modern Islam. Ummayad palaces on the fringe of Syria are as tantalizing as works of Gandhara art: their stance between East and West is still undecided.[11]

8. Peter Brown, *The World of Late Antiquity* (London, 1971), pp. 172–76 and the important work on late sixth-century Constantinopolitan culture by Averil Cameron, see below, p. 275, n. 109. On the plague of 543 as the end of an epoch of East Roman social history: Evelyne Patlagean, *Pauvreté économique et pauvreté sociale à Byzance* (Paris, 1977), pp. 84–92. There is also a turning point in the relations between Byzantium and the barbarian kingdoms, who, for the first time, felt that they had come to stay: W. Goffart, 'Rome, Constantinople and the Barbarians', *American Historical Review* (to appear).

9. Pirenne, *Mohammed and Charlemagne*, pp. 147–52. 'When it was converted to Christianity, the Empire, so to speak, underwent a change of soul; when it was converted to Islam, both its soul and its body were transformed' (p. 152).

10. Franz Rosenthal, *The Classical Heritage in Islam* (Berkeley and Los Angeles, 1975); P. Kunitsch, 'Über das Frühstadium der arabischen Aneignung antiken Geistes', *Saeculum* XXVI (1975): 268–82.

11. The Late Antique elements in early Islamic art and civilization are brilliantly exposed by U. Monneret de Villard, *Introduzione allo Studio dell'Archeologia Islamica* (Venice, 1966). Unfortunately, P. Crone and M. Cook, *Hagarism: The Making of the Islamic World* (Cambridge, 1977), though thought-provoking, represents a missed opportunity: see Peter Brown, 'Islam', *New York Review of Books* XXVI

Indeed, the battle for control of the Mediterranean was fought within Islam itself, between Syria and Iraq—between old Roman Damascus and new Baghdad, heir to the majesty of the Sasanian Empire.[12] It was the last round of a battle that had been fought from the days of the Achaemenids to determine whether the Mediterranean would sink to the status of a distant fringe area of a Eurasian empire. The constant military and diplomatic initiative enjoyed by the Persian court of Ctesiphon over the emperors of Constantinople in the sixth century contained the ingredients of the final victory of Baghdad. An Arabic teller of Persian fairy-tales (distant harbinger of *The Thousand and One Nights*) already threatened to draw away Mohammed's audience in the marketplace of Mecca.[13] Even Sinbad the Sailor had already made his *début*. The recently published discoveries of the British Institute at Teheran in their archaeological expedition to Siraf on the Persian Gulf give an impression of a Sasanian maritime trade that must have formed the basis for the Arab commercial empire in the Indian Ocean.[14] These are clear rumblings of the vast subsidence that shifted the centre of gravity of Near Eastern civilization away from the Mediterranean. Around the shores of the Mediterranean, the true battle for the survival of *Romania* was waged not for control of the salty sea itself, but by sturdy farmers—in the Upper Nile, in Nubia, and in the great olive plantations of North Africa—

(1979): 32–33. See Myriam Rosen-Ayalon in *Israel Exploration Journal* XXVI (1976): 104–19, for the bizarre juxtaposition on the same mosaic in Ramlah of a florid Late Antique leopard and the first example of the Islamic mihrāb: Ummayad Islam is full of such surprises.

12. Monneret de Villard, *Introduzione*, pp. 165–79; C. Moroney, 'The Effects of the Muslim Conquest on the Persian Population of Iraq', *Iran* XIV (1976): 41–60; R. Ettinghausen, *From Byzantium to Sasanian Iran and the Islamic World* (Leiden, 1973) on the Sasanian prototypes of the reception hall of Khirbet al-Mafjar: on which see E. Baer, 'A Group of North Iranian Craftsmen among the Artisans of Khirbet al-Mafjer?', *Israel Exploration Journal* XXIV (1974): 237–41.

13. A. Guillaume, *The Life of Muhammad. A Translation of Ibn Ishaq's Sirat ar-Rasūl Allah* (Oxford University Press at Lahore, 1968), p. 136.

14. D. Whitehouse and A. Williamson, 'Sasanian Maritime Trade', *Iran* XI (1973): 29–50.

for control of the irrigation that held their precious rainwater against the blind pressure of the nomads. Polish and British archaeologists have discovered, at Faras and at Kasr-Ibrahim in the Assuan province of Egypt, a little *Romania*, an amazing miniature Byzantium that held onto its water and so to its sixth-century Christian culture up to the age of Joan of Arc.[15]

Standing between the modern student and unqualified acceptance of the main line of the argument of *Mahomet et Charlemagne* are the facts that *Romania* was dilapidated by fissures more ancient and more paradoxical than those stressed by Pirenne, and that Islam's deeper rhythms, in relation to *Romania*, coincide at few points with the tempting juxtaposition to which Pirenne first drew attention. To these I must add that among western medievalists, there has been a revived appreciation of the northern world slowly and obscurely taking shape in this period, often along sea routes that had changed little since the age of the Megaliths,[16] and a steady depreciation and redefinition, particularly among economic historians, of the significance of the movement of luxury goods and bullion as factors in the style of Mediterranean civilization: to both these points I shall return.

Pirenne, however, chose his evidence as he did because what interested him was civilization and its material basis. Differing ways of life and their material foundations drew his unfailing attention. How the style of one civilization differed from that of another—this Pirenne would seize upon and lay bare with unfailing clarity and zest in terms of a landscape, of an economic situation, or of a form of social organization. His *Histoire de Belgique* is *Mahomet et Charlemagne* without the cramping necessity for a single explanation; here he deals not

15. W. H. C. Frend, 'Nomads and Christianity in the Middle Ages', *Journal of Ecclesiastical History* XXVI (1975): 209–21.

16. J. N. Hillgarth, 'Visigothic Spain and Early Christian Ireland', *Proceedings of the Royal Irish Academy* (1962): 167 ff.; H. Jankuhn, 'Frühe Städte im Nord- und Ostseeraum (700–1100 n. Chr.)', *Settimane di Studi del Centro Italiano di Studi sull'Alto Medio Evo* XXI (Spoleto, 1974): 153–201; P. H. Sawyer, 'Kings and Merchants', *Early Medieval Kingship*, ed. P. H. Sawyer and I. N. Wood (School of History, University of Leeds, 1977), pp. 139–58.

with two successive and contrasting styles of civilization, but with a spectrum of contrasting ways of life, contemporary in time and contiguous in space, each firmly set by Pirenne in its own economic and social context, each explored as a bundle of distinctive human possibilities. In a masterly survey of the fourteenth-century Netherlands, for instance, Pirenne describes how Flanders slowly took on its non-French, Flemish face as the sea routes from the Atlantic ousted the land routes across the kingdom of France; it was a Flemish face, also, because the local producers at Bruges and Ghent no longer depended on the merchants who had previously controlled the distribution of cloth along the roads into the French-speaking south.[17] In a few, lucid pages he analyses a revolution in social structure and cultural horizons of momentous importance for the history of modern Belgium.

In the 1920s and 1930s this particular manner of grasping the folds in the landscape of medieval Europe called for deep serenity of vision. Pirenne came from a family of Walloon industrialists, yet he was professor at the predominantly Flemish-speaking University of Ghent. What mattered for him was the shifting pageant of varying social structures, not the Romantic shibboleths of race and language. There is real personal warmth in his appreciation of Jean Froissart—chronicler, man of the world, true cosmopolitan, a fitting symbol of the human diversity and tolerance that Pirenne admired in the fourteenth-century Netherlands.[18] Race and language, for Pirenne, were infinitely plastic.[19] His heavy emphasis on the continuity of *Romania* as a social and economic unity based on the Mediterranean was forced into prominence by his steadfast refusal, as a cultivated European of the 1920s, to admit that, by virtue of their race alone, the

17. Henri Pirenne, *Histoire de Belgique*, II (Brussels, 1903), 51–68.
18. Ibid., p. 424: 'à la fois neutre et cosmopolite'.
19. See Pirenne to H. Sproemling, 31 May 1931 in Lyon, *Henri Pirenne*: 'La Belgique se prêtait particulièrement bien à son étude! [of economic history as the moving force in social and cultural change] En outre les influences des races y sont reduites à leur minimum. De là vient le peu d'importance que je leur ai attribué . . .' (p. 380).

Germanic invaders could have offered any alternative to it. It took more than a Romantic emphasis on the supposedly distinctive nature of Germanic political and legal institutions to convince this Belgian that the Germanic invaders had anything to offer to a civilization based on such tangible and massive realities as a network of ancient towns, a disciplined tax-system, and a living commerce.[20]

Early in his career, Pirenne opted for Paris against Germany. He opted for the conviction of Fustel de Coulanges, that the documents of the early Middle Ages, if left to speak for themselves in their rough Latin, would, to the unprejudiced reader, speak of a late Roman social scene prolonged untidily into the Merovingian period, and not of any new Germanic principles of social organization. Pirenne first conceived the main theme of *Mahomet et Charlemagne* in an internment camp in Germany after 1914, to which he had been sent for refusing to collaborate with the German attempt to re-open the University of Ghent as a 'nationalist', Flemish university. This goes some way to explain why he upheld its paradoxes with such sharpness: for Pirenne, the traditional equation of a western European of the early twentieth century in explaining his own past had had one crucial element removed—the Germanic invaders were not a significant factor in the history of the early medieval period. If he could turn neither to Alaric nor to Clovis to account for the developments that led to the empire of Charlemagne, why not to the only genuinely creative non-Roman left on the horizon—Mohammed?

Rereading Pirenne's canny narrative about the early settlements of Germans around the Mediterranean makes one appreciate the vital contribution made by Marxist and Marxist-influenced historiography to the history of the barbarian invasions. Here, as in Pirenne, is history 'demythologized', rendered antiseptic to the myth of race by stern attention to the grey, common humanity which, in late Roman condi-

20. Pirenne, *Mohammed and Charlemagne*: '"Romania" survived by virtue of its inertia. There was nothing to take its place' (p. 45).

tions, rapidly turned German warlords into great landowners and starving pillagers into serfs. Whether the organizing principle at issue is the *Romania* of Pirenne or the class struggle of Marx, the history of the barbarian invasions has been made more intelligible through the choice of a principle different from those which guided generations of 'Romanist' and 'Germanist' studies.[21]

One can appreciate how *Mahomet et Charlemagne* is the sort of classic that can render itself unnecessary. In one firm stroke, Pirenne released the study of Late Antiquity from the *impasse* created by the rival claims of 'Romanist' and 'Germanist' legal historians. Naturally, scholarship has raced ahead, without bothering to look back. The debate over the 'Pirenne thesis' quickly moved to areas where Pirenne's knowledge lagged behind his intuitions: in fact, the most stimulating contributions have been made by Byzantinists and Islamic scholars.[22]

This is easy to understand. Pirenne's book, the work of a master of northern European history, was also the historical testament of a generation of Byzantine studies. The discovery of the social and economic achievement of Byzantium was the most exciting feature of early medieval studies in Pirenne's generation. To the historian of the transition from the ancient to the medieval idea of the state the Byzantine Empire was a surviving example of the ancient bureaucratic polity: a state supported by a high rate of taxation, soundly based on mercantile cities and a prosperous peasantry, able to maintain a professional army, a salaried bureaucracy and a prestigious gold currency. By this high yardstick of achievement, the 'feudal' society of the medieval West was measured

21. Hence the importance of the classic studies of E. A. Thompson, notably 'The Settlement of the Barbarians in Southern Gaul', *Journal of Roman Studies* XLVI (1956): 65–75.

22. R. S. Lopez, 'Mohammed and Charlemagne: A Revision', *Speculum* XIX (1943): 13–38; D. C. Dennett, 'Pirenne and Muhammed', *Speculum* XXIII (1948): 165–90; M. Lombard, 'Mahomet et Charlemagne: le problème économique', *Annales* III (1948): 188–99 (all in *Bedeutung und Rolle des Islam*). M. Lombard, *Espaces et réseaux du haut moyen-âge* (Paris, 1972); E. Ashtor, 'Aperçus sur les Radhanites', *Schweizerische Zeitschrift für Geschichte* XXVII (1977): 245–75.

and found wanting. Pirenne's fertile intuition—an intuition not shared by every scholar of the later Roman Empire, many of whom still stress the long-standing social and cultural differences between eastern and western Mediterranean society in Late Roman times[23]—was to apply this idea of Byzantium to western Europe before the Islamic conquests. *Romania*: for Pirenne this word (revealingly, a word coined in the eastern Mediterranean where it remained current up to Ottoman times) seemed to sum up exhaustively the shabby, but solid, social and cultural furniture of Merovingian Gaul. He saw western Europe as a substandard Byzantium: 'Until the eighth century, the only positive element in history was the influence of the Empire.'[24]

This was perhaps, too narrow a definition of Mediterranean civilization in the Late Antique period. The traveller who drives along the coastline of the Mediterranean, always aware of the grey band of mountains to the north, massive forerunners of the Alps, that dwarf the plains covered with vineyards and the porphyry escarpments heavy with the scent of cistus, might be reminded that, in a similar way, alternative styles of life to the clearly defined *Romania* of Pirenne had existed as palpable presences for Mediterranean men many centuries before Charlemagne. A history of western European civilization in the early Middle Ages is today better able to find room for an element trenchantly excluded by Pirenne: the distinctive style of the civilization of the north. The recent achievements in Irish and Anglo-Saxon studies have revealed an insular world in the late sixth and seventh centuries of vast creativity, only partly dependent on *Romania*.[25] The work of social anthropologists (more fruitfully allied with Dark Age studies than with any other period of history except that of Ancient Greece) has induced a sober respect for the skill with which preliterate and technologi-

23. See below, pp. 167–168.
24. Pirenne, *Mohammed and Charlemagne*, p. 73.
25. This is summed up in the work of J. M. Wallace-Hadrill, most notably his *Early Germanic Kingship in England and the Continent* (Oxford, 1971).

cally primitive societies have been observed to create a resilient 'technology of human relations'. A connoisseur of the intricate codes of behaviour revealed in *Beowulf* and confirmed in the life of African tribes might still find the Merovingian court, as Pirenne found it, 'a brothel', but its violences were governed by the law of the blood feud—and this was not the 'law of the jungle'.[26] The claims of a new generation of historians working on the culture and social mores of Dark Age northern Europe are more solid than earlier claims based on a Romantic—and later brutally racist—idealization of the 'Germanic' contribution to early medieval Europe, against which Pirenne so rightly set his face in the 1920s and 1930s. These new studies reveal values and social habits which were resilient and apposite, even in *Romania*; their rise to prominence in the civilization of the age of Charlemagne need not be regarded as due to the closing down of some infinitely richer alternative.

Pirenne's approach is most revealing where he touches most closely on cultural history. The evidence of the conscious values of groups supports his perspective better than does the fragmentary and ambiguous evidence for their economic activities. Surprisingly enough, it is the historian of the Christian Church, and not the economic historian, who finds Pirenne's vision of the early medieval period most helpful. The Christian religion identified itself almost from its origin with the urban civilization of the Mediterranean; it penetrated into the sprawling countryside of Western Europe along trade routes that linked it with the 'boom' towns of Asia Minor, and it fed its imagination on Palestine and Syria and found that its intellectual powerhouse, in the Latin world, was North Africa.[27] Indeed, the history of the Christian Church in the early Middle Ages is the history of *Romania à la Pirenne*. A student of religious sentiment and its visual expression in the eastern Mediterranean, who sets out

26. See especially, J. M. Wallace-Hadrill, 'The Blood-Feud of the Franks', *The Long-Haired Kings* (London, 1962), pp. 121–47.

27. See below, pp. 168–173.

to trace the evolution of the Byzantine iconostasis only to find the missing link in the surviving evidence in a description of a church in seventh-century County Kildare, returns to his task with a sober respect for the taproots that the culture of the Christian Church sank into the ancient soil of *Romania*.[28]

The scholar who scrutinizes the evidence for commercial contact between Gaul and the eastern Mediterranean in the sixth century must surely come away with the odd feeling that somehow the glass that he holds in his hand for this meticulous task tells him far more about the quality of Mediterranean civilization than do the fragments caught in its focus. The whole text he has read has something to say to him. Rather than turn over yet again references to Syrian merchants and Egyptian papyrus in the *History of the Franks* by Gregory of Tours, it might be more rewarding to attempt to delineate the mental horizons of Gregory himself—a delicate, but better-documented task, promising more sure conclusions. What did *Romania* really mean to Gregory? How deeply were the ancient ways still sunk into his mind and categories of behaviour? Did his expectations of a miracle, his characterization of a holy man, his instinctive reactions to the ways of God with men still move to the same rhythms as Syria and Cappadocia?[29] This enterprise, an examination of the respective ease or difficulty with which Mediterranean men and their neighbours throughout *Romania* could lift the heavy legacy of the ancient world from their minds, might illuminate some of the greatest unsolved problems of medieval history.

However, it would not, I suspect, have satisfied Pirenne to rest his thesis on the atavisms of Christian bishops. He wanted more from a civilization: he wanted towns and mer-

28. M. Mesnard, 'L'église irlandaise de Kildare d'après un texte du viiie. siècle', *Rivista di archeologia cristiana* XIX (1932): 37. See now, for Northumbria, P. Meyvaert, 'Bede and the Church Paintings at Wearmouth-Jarrow', *Anglo-Saxon England* VIII (1979): 63–77.

29. See below, pp. 185–194.

chants. This accounts, perhaps, for the most hotly contested element in the 'Pirenne thesis': Pirenne's insistence that the long-distance trade conducted by Syrian merchants was the distinguishing characteristic—indeed the *sine qua non*—of the *Romania* of the pre-Islamic era.

Here again we touch on the outstanding quality of Pirenne's life work: his understanding of the medieval city. The full meaning of the age of Charlemagne, as presented in *Mahomet et Charlemagne*, is not only that it marks the end of the ancient world, but that it serves as the backdrop to *Medieval Cities*.[30] Pirenne's brilliant sketch, *Medieval Cities*, begins with a world that had recently, in the Carolingian Age, lost its cities and their merchants. Nobody knew better than Pirenne how different the ancient city was from the medieval city—the creation of merchants alone. Yet one cannot resist the impression that Pirenne, looking back, past the band of shadow that fell over urban life in the age of Charlemagne, into the *Romania* of Merovingian times, saw the same shade of light on both sides of the darkness. In *Medieval Cities*, Pirenne describes the revival of trade in tenth-century Europe as sweeping 'like a beneficent epidemic' from Venice.[31] Venice, to Pirenne, was a survival of the old, mercantile style of the Roman Mediterranean, a tenacious colony of 'honorary Syrians' perched on the edge of the landlocked Carolingian West.

In *Mahomet et Charlemagne* the merchant is as much a symptom as the cause of a style of civilization of which Pirenne evidently approved: 'the south had been the bustling and progressive region.'[32] In fact, however, when disentangled from the skein of related phenomena that made up Pirenne's *Romania*, the Syrian merchant cuts a poor figure. In the later Empire, he was a stopgap who replaced the more solid commercial ventures of the classical Roman period. In

30. H. Pirenne, *Medieval Cities* (Princeton, 1925; Anchor Books, 1956), pp. 39–74.
31. Ibid., p. 74.
32. Pirenne, *Mohammed and Charlemagne*, p. 236.

Italy, it has been shown, the merchants spent their money on land and vanished, like water into sand: no Mediterranean-wide horizons for the soapmaker whose fortunes were safely invested in estates·near Ravenna.[33] The discreet ministrations of merchants of luxury goods survived the Arab invasions precisely because they had always been sporadic and marginal. One might look for the genuine article far into the East —in the villages of Mesopotamia and the Sassanian capital at Ctesiphon (whither the brother of one family of Syrian merchants vanished for twenty years in the sixth century),[34] in the Isle of Kharg in the Persian Gulf,[35] in the camp of nomad chieftains on the ends of the silk ways of Central Asia,[36] in the wake of Persian *condottieri* on the western frontiers of China where Christianity was described (in newly discovered Chinese Christian documents of the late seventh century) as 'the religion of Antioch'.[37] There we could find a merchant and his distinctive culture after the heart of Pirenne, but it would be the culture of the caravan routes of Asia, not of the Mediterranean.

It was as a symbol of a style of life that Pirenne stuck to the role of the Syrian merchant in creating the *Romania* of post-Roman western Europe. For Pirenne had that capacity of the greatest historians of civilization, and especially of historians who attempt to deal with the problem of changing styles of civilization: a warm blush of romantic fervour that led him to identify himself wholeheartedly with one style of

33. L. Ruggini, 'Ebrei ed orientali nell'Italia settentrionale tra il iv. ed il vi. secolo', *Studia et Documenta Historiae et Iuris* XXV (1959): 180–308.

34. John of Ephesus, *Lives of the Eastern Saints*, ed. and trans. E. W. Brooks, *Patrologia Orientalis* XVIII, p. 376; U. Monneret de Villard, 'La fiera di Batnae e la traslazione di san Tommaso a Edessa', *Rendiconti dell'Accademia nazionale dei Lincei*, s. 8, VI (1951): 77–104.

35. R. Ghirshman, *The Island of Kharg* (Teheran, 1970); B. E. Colless, 'Persian Merchants and Missionaries in Medieval Malaysia', *Journal of the Malaysian Branch of the Royal Asiatic Society* XLII (1969): 10–47.

36. N. Pigulewskaja, *Byzanz auf den Wegen nach Indien* (Berlin, 1970).

37. K. Enoki, 'The Nestorian Christians in China', *L'Oriente cristiana nella storia della civiltà*, Accademia dei Lincei. Problemi attuali di scienza e cultura LXII (Rome, 1964), p. 46.

life, and so to follow its development and modification with a passionate interest heavy with love and concern. Pirenne for the Middle Ages; Rostovtseff for the ancient world:[38] each in his way was a great European *bourgeois*, studying with deep commitment the fate of civilizations based on cities.

38. A. D. Momigliano, 'M. I. Rostofftzeff', *The Cambridge Journal* VII (1954): 334–46 in *Studies in Historiography* (London, 1966), pp. 91–104.

PART II
SOCIETY AND THE HOLY

The Last Pagan Emperor:
Robert Browning's *The Emperor Julian*†

JULIAN REIGNED AS EMPEROR FOR TWO YEARS AND
five months, from 360 to 363. In that time, he had moved
from Paris to the foothills of the Zagros mountains.
There he met his death in an untidy skirmish, having
failed to bring to a successful conclusion one of the most
determined incursions for centuries of a Roman army into
the territories of the Persian Empire. In that short period, he
wrote continuously. Frequently on the move, and often in
the tents of his army, Julian fitted with gusto into the image
of the late Roman gentleman of letters, for whom composi-
tion, even in circumstances of profound leisure, was expected to have a quality of frenzied 'action-painting'. Laws,
letters, propaganda-speeches and religious tracts poured
from him. British standards of reticence did not hold sway in
the fourth-century Mediterranean. Some months before his
death, for instance, the citizens of Antioch had taken to lam-
pooning his policies, his religious beliefs and his long beard
—the last a pointed reminder, after generations of government by clean-shaven Christian generals, that a Late Antique
intellectual was now on the throne. Julian, of course, answered with a counter-lampoon. The *Misopogon* or *Beard
Hater* was posted up 'on the Elephant Arch, just outside the

†Review of Robert Browning, *The Emperor Julian* (London, 1975) in *The Times
Literary Supplement* (London), 8 April 1977, pp. 425–26.

palace, for all to read and copy.'[1] This very morning, perhaps, the citizens of Peking may have wakened to relish, in much the same manner, yet another rash of *graffiti* from high quarters pasted on the palisades of the outer courtyard of the Forbidden City.

Julian was a university man. His collected works take up three volumes of the Loeb Classical Library.[2] The best that he could say of his cousin and predecessor, Constantius II, was that, unlike the kings of Sparta, Constantius had had an education totally different from that of other men—by which Julian, recently returned from his studies at Athens, implied that, in his opinion, his cousin had had no education whatsoever.[3] Altogether, both as a general and as a writer, the man who died at the age of thirty-two had been a memorable emperor.

History has given him even greater prominence. For Julian was the last pagan emperor of Rome. Apart from the Muslim rulers of Spain, the spine-chilling sea-kings of Dark Age Scandinavia, and the occasional lord of the steppe-lands of Eastern Europe (joined, for one ugly moment, by a thirteenth-century king of Hungary—Ladislas 'the Cuman'[4]) no major king of a settled European territory has, since the reign of Julian, publicly declared himself not to be a Christian. Posterity came to know Julian as Julian the Apostate. Whatever Julian may have thought about the Christians, and whatever were his long-range intentions against the Christian Church—and intellectuals and emperors, we must remember, are busy men, so that he may have spent less time and energy on Christians than we might suppose—we know in no uncertain terms what the Christians thought of Julian.

1. Browning, *Julian*, p. 158.
2. *The Works of the Emperor Julian*, ed. and trans. W. C. Wright, 3 vols., Loeb Classical Library (London, 1949–54), cited below as *Works*.
3. *Panegyric in Honour of Constantius*, in *Works*, I, 34–38.
4. On the cultural background to this strange incident, see J. Szücs, 'Theoretical Elements in Master Simon of Kéza's Gesta Hungarorum', *Studia Historica Academiae Scientiarum Hungaricae* XCVI (Budapest, 1975).

When the broken remnants of the Roman army trailed past the walls of Nesibin, the Christian Ephraim came out to look: 'I went, my brothers, and approached the corpse of the unclean one, I stood over him and mocked his heathendom and I said, "Is this the one who raised himself against the living name and forgot that he is dust? God has let him return to dust that he may learn that he is dust."'[5] In distant Alexandria, Christians had hoped for just that: 'The holy bishop Epiphanius related that some crows, flying all around the temple of Serapis, in the presence of blessed Athanasius, cried without interruption, "Caw, caw". Then some pagans, standing in front of the blessed Athanasius cried out, "Wicked old man, tell us what these crows are crying." He answered, "These crows are saying, Caw, caw—*cras, cras* [Latin for "tomorrow"]. He added, "Tomorrow you shall see the glory of God." Just afterwards, the death of the Emperor Julian was announced.'[6]

At the end of 363, it was a relief to be wise after the event. 'It is a small cloud,' Athanasius was believed to have said. 'It will pass.'[7] But the cloud had cast such a chill shadow that, from then onwards, Christian bishops never let the Emperor out of their sight for a moment; and the modern historian has to unravel much of the truth about Julian from a tissue of black rumours that still needed to be circulated by Christian historians writing two generations after his death. Paradoxically, Julian the university man also held the fascination of a Christian reading public. A lichen of forgeries runs along the side of his genuine letters: these emphasize polished exchanges with philosophers—with men who read books, as their stage coach trundled, at ruinous official expense, across the roads of Asia Minor;[8] they even attempt to edge a galaxy of well-known Christian bishops into the charmed circle of

5. Ephraim the Syrian, cited by Browning, *Julian*, p. 217.
6. *Apophthegmata Patrum*, Epiphanios 1, *Patrologia Graeca* 65:161C–163A; trans. B. Ward, *The Sayings of the Desert Fathers* (Oxford, 1975), p. 48.
7. Browning, *Julian*, p. 219.   8. *Ep.* 83, *Works*, III, 290–92.

85

his correspondents.[9] Quite apart from later myth, Julian was 'copy' for Late Antique men.

It is typical of late Roman studies that, like the inhabitants of a placid provincial town, late Roman scholars pay very little attention to the extraordinary cathedral perched in their midst. *Les savants ne sont pas curieux.* With a few memorable exceptions (Edward Thompson's masterly study of the main source for the reign of Julian, the historian Ammianus Marcellinus,[10] and J. P. C. Kent on the Emperor's coinage[11]) frontal attacks on individual problems raised in the abundant evidence for the religious, cultural, social and military history of Julian's reign have been few and far between—one proof among many that the average graduate student still considers himself to be an angel, and so not obliged to give serious and prolonged attention to issues sufficiently profound as to make him appear, for a probationary period, a fool. To have a complete biography of the Emperor Julian from the pen of one of the most distinguished English Byzantinists is, therefore, an important event. It is a pity that it should also have rarity value.[12]

Robert Browning's *The Emperor Julian* is written with style, by an author of wide and discriminating culture, and, most important of all, by a historian of early Byzantine society who never relaxes his grip on the realities of Julian's situation. Browning knows more than most of us about the function of classical culture in the Byzantine world, and

9. E.g., *Epp.* 26 and 82, *Works*, III, 80–82, 288–90: Julian imagined in two very different moods to Basil of Caesarea.

10. E. A. Thompson, *The Historical Work of Ammianus Marcellinus* (Oxford, 1947).

11. J. P. C. Kent, 'An Introduction to the Coinage of Julian the Apostate', *Numismatic Chronicle* XIX (1959): 109 ff.

12. I spoke too soon: see now the important study of G. W. Bowersock, *Julian the Apostate* (Cambridge, Mass., 1978) and the article of Polymnia Athanassiadi, 'A Contribution to Mithraic Theology: The Emperor Julian's *Hymn to King Helios*', *Journal of Theological Studies*, n.s., XXVIII (1977), 360–71, to be followed by a full-scale study to appear in the Oxford University Press; Diana Bowder, *The Age of Constantine and Julian* (London, 1978); *L'Empereur Julien: de l'histoire à la legende (331–1715)*, ed. R. Braun and J. Richer (Paris: Les Belles Lettres, 1978).

about the social position of the groups who maintained it. It is with an interest long-whetted by Browning's articles on Antioch in the fourth century, on the intellectual renaissance in eleventh-century Byzantium, and by his books on Justinian and Theodora and on Byzantium and Bulgaria, that we turn to his study of a man who foreshadows all that puzzles us most in Byzantines of succeeding centuries—a rare combination of opportunism, preciosity and the sense of divine mission.[13] Browning's Julian is seen most clearly when he is seen at his most 'Byzantine'. After all, it would be no more strange, to the average Byzantine reader, that an emperor should write in defence of his beard on the eve of a major campaign against Persia than that, eleven centuries later, the Emperor Manuel II should write a tranquil and reassuringly old-fashioned dialogue between a Christian and a Muslim, at the very moment when the Ottoman Turks had established an inexorable grip around Constantinople.[14]

The greatest merit of Browning's book is his unfailing sense of the concrete. Julian was an emperor; and ruling the Roman Empire meant war, torture and execution. In recent years we have gained immeasurably in our knowledge of those relatively peaceful arts of administration, landholding and patronage that would ensure that a Roman style of life survived around the Mediterranean basin long after the Roman Empire itself had collapsed in Western Europe. But in Julian's age, in the middle of the fourth century, the Empire was still functioning; so Browning's book is at its best when he deals with power, not influence, and with war, not with

13. R. Browning, 'The Riot of 387 in Antioch', *Journal of Roman Studies* XIII (1952): 23–30; *Justinian and Theodora* (London, 1971); *Byzantium and Bulgaria: A Comparative Study across an Early Medieval Frontier* (London, 1975); 'Enlightenment and Repression in Byzantium in the Eleventh and Twelfth Centuries', *Past and Present* LXIX (1975): 3 ff.; 'Literacy in the Byzantine World', *Byzantine and Modern Greek Studies* IV (1978): 39 ff.

14. *Manuel II Palaiologos: Dialoge mit einem Perser*, ed. E. Trapp (Vienna, 1966); *Manuel II Paléologue: Entretiens avec un Musulman, 7e. Conférence*, ed. and trans. T. Khoury, Sources chrétiennes 115 (Paris, 1966). See C. Mango, *Journal of Theological Studies*, n.s., XIX (1968): 'One of those mysteries of the Byzantine temperament that cannot fail to puzzle the modern historian' (p. 353).

administration. The finest pages are those that describe the slow loss of orientation in the Roman army as it wandered deeper into Mesopotamia, shadowed by the mail-clad Persian cavalry, 'And mingled with the neighing of their horses, came a new and more ominous sound, the trumpeting of their elephants.'[15] The most successful politics in the later Empire were, of course, the most silent. Yet when Browning gives his opinion as to why the young Julian was, first of all, spared by his cousin Constantius, was unexpectedly brought back to act as Constantius' viceroy—his 'Caesar'— in Gaul, in November 355, and how, at the end of a series of embarrassingly fortunate coincidences, he was crowned Emperor by the mutinous army in Paris, in February 360, and thus committed to an open civil war for the control of the Empire, we can trust him.[16] Given Browning's sober and alert perspective, it is not surprising that it is Constantine, Julian's hated uncle and the founder of the Christian autocracy, whose figure dominates the clear and compact introductory chapter on the age of Julian: for Constantine 'understood and enjoyed power'.[17]

Brought up as a Christian, Julian became a pagan in his early teens. That tantalizing event is the only conversion in the fourth century, apart from the *Confessions* of Augustine, of which we possess an autobiographical account. Once again, what Browning can communicate best is not the conversion itself, but what it was like to live, from then onwards, with opinions subversive to a Christian régime. Browning catches the thrills and the *camaraderie* of an intellectual 'underground', living on the edge of a court that was all the more dangerous for being random. He has rare sympathy for cultivated and talented men who moved in 'that grey area between the permitted and the illicit'.[18] He not only knows his heroes—he knows why they are heroes. This is the ex-

15. Browning, *Julian*, p. 205.
16. Ibid., pp. 99–122: now compare Bowersock, *Julian the Apostate*, pp. 33–54.
17. Browning, *Julian*, p. 18.   18. Ibid., p. 59.

traordinary Maximus of Ephesus: 'The very pupils of his eyes seemed endowed with wings . . . his beard was long and gray, his eyes revealed the impulses of his soul. Both to eye and ear his person had a kind of harmony.'[19] It is right that Browning should point out that this is a contemporary description of a man who had already been under torture, and who had seen his wife commit suicide before his eyes.[20] Now Maximus is not everybody's cup of tea. He had his own, strange ways of mingling with the unseen. Like the court magicians of the Renaissance (or, indeed, the technological advisers of many a modern government) Maximus tried to reconcile expertise with the exercise of power—an attempt which his academic colleagues, predictably, regarded as bound to come to no good.[21] Yet Browning's sense of the realities of life under a hard régime saves him from accepting without question the conventional impression, which he conveys in other parts of the book, of the pagan intelligentsia of the early fourth century. Maximus was no Aleister Crowley; and he and his circle were not 'remote and ineffectual dons'.

Unfortunately, this excellent study of the rise to power and the failure of the last pagan Emperor, and of the groups within the Roman world who welcomed him, dreaded him or just waited to see, remains unsatisfactory as a portrait of Julian himself. Julian is swallowed up in his age. 'Julian seems to me', Browning writes, 'very much a man of his time . . . a man of his age grappling with the problems of his age.'[22] These are words of unexceptionable caution. They are written as a stern warning to those, from Ephraim the Syrian to Gore Vidal, who wish to present a Julian larger than late Roman life. Hence, Browning's deliberate reliance on the most up-to-date outline accounts of the later Roman Empire.

19. Eunapius of Sardis, *Lives of the Sophists*, 473.

20. Browning, *Julian*, pp. 56–57.

21. Peter Brown, *The Making of Late Antiquity* (Cambridge, Mass., 1978), pp. 59–62.

22. Browning, *Julian*, p. xi.

Hence, therefore, the failure of the book. For the age we get is narrower than it was; and its inconsistencies, as they are held to have been summed up in extreme form in the person of Julian, are, most of the time, inconsistencies within the tradition of modern late Roman studies. This tradition is notoriously prone to see inconsistency in the eyes of fourth-century men rather than methodological confusion and the lack of elementary home-work in its own.

The result is sad. We are given a thin-blooded portrait of Julian: a lonely man, condemned by childhood trauma and adolescent escapism to retreat into a dead world that was unrelated to the realities of fourth-century life. His character, therefore, was 'riddled with inconsistencies and conflicts',[23] and his pagan revival was condemned to failure as no more than another example of the Late Antique 'dream of turning the clock of history backwards'.[24] We might have hoped to touch in Julian—in his prodigious output, in his studiously unconventional gestures, in his deep religious anger, right down to that lice-ridden beard reeking with the blood of sacrifice as he stood at the altar of his gods and 'shuddered at the thought of the unseen presences that look out at him from the other world'[25]—something of the raw and magnificently unclassical vigour of fourth-century men, pagan and Christian alike, that made young Ephraim come out to look with relief that such a man was dead. Altogether, they make a challenging pair: Ephraim, 'the greatest poet of the patristic age, and, perhaps the only *theologian-poet* to rank beside Dante';[26] and Julian, the pagan intellectual and Emperor. They are big fish, not easily caught in the net of conventional late Roman scholarship.

In the first place, it is too easy to 'psychologize' Julian; for in so doing, we slide imperceptibly into a self-supporting

23. Ibid., p. 134.   24. Ibid., p. 132.
25. *Letter to a Priest*, 294 D, *Works*, II, 310.
26. Robert Murray, *Symbols of Church and Kingdom: A Study in the Early Syriac Tradition* (Cambridge, 1975), p. 31.

argument. Julian, it is said, grew up cut off from the real world. The classical paganism that he adopted and the pagan intellectuals among whom he moved were cut off from the real world also. It makes a difference whether we can accept either of these two statements as true, and whether our confidence in the truth of the one is not subtly bolstered by misplaced certainty about the other.

We are presented with a lonely boy, the survivor of a family blood-bath, whose love of the literature of the pagan past carried him poignantly out of touch with the realities of his age: 'His own personal attitude was probably strongly coloured by the experiences of his youth and young manhood, and the extraordinary isolation in which he found himself. It was perhaps the very strength of his emotions that made it difficult for him—intelligent and sincere as he certainly was—to think through this complex of problems rationally. Instead he took refuge in a return to the past which, like so many historical pasts, was in part mythical.'[27] Even this is far from certain. To be by oneself is no bad thing for a growing lad; and a country estate in Cappadocia (a province which could produce such hardy stock as Julian's contemporary, St Basil of Caesarea, who shared the Emperor's combination of high-mindedness and canny obstinacy) need not amount to acute deprivation. To grow up in similar conditions of dangerous seclusion did not lead to 'an undervaluing of the contemporary world' in either Queen Elizabeth of England or in Peter the Great of Russia.

Thus, if we think that we can conclude from the meagre evidence of Julian's childhood that his sense of reality must have been crippled, it is largely because we are already convinced that Julian's ferocious love for the old gods, his wish to retain the means of expression of classical literature, and his attempt to recapture in his relations with his more privileged subjects some of the consensual atmosphere of the Antonine Age were endeavours misplaced to the point of neu-

27. Browning, *Julian*, p. 131.

rosis in the conditions of the fourth century. This, again, is far from certain. In any society but the Roman Empire, scholars tend to associate punctilious adherence to a classical idiom with confidence and with discreet solemnity in the exercise of power—not with an escape from reality. The fact that the late Chairman Mao wrote verses on painted landscape scrolls has not (in western circles at least) been held against him.

The *ars artium* of Late Antique studies consists in avoiding premature judgment as to the 'unreality' of the classical tradition as it was used by Late Antique men. We frequently find that, even in the most traditionalist circles, the ancient language is being discreetly manipulated to act as an enabling formula, or as a commonly-agreed shorthand with which to sum up and so to render manageable strictly contemporary situations.[28] As late as the eleventh century, a half-verse of Homer was enough to set the tone for the court's reaction to the Emperor's new Circassian mistress.[29]

Nor was this classicism a mere appendage of 'exquisite good taste'. In a world still dominated by ties of family and patronage relations, where communications had remained so stable that the sailing-time between Crete and Egypt was the same for Strabo as it had been for Homer, where economic growth was held in a pincer grip of seemingly immoveable factors, the guidelines of Mediterranean life as the art of the possible could be summed up in the writings of Homer precisely because no discontinuity even remotely like that to which a modern, post-industrial society can be exposed had come between the men of the fourth century and their models. It is only with the nineteenth century that the teaching of the classics finally reached that degree of preciosity and inapplicability to the present that we judge so harshly in fourth-century men. For it is we, and not Julian, who read our Ho-

28. Above, p. 44, n. 56.
29. N. H. Baynes, 'The Hellenistic Civilisation and East Rome', *Byzantine Studies and Other Essays* (London, 1960), p. 23.

mer and conjure up the myths of the gods as if they were dream memories of a long-lost world. For the men of Late Antiquity, the classical past—and especially the gods, who hung so close to them in the planets and in the heavy clusters of the Milky Way—were not yet 'the past'. It was not an option that could be 'revived' or 'abandoned', 'applied' or deemed 'irrelevant'. It was part of the air that men breathed; and it is incautious to assume precipitately that, any more than in classical China or in the Islamic world, this mellow air did not contain most of the elements necessary for continued, healthy respiration.[30] It has become fashionable to talk of late Roman and Byzantine literature as a 'distorting mirror'. Yet the more intimate our knowledge of the period becomes, the more attention that is given to the manner in which men threaded their way through 'life's great casuistry' in a Mediterranean society, the less certain we have become that it is not we who have distorted those parts of reality that the old mirror continued to reflect none too badly.

What this book makes plain is that we need a new sense of scale in Late Antique studies. Julian, we are told, was a man of his age. But when did the age of Julian begin? Late Antiquity is always later than we think. It rests upon centuries of silent change. The best book on late Roman paganism is still Johannes Geffcken's, *Der Ausgang des griechisch-römischen Heidentums* precisely because Geffcken began with Plutarch and, like Gibbon before him, regretted that he had not begun a century earlier. English scholarship dearly needs

---

30. In this context, one cannot cite too often the wise remarks on Hellenistic and Late Antique culture by H. I. Marrou, *A History of Education in Antiquity*, trans. George Lamb (London, 1956): 'It is a mistake to say, as is often said by its detractors, that it was 'born with its head back to front', looking back to the past. It is not autumnal, tormented with nostalgic regrets for a vanished spring. On the contrary, it looks upon itself as firmly established in an unchanging present, in the full blaze of a hot summer's sun. It knows what mighty reserves it possesses, what past masters it has had. The fact that these appeared at certain moments of time, under the influence of certain historical forces, is unimportant. What matters is that they exist and can be re-discovered in the same way, again and again, by each successive generation' (p. 161).

a substitute for or a translation of this fundamental treatment.[31] For to recapture Geffcken's sense of scale is crucial if we wish to enter into the religious mentality of Julian's age. The conflict of Christianity and paganism in the fourth century takes on a breathless urgency largely because we insist in cramming the conflict into the narrow space of one century. In reality, the problems raised by the rise of Christianity in the Roman Empire and the changing sensibility of paganism itself had been on man's horizons for a good two centuries. They had the manageability that comes from prolonged familiarity. It is, therefore, subtly misleading to speak of Julian's reign as a pagan 'reaction', as if a policy of reviving and supporting the pagan cults were an anachronistic attempt to reverse the trend of history at the last moment—to turn 'the clock of history backwards'.

Things may have looked different to Julian. The only 'dream' he knew of was the bad dream of two generations of impious rule by a Christian dynasty. This was a tiny cloud compared with the long period in which men had already had time to square up to the new religion, and where he knew that they had adopted stances similar to his own. Julian knew more about his immediate past than we can ever hope to know about it. Recent discoveries, small enough in themselves, nevertheless show that his reading of the Roman past, and especially of the third century, may have been more accurate than that presented to us by modern text-books. In Italy, for instance, an inscription has been uncovered that acclaimed the mid-third-century Emperor Decius as 'Restorer of the Cults'. Decius had persecuted the Christians and had insisted on the performance of sacrifice throughout the Empire. Until now, however, that heavy phrase, 'Restorer of the Cults', had only been known in connection with Julian.[32] 'Restoration', therefore, had been in the air for a century. It

31. J. Geffcken, *Ausgang des griechisch-römischen Heidentums* (Heidelberg, 1929; Darmstadt, 1972). A translation is now available, with up-dated footnotes: *The Last Days of Greco-Roman Paganism*, trans. Sabine MacCormack (Amsterdam: North Holland, 1978).

32. *Année Épigraphique* 1973, no. 235.

94

required no eccentric leap across the ages to link up with that continuum of Roman imperial attitudes. Before we accuse Julian of wishing to 'put the clock back' we have to be very sure indeed that in the notoriously slow-moving world of the Roman Empire—and especially in Roman attitudes to the gods, who, after all, being immortal, changed as little as the face of the heavens—the finger of the dial had even moved appreciably.

Julian's 'reactions', therefore, took the form of rather deeper breaths of an air that was still part of the atmosphere of the Roman Mediterranean. His reforms, also, emerged all the more built to last for having been slowly prepared, and in a more self-confident environment than the tone of Browning's book suggests. Julian's restructuring of the provincial priesthoods of Asia Minor, his letters on the duties of a priest and the handbook, *On the Gods and the World*, that was written by his friend, Sallustius, have all been presented as a confession of the need to reform paganism in order to meet the challenge of the Christian Church. To say this overlooks those long, subdued centuries in which pagan belief and practice had changed under its own, inner momentum. We still know very little about the social function and teaching traditions of the Neo-Platonic schools of the late third and fourth century, and of the evolution of pagan attitudes at that time. When Browning presents the scholarly consensus of this century on the nature of the pagan intelligentsia among which Julian moved, and from whom he derived many of his religious attitudes—and a rum lot they are made to seem—we can only say:

> Oh, let us never, never doubt
> What nobody is sure about.

In fact, the balance of rational and irrational elements in later Platonism and the intention of the authors who have left us such strange vignettes of the behaviour of professors just have not received the slow and patient attention to detail on which a true tradition of scholarship must be based. The paganism of the later Empire still awaits an equivalent to Keith Thomas' *Religion and the Decline of Magic*. We would emerge from it, I suspect, with more insight and with fewer *frissons*.[33]

To take two examples: given the evolution of pagan thought and teaching-methods, it is not very strange that a fourth-century pagan such as Sallustius should have wished to write a systematic handbook *On the Gods and the World*. To write as he did would have been a pleasure to him; he may not have been over-concerned 'to fit (the pagan) religious heritage to compete with Christianity—organised, articulate and polemical'.[34] Rather, pagan thought had tended to become 'organised, articulate and polemical' as part of a change in which paganism and Christianity themselves were no more than arcs on an even wider circle. To be abstract and orderly, and to wish to teach others is an option which ancient men could take without looking over their shoulders at the local Christian bishop. When such men sat for their portraits, for instance, similar qualities emerge, all the more authentically for having emerged *sine ira et studio* from the sculptor's block.[35]

It is the same with Julian's reforms of the pagan priesthoods. The priests that Julian wanted were plainly not the priests we associate with classical paganism. Yet, just because they are different from their predecessors, there is no reason

33. C. Zintzen, 'Die Wertung von Mystik und Magie in der neuplatonischen Philosophie', *Rheinisches Museum* CVIII (1965): 71–100, still offers standard fare; but see A. Smith, *Porphyry's Place in the Neo-Platonic Tradition* (The Hague, 1974), pp. 81–150, for a significantly different presentation of theurgy. We can expect illumination from the translation and commentary on the *Life of Isidore* by Damascius being prepared by Stewart L. Karren.

34. The point has been well made by Oswyn Murray, *Journal of Roman Studies* LXIX (1969): 263, talking of the apparent 'rise' of the occult sciences in Late Antiquity: 'There is a relation between the systematization of astrology and magic, and the forces which led to similar, more rigid systematization in government, rhetorical theory, law, philosophy, geography, medicine, and religion, whether Jewish, Christian or pagan.' This, and not simply 'apologetic' needs, seems to be the most fruitful, and as yet largely unexplored, explanation of a book such as Sallustius'.

35. H. P. L'Orange, *Art Forms and Civic Life in the Later Roman Empire* (Princeton, 1966), pp. 105–125.

to jump to the conclusion that this difference is due to conscious modelling on the Christian hierarchy. Julian's priests
were home-grown figures, who may have sprung quite naturally from the rich soil of Asia Minor, a soil better known to
Julian (and to the fortunate epigraphist) than to the average
classical scholar.[36]

Instead, we should look at the facts. Julian was an emperor. All his life he had watched emperors. He would have
agreed with J. B. Bury that, 'It must never be forgotten that
Constantine's revolution was perhaps the most audacious act
ever committed by an autocrat in disregard and defiance of
the vast majority of his subjects.'[37] Constantine's reign had
shown what the continued and articulate support of an emperor for the religion of his choosing could mean in the Roman world. Julian would have read Fergus Millar's *The Emperor in the Roman World* with sombre satisfaction. More than
any other recent book, the sheer size and multiplicity of the
imperial machinery of patronage, as revealed by Millar,
would have proved him right.[38] His business was not to 'reform' paganism by making it into a counterfeit of the Catholic hierarchy: it was to out-Constantine Constantine in supporting his own religion. The provincial priest of Galatia
received thirty thousand bushels of wheat and sixty thousand
pints of wine to distribute to the poor, together with a lecture
on Christian alms-giving: 'Do we not see that what has most
contributed to the success of atheism is its charity towards
strangers, the care it takes of the tombs of the dead, and
its feigned gravity of life?'[39] It is not so often realized that
the Christianity that Julian was combatting was not the religion of charity whose success among the masses was guaran-

36. See the remarkable early fourth-century cases discussed by L. Robert, *Études anatoliennes* (Paris, 1937), pp. 131–32.

37. J. B. Bury, *A History of the Later Roman Empire*, I (New York: Dover Books, 1958), 360.

38. F. Millar, *The Emperor in the Roman World* (London, 1977), esp. pp. 133–34, 583. For the overwhelming impact of Constantine's munificence in the churches of Rome, C. Pietri, *Roma christiana* (Paris, 1976), p. 84.

39. *Ep.* 22, 429E, *Works*, III, 68.

teed by a doctrine of neighbourly love: it was a Christianity whose bishops and clergy had had their social horizons blown wide open by finding the open-handed Constantine in their midst.[40] Constantine would buy up a whole town: 'being anxious that here also as many as possible might be won to the truth, [he] bestowed abundant provision for the necessities of the poor.'[41] What Julian was up against was the sheer purchasing power of imperial munificence.

Least of all can we be certain that Julian's paganism could not be expected to touch 'the man in the street'. Two tacit judgements are contained in this assertion. The first is revealed in Browning's index: 'paganism *see* Neoplatonism'. Browning's Neo-Platonism does not inspire confidence: 'At its best it was an impressive, and for some minds a satisfying world-picture. At its worst it could be a tawdry rationalization of magic and popular superstition.'[42] To base a successful pagan revival on such stuff would be like trying to place an altar on a soap-bubble.

The second is 'the man in the street'. This unknown hero of historical writing, who understands very little in most ages, has been somewhat overworked of late to cover our own genuine difficulties in coming to grips with the content of late Roman thought and the manner in which ideas percolate in a society of restricted literacy. What we have begun to know about the 'man in the street' is that, on the whole, he lived in cramped, and stable *quartiers*; that he disliked change; that he enjoyed processions; that chronic underemployment gave him too much time on his hands and so, as contemporary Christian theological disputes show, he took a genuine, Cockney pride in following ruminations which seem difficult to us largely because we lack the long, hot hours of a Mediterranean summer. Precisely the issues that worried Sallustius can still provide mileage for the visitor to Yazd or to Herat.

40. As was realized by A. Harnack, *Mission und Ausbreitung des Christentums* (Leipzig, 1906), pp. 143–45. See now R. M. Grant, *Early Christianity and Society* (New York, 1977), pp. 142–45.

41. Eusebius of Caesarea, *Vita Constantini* 3, 58.

42. Browning, *Julian*, p. 41.

Above all, he worried constantly about the harvest.[43] In 361, the gods had been there for a long time; their worship did not lack pomp (and 'pomp' derives from those long, hot cavalcades, carrying the holy statues, enlivened by banquets and the judicious distribution of sweet-meats and free perfume for the women, which, as good Christian children we still have to renounce, along with the Devil, in the Anglican catechism);[44] and in most areas, the gods had kept a firm grip on the rhythms of the countryside, and so on the weather and the food.[45]

To enjoy 'fine-spun' literary activity about the gods was a bonus to Late Antique men, which they could never resist: the literary man, said Basil of Caesarea, must always sing like a nightingale in the spring nights of classical leisure.[46] But we live in an age where the concrete, cultic content of religion is so attenuated that it is difficult to enter into a world where the works of Julian were an agreeable background noise to the bedrock of real religious practice. The Christian Church, after all, had previously passed through a spasm of *odium theologicum* on the nature of the Trinity which, quite as much as any work of Julian's, 'presupposes a philosophical understanding that only the most highly educated possessed'. But with the Emperor Constantine as patron, the opulent new basilicas had remained open, the Holy Places of Jerusalem were thronged, imperial mausoleums lay on the threshold of the martyrs' shrines—and the temples had stood closed.

So the problem can be reduced to manageable dimensions: could Julian, had he lived, have exercised the same amount of power in favour of paganism as Constantine had done in favour of Christianity? Browning considers that this would have been highly unlikely: 'compulsive communica-

43. Brown, *Making of Late Antiquity*, pp. 3–4.
44. For vivid examples continuing up to the early fourth century, see the case of Stratoniceia, *Bulletin de correspondance hellénique* XII (1888): 101.
45. See the telling juxtaposition of gods, sacrifice and a full harvest in the late third-century Boglio Stele from Siliana in North Africa, in R. Bianchi-Bandinelli, *Rome: The Late Empire* (London, 1966), pl. 200 at p. 217.
46. Basil of Caesarea, *Ep.* 20.

tor though he was, he had not found a way to speak to the common man.'[47]

We have seen, so far, that we cannot assume the interpretations on which this judgement rests. The classical idiom did not encapsulate men from their contemporary realities. The intellectual and religious resources of Julian form part of a more resilient continuum than we had thought. The 'man in the street' would have got what he liked. The last issue remains: was Julian's personal exercise of power too eccentric to carry conviction?

Again, it is worthwhile remembering that Julian appears so complex to us because we know more about him than about most other Roman emperors. In order to rule the Roman world effectively, the Roman emperor had to be larger than life; and that usually meant that he had to be odder than life. Emperors were actively expected to be over-articulate. If they were to be heard at all, over the vast distances of the Empire, they had to approach every problem with an open mouth.[48] Constantine, we are told, wrote and preached frequently. It is merciful to his reputation that so little of this has survived. What little we know is ominous.[49] Constantine, *chez soi,* would have been as febrile an intellectual as Julian.

It is the same with the imperial deportment. Here Browning stresses what appears to him as an inconsistency: 'Throughout his reign there was a conflict between the role of "democratic prince", which he wished to play, and that of a remote half-divine ruler, which the mass of his subjects expected, and which may have been what the situation called

47. Browning, *Julian,* p. 143.
48. On this style of address, which was by no means prevalent only in the later Empire, see Paul Veyne, *Le Pain et le Cirque* (Paris, 1976), pp. 549–50.
49. See T. D. Barnes, 'The Emperor Constantine's Good Friday Sermon', *Journal of Theological Studies,* n.s., XXVII (1976): 414–23, with the harsh judgement of Harnack, *Mission und Ausbreitung:* 'Die "Rede" Constantins ist vielleicht—auch abgesehen von ihrem Autor—die eindrucksvollste Apologie, die geschrieben worden ist . . . eindrucksvoll für halbgebildete Leser, d. h., für das gebildete Publikum, wie es damals war' (p. 195, n. 3).

for.'[50] Yet we tend to exaggerate the majesty of the late Roman imperial image. An effective emperor would use this majesty and inaccessibility in order to exploit all the more effectively carefully-rationed doses of intimacy and 'the common touch'.[51] It is the combination that was so overpowering. Constantine arrived at the Council of Nicaea in his full regalia, 'like an angel of the Lord', and then sat down on a low chair, cracking jokes with the bishops in kitchen Greek. After this, unanimity on the Trinity came surprisingly quickly.[52] Julian may have erred on the side of ostentatious familiarity. Important people like to bask in the glory of even more important people—and the newly-founded Senate of Constantinople needed more than most bodies to feel important.[53] Yet if Julian erred, he erred in his dosage of a well-known late Roman mixture, not because he wished to abandon the mixture altogether for unrealistic flight to the courteous affabilities of the age of the Antonines.

These are some of the main problems raised by Browning's book, and by the tradition of scholarship from which Browning, and all of us concerned with Late Antiquity, have drawn with gratitude. In his elegant and deeply sane study, they appear carefully enunciated and firmly held within the bounds of common-sense. They obtrude all the more clearly, therefore, as marking the limits beyond which modern scholarship on Julian, and, by implication, research on the role of paganism, of the classical tradition and of the Emperor in late Roman society, has not yet been prepared to go. If we can break through these limits at some points—and it will take slow, patient burrowing to do so—then we may very well find again the Julian that Ephraim the Syrian went out to see: a man who spoke the language of *his* side of a

50. Browning, *Julian*, p. 144.
51. A point well-made by Alan Cameron, *Bread and Circuses: The Roman Emperor and His People* (London, 1973).
52. Eusebius, *Vita Constantini* 3, 10.
53. Thompson, *Ammianus Marcellinus*, pp. 82–83.

complex age, and who spoke it with unnerving confidence and a strange, taut skill.

Right down to his flamboyance and his deadly concern, Julian had lived like a Roman emperor. As a general, he is one of the few who died like one. At Kermanshah, behind the knife-edge of the Zagros mountains, far above the hot plain where the young Emperor fell, Kurdish women in purple trousers, their eyes painted in lapis lazuli blue, now wash their burnished silverware in a stream that flows past the haunting Sasanian rock-carvings of Taq-i Bostan. On the side of the rock, a Persian king stands over the prostrate body of a bearded man, wearing the pearl-studded diadem of a Roman emperor.[54] As Professor Browning says: 'In a sense all historical figures are tragic for us, since we know what for them was unknowable—the future.'[55]

54. L. Trümpelmann, 'Triumph uber Julianus Apostata', *Jahrbuch für Numismatik und Geldgeschichte* XXV (1975): 101–11. The king, however, is not Shapur II, but Ardashir II, his successor: V. G. Lukonin, *Kultura sasanidskogo Irana* (Moscow, 1969), p. 195. Seen from Persia, Julian was merely a symbolic conquered Roman emperor!

55. Browning, *Julian*, p. 224.

The Rise and Function
of the Holy Man
in Late Antiquity[†]

TO STUDY THE POSITION OF THE HOLY MAN IN Late Roman society is to risk telling in one's own words a story that has often been excellently told before. In vivid essays, Norman Baynes has brought the lives of the saints to the attention of the social and re-

---

[†]*Journal of Roman Studies* LXI (1971): 80–101. A first draft of this paper was read at Professor Momigliano's seminar in London. I owe to the work of Dr. Mary Douglas an inspiration that has guided me toward this, and related, topics; and the unflagging enthusiasm and acuteness of Professor Momigliano, with that of Dr. S. C. Humphreys, have instilled in me a salutary *esprit d' escalier*, in raising problems worth following through for many years to come.

I have adopted the following abbreviations for recurrent citations:

A.P.=*Apophthegmata Patrum. Patrologia Graeca* LXV, 71–440 (by name and number of the saying and column).

H.L.=Palladius, *Historia Lausiaca*, ed. C. H. Butler, *Texts and Studies* VI, 2 (1904).

H.R.=Theodoret, *Historia Religiosa, Patrologia Graeca* LXXXII, 1283–1496 (by column).

Sym. Styl.=H. Hilgenfeld. 'Syrische Lebensbeschreibung des heiligen Symeons' in H. Lietzmann, *Das Leben des heiligen Symeon Stylites* (Text und Untersuchungen XXXII, 4) (1908), pp. 80–187.

V. Alex.=*Vie d'Alexandre l'Acémète*, ed. J. de Stoop,*Patrologia Orientalis* VI, pp. 659–701.

V. Dan.=*Vita Danielis*, ed. H. Delehaye, *Les Saints Stylites* (1923), pp. 1–94.

V. Euthym.=Cyril of Scythopolis, *Vita Euthymii*, ed. Eduard Schwartz, *Kyrillos von Skythopolis* (Texte und Untersuchungen XLIX, 2) (1939).

V. Hyp.=Callinicus, *Vita Hypatii* (Teubner, 1895).

V. Sab.=Cyril of Scythopolis, *Vita Sabae*, ed. Eduard Schwartz, *Kyrillos von Scythopolis*, o.c.

V. Sym. Jun.=*Vita Symeonis Junioris*, ed. P. van den Ven, *La vie ancienne de saint Syméon Stylite le Jeune* I (1962).

V. Theod.=*Vita Theodori Syceotae*, ed. Th. Ioannou, Μνημεῖα ἁγιολογικά (1884),

ligious historian of Late Antiquity.[1] The patient work of the Bollandists has increased and clarified a substantial dossier of authentic narratives.[2] These lives have provided the social historian with most of what he knows of the life of the average man in the Eastern Empire.[3] They illuminate the variety and interaction of the local cultures of the Near East.[4] The holy men themselves have been carefully studied, both as figures in the great Christological controversies of the fifth and sixth centuries,[5] and as the arbiters of the distinctive traditions of Byzantine piety and ascetic theology.[6]

pp. 361–495. [Now ed. A. J. Festugière, *Vie de Théodore de Sykéôn*, Subsidia Hagiographica XLVIII (Brussels, 1970).]

Admirable translations and commentaries are available for most of these, and others besides, by E. Dawes and N. H. Baynes, *Three Byzantine Saints* (1948) (*V. Dan.* and *V. Theod.*); by A. J. Festugière, *Les Moines d'Orient*, I-IV (1961–65) (*V. Hyp.* and *V. Dan.* in vol. II, *V. Euthym.* in vol. III/1, and *V. Sab.* in vol. III/2); and by van den Ven, ed. cit., II (1970), 1–248 (*V. Sym. Jun.*). [The following further translations are available: Benedicta Ward, *The Sayings of the Desert Fathers* (London and Kalamazoo, 1975); Apostolos N. Athanassakis, *The Life of Pachomius (Vita Prima Graeca)* (Missoula, Mont.: Scholars Press, 1975). J. W. Nesbitt, 'A Geographical and Chronological Guide to Greek Saints' Lives', *Orientalia Christiana Periodica* XXXV (1969): 443–89 is helpful.]

1. N. H. Baynes, 'The Thought World of East Rome', *Byzantine Studies and Other Essays* (1960), pp. 24–46; 'The Pratum Spirituale', ibid., pp. 261–70.

2. E.g., F. Halkin, 'L'hagiographie byzantine au service de l'histoire', *XIIIth International Congress of Byzantine Studies* (Oxford, 1966), Main Papers XI, pp. 1–10.

3. E. Patlagean, 'À Byzance: ancienne hagiographie et histoire sociale', *Annales* XXIII (1968): 106–23, is the most thought-provoking study.

4. P. Peeters, *Le tréfonds oriental de l'hagiographie byzantine* (1950).

5. H. Bacht, 'Die Rolle des orientalischen Mönchtums in den kirchenpolitischen Auseinandersetzungen um Chalkedon (431–519)', *Das Konzil von Chalkedon*, II (1954), 193–314. [W. H. C. Frend, *The Rise of the Monophysite Movement* (Cambridge, 1972), pp. 104–42.]

6. K. Holl, *Enthusiasmus und Bussgewalt beim griechischen Mönchtum* (1898); A. Vööbus, *A History of Asceticism in the Syrian Orient*, II (Louvain, 1960); *La Théologie de la Vie monastique* (Théologie 49; Lyon, 1961); D. Chitty, *The Desert a City* (1966). Brevity has determined that this list should be not a guide to the vast literature, but rather the expression of my debt to those works cited. [Jaroslav Pelikan, *The Spirit of Eastern Christendom (600–1700)* (Chicago, 1974); Roberta C. Chesnut, *Three Monophysite Christologies* (Oxford, 1976) and 'The Two Prosopa in Nestorius' Bazaar of Heracleides', *Journal of Theological Studies*, n.s., XXIX (1978): 392–409; R. C. Gregg and D. E. Groh, 'The Centrality of Soteriology in Early Arianism', *Anglican Theological Review* LIX (1977): 260–78, and by the same authors, *Early Arianism: A View of Salvation* (Philadelphia, 1980)—a model book. These studies,

The intention of this paper is to follow well-known paths of scholarship on all these topics, while asking two basic questions: why did the holy man come to play such an important role in the society of the fifth and sixth centuries? What light do his activities throw on the values and functioning of a society that was prepared to concede him such importance? It is as well to ask such elementary questions. For there is a danger that the holy man may be taken for granted as part of the Byzantine scene. Most explanations of his position are deceptively easy.

In the first place, because many social historians have been led to such evidence mainly to satisfy their interest in the life of the lower classes of the later Empire, they have tended to stress the spectacular occasions on which the holy man intervened to lighten the lot of the humble and oppressed: his open-handed charity, his courageous action as the spokesman of popular grievances—these have been held sufficient to explain the role of the holy man. The holy man's popularity is explained as a product of the oppression and conflict that the social historian often tends to see as a blatant feature of East Roman society.

Such a view sees too little of the life of the holy man. It was through the hard business of living his life for twenty-four hours in the day, through catering for the day-to-day needs of his locality, through allowing his person to be charged with the normal hopes and fears of his fellow men, that the holy man gained the power in society that enabled him to carry off the occasional *coup de théâtre*. Dramatic interventions of holy men in the high politics of the Empire were long remembered.[7] But they illustrate the prestige that the

each in their different way, have the singular merit of presenting the manner in which the seemingly metaphysical controversies on the Trinity and the nature of Christ condensed, in some measure, concrete problems of the nature and the potentialities of the human personality as this was revealed and tested in the new ascetic milieus: piety, self-knowledge and theological speculation were more closely connected than we had thought.]

7. Libanius, *Oratio* I, 2 (ed. A. F. Norman, *Libanius' Autobiography* (1965), pp. 2–3) shows how the reputation of a local family depended on members who were

holy man had already gained, they do not explain it. They were rather like the cashing of a big cheque on a reputation; and, like all forms of power in late Roman society, this reputation was built up by hard, unobtrusive (and so, for us, partly obscure) work among those who needed constant and unspectacular ministrations.[8]

Secondly, it is a simple matter for the religious historian to use the literature of the ascetic world to evoke the feelings that crystallized around the holy man. Here was a man who had conquered his body in spectacular feats of mortification. He had gained power over the demons, and so over the diseases, the bad weather, the manifest disorders of a material world ruled by the demons. His prayers alone could open the gates of heaven to the timorous believer.[9] Yet a description of the power attributed to the holy man cannot, of itself, explain why, at a precise time, the majority of men were prepared to see a small number of their fellows in so dramatic a light. Furthermore, the picture stands *in vacuo*. To leave it like that is to miss an opportunity. In studying both the most admired and the most detested figures in any society, we can see, as seldom through other evidence, the nature of the average man's expectations and hopes for himself. It is for the historian, therefore, to analyse this image as a product of the society around the holy man. Instead of retailing the image

---

famous 'in the oratory which opposes itself to the ill-temper of governors'. The circles around holy men delighted in similar incidents: *V. Theod.* c. 142: 'The consul (Bonosus) stood but did not bend his neck, so the saint took hold of the hair of his forehead and pulled it and in this way bent his head down . . . We who were present were thunderstruck and terrified at the just man's daring.' [On freedom of speech in the pagan world and its severe limitations: H. Musurillo, *Acts of the Pagan Martyrs* (Oxford, 1954), pp. 269–70 and A. D. Momigliano, 'La libertà di parola nel mondo antico', *Rivista storica italiana* LXXXIII (1971), esp. pp. 521–23.]

8. Macedonius boldly halted the military commissioners on their way to punish the city of Antioch in 387 (*H.R.* 1404 C); but he had already created a clientèle among the military—he had impressed a general on a hunt, and had prophesied for Count Lupicinus on the outcome of grain-speculations (*H.R.* 1404 B). Alexander the Sleepless, who attempted to rebuke officials without such preparation, was summarily exiled both from Antioch (*V. Alex.* c. 39–40, pp. 687–89) and Constantinople (*V. Hyp.* c. 41).

9. N. H. Baynes, in Baynes and Dawes *Three Byzantine Saints*, pp. ix–xii.

of the holy man as sufficient in itself to explain his appeal to the average late Roman, we should use the image like a mirror, to catch, from a surprising angle, another glimpse of the average late Roman.

Lastly, the rise of the holy man to such eminence in the later Empire has long been attributed, in the sweeping and derogatory perspective of many classical scholars, from Gibbon onwards,[10] to the decline of Greek civilization in the Near East. For just as the lives of saints have been quarried by the social historian for evidence of the life of the man in the street, so have they been used, in this past century, as a sort of bathyscope, that enables the religious historian to penetrate into what he regards as hitherto untouched depths of popular superstition; it is assumed that the study of such documents must necessarily be akin to deep-sea diving.[11] This impression was reinforced, at the turn of the century, by the influence of a Darwinian theory of evolution that dominated the anthropological study of religion. 'Popular' belief was treated as the belief of populations at a lower stage of moral and intellectual evolution. This approach produced an exceptionally static and élitist view of ancient belief: beneath a Greco-Roman élite, the populations of the Mediterranean and the Near East were each thought of as living at a lower stage of evolution—a stage that was basically similar to other lower stages of evolution in different areas and different ages.[12] Hence the ease with which some of the very best

10. E. Gibbon, *The Decline and Fall of the Roman Empire*, ch. 37: 'If it be possible to measure the interval between the philosophic writings of Cicero and the sacred legend of Theodoret, between the character of Cato and that of Simeon, we may appreciate the memorable revolution which was accomplished in the Roman empire within a period of five hundred years.'

11. This has been rebutted, and most acutely, in only one study known to me: Patlagean, 'À Byzance' (n. 3), pp. 106–10.

12. E.g., F. Steinleitner, *Die Beicht im Zusammenhang mit der sakralen Rechtspflege in der Antike* (1913), p. 99. 'Diese Glaube [on the relation between sin and illness] ist für alle niederen Stufen ethischer Betrachtung charakteristisch'—not surprisingly, therefore, the religious practices of the nineteenth-century Aargau (p. 127, n. 1) conclude a monograph on second-century Asia Minor! [See above, pp. 8–12, and Peter Brown, *The Cult of the Saints: Its Rise and Function in Latin Christianity* (Chicago, 1981), pp. 12–22.]

monographs in the *Religionsgeschichtliche Versuche und Vorarbeiten* pass, in their footnotes, from cuneiform texts, through the folklore of Ancient and Modern Greece, to the gnarled practices of near-contemporary Swiss and German villages.

The modern historian of late Roman culture is too often the unwitting heir of this monotonous perspective. For it is this view of 'popular' belief that has lent authority to the opinion, proposed by Rostovtzeff and elaborated as the guiding-line of many modern interpretations of the cultural changes of Late Antiquity, that the end of the ancient world was marked by the rapid democratization of the culture of the Greco-Roman élite, and so by a catastrophic dilution of the religious ideas of an enlightened minority, by the beliefs of the more primitive majority of the provincials. Like an antediluvian sea bed placed by some convulsion at the crest of a mountain range, the hagiographical literature of Late Antiquity is treated as representing the intrusion into the upper classes of the Roman world of ideas whose rightful place was among the more primitive masses of the Near East.[13]

To take issue with such a view would involve rewriting the social and religious history of the Roman world. It is sufficient to say, in connection with the holy man, that this explanation of the arrival of the holy man, though temptingly simple, throws no light whatever on his continuing function in late Roman society. It places too much emphasis on the origins of certain ideas, without paying attention to the distinctive manner in which these ideas were combined and used for new purposes in the late Roman period. It is as if an archaeologist should attempt to use a rude piece of late Roman village craftmanship to explain the style of a masterpiece such as the Ravenna mosaics.[14]

13. Festugière, *Les Moines d'Orient* I, 21: 'Ce que Gilbert Murray a nommé "the failure of nerve" à propos du goût de l'irrationel dans le Bas-Empire, ne doit pas être regardé comme une décadence des esprits cultivés (à preuve Plotin, Ambroise, Augustin, Boèce, Cassiodore) que comme l'apparition, dans la littérature . . . des croyances et des sentiments du vulgaire.'

14. A. Grabar, *Christian Iconography* (1969), p. 65, rightly criticizes an account of the growth of the Late Antique portrait by an author who 'chiefly stressed this

Altogether, the student of late Roman society can no longer be content with *prima facie* conclusions from the evidence. He must be prepared to be wary and undramatic. If we are to understand the position of the holy man in this period, it might be as well to begin by treating him as one of those many surprising devices by which men in a vigorous and sophisticated society (as the East Roman Empire of the fifth and sixth centuries now appears to have been) set about the delicate business of living.

First we must find our holy man. There was little doubt about this for late Roman men: Syria was the great province for ascetic stars.[15] This fact in itself calls for explanation. Egypt was the cradle of monasticism. It was in Egypt that the theory and practice of the ascetic life reached its highest pitch of articulateness and sophistication. Yet the holy men who minted the ideal of the saint in society came from Syria, and, later, from Asia Minor and Palestine—not from Egypt. This lacuna has little to do with the isolation of Egypt under the Monophysite Patriarchs: such isolation has been exaggerated.[16] Rather, the holy man in Egypt did not impinge on society around him in the same way as in other provinces. Egypt provides the first evidence for the formation of a lay and clerical clientèle around the holy man;[17] the violences of the monks in Egypt are notorious:[18] yet the ferocious independence, the flamboyant ascetic practices, the rapid rise and

---

simplification, which he attributed to the influence of artisans who came from the masses and to poorly defined "oriental influences". . .' The historians of Late Antique art are, on the whole, more sophisticated in their approach to such problems than are the historians of late Roman society.

15. *V. Alex.* c. 6, p. 661.

16. Rectified by C. Detlef G. Müller, 'Die koptische Kirche zwischen Chalkedon und dem Arabereinmarsch', *Zft. f. Kirchengesch.* LXXXV (1964): 271–308; M. P. Roncaglia, 'La chiesa copta dopo il Concilio di Chalcedonia: monofisismo reale o monofisismo nominale?', *Rend. Ist Lomb.* CII (1968): 493–514. [Peter Brown, *The Making of Late Antiquity* (Cambridge, Mass., 1978), pp. 81–82.]

17. H. I. Bell, *Jews and Christians in Egypt* (1924), ch. III ('The correspondence of Paphnutius'), pp. 100–20; cf. A.P. Daniel 3 (95), 153C. [Philip Rousseau, *Ascetics, Authority and the Church in the Age of Jerome and Cassian* (Oxford, 1978), pp. 9–32.]

18. See recently, J. Barns, 'Schenute as an Historical Source', *Actes du Xème Congrès International des Papyrologues* (1964), at pp. 153 54 and 157.

fall of reputations, and the constant symbiosis with the life of the surrounding villages—these are the distinctively Syrian features that were welcomed in Byzantine society.[19] They were virtuoso cadenzas on the sober score first written by the 'Great Men' of Egypt.

This difference is written into the landscape and climate of the two areas. In Egypt, the antithesis between desert and settled land—between ἔρημος and οἰκουμένη—was stark enough in reality (the rainfall of Egypt is 1.1 inches per year) and absolute in the imagination of the Egyptians. The links between the holy man and society constantly yielded to the pressure of this great fact. To survive at all in the hostile environment of such a desert, the Egyptian had to transplant into it the tenacious and all-absorbing routines of the villages of the οἰκουμένη. To live at all, the man had to remain in one place, earning his living from manual labour, from pottery and reed-weaving.[20] Groups had to reproduce exactly, on the fringe of the desert, the closed-in, embattled aspect of the fortified villages of Upper Egypt. The monastery of Pachomius was called quite simply The Village.[21] The Egyptian desert, therefore, exercised a discreet and irresistible pressure in the direction of an inward-looking and earnest attention to the hard business of survival. It stimulated a rapid elaboration of the skills of organization, an emphasis on stability and introspection, a piling up, in the *Apophthegmata Patrum*, of

19. G. Tchalenko, *Villages antiques de la Syrie du Nord* I (1953), p. 226 (on Symeon Stylites): 'Sa vie est un exemple typique du monachisme syrien qui savait concilier l'isolement et la discipline la plus sévère avec la participation directe à toutes les manifestations de la vie temporelle et religieuse, en contact journalier avec le peuple.'

20. E.g., *A.P.* Esias 5, 181B—sharecropping; Isidore 7 (20), 221B—sale of pots; John the Persian 2 (50), 237—working flax; Lucius (75), 253C—earns 16 νομίσματα per day; Megethius 1, 30D—is totally independent on 3 baskets a day. [On the earning capacities of the free artisan and seasonal labourer in Egypt, see I. F. Fikhman, *Egipet na rubezhe dvukh epokh* (Moscow, 1965). E. A. Judge, 'The Earliest Use of Monachus for "Monk", (P. Coll. Youtie 77),' *Jahrbuch für Antike und Christentum* XX (1977): 72–89.]

21. A. Veilleux, *La liturgie dans le cénobitisme pachômien au IVème siècle* (Studia Anselmiana LVII, 1968), p. 186, n. 91. [H. Torp, 'Murs d'enceinte des monastères coptes primitifs', *Mélanges d'archéologie et d'histoire*, LXXVI (1964): 173–200. On the growth of monastic landholdings: E. Wipszycka, 'Les terres de la congrégation

an unrivalled collection of proverbial wisdom.[22] As many
an Egyptian anecdote shows, the free floating ideal of the
'angelic life'—the dᶜmū±ā dᶜmala'kē—that summed up the
style of Syrian asceticism, was not viable in the πανέρημος,
the Deep Desert, of Egypt.[23] In the Syrian provinces, ἔρημος
and οἰκουμένη were not sharply contrasted. Instead, they
interlocked like the pieces of a jigsaw. Theodoret wrote of
Osrhoene, χώρα δὲ παμπόλλη μὲν οἰκουμένη παμπόλλη δὲ
ἀοίκητός τε καὶ ἔρημος,[24] and of his own territory of Cyrrhus—'It includes many high mountains, some wholly bare,
and some covered with unproductive vegetation.'[25]

The desert of Syria was never true desert. In the steppe-
lands of Chalcis, occasional showers ensured that water was
always near the surface; the ruins of deserted Roman forts
trapped enough to support a hermit all the year round.[26] The
mountains had the same quality. To go to the ἔρημος in Syria
was to wander into the ever-present fringe of the οἰκουμένη;
it was not to disappear into another, unimaginable world.
The desert was a standing challenge on the very edge of the
village: 'The ravens that fed Elijah cry, Leave the plough.'[27]

Yet, just because the desert was more mild, the human
contrast between the man in the desert and the man in the

pakhômienne dans une liste de paiements pour les *apora*,' *Hommages C. Préaux*
(Brussels, 1975), pp. 625–36.]

22. See *A.P.* Zeno 3 (38), 176 C on the Egyptian pride in scrupulous self-
examination.

23. See Vööbus, o.c. (n. 6), ch. 9, pp. 292–315. [A Guillaumont, 'La
conception de désert chez les moines d'Egypte', *Revue de l'Histoire des Religions*
CLXXXVIII (1975): 3–21; R. Kasser, 'Sortir du monde. Réflexions sur la situation
et le développement des établissements monastiques aux Kellia', *Revue de Théologie
et Philosophie* CXIX (1979): 111–24; T. Baumeister, 'Die Mentalität des frühen
ägyptischen Mönchtums', *Zeitschrift für Kirchengeschichte* LXXXVIII (1977): 145–
60. Compare the Syrian emphasis on continual migration: A. Guillaumont, 'Le dé-
paysement comme forme d'ascèse dans le monachisme ancien', *Annuaire de l'École
Pratique des Hautes Études: Ve. Section* LXXVI (1968–69): 3–58.]

24. *H.R.* 1305 C, 'a countryside where much is settled land and much is unin-
habited and desert.'

25. Theodoret, *Ep.* 42.

26. A. Poidebard, *La trace de Rome dans le désert de Syrie: le limes de Trajan à la
conquête arabe* (1934), pp. 13–16 and Vööbus, o.c. (n. 6), p. 165, n. 21.

27. Vööbus, o.c. (n. 6), p. 151, n. 24.

world was heightened. The Egyptian had to take the habits of the οἰκουμένη with him if he were to survive at all. The Syrian could live with his desert as long as he was prepared to merge into it, to adopt the total informality and lack of structure of wild life, to keep constantly on the move in search of food and water, to live off roots,[28] to be equated with the beasts and especially with the birds—ambivalent symbols, for late Roman men, of both the free and the de-monic.[29] The ascetics of Syria called themselves the tūraiē—the men of the mountains—and the ra'iē—the shepherds. Many simply merged back into the semi-nomadic fringe of the life of the Fertile Crescent. The Beduin were among the first clients of many Syrian and Palestinian holy men.[30] Many a holy man had lived this free and rootless life before. Symeon Stylites had guarded his brother's herds on the mountains around Ṣiṣ (near Nicopolis): deeply under-Christianized, his early piety was moved by ancient memories of sacrifice and prophecy on the high places.[31] Near to the coast, the distinction between ἔρημος and οἰκουμένη was one of height. The hermit deliberately placed himself on the mountain tops, as a usurper of the power of the ba'alīm.[32] From such tops, he could look down on prosperous villages and on the farmers working on the slopes.[33] He belonged to a world that was not so much antithetical to village life as marginal. He was known to the hunter: he too was on the mountain-side 'to stalk his god'.[34]

To the fluidity and the informality of the life of the individual in the desert, we should add the fluidity of the village population of Syria. Then as now, massive under-employ-

28. Vividly described by Cyril of Scythopolis, esp. *V. Cyriaci* c. 8 (Festugière, o.c. (n. 13), p. 44).

29. Vööbus, o.c. (n. 6), pp. 25–27; and *V. Sab.* c. 27.

30. *H.R.* 1360 C-D; 1476 D (Symeon Stylites and the Beduin); *V. Euthym,* c. 15; *V. Alex.* c. 33, p. 683.

31. Sym. Styl. cc. 2–5, pp. 80–82.

32. *H.R.* 1453B: καὶ τὸν ὕπαιθρον βίον ζηλώσας κορυφὴν ἑτέραν κατέλαβε κώμης τινὸς ὑπερκειμένην, 'and in his zeal for the life of the open wilds he chose another mountain peak, rising above a village'; cf. *H.R.* 1365 B; 1417 C; 1456 D; 1488 A.

33. *H.R.* 1340 C-D.   34. *H.R.* 1404 B.

ment was the norm of peasant life.[35] After the harvest and the threshing, the crowd would build up throughout the high summer and autumn. The development of the olive plantations around the Limestone Massif produced a reservoir of mobile manpower: a fluid population was mobilized from November to April to deal with the olive harvest.[36] In between it produced the gangs of skilled craftsmen that roamed the mountain villages, whose fine products still impress the archaeologist.[37] The same men also built the reputation of the Syrian holy man.[38] The crowd is an essential element in the life of the holy man in Syria.[39] In the late summer, the unemployed would stream from the villages to the death-bed of the holy man (in the hope of snatching his body as a relic).[40] Later, mass-meetings were held at the foot of the column of St Symeon Stylites at Telnesin.[41] To the ever mobile crowd, we should add the traveller.[42] The villages around Antioch supplied themselves at great fairs.[43] It was at one such fair, at Imma (Yeni Šehir, still a caravanserai village), on the road from Antioch to Berrhoea, that one holy man first made his reputation.[44] Jewish peddlers carried the news to Cyrrhus that one hermit kept tame lions.[45] The most important travellers, for the reputation of the holy man, were the soldiers of

35. M. du Buit, 'Note sur la Palestine byzantine', in Festugière, Les Moines (above, n. 13), III/1, p. 47. [For what follows see the outstanding study of Evelyne Patlagean, Pauvreté économique et pauvreté sociale à Byzance: 4e.–7e. siècle (Paris, 1977), both a gold mine for information on the life of the lower classes of town and country alike in the Eastern Empire, exclusive of Egypt, and a model of alert and original interpretation.]

36. Tchalenko, o.c. (n. 19), p. 70.

37. Ibid., pp. 419–21, n. 3. [Patlagean, Pauvreté, p. 270–71, 301–40.]

38. H.R. 1400 D: Macedonius had to move to avoid the crowds.

39. The miracles of Symeon Stylites are crowd-phenomena: Sym. Styl. c. 61, p. 111, 13; c. 65, p. 113, 34–114, 14 and especially c. 109, pp. 156–58. For the rôle of the crowd in such a situation, see E. Peterson, Εἰς θεός. Epigraphische, formgeschichtliche und religionsgeschichtliche Untersuchungen (1926), esp. 181–95.

40. H.R. 1433 C.

41. See Peeters, Le tréfonds . . . , cit. (n. 4), p. 124, n. 1, on the great festival at the foot of the column timed for 27 July.

42. Tchalenko, o.c. (n. 19), p. 373.   43. Libanius, Or. XI, 230.

44. H.R. 1365 B; Tchalenko, o.c. (n. 1), p. 23; and p. 93.

45. H.R. 1375 D.

the garrisons of inland Syria.[46] The soldiers were strangers themselves; like the holy man they were notorious intruders into the settled patterns of social relationships; they were the most influential single group among the clientèle of the holy man.[47]

Recruitment to the ascetic life betrays the same deep informality. A holy man could collect up to one hundred followers in a season.[48] Some drew on the great fluidity of misery: gangs of blind unemployed settled around one such.[49] Sudden conglomerations of this kind could survive only by going wild. Alexander the Sleepless lived with four hundred followers by roaming the steppeland for a year, until hunger drove them down to Palmyra. The townsmen shut the gates against his band: for what they saw was the old curse of the Fertile Crescent in a new form—a Beduinization of the ascetic life.[50]

All this was no recommendation for the holy man to the settled population. For the ecclesiastical authorities, Syria was notoriously the Wild and Woolly West of ascetic heresy: the Manichaean elect and, later, the Messalian monks were brutally contained by the bishops.[51] The hermit, an unattached stranger on the edge of the village,[52] had an uphill task to allay initial hostility and suspicion: he could be framed in a murder;[53] he was often held responsible for pregnancies among the village girls;[54] he had the evil eye.[55] To understand

46. L. Harmand (cited below, n. 60), 150–56. These were later maintained to guard the cities from the Isaurian raids: *Sym. Styl.* c. 8, p. 85, 14 and n. 5. Theodoret, *Comm. in Ezech.* 3, 17 (*PG* LXXXI, 848 C) describes watchtowers to give warning of such raids.

47. *H.R.* 1329 B on the close relations of Marcianus of Cyrrhus with a general at Beroea; and *Sym. Styl.* c. 9, p. 86, 12.

48. *H.R.* 1308 B.   49. *H.R.* 1456 B.

50. *V. Alex.* c. 34–35, pp. 684–86.

51. Vööbus, o.c. (n. 6), pp. 120–23; and P. Brown, 'The Diffusion of Manichaeism in the Roman Empire', *JRS* LIX (1969): 96 (= *Religion and Society in the Age of St. Augustine*, 1971, 104). [Patlagean, *Pauvreté*, pp. 141–43.]

52. *H.R.* 1360 C—in a little house by the threshing floors.

53. *H.R.* 1365 B.   54. *A.P.* Macarius the Egyptian I (80), 256 C.

55. *Marc le Diacre, Vie de Porphyre*, ed. Grégoire-Kugener (1930), c. 19, p. 16 and 95; *V. Alex.* cc. 11, p. 665 and 40, p. 689.

how so unlikely a candidate for eminence gained his position in Syrian society, as elsewhere, we should look more closely at the problems of the οἰκουμένη, especially at the conditions of the village life in the eastern provinces in the fourth and fifth centuries.

The evidence that we have for the Syrian countryside suggests strongly that, in the fourth and fifth centuries, the villagers of those areas where the holy man was to be most active were passing through a crisis of leadership. The prosperity of the Syrian countryside shows every sign of increasing, and with it the population.[56] Whether we read Libanius, Theodoret or the inspired evocation of a distinctive area by Tchalenko, we are in a world of thriving villages: the holy man is regularly settled beside the κώμη ... μεγίστη καὶ πολυάνθρωπος.[57] The archaeological and epigraphic evidence points to an increase of a new class of independent and self-respecting farmers—ἐσθλῆς ἐκ γεωργείης[58]—to the break-up of the previous great estates, and consequently to the emergence of a new, more egalitarian society, whose solid and unpretentious farmhouses survive to this day.[59] The holy man did not arise from any *misère* of the country folk, as is too often stated.

Nor does *misère* explain the appearance of that other figure on the Syrian scene, the rural patron, the προστάτης.[60]

56. R. Rémondon, *La crise de l'empire romain* (1964), pp. 302–308, provides an excellent survey of recent studies and discoveries; and, now, E. Patlagean, 'Sur la limitation de la fécondité dans la haute époque byzantine,' *Annales* XXIV (1969): 1353–69 esp. at p. 1368.

57. *Gindaros*, H.R. 1313 C, 'the great and populous village'; and *Sym. Styl.* c. 98, pp. 143–44; Nicerta, *H.R.* 1325 D; Teleda (Tel 'Ade) *H.R.* 1340 D; Immai (see n. 44) 1365 A.

58. L. Robert, *Hellenica* XI–XII, 1960, esp. 321–27 on inscriptions in the Hauran: 'honourable from working the land.'

59. Tchalenko, o.c. (n. 19), pp. 317 and 385 ff.

60. See Libanius, *Or.* XLVII in L. Harmand, *Libanius, Discours sur les patronages. Texte traduit, annoté et commenté* (1955) (cited henceforth in this edition). [For an excellent new translation and introduction: A. F. Norman, *Libanius, Selected Works* II, Loeb Classical Library (London, 1977), pp. 491–535, whose divisions of the text are the same as those used by Harmand.] I owe to W. Liebeschuetz's *Antioch: City and Imperial Administration in the Later Roman Empire* (Oxford, 1972), pp. 192–208, a different perspective from that adopted by Harmand.

Too sombre a preoccupation with the long-term evils of the growth of rural patronage (for which the evidence is effectively limited, for the fifth century, to Gaul and Egypt only) has led us to neglect the excellent evidence that we do have from Syria, for the immediate and unspectacular roots of a patron's activity in a village.[61] From the *De patrociniis* of Libanius and the *Historia Religiosa* of Theodoret it is possible, as seldom elsewhere, to see the patron as a necessary figure of village life.

Patronage was a fact of life. What Libanius regretted was that it was being exercised by the wrong people[62]—by the military to the exclusion of the traditional leaders of society, the urban landowners of Antioch 'even though these are villages of noble men, men well able to stretch out a helping hand to those in distress'—καὶ τῶν οἵων τε ὄντων χεῖρα ὀρέξαι λυπουμένοις.[63] What the patron could offer was power on the spot. Δύναμις, 'power', is a central element in the rôle of the patron.[64] By means of such δύναμις, he could help the villagers to conduct their relations with the outside world: he would forward their lawsuits;[65] his protection might cover their feuds with other villages;[66] he might arrange for them to meet tax demands, and not necessarily to evade them.[67] The patron appears as a disruptive figure only when his activities threaten the traditional links between the village and the outside world—when he had gained a strong enough position, that is, to intercept rents and taxes.[68] But the bond between village and patron was strengthened by services of-

61. Harmand, esp. p. 181, tends to conflate the evidence from Salvian of Marseilles with that of Syrian conditions.

62. *Or.* XLVII, 6–7 (p. 16, 20–33). [J. M. Carrié, 'Patronage et propriété militaire au ive. siècle. Objet rhétorique et objet réel du discours, Sur les Patronages, de Libanius', *Bulletin de Correspondance Hellénique* C (1976): 159–76, sees this clearly.]

63. *Or.* XLVII, 11 (p. 17, 24).

64. Harmand, p. 123. This is what the traditional landowners were thought to lack: *Or.* XLVII, 22 (p. 19, 30): τί οὖν, φησί, εἰ τῆς χρείας ἐλάττων ὁ τὸν ἀγρὸν ἔχων εἴη καὶ δέοι δυνατωτέρας κεφαλῆς; '"Well," it may be said, "what happens if the landlord is incapable of doing the job, and some more powerful personage is needed?"'

65. *Or.* XLVII, 13 (pp. 17–8).   66. *Or.* XLVII, 4 (p. 15, 28–30).

67. See p. on *H.R.* 1420 C—1421 B.

68. *Or.* XLVII, 4 (p. 15, 25); 6 (p. 16, 23–7).

fered within the village itself. Libanius describes the good patron: he is a man who would use his δύναμις to smooth over the thorny issues of village life. He would provide—and help distribute—the all-important water supply of the village.[69] He would arrange the cancelling of debts.[70] He could settle disputes among the villagers on the spot, and so save them the long trek to the local town to conduct their litigation.[71] To offer such services was time-consuming. Libanius and many urban landowners only paid lip service to the ideal of the 'good patron'. They did not want duties that took them far into the countryside, away from the politics of the city and the delights of the great suburban villas at Daphne. They were outclassed by the military. The military often possessed δύναμις in the form of a garrison in the neighbourhood of the village;[72] they enjoyed exceptional facilities for transport—a decisive element in the exercise of power in the Roman world; they dug themselves in vigorously at the expense of the traditional landowners by being sensitive to the needs of the villagers. The hard work of patronage, which Libanius dismissed contemptuously as 'slaving for the country folk', was the only way in which men whose careers lay on the fringe of the traditional landed aristocracy could gain access to the one permanent source of wealth and prestige in the ancient world, to the land.[73] We can even watch the rise of

69. *Or.* XLVII, 19 (p. 19, 9–10). It is notable (if not very surprising) that the most memorable miracles of holy men affected just this issue—the finding, diverting, distributing of water: e.g., *H.R.* 1389 A ὥσπερ ὑπό χεῖρα ἔχων τὴν τῶν ὑδάτων φόραν, 'as if he had the flow of the water under his hand.'; 1392 D; *Sym. Styl.* c. 72, p. 119.

70. *Or.* XLVII, 19 (p. 19, 10–12); *Sym. Styl.* c. 57, p. 108, 27.

71. *Or.* XLVII, 19 (p. 19, 12–4): cf. H. I. Bell, V. Martin, E. G. Turner and D. Van Berchem, *The Abinnaeus Archive. Papers of a Roman Officer in the reign of Constantius II* (1962), no. 28, p. 77: 'For my intention was to go up to the city . . . but first of all I have written to you, my master, to do me justice.' cf. H. Braunert, *Die Binnenwanderung. Studien zur Sozialgeschichte Ägyptens* (Bonner Historische Forschungen, 28) (1964), p. 144.

72. Harmand, pp. 148–68, esp. pp. 155–56; cf. R. Rémondon,' Militaires et civils dans une campagne égyptienne au temps de Constance II', *Journal des Savants* (1965): 132–43.

73. Libanius: *Or.* XXXIX, esp. 10 (Förster III, p. 270), where a friend of Li-

a patron. Abraham the hermit came to a pagan village in the Lebanon. It was, Theodoret was careful to point out (in exactly the same terms as Libanius had done), a village of many owners—a village, that is, of independent farmers. He rented a house and settled down as an agent for the walnut crop. He sang the Psalms. His neighbours promptly blocked the entrance of his house with refuse. But, when the tax collector came, it was Abraham who was able through friends in Apamaea to arrange a loan for the village. From then on he was declared to be προστάτης of the village.[74]

This process does not show peasants fleeing to an overmighty protector, as has too often been supposed; rather, it points to a relationship which in its initial stages was strictly bilateral. Very often it was the village that called the tune. Patronage was the lever by which the astute and self-confident farmers of late Roman Syria and Egypt managed to shift the structure of land-holding to their advantage, by exploiting the rivalries of prospective patrons.[75] Jewish tenants of Libanius, Ἰουδαῖοι τῶν πάνυ, 'real, proper Jews,' got the better of him by promptly paying court to a general.[76] The mutual exploitation of the relations of patronage became acute in the late fourth century. What Libanius complained of was a 'hunting after patrons' among the villagers of Syria.[77] This was because the new προστάτης filled a gap in rural society. Villagers needed a hinge-man, a man who belonged to the outside world, and yet could place his δύναμις, his know-how and (let us not forget) his culture and values at the disposal of the villagers.[78] The crisis of the late Roman Empire is precisely the crisis by which the traditional hinge-man withdrew from the village scene. In Syria, as in Egypt, it appears that substantial landowners, who had connections with the city and the Imperial government, resided less often on the

---

banius is consoled for having as an enemy Mixidemus, a lawyer who had gained his wealth by this and other distasteful means.

74. *H.R.* 1420 C—1421 B.

75. Rémondon, *La crise* (above, n. 56), pp. 303–304.

76. *Or.* XLVII, 13 (pp. 17, 39–18, 10).   77. *Or.* XLVII, 17 (p. 18, 36).

78. See R. Redfield, *The Little Community* and *Peasant Society and Culture* (Phoenix Books, Chicago, 1960), esp. *Peasant Society and Culture*, pp. 36–38.

threshold of the village. In the Limestone Massif, the large villas, the demesnes and the ostentatious family tombs of the Roman citizens of the second and third century disappear.[79] They are replaced by a self-confident and idiosyncratic local style:[80] 'vor allem zerrissen nun auch mehr und mehr die geistigen Fäden zwischen Stadt und Land.'[81] It was the villagers who had to look around to recreate, with the human material that lay to hand, the vital figure of the hinge-man.[82]

Furthermore an effective patron was essential to the internal working of the villages at a time of growing prosperity. Communities of small farmers on the make needed an arbitrator to settle their disputes. The villagers of the Limestone Massif appear to have needed this service most acutely. The prosperity of the individual houses contrasts significantly with the total absence, before the late fifth century, of any sign of communal building. The sense of community was weak. Private water-cisterns relieved the villages of the hills from the hard discipline of co-operation imposed on the peasantry of Egypt by the river Nile.[83] Villages that were only governed by a council of elders, that is by their equals,

79. Tchalenko, o.c. (n. 19), pp. 408–409. 80. Ibid., p. 142.

81. Braunert, o.c. (n. 71), p. 291.

82. In this context, it is important to stress that the ascetic movement in Syria was far from being a movement of the lower classes. Its leading figures would have come from families used to exercising the powers of the good patron: e.g. Marcianus of Cyrrhus, a local notable and former courtier, an acquaintance of a general at Beroea, uncle to a πρωτεύων of Cyrrhus (H.R. 1324 D; 1329 B and 1333 D). Symeon was a comfortable farmer, who could feed the village poor off his land, and needed a camel to carry his valuables to a monastery: Sym. Styl. cc. 11–13, pp. 86–87. His impresario, the περιοδευτής Bassus, came from a curial family of Edessa: Sym. Styl. c. 51, p. 104, 26 and n. 4. To speak of the early monks as simple and ignorant peasants is to forget both that, whatever their former education, they depended for their position precisely on standing outside culture (see below, p. 131), and that many came from a local aristocracy which was well-lettered in Syriac. To prefer the desert to a late Roman town and Syriac to Greek is quite credible for such a man, and no sign that he is a country bumpkin of low social standing. If anything, the rise of asceticism in Syria is a sign not of a brutal 'democratization' of the upper classes, so much as of a 'fragmentation' of what had liked to consider itself a homogeneous urban aristocracy, so that generals and abbots came to compete with men like Libanius.

83. See Tchalenko, o.c. (n. 19), pp. 46 ff; Sym. Styl. c. 65, p. 113, 26—a rain-miracle fills these cisterns. Olive-harvesting made co-operation desirable, without creating year-long habits of communal work; see Tchalenko, p. 386.

threatened to explode without the intervention of an influential outsider.[84] As in the modern Near East, a village with a weak patron was a village made intolerable by quarrels: the ideal was a patron 'during whose days none could open his mouth.'[85]

Rural patronage in Syria was not a symptom of decline. It was like the governor of an engine, in that it enabled the inland villages to pass through a period of rising prosperity without over-heating. It is a significant facet of that seismic shift that enabled new classes in the empire to make their creativity felt by throwing up new forms of social relations, and by moulding to their own advantage the old features of public life.

It is precisely at this point that the holy man came to the fore as a figure in village society and in the relation between the village and the outside world. For what men expected of the holy man coincides with what they sought in the rural patron. The *Historia Religiosa* of Theodoret deserves careful attention from this point of view. It was written to validate and publicize the local traditions surrounding the holy men of Syria, and so it reflects all the more faithfully what Theodoret and his informants wanted from a holy man.[86] They knew exactly what they wanted—a version of the good pa-

84. See Tchalenko, p. 317 on the egalitarian tone of the farmhouses at Bamuqqa. Frequent late Roman inscriptions against envy and the evil eye are not an argument for neighbourliness among Syrian house-holders: E. Peterson, o.c. (n. 39), pp. 34–36 and L. Robert, *Hellenica* XI–XII (1960): 298, n. 1 and p. 299; and XIII (1965): 265–71. [Patlagean, *Pauvreté*, pp. 343–45. For the function of a holy man in an analogous situation—the role of Wulfric of Haselbury in the expanding villages of twelfth-century Somerset: H. Mayr-Harting, 'Functions of a Twelfth Century Recluse', *History* LX (1975): 337–52, especially pp. 340–41.]

85. Hamed Ammar, *Growing Up in an Egyptian Village. Silwa, Province of Aswan* (1954), p. 80.

86. Peeters, o.c. (n. 4), p. 95. See also P. Canivet, 'Theodoret et le Monachisme syrien avant le concile de Chalcédoine', *Theologie de la Vie monastique*, cit. (n. 6), pp. 241–82; A. J. Festugière, *Antioche päienne et chrétienne* (1959), pt. II, especially pp. 244–506. [P. Canivet, *Le monachisme syrien selon Théodoret de Cyr*, Théologie historique XLII (Paris, 1977); *Théodoret de Cyr, Histoire des moines de Syrie: Histoire Philothée i-xiii*, P. Canivet and A. Leroy-Molinghen, *Sources chrétiennes* CCXXXIV (Paris, 1977); E. Bellini 'L'opera sociale de Teodoreto di Ciro alla luce del suo Epistolario', *Augustinianum* XVII (1977): 227–36.]

tron of Libanius, a man with sufficient power to 'reach out a hand to those in distress'.

Above everything, the holy man is a man of power. In Theodoret's account, the Syrian countryside is shown dotted with figures of supernatural δύναμις quite as palpable, as localized, and as authenticated by popular acclamation as were the garrison posts and the large farmhouses. To visit a holy man was to go to where power was.[87] The *Historia Religiosa* is a study of power in action—χάρις ἐνεργοῦσα.[88] Hence the emphasis even on the detail of the stylized gestures by which this power was shown.[89] Theodoret's accounts of his holy men in action are as precisely delineated as a Late Antique artist's formal representation of the gestures of Christ as He performs His miracles. The scene is grouped around the hand of the holy man—an ancient and compact symbol of power.[90] Hence a certain monotony in the account, and even a misleading *sprezzatura*. There are few long miracle stories. That this is so is due to no Hellenic humanism on the bishop's part,[91] but rather to his serious preoccupation with the absorbing topic of power.[92] The miracle is felt to be secondary: for it was merely a proof of power—like good coin, summarily minted and passed into circulation to demonstrate the untapped bullion of power at the disposal of the holy man.[93]

These miracles are of the sort that assume that the holy man is there to play a rôle in society based on his power. Furthermore, just as the miracle demonstrates a hidden, intangible nucleus of power, so the miracle story is often no

87. *H.R.* 1364 D: it was a power in Heaven that reached its zenith after death: Ἐγώ δὲ τῆς νῦν δυναστείας αὐτοῦ καὶ πρεσβείας ἀπολαῦσαι ἀντιβολῶ; 'I pray to derive benefit from the power he now wields and from his intercession.'

88. *H.R.* 1392 D: 'the grace (of God's power) in action'.

89. *H.R.* 1312 C and 1328 D.

90. O. Weinreich, *Antike Heilungswunder* (1909), pp. 13, 29–30, 49.

91. As assumed in A. Adnes and P. Canivet, 'Guérisons miraculeuses et exorcisme dans l'*Histoire Philothée* de Theodoret', *Rev. Hist. Religions* CLXXI (1967): 53–82.

92. *H.R.* 1365 D: Ἱκανὸν γὰρ ἦν τὸ θαῦμα δεῖξαι τὴν παρὰ τῷ θεῷ τοῦ ἀνδρὸς παρρησίαν; 'this miracle is enough to show the strength of this man's intercession with God'.

93. *H.R.* 1360 C: οἷόν τινα χαρακτῆρα; 'like a coin type'.

more than a pointer to the many more occasions on which the holy man has already used his position in society. The miracle condenses and validates a situation built up by more discreet means. We must examine two groups of miracles in the light of this caution—the curse and the exorcism. Both are sufficiently colourful to have been misleading.

The Syrians were notable cursers. We begin the *Historia Religiosa* with Jacob of Nisibis. He cursed laundry girls, so that their long tresses floated down the river like autumn leaves.[94] He cursed a Persian judge who had given an unjust judgment, so that a boulder exploded beside him.[95] From the toppling walls of Nisibis, he cursed the army of the King of Kings himself.[96] Yet, in the majority of cases, the exercise of the curse points backwards to the position of the holy man as an arbitrator and mediator.[97] The vengeance of God falls only on the man whose case the holy man has rejected.[98] Thus Symeon Stylites 'prophesied' the death, within nineteen days, of an opponent of Theodoret.[99] Had the bishop made one of his rare journeys to Telnesin precisely in order to place his law suit before the holy man, as so many had done?[100] Again, the holy man could lift the vengeance of God from a man who sought his mediation. A peasant whose grain was menaced by fire (sent, so they said, from Heaven) was enabled by the local holy man to make his peace with angry neighbours, whose grain he had appropriated on the communal threshing floor[101]—this was a seasonal grievance among villagers, to which any local patron must have been inured.[102] Successful mediation passed off without a curse: it is only through a few memorable instances of failure, there-

94. *H.R.* 1296 A. [s.v. 'Fluch', *Reallexikon für Antike und Christentum* VII (Stuttgart, 1969), pp. 1245–85.]
95. *H.R.* 1297 B.   96. *H.R.* 1304 D.
97. See esp. *A.P.* Gelasius 2, 148 CD—on Symeon Stylites.
98. *Sym. Styl.* c. 77, 124–125—a decision in favour of a poor man's right to his cucumber-patch.
99. *H.R.* 1486 A.   100. *Sym. Styl.* c. 55, p. 107, 18.
101. *H.R.* 1360 C-D.
102. *Abinneaus Archive*, cit. (n. 71), no. 50, p. 109: 'The same Aion, after I had finished winnowing the threshing floor, carried off my own corn and took it away to

fore, that we can glimpse the day-to-day activity of a man like Symeon Stylites. He is not as unlike Libanius as we might think. Symeon, also, stands up for the oppressed guilds of Antioch;[103] Symeon, also, has a soft spot for deserving young men in danger of forcible enrolment in the town council.[104] We should, at least, be no more credulous than our late Romans. The curse merely highlighted a δύναμις, a power, created by hard work and exercised by much the same skills as those practised by any other effective patron.

Exorcism takes us into deeper waters. When little girls played games in fourth-century Syria, they played at monks and demons: one, dressed in rags, would put her little friends into stitches of laughter by exorcising them.[105] The history of exorcism in the ancient world has been carefully studied.[106] Modern anthropological studies may help the historian to see the wood for the trees.[107] These studies have recently stressed the relation between the possessed and the community, represented, in this case, by the exorcist. In this relationship the anthropologists have tended to single out as significant the *aspect théâtral* that links both parties.[108] Highly individual though the experience of possession may be, its handling tends to be acted out as a duet between the possessed and the non-possessed. In such a duet, each side has a rôle; each unconsciously follows a score. The dialogue between the possessed and the community, therefore, tends to have the stylized, articulated quality of an operetta. Possession and its working through is a way in which a small community can both admit and control disruptive experiences by playing them out.

---

his own place, and carried off my half share . . . Having neither fear of God nor of you, my lord . . .'

103. *Sym. Styl.* c. 92, p. 135.   104. *Sym. Styl.* c. 95, pp. 137–38.

105. *H.R.* 1384.

106. S.v. 'Exorzismus' (K. Thraede), *Reallexikon für Antike und Christentum* VII (1969): pp. 44–117.

107. See most recently, *Spirit Mediumship and Society in Africa* (ed. John Beattie and John Middleton, 1969).

108. See M. Leiris, *La possession et ses aspects théâtraux chez les Ethiopiens de Gondar* (1958).

This is particularly true of exorcism in the late Roman period. For, compared with many African tribes, the late Roman operetta is, with few exceptions,[109] brutally simple. It is on the theme of violence and authority. By exorcism, the holy man asserts the authority of his god over the demonic in the possessed. The dialogue between the exorcist and the possessed locates and measures precisely the power of the holy man. The demon in one possessed 'had the rank of a World Ruler'; only Paul the Simple could command him.[110] Furthermore, the dialogue is worked out as a controlled explosion and interchange of violence.[111] The demon in the possessed abuses, and even attacks the holy man:[112] and the holy man shows his power, by being able to bring into the open and ride out so much pent-up rebellion and anger.[113] It is a dramatic articulation of the idea of the power of the holy man.[114]

This was plainly the sort of operetta which late Roman men felt that they needed to play out to a happy ending. Violence was a constant problem in late Roman society, all the more so as this society's image of itself had been so resolutely urban and civilian. Violence in society had long been articulated in terms of the demonic. For such a society, the holy man was very necessary. Like the shaman of Siberian tribes, he could master, by diagnosing, by entering into relation with, by solemnly overpowering, those inexplicit undertones of aggression, envy and mutual recrimination that build up so easily in the relatively small groups with which the historian of exorcism deals.[115] The traditional idiom of

109. *V. Sym. Jun.* c. 118 provides a fascinating exception: the acting out of a woman whose demon thought of itself as more married to her than was her husband.

110. *H.L.* c. XXII, 11–13.   111. E.g., *V. Theod.* c. 46.

112. E.g., *A.P.* Daniel 3 (95), 156A; *V. Theod.* c. 71. That the 'demon' is an articulation of a relationship crystallized toward the holy man, is indicated by the way in which it was believed that the same 'demon' could 'pass' from one client to another, who were strangers to each other: *V. Dan.* c. 33.

113. *V. Theod.* c. 84, 108 and 132.

114. *H.R.* 1329 D, by which the authority of the holy man is shown even at a distance.

115. S. M. Shirokogoroff, *The Psycho-Mental Complex of the Tungus* (1935),

possession both enabled the forces to be pinpointed and designated a man able to resolve them. The many villages that called in Theodore of Sykeon, for instance, lived through dramatic crises of 'possessed' disruption, followed by re-integration gained through an assertion of authority over the demons on the part of the holy man. Significantly enough, the crisis in these particular villages was generally provoked by some enterprising villager who, it was held, had attempted to alter to his personal advantage the immemorial boundaries of the village. Actual physical violence among the villagers was usually imminent on these occasions;[116] but the resolution of the crisis took the form of a rousing opera in which the holy man challenged and mastered the demonic in the village.

'When Theodore drew nigh to the village the spirits which were afflicting men felt his presence and met him howling out these words: "O violence! why have you come here, you iron eater, why have you quitted Galatia and come into Gordiane? There was no need for you to cross the fron-

---

esp. pp. 264–68. That it was a genuine group-experience is shown by the articulation of a mass-panic by a possessed man in Trier, and its successful pacification, by St Martin: Sulpicius Severus, *Vita Martini* c. 18, 2 (*CSEL* I, p. 127): 'tum confessus est decem daemones secum fuisse, qui rumorem hunc per populum dispersissent, ut hoc saltim metu ex illo Martinus oppido fugaretur: barbaros nihil minus quam de irruptione cogitare. ita cum haec immundus spiritus in media ecclesia fateretur, metu et turbatione praesenti civitas liberata est.' 'The possessed confessed that he had ten demons with him who had spread the rumour among the people, hoping that fear of the attack, if nothing else, would drive Martin from the city, though nothing was further from the minds of the barbarians than an invasion. This confession, made by the unclean spirit in the middle of the church, freed the city from the fear that was troubling it' [One is reminded of St Francis who exorcised the demons of discord from Arezzo: *Scripta Leonis, Rufini et Angeli* 81, ed. and trans. R. Brooke (Oxford, 1970), pp. 228–30; the scene is shown in the fresco in San Francesco in Assisi.] Moments of uncertainty about authority were also pinpointed: in the late seventh century, a 'demon' in Rome would not be expelled: he was called 'Philippicus'—the name of a usurper at Constantinople against Anastasius II: (the name, also, of the holy man): *Analecta Bollandiana* XI (1892): 233–41.

116. See esp. *V. Theod.* c. 114: 'They grew mad against the householder and rushed to burn down him and his household as being responsible for their ill-fortune. But as this attempt was foiled by those who held the highest positions in the village and wished to restore peace, they sent to the monastery begging the saint and servant of Christ, Theodore, to come to the village and free them from the evils that had befallen them.' Cf. *V. Theod.* c. 116.

tier. We know why you have come, but we shall not obey you as did the demons of Galatia; for we are much tougher than they and not milder." When he rebuked them they at once held their peace . . . But one very wicked spirit which was in a woman resisted and would not come out. Then the Saint caught hold of the woman's hair and shook her violently and rebuked the spirit by the sign of the cross and by prayer to God and finally said, "I will not give way to you nor will I leave this spot until you come out of her!" Then the spirit began to shriek and said, "O violence, you are burning me, iron eater! I am coming out, I will not resist you . . ." And through the grace of God they (the spirits) were all collected, and to some who saw them they looked like flying bluebottles or hares or dormice, and they entered into the place where the stones had been dug out, which the Saint then sealed with prayer and the sign of the cross, bade the men fill up the hole and restore it as it was before . . . And from that time on that place and the inhabitants of the village and all the neighbourhood remained safe from harm.'[117] Far from being bizarre fragments of folk-lore, such incidents have a social context: they condense—in the same manner as did the belief in the curse of the holy man—a widespread preoccupation among small, fissile communities to find some figure who would resolve tension and explosions of violence in their community.

The evidence all points to the vital importance of the holy man as a mediator in village life. Anthony was immediately mobbed: he became 'a doctor to all Egypt'; 'χάριν τε ἐν τῷ λαλεῖν ἐδίδου [ὁ θεὸς] τῷ Ἀντωνίῳ καὶ οὕτω πολλοὺς μὲν λυπουμένους παρεμυθεῖτο, ἄλλους δὲ μαχομένους διήλλαττεν εἰς φιλίαν . . .'[118] The holy man of sixth-century Asia Minor continued this tradition: 'when men were at enmity with each other or had a grievance one against another he rec-

---

117. *V. Theod.* c. 43.

118. Athanasius, *Vita Antonii* c. 14 (*PG* XXVI, 865 A). 'And the Lord gave him a gift for speaking, and so he consoled many who were saddened, and made friends among others who were locked in disputes.'

onciled them and those who were engaged in lawsuits he
sought to bring to a better mind counselling them not to
wrong each other.'[119] It was by the intervention of such men
that the villagers sought a sense of communal identity. He
placed some check on the strong centrifugal tendencies of late
Roman agricultural life. The holy man, for instance, insisted
that misfortune should be coped with by ceremonies that
emphasized the communal activity of the village. Villages attacked by were-women in the Lebanon were told to get
themselves all baptized and to take collective ritual measures.[120] By the sixth century, we have already entered a
world of carefully organized village processions, through
which the holy man recaptured, by solemn junketing, the
ancient ideal of the great benefactor, presiding over the good
cheer—the εὐφροσύνη—of a united community.[121] Above
all, the holy man insisted that misfortune could be averted
only by penance, and that penance meant, quite concretely, a
'new deal' among the villagers.[122] It is here that we meet
Symeon Stylites at work. What we know of Symeon's ac-

119. *V. Theod.* c. 147. Theodore was, for part of his life at least, a bishop. Such
was the normal function of the *audientia episcopalis*: H.R. 1356 D—it was a bishop's
life: καὶ νῦν μὲν τῶν ξυγομαχούντων τὰς ἔριδας διαλύων; 'and at times he would be
resolving the conflicts of litigants'; cf. Possidius, *Vita Augustini*, c. XIX and
P. Brown, *Augustine of Hippo* (1967), pp. 195–96. In the towns, such a duty was a
compromising corvée, and the *rabbi* often did it better, see John Chrysostom, *Adversus Judaeos* I, 3 (*PG* XLVIII, 847 ff.). The holy man occasionally fell foul of the clergy
through competing with this jurisdiction: *V. Alex.* c. 40, p. 689. [We should not
overlook the continuity between expectations of the role of the bishop in the early
Christian communities and that of the later holy man: both were valued as endowed
with charismatic powers to arbitrate and 'search hearts': Brown, *Making of Late
Antiquity*, pp. 95–96.] The holy man could offer resolution, even in the towns, on
the more intangible tensions articulated by sorcery-accusations, in those areas of
society where they were most prevalent: see P. Brown, 'Sorcery, Demons and the
Rise of Christianity', *Witchcraft Confessions and Accusations* (Association of Social Anthropologists, no. 9) (1970): 17 ff. at pp. 20–26 and 32–33 (= *Religion and Society in
the Age of Saint Augustine* (1971), pp. 123–31). See H.L. XVII, 6–7; *Sym. Styl.* c. 76,
p. 124, 4; *V. Hyp.* c. 12, 15, 22 and 28: *V. Euthym.* c. 57 (ended, significantly, with a
village-banquet); *V. Theod.* c. 35 and 38.
    120. *Sym. Styl.* c. 97, 140–3, cf. c. 73, pp. 119–20 and 75, pp. 121–22.
    121. *V. Euthym.* cc. 45 and 57, with Festugière, *Moines d'Orient* III/1, 121, n.
147 and L. Robert, *Hellenica* X (1955): 199–200.
    122. *Sym. Styl.*, *Vorschriften und Ermahnungen*, p. 181, 27.

tivity as a mediator in the villages is all the more impressive as our main source takes it entirely for granted. The Syrian author of the panegyric most readily available to us was plainly concerned to add exotic trimmings to a local reputation so firmly established as hardly to bear repeating: Persian princesses, merchants from central Asia, Yemeni sheiks[123]— these interested the writer and his audience more than did the constant trickle of delegations from neighboring villages, headed by their priest and elders, who trooped up the side of the mountain to hear 'the lion roar' as to how they should order their affairs.[124] It is only in passing that we learn that Symeon had law suits entrusted to his arbitration;[125] that his curse had sanctioned water rationing in a large lowland village (and even then, one enterprising farmer had slipped out of church on Sunday to have a sly dip at the fountain);[126] and that he had negotiated an agreement on the collection of tithes—a thinly Christianized version of the running battle between urban landowners and villagers as to exactly how much of the crop should be taken and when it should be harvested.[127]

Fortunately, we also have a letter from the priests and notables of one village, acknowledging the commands of Symeon. They are extraordinarily detailed. They would cancel debts. They would observe their neighbours' boundaries.[128] They would loan money at low rates of interest.[129] This last is the most revealing: rather than do away with interest, Symeon and the villagers plainly preferred the subtle

123. *Sym. Styl.* cc. 66–70, pp. 114–18; 101–107, pp. 146–56. Further testimony surely, to the rôle of the merchant in spreading the reputation of saints: see inf. n. 186.

124. *Sym. Styl.* c. 72, p. 119—from seven days' journey away; c. 73, pp. 119–20 and c. 75, pp. 121–22.

125. *Sym. Styl.* c. 55, p. 107, 18: it was a *charisma* bestowed on him by the prophet Elijah—some indication of the difficulty of the job! c. 81, p. 127, 28.

126. *Sym. Styl.* c. 98, pp. 143–44, at Gindaros; cf. *H.R.* 1313 C and above n. 69.

127. Compare *H.R.* 1413 B.

128. *Sym. Styl.* 'Brief des Cosmas', p. 186, 17.

129. *Sym. Styl.* c. 57, p. 108, 33; *Vorschr. und Ermahnungen*, p. 183, 23.

network of mutual advantage and obligation created in the
village by frequent loans at moderate rates of interest, to having no loan at all.[130] Symeon Stylites was 'the wall',[131] 'the
tower'—and, in a less classical epithet, equally suited to the
needs of the hard and ebullient world of the Syrian villages,
he was 'the lion'.[132] 'The oppressed shuddered at his memory
. . . and sighed to each other in their sorrow . . . whom shall
we beg now to awaken the lion, who sleeps now in the slum-
ber of death, before whose roar the oppressors trembled, at
the sound of whose mighty voice they slunk like foxes into
their holes.'[133] In a word, Symeon, the model holy man of
the early Byzantine world, was the 'good patron' writ large.

The holy man first established a position for himself in
late Roman society in the Syria of the fourth and fifth centuries, in conditions that we are fortunate to be able to trace
in considerable detail. Such conditions were distinctive in
Syria; but they were not exclusively Syrian. They were to be
found elsewhere in the Eastern Empire. Thus, in Asia Minor,
we also find, in a slightly later period, the development of a
society of prosperous and obstreperous villages.[134] In Asia
Minor, also, ἔρημος and οἰκουμένη interlocked in a manner
that echoed Syrian conditions: the Olympus range at Prusa
(Brousse), ringed by bandit-patrols in the second century
A.D., came to shelter influential colonies of hermits throughout Byzantine times.[135] It is hardly surprising, therefore, that
the villages of sixth-century Asia Minor should produce holy
men of similar stature and accomplishments to those produced by similar conditions in Syria in the fourth and fifth
centuries.

130. *Sym. Styl.* 'Brief des Cosmas', p. 187, 4.
131. *Sym. Styl.* 'Brief des Cosmas', p. 184, 32.
132. Used of God—from *Amos*, 3, 8: *Sym. Styl.*, *Vorschr. und Ermahnungen*, p. 180, 14.
133. *Sym. Styl.* c. 128, p. 173, 6.
134. Justinian, *Nov.* 24, I . . . κῶμαι μέγισται . . . καὶ πολυάνθρωποι καὶ πολλάκις πρὸς αὐτοὺς (i.e. τοὺς δημοσίους φόρους) στασιάζουσαι; 'great and populous villages, and frequently in a state of revolt against the public taxes.'
135. L. Robert, *Études anatoliennes* (1937), pp. 99–107; see *Vita Sancti Johannicii* II, 5, *Acta Sanctorum Novembris*, II (1894), p. 337 A, and commentary at pp. 322–25.

We can, therefore, trace the 'rise' of the holy man back into the narrow exigencies of the village communities of the eastern Mediterranean. Yet, we can never simply reduce the holy man to the rôle of a charismatic *ombudsman* in a tension-ridden countryside. There were elements in his power that stretched far beyond a village setting: he played a rôle that was applicable to urban conditions; his person summed up widespread ideals, common to Byzantine culture as a whole, in town and country alike; he could be approached, therefore, to minister to needs both more intimate and more universal than arbitration on the loans and boundaries of farmers.

In the second part of this paper, therefore, we must survey the holy man at work in Byzantine society at large. We must first examine those elements in his position that were most valued by his contemporaries, in Syria and elsewhere; and then we must touch upon the personal needs that he was thought to satisfy. Both in geographical range and in timescale, such an examination must take us far beyond the Syria of Symeon Stylites, as far as Constantinople in the High Middle Ages. Yet the examination will do no more than trace the further circulation of the quite distinctive 'coinage', first 'minted' by the Syrian holy men known to us from Theodoret of Cyrrhus.

We can know, from our Syrian evidence, what problems the holy man was increasingly called upon to resolve. We still have to explain why, when faced with a choice of possible arbitrators and leaders, the villagers—and, to a lesser extent, the townsfolk—picked on the unlikely figure of the lone hermit, in so many different areas and for so many centuries. We may come a little closer to the appeal of the holy man, if like the inquisitive layman in the *Historia Religiosa*, we climb up the ladder to Symeon Stylites and pose the crucial question: 'Are you human?'[136] The answer for the sociologist was quite definitely, 'no.' In late Roman society, the holy man was deliberately not human. He was the 'stranger' *par excellence*.

136. *H.R.* 1481 B: ἄνθρωπος ει ἢ ἀσώματος φύσις;

Now it has been observed, in the study of many small communities, that the burden of difficult or of unpopular decisions inevitably comes to rest on the individual who is the 'stranger'—the churchman in a chapel village in Wales, the dissociated medium in an African tribe.[137]

The life of the holy man (and especially in Syria) is marked by so many histrionic feats of self-mortification that it is easy, at first sight, to miss the deep social significance of asceticism as a long drawn-out, solemn ritual of dissociation—of becoming the total stranger.[138] For the society around him, the holy man is the one man who can stand outside the ties of family, and of economic interest;[139] whose attitude to food itself rejected all the ties of solidarity to kin and village that, in the peasant societies of the Near East, had always been expressed by the gesture of eating.[140] He was thought of as a man who owed nothing to society. He fled women and bishops, not because he might have found the society of either particularly agreeable, but because both threatened to rivet him to a distinct place in society. His very powers, as we shall see, were entirely self-created. The holy man is frequently confused with the θεῖος ἀνήρ, 'the divine man', of late classical times, merely because both share an ability to perform miracles. This is a superficial parallel: for while the θεῖος ἀνήρ continued to draw his powers from a bottomless sense of occult wisdom preserved for him in and by society—whether this is the παλαιὸς λόγος, 'the Ancient Wisdom', of the Neo-Platonists, the Egyptian temple lore of the astrologer or the *Torah* of the Rabbi[141]—the holy man

137. See esp. G. Kingsley-Garbett, 'Spirit Mediums as Mediators in Valley Kore-kore Society', *Spirit Mediumship and Society*, o.c. (n. 107), 104–27.

138. Vööbus, o.c. (n. 6), p. 299 is unduly impressed by the 'hyperasceticism' of the Syrian hermits. Rather, men constantly in contact with the surrounding society—see Tchalenko cited in n. 19—needed to act out a more elaborate and dramatically 'inhuman' ritual, if they were to maintain their position as 'the stranger'. Symeon, significantly, would have been 'ashamed' had he been seen on ground-level: *Sym. Styl.* c. 116, p. 163, 16–19.

139. *Sym. Styl.* c. 38, p. 100, 2.

140. *Sym. Styl.* c. 17, p. 90, 26: Symeon even rejected the Eucharist if it tied him to his fellow-monks.

141. See the most illuminating discussion of J. Neusner, *A History of the Jews in*

drew his powers from outside the human race: by going to live in the desert, in close identification with an animal kingdom that stood, in the imagination of contemporaries, for the opposite pole of all human society.[142] Perched on his column, nearer to the demons of the upper air than to human beings, Symeon was objectivity personified.

It is one of the most marked features of late Roman society that it needed objective mediators, and that it was prepared to invest a human being with such a position. It was as a 'stranger' that Ephraim was able to administer food supplies in Edessa during a famine, for none of the locals could trust one another.[143] He kept his reputation as a stranger to the last. After twenty years of active life in Edessa, he insisted that he should be buried in the stranger's plot.[144] One of the sober delights of the Byzantine historian is to study the astuteness with which the great stars among the holy men avoided committing themselves to any one faction in the Eastern Empire.[145] Constantinople, it was agreed, was the toughest consignment for such a man.[146] Take Daniel the Stylite in the late fifth century. Daniel's reputation owes little to his feats as a thaumaturgist. It was solidly based on a dogged defence of his status as a total stranger in a faction-

---

Babylonia IV (1969), pp. 297–402, whose rabbis resemble the θεῖος ἀνήρ of Late Antique paganism far more than either resembles the holy man.

142. See P. Brown, [*Making of Late Antiquity*, pp. 86–94; H. J. W. Drijvers, 'Spätantike Parallelen zur christlichen Heiligenverehrung', *Aspekte der frühchristlichen Heiligenverehrung*, Oikonomia VI (Erlangen, 1977), pp. 54–76, esp. pp. 71–72.]

143. *H.L.* XL, 2: Apollonius of Tyana did the same, and, also, as a total 'stranger', 'dissociated' by the Pythagorean vow of silence: Philostratus, *Vita Apolonii* I, 15 (Loeb edn. I, pp. 38–42). Cf. Severinus of Noricum, Eugippius, *Vita Severini* iii, 2. He, also, was so total a stranger to Noricum, as to be believed by some to be a fugitive slave: ibid., appendix c. 9. Severinus has kept us guessing up to the present: see F. Lotter, *Deutsches Archiv* XXIV, (1968): 309 and F. Prinz, ibid. XXV (1969): 531. [F. Lotter, *Severinus von Noricum. Legende und historische Wirklichkeit* (Stuttgart, 1976).]

144. Vööbus, p. 91.

145. As did the influential Marcianus; *H.R.* 1332 C—a stroke of diplomacy appreciated by Festugière, o.c. (n. 13), p. 254. Marcianus even ensured that no one party had his body for burial! *H.R.* 1336 A.

146. *V. Dan.* c. 57.

ridden city.[147] To begin with, he had the advantage of speaking only Syriac—his orthodoxy, therefore, was impenetrable.[148] Soon his clientèle embraced representatives of the conflicting factions of the previous generation.[149] Later, his blessing validated the purges that marked the rise of the Isaurians at the expense of the Goths;[150] and, behind this blessing, there lay a heavy work of reconciliation, and the burying of hatchets among conflicting generals through the mediation of the holy man.[151] Like Symeon, he decided law suits; but this time, the holy man provided the sanction for international arbitration.[152] Throughout, Daniel avoided being placed. He refused to be ordained by the patriarch. He held out until it was recognized that he was ordained 'by the hand of God' alone:[153] it was a free-standing position which only the Emperor enjoyed.[154] During the crisis of the usurpation of Basiliscus, Daniel showed his gifts at their full stretch. Not only did he show himself a master of the arts of peaceful protest marches,[155] he discreetly set the pace of the negotiations between Basiliscus and the patriarch by a sleight of hand. A patrician lady wished to be blessed so that she would

147. The parallel of Rasputin, adduced by Delehaye, o.c. (note †), p. LV, is trivial compared with the diplomacy required of Daniel. For the pressures to which a holy man was subject in Constantinople, see *V. Hyp.* c. 32—trick questions posed by Nestorius; c. 39—tactful lobbying by supporters of Nestorius!

148. *V. Dan.* c. 17.

149. *V. Dan.* cc. 31–32; Cyrus of Panopolis and Gelanios, a supporter of the eunuch Chrysaphius.

150. *V. Dan.* cc. 55 and 65.   151. *V. Dan.* c. 49.

152. *V. Dan.* c. 51.

153. *V. Dan.* c. 43. [This had been the privilege, also, of the *confessor* in the early Church: *Testamentum Domini Nostri* XXXIX, ed. I. E. Rahmani (Mainz, 1899): 92–93. I would now see a real element of continuity between the position of the *confessores* in the early Church and that of the ascetic holy men: B. Kötting, 'Die Stellung des Konfessors in der alten Kirche', *Jahrbuch für Antike und Christentum* XIX (1976): 7–23; T. Baumeister, 'Ordnungsdenken und charismatische Geisteserfahrung in der Alten Kirche', *Römische Quartalschrift* LXXIII (1978): 137–151.]

154. On the 'Hand of God', see A. Grabar, 'Recherches sur les sources juives de l'art paléochrétien (III)', *Cahiers archéologiques* XIV (1964): 49–57, at 53–57. [D. Miller, 'The Emperor and the Stylite: A Note on the Imperial Office', *Greek Orthodox Theological Review* XXV (1970): 203–12.]

155. *V. Dan.* c. 75.

bear a son. Of course Daniel would bless her, provided, he said—in the crowded audience hall—provided that she called the boy . . . Zeno.[156] Zẹno, the fallen Emperor, was rallying his forces in the east. Only a holy man could thus mention the unmentionable. The dénouement shows how both sides needed such a stranger in their midst if they were to save face. A Byzantine emperor could never be seen to give way to his patriarch. So both Emperor and patriarch ended up, stretched full length, at the feet of the holy man.[157] It was by such astute devices that church and state in the Eastern Empire preserved the great myth of unanimity.

The rise of the holy man as the bearer of objectivity in society is, of course, a final playing out of the long history of oracles and divination in the ancient world. The 'god-bearing' hermit usurped the position of the oracle and was known to have done so. 'While the Great One (Anthony) is still alive . . . go to him . . . and wait until Anthony comes out from the cave and refer the case to him. And whatever he says to you, go by his decision, for God speaks to you by him.'[158] John of Lycopolis had a hall to house one hundred consultants at a time.[159] The lonely cells of the recluses of Egypt have been revealed, by the archaeologist, to have had well-furnished consulting rooms.[160]

That this should have happened takes us to the heart of the religious revolution of Late Antiquity. Yet we should stress some of the significant differences between the old oracle and the new 'stranger'. The distinctive feature of the late Roman holy man is that he gained the position of a stranger among men without being possessed by a god. The old προφήτης tended to be dissociated from his fellows by losing his identity: 'and the spirit of the Lord will come upon thee, and thou shalt prophesy with him, and shalt be turned into

156. *V. Dan.* c. 82.   157. *V. Dan.* c. 83.   158. H.L. XX, 7, 10.

159. H.L. XXV, 4 and Festugière, *Les Moines*, cit. (n. 13), I, p. 46.

160. S. Sauneron, *Bull. de l'Inst. fr. d'Arch. orientale* LXVII (1969): 110, on the hermitages at Esna. [S. Sauneron and J. Jacquet, *Les Ermitages chrétiens du désert d'Esna: Archéologie et inscriptions*, Publications de l'Institut français d'archéologie orientale du Caire, Fouilles de l'Institut 29/1 (1972).]

another man.'[161] The late Roman holy man kept his identity intact. His very real position as an arbiter in society made it essential that he should keep his wits about him.[162] An exacting and frankly histrionic ritual of dissociation replaced the trance.[163]

This is the sign of a shift in a whole society, towards greater explicitness and harder boundaries. Breaching the identity by trance was treated with genuine distaste—it was demonic.[164] What men needed more in the later Empire was the acting out of clearly defined rôles by figures with a function in society. The portraiture of the age shows that a philosopher had to be seen to be a philosopher.[165] In this ritual of self-definition, the holy man led the field. The imperial ceremonial, which attracts the attention of most historians, was but an intermittent flickering compared with the lifetime's work of true professionals at self-definition. In a procession in Rome, Constantius II stood bolt upright and refrained, for a few hours, from spitting:[166] but Symeon Stylites stood without moving his feet for nights on end;[167] and Macarius the Egyptian had not spat since he was baptized.[168] It is perhaps one of the most faithful indications of the whole style of late Roman society that the objectivity that men so desperately needed was less often vested in impersonal institutions,

161. *I Samuel* 10, 6.

162. *H.R.* 1369 C–1373 A–B, on Aphraat the Persian. His guarded and homely parables, delivered in pidgin-Greek, are rightly relished by Festugière, o.c. (n. 13), pp. 259–60, as part of a long tradition.

163. Salamanes of Capesana, who was transported, cell and all, from his adopted village to his native village and back again, was the ideal of a man impassive but not in a trance: *H.R.* 1428 D–1429C.

164. J. Fontaine, 'Démons et sibylles: la peinture des possédés dans la poésie de Prudence', *Mélanges Jean Bayet* (1964), pp. 196–213. On the possible implications of such a shift, Mary Douglas, *Natural Symbols. Explorations in Cosmology* (1970), pp. 65–98, which forms an admirable starting-point for many trains of thought relevant to the historian of Late Antiquity. [R. F. Newbold, 'Boundaries and Bodies in Late Antiquity,' *Arethusa* XII (1979): 93–114.]

165. See esp. Helga von Heintze, '*Vir gravis et sanctus*, Bildniskopf eines spätantiken Philosophen', *Jahrbuch für Antike und Christentum* VI (1963): 35–53.

166. Ammianus Marcellinus, XVI, 10, 10.

167. *Sym. Styl.* c. 10, p. 86, 20.   168. *H.L.* XVIII, 28.

such as the oracle site, or in depersonalized figures, such as the possessed medium, but was only thought acceptable in a man who could be closely observed to be in the act of forging total dissociation in himself, by hammering it out like cold metalwork, from a lifetime of asceticism.[169]

It is here that we see most clearly the moulding force of the expectations and practices of late Roman society in forming the image and the habits of the holy man. The holy man stands so still because he is pleading for men before the King of Kings in the *consistorium* of heaven.[170] Men entrusted themselves to him because he was thought to have won his way to intimacy with God—παρρησία. This word has a long history.[171] It was only in Syria in the fourth century that it took on the final harsh contours that the word implied in Byzantine piety.[172] For the παρρησία enjoyed by the Byzantine saint is subtly different from the delicate artifice of intimacy affected by rulers and their circle in Hellenistic times. It was a dizzy privilege, earned by a lifetime of tremulous obedience and hard work at the court of an absolute monarch. 'One day the old man took a fig-seed, and said to his disciples . . .

169. Closely observed: a layman counted Symeon bending to his toes in prayer 1244 times, then gave up! *H.R.* 1481 A. Meticulously recorded: on the circumstantial accounts of the exact periods of asceticism 'done' (ἐποίησεν) by the holy men, see Festugière, *Moines,* cit. (n. 13), III/1, 68, n. 1. This was because a holy man's claims on God—and so on his clientèle—depended directly on the πόνοι he had been assumed to have undergone (cf. below, n. 182). *H.R.* 1417 C ὁ δὲ ἀγωνοθέτης τοῖς πόνοις τήν χάριν ἐπεμέτρησεν—'The (divine) Master of the Games measured out the grace as reward suitable to his labours'—sums up the backbone of every account of the powers of a late Roman holy man. [Brown, *Making of Late Antiquity,* pp. 13, 92–94.]

170. *H.R.* 1452 B, cf. Neusner, o.c. (n. 141), p. 327 for Jewish parallels.

171. E. Peterson, 'Zur Bedeutungsgeschichte von Παρρησία,' *Festschrift Reinhold Seeberg* 1 (1929), 283–97.

172. See Holl, o.c., pp. 85–90 on sixth-century Palestinian usage. This is exactly paralleled in Theodoret, *H.R.* The newly discovered Manichaean codex, a translation from a Syrian environment, shows the frankly social meaning of the word: *Pap. Colon.* inv. no. 4780, 102, 5–11, (*Zeitsch. für Papyr. und Epigr.* V, 2 (1970): 177, n. 201) ἐν τε τῶι πλούτωι αὐτῶν καὶ τῆι παρρησίαι καὶ τοῖς χρήμασι; 'in their wealth, freedom of speech with the great and possessions'. In Egypt, by contrast, it remained a negative quality: *A.P.* Agatho I (8), 109 A; Daniel 8, 160 B and Festugière, *Moines* III/1, 66, n. 27.

"Listen, my children, if God in His mercy shows His favour to this seed and gives this bare rock power to give forth fruit, then know that God has given me the Kingdom of Heaven as His reward."'[173]

The power so gained was the reward of service. The labours of the holy man echo the 'sweat'—the *sudor*—of the new nobility of service of the East Roman state.[174] Power gained in this way had to be seen to exist. After Martin's first miracle, 'ab hoc primum tempore beati viri nomen enituit, ut qui sanctus iam ab omnibus habebatur, potens etiam et vere apostolicus haberetur.'[175] Continuing a classical habit, sharpened by late Roman conditions, the *potens* needed a crowd. 'As the holy man with the crowd approached the palace of Hebdomon, a Goth leant out of a window and, seeing the holy man carried along, he dissolved with laughter and shouted, "See here is our new consul!"'[176] He fell out. But he was right. The holy man was able, while remaining a stranger, to draw on himself, in a great surge, the ancient theatrical sense of the masses of the towns, which had found so many new forms of expression in the late Roman period.[177]

We are perhaps unduly interested in consuls. The ceremonial life of the East Roman towns had always happened a little below the brittle rituals of the capital. The charioteer, the athlete and the gladiator were more firmly rooted in the imagination of the average man. The theatre remained the main source of the styles of public life.[178] It is worthwhile stressing this: so many of the ideas and forms of expression in

173. Cyril of Scythopolis, *Life of John the Hesychast* c. 25 (Festugière, o.c. III/3, p. 32).

174. See the career of Flavius Philippus: *AJP* LXXXIII (1962): 247–64.

175. Sulpicius Severus, *Vita Martini* 7, 7 (*CSEL* 1, 118, 11).

176. *V. Dan.* c. 75.

177. See esp. Ramsay MacMullen, 'Some Pictures in Ammianus Marcellinus', *The Art Bulletin* XLVI, (1964): 435–55. [K. M. D. Dunbabin, *The Mosaics of Roman North Africa: Studies of Patronage and Iconography* (Oxford, 1978), pp. 65–108.]

178. It was recognized in military manuals that the personnel of the theatre provided the skilled leadership for all public ceremonies: *Griechische Kriegsschriftsteller* (ed. H. Köchly and W. Rüstow, 1855), ii, 2, 55. [Alan Cameron, *Porphyrius the Charioteer* (Oxford, 1973), and *Circus Factions* (Oxford, 1976).]

the early Church can be precisely located in the crucial area of ancient show-business.[179] The reputation of the holy man (and earlier of the martyr, frankly identified with the gladiator), rested on the bed-rock of long established popular attitudes.[180] The holy man was the 'athlete'.[181] This is far more than a turn of phrase. By spectacular labours, by frequent victories in intense competition, by an enviable mobility, the athlete summed up for the average late Roman, as effectively as did the figure of Napoleon for a Julien Sorel or a Raskolnikov, the figure of the self-made man—ἀπὸ πρώτης ἡλικίας εἰ[ς τὰς ὁ]δούς τῆς ἀρετῆς τραπεὶς ἱδρῶσι [καὶ πό]νοις ἐκτήσατο τὴν εὐκλεῆ δόξαν.[182] In the literature surrounding the holy man we breathe the same heavy air. Like Henry James at the amphitheatre of Arles, the reader of the lives of the Byzantine saints can imagine 'the murmurs and shudders, the thick voice of the circus that died away fifteen hundred years ago'.

We are faced, therefore, with a delicate and enthralling situation. For here was power in society that was blatantly based on 'achieved status'. It could never be pinned down satisfactorily in any recognized niche in the hierarchy of church or state. A woman dreamt that her daughter could be healed at a monastery. On her arrival, they brought her the abbot. 'No,' she said, 'that is not the man I saw. Bring me the red-faced one with warts on his knees.'[183] The Byzantine

179. A fact almost too large to be seen, and so seldom applied to precise details: now recognized by Grabar, o.c. (n. 14), p. 16.

180. For the parallels in expression, see L. Robert, *Hellenica* XI–XII (1960): 355–58.

181. Canivet, o.c. (n. 86), p. 247.

182. Le Bas-Waddington, no. 1620, 7–10, 'treading the paths of virtue from earliest youth, by sweat and hard labour he has acquired his glorious renown', discussed, with further examples, by L. Robert, *Hellenica* XI–XII (1960): 347 and XIII (1965): 141. Compare *A.P.* Arsenius, 5 (49), 89 A, the comment of a cultivated man on Egyptian holy men: ἀπὸ τῶν ἰδίων πόνων ἐκτήσαντο τὰς ἀρετάς; 'from their own hard labours they have acquired their virtues.' One hardly need add that competition between holy men had a similar fullblooded quality: despite elaborate self-abasement, some hoped to be 'stars'. In *V. Hyp.* c. 42, the Devil told one: 'You are more just than all the others. You have practised ascesis more than they. Jesus loves you and lives in you and speaks by your mouth . . .' The Devil, in fact, had revealed to the poor young man the banal *recipe* for all Byzantine hagiography! V. sup. n. 169.

183. *H.R.* 1340 A.

Empire must be thought of as ringed with holy men, each of whose resources were as firmly hidden in the courts of heaven, as fortunes in a Geneva bank. The resources, as we have seen for Syria, were a matter of local opinion. They could become issues of local pride. Of course no Emperor could have his child exorcised at Constantinople, wrote a Copt; but in Schiît, 'they are great men in the religious life and we believe that God will grant her healing by their prayers.'[184] Galatian pilgrims knew about Theodore of Sykeon. 'They spoke about him in the holy city and in the monasteries to those they chanced to meet and said, "We have a holy father in our country who by one single prayer can fill the whole world with rain."'[185] The diffusion of the reputation of holy men in the later Empire is as absorbing and as delicate an aspect of ancient mobility as is the better-known topic of the diffusion of the oriental cults.[186] In such a situation, there was even room for delightful paradox. At any given time, no one could know for certain which man enjoyed most παρρησία in the court of heaven: he might be a doctor in Alexandria;[187] a simple farmer in an Egyptian village;[188] even—who knows?—an inspector of the Alexandrian brothels.[189]

Much of the contrasting development of western Europe and Byzantium in the Middle Ages can be summed up as a prolonged debate on the precise *locus* of spiritual power. In western Europe, the circle of spiritual power was drawn from a single *locus*. The clergy stood unchallenged, under the awesome shadows of the long-dead heroes of the faith. Even in fourth-century North Africa, a province which bears so

184. N. Giron, *Légendes coptes* (1907), p. 51.   185. *V. Theod.* c. 50.

186. To the examples of Symeon's reputation, spread by Syrian merchants, v. sup. n. 123, we could add that of John of Lycopolis, spread by members of the family of Theodosius I, see P. Devos, *Analecta Bollandiana* LXXXVII (1969): 189–212, and of St Phocas of Sinope, spread throughout the Mediterranean by Black Sea sailors: Asterius of Amasea, *Hom. ix. in S. Phocam* (PG XL, 309–312).

187. *A.P.* Anton, 25, 84 B.

188. *A.P.* Eucharistos 1 (24), 169 A.

189. Paul of Monemvasia, ψυχωφελεῖς ἱστορίαι, see G. Schirò, *Riv. di cultura class. e medievale* VII (1965): 1006–16.

close a resemblance in many ways to Asia Minor and Syria, the relic of the dead martyr, patronized by the bishop of the town, was the sole centre of χάρις ἐνεργοῦσα in the towns. Men who claimed to heal were dismissed as frauds.[190] In Byzantium, the *locus* of spiritual power wavered as paradoxically as did the fluid society in which it was exercised. With only a passing challenge, from the Iconoclast Emperors, the charge that surrounded the 'God-bearing man' of the fourth and fifth centuries readily spilt over to invest the 'God-shadowed' image with much the same efficacy.[191] In Byzantium there was a proliferation of little centres of power that competed with the vested hierarchy of church and state. The clear outlines of the meticulously articulated imperial bureaucracy strike the casual observer of the Byzantine scene:[192] but they were incessantly obfuscated by a fibrous growth of informal, unarticulated relationships—relations between patron and client, between spiritual brothers, between fellow godparents.[193] In much the same way, on the edge of the hierarchical structure of the Byzantine church spiritual power flickered in and out like St Elmo's fire. The bishops might wield the *mysterium tremendum* of the Eucharistic sacrifice. In the hands of a courageous bishop this could be no mean weapon, as the career of Ambrose of Milan shows:[194] in this detail, as in so much else, Ambrose is part of a common early Byzantine world, that followed the imperial court from Antioch to Trier. But it was the holy man who, through his unassessible παρρησία with God, kept his grip on the keys of heaven. In the tenth century, a patriarch might try to browbeat the Tsar of Bulgaria by threatening to use his παρρησία to stand

190. See P. Brown, o.c. (n. 119), pp. 413–14.

191. See below, pp. 268–72.

192. As it struck, and misled, Western medieval statesmen: R. W. Southern, *Western Society and the Church in the Middle Ages* (Pelican History of the Church 2, 1970), pp. 75–76.

193. See esp. H. G. Beck, 'Byzantinische Gefolgschaftswesen', *Sitzungsberichte d. bayer. Akad. der Wiss.* (1955), no. 5. [E. Patlagean, 'Christianisation et parents rituels: le domaine de Byzance', *Annales* XXXIII (1978): 625–36.]

194. Ambrose. *Ep.* 41, 28.

against him at the Day of Judgement.[195] But half of Constantinople was convinced that, on that dread day, the patriarch himself stood a very slim chance. They had already invested their hopes in more reliable professionals: the dying Emperor had committed to three hundred holy men a book containing the list of his sins. After days of incessant prayer the list was found expunged![196] In such a society, a Hildebrand was inconceivable.

Earlier in the Middle Ages, Byzantine attitudes already puzzled western observers. Had the protospatharius Theodore been properly shriven by a priest? The delegate of the most holy see of old Rome said: 'What was the name of your confessor?' 'I don't know. I only know that he was in the imperial chancellery. He became a monk. He did (*fecit*!) forty years on a pillar.' 'But was he a priest?' 'I don't know, he was a holy old man, and I put my trust in the man . . .'[197].

With this incident, we return to the holy man at his humble routine. An analysis of his rôle in terms of the conditions and aims of the exercise of power in late Roman society can only take us so far; for it restricts us to particular environments and to occasional circumstances. The universal and enduring appeal of the holy man, throughout Late Antiquity and the Byzantine Middle Ages, takes us into more intimate places. Briefly, it was with the help of the holy man, that the East Roman hoped to cope with 'life's casuistry'.[198] To appreciate what light this rôle throws on the mood of late Roman society, we should look more carefully at the holy man in action with his clientèle, as healer and as confessor.[199]

Faced by so many accounts of the miraculous, the histo-

195. Nicholas Mysticus, *Ep.* 5 (*PG* cxi, 56 C).

196. *Theophanes Continuatus*, ed. Bonn., pp. 439–40.

197. Mansi, *Concilia* XVI, 150 D (Synod of A.D. 869). [See below, pp. 191–95.]

198. Baynes, 'The Hellenistic Civilisation and East Rome', o.c. (n. 1), p. 5. 'It was on life's casuistry—on the moral problems of the individual in a dangerous world—that attention was concentrated.'

199. Fairy von Lilienfeld, 'Anthropos Pneumaticus—Pater Pneumatophorus', *Studia Patristica* V, *Texte und Untersuchungen* LXXX (1962): 382–92, is particularly

rian of Late Antiquity usually relieves the strain placed on his own credulity by vastly inflating the credulity of his subjects. It is possible to say, with Lucian, that 'that pair of tyrants, Hope and Fear' account for so widespread a belief in miracles. To be content with such a judgment is of no help to the historian whatsoever. He has to seize the precise and individual character of an age. What we have is of great value— abundant evidence, not of *why* men sought cures in the way they did, but of *what* kind of cure satisfied them.[200] The history of what constitutes a 'cure' in a given society is a history of that society's values: for the rhythm of the cure shows what is acceptable in that society as a plausible way of giving form, and so the hope of resolution to what is experienced— in all ages—as the nebulous and intractable fact of suffering and misfortune. For the late Roman period the question can be answered quite succinctly. Cures effected by the holy man almost invariably involved a process of 'focusing'. Exorcism was the classic cure associated with the holy man; for it involved both the formal designation of an authoritative healing agent, on which the sufferer and his companions could focus their hopes, and the equally precise isolation and extrusion—often in a satisfactorily visible form—of the disturbing element.[201] Other forms of healing follow the same rhythm. Many are connected with the administration of an innocuous *placebo* that is charged with the blessing of the holy man.[202] The blessing gives reality and efficacy to what were thought of as the inscrutable workings of providence. Water is given, 'πίε τοίνυν καὶ τῆς θείας ἐπικουρίας αἰσθήσῃ'.[203] To dismiss such practices as a legacy of magical beliefs is singularly unhelp-

revealing: see p. 382: 'Begreift man ihn recht (this aspect of the rôle of the holy man), so möchte man die inneren Gründe jener erstaunlichen Blüte des Mönchtums im 4. Jahrhundert erspüren können.'

200. [See now the excellent study of Aline Rousselle, 'Du sanctuaire au thaumaturge: la guérison en Gaule au ive. siècle', *Annales* XXXI (1976): 1805–1807; and Brown, *The Cult of the Saints*, pp. 113–118.]

201. E.g., *V. Theod.* cc. 84, 86, and 108.

202. E.g., *Sym. Styl.* cc. 27, p. 95; 31, p. 97, 8; 34, p. 98, 14; 35, p. 98, 30.

203. *H.R.* 1409 C, 'Drink now, and feel the divine protection.'

ful.[204] The fastidious label obscures both the poignant need of sufferers, in all ages, our own included, to focus their hopes on a single agent of cure;[205] and it ignores the fact that the vesting of the object is merely a minor case of the whole movement of late Roman opinion which, as we have seen, was towards charging the person of the holy man himself with utterly objective, inalienable power.[206] As we have seen, the holy man was expected to establish himself almost as a 'blessed object' in the midst of his fellows. Merely to see a holy man stirred East Romans deeply.[207] Right down to his rigid stance, his figure was a precipitate of the unfulfilled needs of an ill-oriented and highly competitive society. What needs, therefore, did his person fulfil?

In the first place, the holy man resolved a dilemma inherent in early Christian piety. Like the Emperor, God was at one and the same time remote and unflinching, and yet, ideally, the ever-loving Father of his people. Contemporaries had some chilling visions of the justice of such a God. 'It seemed to me that I was standing before someone on a high throne. Many thousands stood round him, begging and pleading with him; but he remained unbending. Then I saw a lady robed in purple come before him, who fell to the ground saying, "At least give a favourable answer for my sake." But He (Christ) remained no less inflexible.'[208] Next day, the terrible earthquakes began. The holy man carried the burden

204. As K. Holl, 'Der Anteil der Styliten am Aufkommen der Bilderverehrung', *Gesammelte Aufsätze zur Kirchengeschichte* II (1928), pp. 388–98 (at p. 395).

205. C. Binger, *The Doctor's Job* (1946), p. 48.

206. The artistic development of the reliquaries associated with the Stylite saints shows the same evolution: see Tchalenko, o.c. (n. 19), III, 17–18: 'il n'y a probablement dans ses dessins géométriques nulle maladresse, nulle inexpérience primitive, mais, semble-t-il, l'expression finale d'un penchant que les Syriens ont souvent montré pour l'image religieuse abstraite'—and, one might add, for the 'abstract holy man'; v. sup. n. 163.

207. I. Hausherr, *Penthos* (Orientalia Christiana Analecta 132) (1944), pp. 81–85. [W. Kahle, 'Die Tränen der Frommen in der Gottesbegegnung', *The Ecumenical World of Orthodox Civilisation. Essays in Honor of G. Florovsky* (Paris, 1974), pp. 191–219.]

208. John Moschus, *Pratum Spirituale* c. 50, PG LXXXVII, 2905 B.

of making such a distant God relevant to the particularity of human needs. In his person, the acute ambivalence of a Christian God was summed up in a manageable and approachable form: for the holy man was both συμπαθητικός, easily moved to tears of compassion, and, at the same time, the heir of the Hebrew prophets. As Elias said, in a vision, to Symeon, 'I am he who in my zeal closed up the rains of Heaven, who gave over Ahab and Jezebel to be devoured by dogs, who slew the priests of Baal.'[209] He could be seen to distribute, with satisfying speed and precision, the blessings and chastisements of an unplumbed divine providence. He could be approached directly, as God never could be.[210] To ask Symeon Stylites to pray for rain was an object lesson in the ability of one man to render manageable and intelligible the dumb hostility of a Syrian drought. Symeon knew why it was happening.[211] He knew what to do about it. The little delegation, chanting its *Kyrie Eleisons*, would be able to focus its hopes on this figure, standing with outstretched arms above them, as, predictably enough, the thunder of the delayed autumn storm rolled nearer.[212]

Secondly, the holy man was the professional in a world of amateurs. The values of the Christian man of the world, the κοσμικός, were, as it were, rendered safe and efficacious by being drained into him. For the piety of the average Byzantine was essentially a piety of discontinuous moments of contrition, κατάνυξις.[213] To seize the spiritual climate of the sixth century, we should not look at the impassive figures of the mosaics but at the illuminations of the *Vienna Genesis*. Here

209. *Sym. Styl.*, c. 80, p. 127, 4.   210. E.g., *H.R.* 1384 A.
211. Hence so many of Symeon's 'prophecies' were, rather, 'explanations': a drought of two years was a 'good beating' for certain sins; that of 36 days, merely a 'switching' by God. *H.R.* 1486 A.
212. *Sym. Styl.* cc. 109–10, 156–60—a vivid scene.
213. See Festugière, *Les Moines* III/1, p. 107, n. 111 and Hausherr, o.c. (n. 207), pp. 14–17. Compare the interesting study of P. Rousset, 'Recherches sur l'émotivité a l'époque romaine', *Cahiers de civilisation médiévale* II (1959), esp. pp. 58–65.

we pass, suddenly, from the delightful *mondanité* of a banquet scene to the shattering grief of the burial of Jacob.[214] Byzantines expected, occasionally, to weep for their own death in sin in that way: 'And by the grace of God the hearts of the faithful people were so touched to the quick that they watered the ground with their tears.'[215] But the κοσμικός knew that such storms of emotion would be wasted on the distant vault of heaven. The holy man was different from him. He had opened his whole life to that bitter tide. 'When he prayed, Hypatios was continually touched with contrition. He wept and cried so hard to God that we, who were weeping, were seized with awe and dread.'[216] Only such a man could hope to commit the case of the penitent to God.

Hence, thirdly, the importance of the holy man as an al-layer of anxiety. It would be inaccurate to call late Romans exceptionally guilt-ridden men: it is rather that they were acutely anxious to control and delimit guilt. Caught between a bottomless God and an archaic system of public penance, laymen flocked to the holy man to know whether there was anything at all that they could do, in their small way.[217] 'Can a man be saved?' This was the blunt question of the κοσμι-κός.[218] Not every answer was reassuring. For the holy man wielded the harsh surgery of the ascetic ἀπόταξις, the ascetic renunciation of the world: for many, total death to the world was regarded as the only remedy for sin.[219] Villagers who asked the question too often found themselves joining the nucleus of a monastic community, such as grew up with sur-

214. See now P. Brown, *The World of Late Antiquity* (1971), p. 159, ill. 105; p. 187, ill. 126; p. 191.

215. *V. Dan.* c. 31.   216. *V. Hyp.* c. 27.

217. See esp. K. Holl, ch. 3 ('Die Binde- und Lösegewalt des Mönchtums'), esp. pp. 287–301.

218. *A.P.* Mios 3 (51) 301 D: εἰ ἄρα δέχεται μετάνοιαν ὁ θεος (the question of a στρατευόμενος); 'does God indeed accept our repentance?' [Rousseau, *Ascetics, Authority and the Church*, pp. 19–20; J. Gribomont, 'Les Apophthegmes du désert', *Rivista di storia e letteratura religiosa* XIII (1977): 534–41.]

219. *H.L.*, XXXV, 5–6: with John of Lycopolis, lay clients were given preference: they were slaves playing truant from their owner, the Devil!

prising and significant rapidity around the local holy man in Syria and Palestine.[220]

What most clients received, however, was a measured penance,[221] a blessing and the far from negligible reassurance that the forgiveness of their sins would be made manifest by increased political success.[222] One such interview stands for them all.[223] The patrician Petronas had been sleeping with a slave girl. He fell ill. Visits to the great incubatory shrine of Sts Cosmas and Damian at Constantinople had had no effect. Typically he needed a precise, focused relationship with a holy man. 'Holy father I am dying.' 'A Christian man does not die.' 'I am a Christian all right, but I have never behaved like a Christian. An evil-looking Ethiopian with a horribly eager look on him came up to me in a dream, and said: "You are mine."'[224] After the interview, Petronas enjoyed his first night of good sleep—with eight pounds of gold off his conscience by way of a fee. From that time, the two men were thought of as inseparable. They even died on the same day.[225] The abiding link established, in this way, between the layman and his πατὴρ πνευματικός, his 'spiritual father', is one of the most profound and touching features of Byzantine lay piety.[226] On death, the spiritual father would draw up and place in the hands of his son a safe conduct to heaven.[227]

Fourthly, the allaying of anxiety made a holy man the *décisionnaire universel* of his locality. 'The inhabitants [of

220. E.g., *V. Euthym.* c. 8.

221. *A.P.* Lot 2, 256 B—can decide the extent of penance for a caster of love-spells: v. Holl. o.c., pp. 315–18.

222. For *not* to be blessed by a holy man was a setback for any Byzantine politician: see the charming story in John of Nikiu, c. 89 (ed. Zotenberg, *Extraits des manuscrits de la Bibliothèque Nationale* XXIV, I, p. 488)—a holy man refused to bless the future Emperor Anastasius because, as a future Emperor, he no longer needed further blessing.

223. F. Halkin, 'Saint Antoine le Jeune et Pétronas vainqueur des Arabes en 863', *Analecta Bollandiana* LXII (1944): 187–225.

224. Ibid., c. 10, p. 216.　　　225. Ibid., c. 20, p. 223.

226. E.g., *A.P.* Daniel 3 (95): 153 C: the πρωτεύων of Babylon has his favourite monk.

227. A. Dmitrevsky, *Opisanie liturgičeskich rukopisej chranjaščichsja v bibliotekach pravoslavnogo vostoka* II (1901), p. 580.

Medaba across the Jordan] were in the habit of going up to visit our holy father Sabas to gain from him all kinds of spiritual consolation.'[228] His judgement decided how Christian ethics might be applied. Should a Christian have baths?[229] Should he consult a doctor?[230] Where, in his new church, should a donor place the sign of the cross and where the delightful late Hellenistic foliage of fashionable mosaics?[231] Altogether, we get a very wrong impression if we look only at the miraculous element in the holy man's relations with his clients. In his relation to contemporary medical science, for instance, the holy man appears far more often than we might at first sight suppose in a merely supporting rôle.[232] Much as the προστάτης, the patron, was thought of as intervening not to disrupt the law but to make it work in particular cases, so the blessing of the holy man did not suspend the normal workings of Byzantine science and their sophisticated methods of dealing with life in the world, but merely strengthened the processes of decision-making involved in the application of these skills. 'Again if any required medical treatment of certain illnesses or surgery or a purging draught of hot springs, this God-inspired man would prescribe the best thing for each . . . He might even recommend one to have recourse to surgery and he would always state clearly which doctor they should employ. In other cases he would dissuade those who wished to undergo an operation or take some medical treatment and would recommend rather to go to hot springs, and would name the springs to which they should go. Or he would prevent those who wished to go to the hot springs at Dablioi or to take the waters, say, at

228. *V. Sab.* c. 45.   229. E.g., *V. Theod.* c. 137.

230. See the fascinating series of answers to clients by the sixth-century hermit Varsanuphius cited by Chitty, o.c. (n. 6), p. 137, whose complete edition is appearing in *Patrologia Orientalis*, 31, 3 [unfortunately interrupted by the author's death; for a translation: L. Regnault, P. Lemaire, and B. Outtier, *Barsanuphe et Jean de Gaza: Correspondance* (Solesmes, 1971).]

231. Nilus, *Ep. ad Olympiodorum*, PG LXXIX, 577 D. [The authenticity of these letters has been questioned: but see now H. G. Thümmel, 'Neilos von Ankyra und die Bilder', *Byzantinische Zeitschrift* LXXI (1978): 10–21.]

232. E.g., *V. Hyp.* c. 40.

Apsoda, and would advise them rather to drink a purging draught instead under a doctor whom he would name.[233]

The little Theodoret long remembered his visits to holy men. 'Daniel used to say, "That boy will be a bishop." But old Peter would not agree with him, knowing how much my parents doted on me. Often he used to put me on his knees and feed me grapes and bread.'[234] A scene like this takes us closer than do a hundred miracles, to the appeal of the holy man in late Roman society.

The rise of the holy man is the *leitmotiv* of the religious revolution of Late Antiquity. A study of the holy man's actual activities might lead us to question whether this revolution can any longer be fruitfully described, as it is so often described, as the rise of more primitive religious sentiments in a depleted and insecure society. One might suggest, tentatively, that the crisis of Late Antiquity was, rather, a crisis of freedom. We have found the holy man central to the way in which different milieus coped with increased freedom and its consequent dangers: for the farmers of Syria, he brought leadership; for the townsmen, the objectivity of a stranger; for innumerable individuals, an oasis of certainty in the conflicting aims and traditions of the world. Such a need for certainty and for leadership is not usually experienced by more stable societies, where the objectivity associated with the supernatural is more securely lodged in impersonal and enduring institutions—in great temple sites, whose prophets are often thought of as totally transparent to the divine and whose grave priests (as in Egypt) emerged only in low relief against the façade of ancient wisdom. We know that the later Roman Empire was the very opposite of such a society.[235] On every level of life, the institutions that had seemed capable of receiving the awesome charge of permanence and divinity in

233. *V. Theod.* cc. 145–46.   234. *H.R.* 1380 D.

235. See esp. R. MacMullen, 'Social Mobility and the Theodosian Code', *JRS* LIV (1964): 49–53, on the variety of careers open to quite humble men. See also *Epistula Ammonis* c. 17 (*Sancti Pachomii vitae graecae*, ed. F. Halkin (1932), p. 106)—a Coptic monk wrestling with the temptation to become a soldier. Peasant, monk, soldier—already an *embarras de richesse*!

classical times either declined or exploded. Men were left with nothing to fall back on than other men. In the early fourth century, the old-fashioned might write as if knowledge and power still resided in the great temples of Egypt;[236] but in Egypt itself, men prayed, 'Send me a man, that I may drink salvation from him.'[237]

So profound a revolution cannot have come unprepared. One might suggest at least two long-term developments within the classical world that merely culminated in the later Empire. First, there was a long-standing uncertainty about the rôle of the father in preserving the traditions of society. The society of the Empire was overtly patriarchal. Respectable provincial families liked to regard their members as so many avatars of the virtues of their forefathers.[238] Yet in reality the father remained a distant and awesome figure compared with the true educators. It was the τροφεύς[239] and the ῥήτωρ, silently but effectively reinforced by the mother,[240] who passed on the values of society to the children of every generation. Nowadays, it is easy to miss the warm emotional undertones of the idea of Christ as the Παιδαγωγός. For so many well-educated young men, the good father was their teacher, not their father. The religious revolution of Late Antiquity contains a surprising number of decisive incidents, each involving the encounter of a lonely and ambitious young man with a man old enough to be his father: Gregory Thaumaturgus with Origen, Julian with the eunuch Mardonius and Augustine with Ambrose.[241] Did the definitive rise of the

236. Porphyry, *Vita Pythag.*, c. 34; cf. F. Cumont, *L'Égypte des astrologues* (1937), pp. 118–70.

237. T. Lefort, *S. Pachomii vitae sahidice scriptae* (1933), pp. 248–51, from the translation of P. Peeters, 'À propos de la vie sahidique de S. Pachôme', *Analecta Bollandiana* LII (1934): 303.

238. L. Robert, *Hellenica* XIII (1965): 226–27.   239. Ibid., p. 22.

240. Women as φιλόλογοι: Robert, ibid., p. 52; cf. Artemidorus, *Oneirocritica* IV, 83—a woman dreams she has a beard on one side of her face: she manages her husband's estates while he is away. Very much the ancestors of St Monica, and of the mothers of Theodoret and of Cyril!

241. See esp. Gregory Thaumaturgus, *In Origenem prosphonetica ac panegyrica oratio* (PG X, 1049–1104), a neglected text, now available: 'Grégoire le Thauma-

πνευματικὸς πατήρ, coinciding as it did with a period when education alone, as opposed to family traditions, partly decided the recruitment of the governing class of the Roman world, represent the final sharpening of the old dilemma?

Secondly, and for a wider stratum of the population than the governing classes, the rise of the holy man has something to do with the silence of the oracles. Plutarch's complaint about the trivialization of the function of the Delphic oracle is relevant to this.[242] Oracles remained active into the late classical period;[243] but they had already become too like their future rival.[244] The holy man merely trumped the oracle, by being both objective and trenchant in an idiom that was more consonant with the habits and expectations of a new, more intensely personal style of society.

What is decisive, and puzzling, about the long-term rise of the holy man is the manner in which, in so many ways, the holy man was thought of as having taken into his person, skills that had previously been preserved by society at large.[245] The word of the holy man was supposed to replace

turge', *Remerciement à Origène*, ed. H. Crouzel (Sources Chrétiennes, 148), 1969. [But see P. Nautin, *Origène. Sa vie et ses oeuvres* (Paris, 1977), pp. 81–86, for doubts on the authorship, but not on the authenticity, of this text.] See *H.R.* 1384 A—the 'netting' of a young man by a spiritual father, with the long classical background of the expression, in Festugière, *Antioche* o.c. (n. 86), p. 258, n. 5.

242. Plutarch, *De Pythiae oraculis* c. 3, 408 B-409 A, is especially revealing. (But, as Professor E. R. Dodds had kindly pointed out to me, the trivialization of oracle-questions was no new thing: Plutarch had pitched his demands rather high.)

243. See esp. L. Robert, *Hellenica* XI-XII, p. 546 (on their continued stabilizing function in times of religious ferment); and "Trois Oracles de la Théosophie et un prophète d'Apollon', *Comptes Rendus de l'Acad. des Inscr.* (December 1968): 568–99. [K. Buresch, *Claros. Untersuchungen zum Orakelwesen der späteren Antike* (Leipzig, 1889), p. 39: "Die grosse Masse wandte sich an die sehr volkstümlich und herablassend gewordenen Orakel wie an vertraute Beichtväter.' There may be more truth in the image than Buresch realized: see Brown, *Making of Late Antiquity*, pp. 36–38.]

244. Already in the third and early fourth century, a 'prophet' had taken on some of the more 'personalized' attributes of a holy man: e.g., the priestess Ammias at Thyateira, and Athanatos Epitynchanos at Akmoneia, discussed with earlier references in L. Robert, *Études anatoliennes* (1937), pp. 131–32.

245. Clearly seen, as the background to the elaborate exorcistic prayers of a holy man, by Robert, *Hellenica* XIII (1965): 267, n. 3.

the prophylactic spell to which anyone could have had access; his blessing made amulets unnecessary; he did in a village what had previously been done through the collective wisdom of the community. He was a ruthless professional; and, as is so often the case, his rise was a victory of men over women, who had been the previous guardians of the diffuse occult traditions of their neighbourhood.[246] The blessing of the holy man, and not an amulet prepared by a wise woman, was what was now supposed to protect you from the effects of a green lizard that had fallen into your soup.[247] If 'the natural death of paganism' is to become something more than a rhetorical phrase, its roots must be sought out in such nooks and crannies of late Roman village life.

The predominance of the holy man, therefore, marked out Late Antiquity as a distinct phase of religious history. The classical period conjures up the image of a great temple; the Middle Ages, of a Gothic cathedral. In between, it is the portraits that strike the imagination, the icons of the holy men, the austere features of the philosophers, the ranks of staring faces in frescoes and mosaics. For some centuries, the *locus* of the supernatural was thought of as resting on individual men. The rise of the holy man coincides, as we have seen, with the erosion of classical institutions; his decline—or rather the levelling-off of the trajectory of his ascent—coincides with the re-assertion of a new sense of the majesty of the community. This is foreshadowed, in the Eastern Empire, by a remarkable revival of the collective sense and morale of the towns, in the late fifth and sixth centuries;[248] and, in the West, by the final organization of the monastic and ecclesiastical hierarchy of the western towns around the tombs of their ancient dead. No holy man was active in Dark Age Rome, but the charged

246. See Neusner, o.c. (n. 141), pp. 348–49, on the rabbi's mother as a source of occult remedies.

247. *V. Theod.* cc. 124 and 143.

248. See now D. Claude, *Die byzantinische Stadt im 6. Jahrhundert* (Byzantinisches Archiv 13), 1969, and A. Grabar, "La mosaique de pavement de Qasr el-Lebya', *C. R. Acad. des Inscr.* (June 1969): 264–82. See below, pp. 275–78.

power of the body of a long-buried martyr was thought enough to strike a workman dead in the catacomb chamber.[249] The great basilica of the martyrs, the incubation church, the icon, and, in the West, the solemn ritual of the great Benedictine monasteries, hemmed in, and over large areas and for long periods eclipsed, the holy man. These impersonal agents had become the bearers of the supernatural among men.[250] Seen in this way, the victory of Christianity in late Roman society was not the victory of the One God over the many; it was the victory of men over the institutions of their past. The medieval papacy, the Byzantine *lavra*, the Russian *starec*, the Muslim Caliphate: these are all, in their various ways, direct results of attempts of men to rule men under a distant high God. The last papyrus in the religious section of Mitteis and Wilcken's *Grundzüge und Chrestomathie der Papyruskunde* (Vol. 1, p. 135) sums up both the late antique revolution and its untold consequences: 'ἐν ὀνόματι τοῦ θεοῦ τοῦ ἐλεήμονος καὶ φιλανθρώπου' ('In the Name of God, the Merciful and the Compassionate. There is no god but God alone.'), it runs, 'οὐκ ἔστιν θεὸς εἰ μὴ ὁ θεὸς μόνος.' It is as we have been told; 'progrès et victoire du monothéisme, ainsi pourrait-on la caractériser d'un mot.'[251] But not quite. Not just the one God. One God *and* His man, for the papyrus continues: 'Μαάμετ ἀπόστολος θεοῦ' ('[and] Muhammad [is] the Apostle of God'). It is this which the historian of Late Antiquity must attempt to understand.

249. See now Peter Llewellyn, *Rome in the Dark Ages* (1971), p. 174.
250. Impressively described by Southern, o.c. (n. 192), pp. 27–33. See below, pp. 317–22.
251. M. Simon and A. Benoit, *Le judaisme et le christianisme antique* (Nouvelle Clio) (1968), p. 2.

Town, Village and Holy Man:
The Case of Syria[†]

T HE PREOCCUPATION OF THIS ESSAY IS THE creation and evolution of a specific form of relationship between town and village in the eastern Mediterranean in the late Roman period. It is a relationship associated with the activities of the Christian holy man in Syria. For in Syria we can follow the genesis and the full development of this relation through a hagiographical tradition that extends from the late fourth to the late sixth centuries from the *Historia Religiosa* of Theodoret of Cyrrhus, through the Syriac panegyric of St Symeon Stylites to the *Lives of the Eastern Saints* of John of Ephesus. Furthermore, the villages of a distinctive region of Syria—the Limestone Massif, which was an area which witnessed the activities of many of the holy men described by Theodoret— have been the subject of the masterly archaeological survey of Tchalenko, *Les villages antiques de la Syrie du Nord*.[1]

It is therefore possible to study a chapter of Late Antique religious history glimpsed against its concrete Late Antique landscape.

For the classical scholar, this is an opportunity not to be missed. Syria, with Egypt, was the scene of one of the most

---

[†] *Assimilation et résistance à la culture gréco-romaine dans le monde ancien*, ed. D. M. Pippidi (Bucharest, 1976), pp. 213–20.

1. Much of the evidence discussed in the following pages is available in my article on 'The Rise and Function of the Holy Man in Late Antiquity', above, pp. 103–52.

momentous transitions from a classical to a medieval world: in it was formed that style of the ascetic life which made the culture of medieval Byzantium discontinuous with so much of its purely secular Hellenistic past. As a result of developments in Syria, the culture of medieval and early modern Eastern Europe and of the Christian Near East allotted a place to the monk and to the hermit as important as that allotted in India to the *Sanyasi*. As in India, it is the non-members of these societies—holy people—who were able to set the tone of the civilization from which they had, technically, totally disengaged themselves.[2] This evolution has long been regarded as a paradigm case of the end of the classical world. As Gibbon said: 'If it be possible to measure the interval between the philosophic writings of Cicero and the sacred legend of Theodoret, between the character of Cato and that of Simeon, we may appreciate the revolution which was accomplished in the Roman Empire within a period of five hundred years.'[3] It is possible, in Syria, to place this revolution in its full cultural and social context as in no other province of the late Roman world. A great work to be done.

My purpose here is to disengage from this vast topic aspects of the theme of assimilation and resistance to classical culture in the Mediterranean.

To begin with I would like to draw attention to an initial difficulty in the theme itself. Assimilation and resistance presuppose a relationship between two elements in a society. If the relationship does not exist, then the theme itself cannot be said to have any significance as a historical process.[4] Many studies of Syria in the Late Antique period have been written in terms of a rhythm, of a dialogue, of assimilation and re-

2. L. Dumont, "La renonciation dans les religions de l'Inde', *Archives de sociologie des religions* VII (1959): 45–69, with an English translation in *Religion, Politics and History in India* (Paris, 1970), pp. 33–60.

3. Edward Gibbon, *The Decline and Fall of the Roman Empire*, IV, chap. 37, ed. J. B. Bury (London, 1929), p. 81.

4. See now the salutary remarks of C. R. Whittaker, *Journal of Roman Studies* LXVIII (1978): 190–92 reviewing M. Benabou, *La Résistance africaine à la Romanisation* (Paris, 1976) and his "Land and Labour in North Africa', *Klio* LX (1978): 331–62.

sistance:[5] but this may be mistaken precisely because they presuppose a relationship between town and village which, in the conditions of the eastern Mediterranean in the later Empire, may never have existed. For there is much evidence, throughout this area, as also for Asia Minor, that the basic and unchanging relationship between town and village was a *non-relationship*. In classical, Byzantine and Islamic times a vast zone of silence opened up between the style of life, the value systems and the rhythms of work of town and village. The extent of this gap should be treated with a sober respect. On both sides, relations were structured according to a tacit model of non-involvement. To Libanius of Antioch, for instance, interest in the villagers meant interest in a world unimaginably alien to his own: it involved relations with men 'who work the land and sleep in hovels with their oxen'.[6] It is a lack of interest which continues unchanged into Islamic times: 'L'État oriental est exclusivement citadin, il ignore les campagnes. C'est donc la ville qui commande et manie seule la machine gouvernementale, qui dispose de la police, de la justice et du fisc.'[7] Normal contact with the village took the form of a strictly delimited infringement of its isolation in the interest of a double constraint: the collection of rent and of taxes. The villagers' side of the picture is less firmly documented; but we can deduce an equally coherent attitude—the town lay beyond the horizon of the village.

This gap dwarfs those other elements of resistance to the classical culture associated by most scholars with the town. Barriers of language, of class, of non-participation in classical culture are peripheral to it. What locked the villager into his own world were the iron laws of peasant life in a Near East-

5. That this can produce bizarre results is shown by Patricia Crone and Michael Cook, *Hagarism: the Making of the Islamic World* (Cambridge, 1977), pp. 60–70, an anatomy of Late Antique Syrians and their culture, which, though conducted with intellectual zest and useful erudition, presents them in a manner frankly unrecognizable to me.

6. Libanius, *Oratio* 39, 10–11.

7. J. Weulersse, *Les paysans de la Syrie et du Proche Orient* (Paris, 1946), and X. de Planhol, *Les fondements géographiques de l'histoire de l'Islam* (Paris, 1966), pp. 46–59.

ern environment. It is essential for the historian, at this juncture, to join forces with the social anthropologist and the human geographer, to measure the sheer extent of this fact of life.[8] That a villager spoke Syriac rather than Greek, that in the course of the sixth century he followed the orthodoxy of Severus of Antioch rather than the 'prevarication' of the Council of Chalcedon matters little compared with the value system in which he was encased. This value system, being the product of the day-to-day commitments of a lifetime, and not the issues which bulk large in our history textbooks, are what made the inhabitant of the village different from the townsman. The non-relationship of town and village was as massive and, basically, as neutral as the alien face of those great mountain sides on which so many of the Syrian villages of Late Antiquity were perched.[9] Hence I would begin by drawing a firm negative conclusion: to write the social and cultural history of late Roman Syria almost exclusively in terms of the resistance of a Syriac speaking village population to the culture of the Hellenistic and post Hellenistic towns, to go on from that to interpret large tracts of the doctrinal history of Syria in the late fifth, sixth and early seventh centuries in terms of a so-called resistance to assimilation by the Chalcedonian orthodoxy of a Greek upper class and, consequently, to ascribe the collapse of Byzantine rule in the province before the Arabs to the final bankruptcy of the assimilating power of Greco-Roman civilization—this is to show a lack of a sense of proportion. The difference in two styles of life, each rooted in the landscape and each gathering momentum from the rhythms of life of millennia, cannot be measured in terms of the protest or resistance of the one to the attempted assimilation by the others. It cut deeper than

8. This has been well done, with reference to modern studies of Near Eastern villages, by Ramsay MacMullen, *Roman Social Relations* (New Haven, Conn., 1974), pp. 15–27.

9. I owe much to the magisterial evocation of the continuity and impermeability of the life-styles of mountain villages in F. Braudel, *The Mediterranean and the Mediterranean World in the Age of Philip II*, trans. S. Reynolds (London, 1971), esp. pp. 34–41, 101–102.

the issues which make up the *Histoire événementielle* of late Roman Syria. To take a small example: the world revealed to us by John of Ephesus in his *Lives of the Eastern Saints* is perched on the extreme eastern frontier of the Byzantine Empire. It is overwhelmingly Syriac–speaking, solidly Monophysite, its rhythms of upper-class life and concepts of social status can be seen to owe as much to Iran as to Byzantium. But the contrast between the style of life of town and country is as sharp, viewed by John from sixth-century Amida, as it was, viewed by Libanius from fourth-century Antioch. John of Urtaya knew what it was like to be 'at first luxurious and delicate and smart as being a city-dweller'.[10]

This first, negative conclusion is necessary in order to appreciate and to delimit the departure from this basic model of non-relationship associated with the activities of the holy man in late Roman Syria.

The background of the activities of individuals aspiring to holiness is the rise of the rural patron in its Late Antique form, and the changing relationship between the town and village associated with the rise of the rural patron. The *On Patronages* of Libanius is the best introduction known to me to the *Historia Religiosa* of Theodoret: and the re-interpretation of the phenomenon of the rise of the rural patron is crucial for our appreciation of the role of men such as Symeon Stylites. Perhaps it is in this way that we can see more clearly the precise roots in the nature of late Roman Syrian society of that revolution which so fascinated and repelled Gibbon.[11]

To sum up a complex subject: the institution of rural patronage cannot be regarded as a purely negative phenomenon. It is not to be treated simply as an abuse, which disrupted the relations between the central government and the municipal administration and their taxpayers, which interposed a new class of *seigneurs* of a quasi-feudal nature between the villagers and their legitimate authorities, and

10. John of Ephesus, *Lives of the Eastern Saints*, ed. and trans. E. W. Brooks, *Patrologia Orientalis* 18, 3, p. 226.
11. For what follows, see above, pp. 115–20.

which led to the loss of freedom by these villagers. It is a phenomenon no longer viewed as a purely unilateral relationship. Instead it has emerged as a bi-lateral relationship, a delicate relationship of mutual advantage, skilfully exploited by the villagers themselves: as the late Roger Rémondon, that most astute student of late Roman social history, has reminded us: 'Mais il y aurait lieu, à mon avis, de rechercher comment ils organisent eux-mêmes leur propre défense . . . Ils opposent les patronages au patronages, en jouant sur les conflits entre catégories sociales (militaires, curiales, clercs, par exemple).'[12] Furthermore, I would tend to emphasize also the role of the patron as a force *within the village itself*, where, in Libanius' view (a view amply supported by other sources) the good patron was encouraged to act as a judge, as an arbitrator, and as a mediator. The need for such patronage relationships within the village was increased by the rise of an equally balanced and evidently prosperous category of farmers in the villagers studied by Tchalenko. Hence, the phenomenon regretted by Libanius—a 'hunting after patrons' in the Syrian countryside.

The expectations centred around the role of the good patron in village society and in the relation between the village and town, mould all accounts of the activity of the holy man in late Roman Syria. The rise of the holy man is a doublet to the rise of the patron. Abraham the hermit—to take one example of many—came to a pagan village. It was a village of many owners, a village, that is, of independent farmers without a landlord who could act as their patron. When the tax collector arrived, Abraham was able through his friend in Apamea to arrange a loan for the village. From then on he was declared patron of the village. Abraham, as patron, became the priest of the village. His position would have been as firm as that of another village priest described in the *Plerophoriae* of John Rufus: 'a man of power and a judge'.[13]

Rural patronage, I would conclude, is the narrow bridge

12. R. Rémondon, *La crise de l'Empire romain* (Paris, 1964), pp. 303–304.
13. John Rufus, *Plerophoriae, Patrologia Orientalis* 13, p. 101.

which spanned the chasm between town and village. In its religious form, in the role of the holy man, we can follow in some detail the logic of the institution of patronage, and through an appreciation of the nuances of this particular logic reach some summary conclusions on the problem of resistance and assimilation as it has usually been treated. First: it has been usual to treat the rise of the holy man in Syria as the rise of an indigenous figure, linked to the villagers and drawing his power from an ability to express the grievances and values of the native Syriac-speaking population in contrast to, and often in opposition to, that of the Greek towns. If, however, the holy man exercises his power on the model of the rural patron, the logic of this particular institution excludes such a simplistic view. The patron was a go-between. He stood between town and village. His position in the village depended on an *ouverture* to the world of the town.[14] (Abraham the hermit, and many like him, would have been helpless without his contacts in cities like Apamea.) His position in the town depended on an unusual sensitivity to the needs of the village. This is what Libanius, too town-bound to make a good patron, objects to in his rival Mixidemus: 'the wretch slaves on behalf of countrymen . . . as letters come in from the fields bidding him do this or that, he cannot sit idle, but has to leap up and put himself at the disposal of this client.'[15]

The novelty of the institution of rural patronage in the later Empire is precisely the growth of classes and categories who could place themselves in such an intermediate position. In the complaints of Libanius, for instance, we see how the self-image of an urban aristocracy which regarded itself as the uncontested master of the Syrian countryside has been splintered by the intrusion of a new category—by the intrusion of the military as rival patrons. It is the fragmentation of the

14. This impression is confirmed, also, by the buildings of the area, which betray the influence of metropolitan Antiochene styles: Christine Strube, "Die Formgebung der Apsisdekoration in Qalbloze und Qalat Siman', *Jahrbuch für Antike und Christentum* XX (1977): 181–91.

15. Libanius, *Oratio* 39, 10.

upper classes, not necessarily any increased resistance or pressure on the part of the villagers, which marks the cultural and social history of late Roman Syria. Men from what had previously considered itself a homogeneous urban upper class were increasingly committed to sharply differing styles of life and outlook, and were basing their social power on different, differing structures of human relationships. The urban aristocracy had to find room from the fourth to the sixth century for the general, for the Christian bishop, and for the Christian holy man.[16]

Second: the cultural consequences of the fragmentation of the upper class cannot be treated in terms of a simple antithesis between the exponents of the classical, Greco-Roman culture and those of a so-called 'new' Syriac culture. Of all the relationships around which to narrate a story of assimilation and resistance, that between Greek and Syriac in the later Empire is about the least helpful. In social terms, as we have seen in the case of town and village, a relationship has to exist in the first place before we can talk of resistance and assimilation. In cultural terms not only does a relationship have to exist, but it must be a relationship tinged with an obscure sense of danger: an awareness of men that another contiguous culture might swamp or modify their own. Now in what Paul Peeters has called *la Syrie bilingue*, there is no evidence for such a sense of danger.[17] The reason is not far to seek. In our appreciation of the role of vernacular languages in the later Empire we have been the unwitting heirs of too unilateral a tradition of classical studies. May I merely remind you, in passing, that not to understand Greek in sixth-century Syria was not considered the mark of barbarism that it might be considered by classical scholars today.[18] Value sys-

16. Hence the urgent need for the publication of a *Prospopography of the Christian Church* for the Eastern provinces, a task which is under way in Paris, and of which Annick Martin, "L'Église dans la khôra égyptienne au ive. siècle', *Revue des études augustiniennes* XXV (1979): 3–26 provides a fascinating first instalment.

17. P. Peeters, *Le tréfonds oriental de l'hagiographie byzantine* (Brussels, 1950), pp. 49–70.

18. This is made plain by Roberta C. Chesnut, *Three Monophysite Christologies*

tems counted for more in Late Antiquity than did the fate of the two classical languages which we usually happen to study.

In the case of the holy man, we have a case of assimilation—of a joining of town and village in a single value system. But it is a case of assimilation made possible by the transcendence of the previous poles of assimilation and resistance. In Syria, the rise of Christianity swallowed up the antithesis between Greek and Syriac, town and countryside. This was possible because of a radical shift of values. The concept of sin and its interpretation, the concept of holiness and its social consequences—these new concepts, or rather concepts articulated in a totally new manner, dominate the cultural history of late Roman Syria.

We can see the practical consequences of the shift in the position of the holy man. Rural patronage is the backdrop to the activities of the holy man. But alas, there are no such simple solutions of continuity for the late Roman historian! The holy man was a patron of a specific type. His role was made effective through being strictly delimited. For he was the ideal patron. Relations with him were shorn of the abrasive qualities of normal patron-client relations. He was a non-participant in society. Sociologically he was not human: he lived the life of an angel, *demutha demal'keh*. In his community he was, officially, the stranger.[19] This meant, in fact, that any obligation incurred towards him was not like the normal, crippling and humiliating obligations that linked the villager to his fellow human beings. The ferocious asceticism, for which Syria was notorious, was the *sine qua non* of the social involvement of the Syrian holy man: for it is the holy man as patron, and not his humble client, who has already taken on himself by ascesis the full load of humiliation—the saint is the

(Oxford, 1976) and Sebastian Brock, 'The Limitations of Syriac in Representing Greek', *The Early Versions of the New Testament*, ed. D. N. Metzger (Oxford, 1977), pp. 243–50 and 'Aspects of Translation Technique in Antiquity', *Greek, Roman and Byzantine Studies* XX (1979): 69–88.

19. See above, pp. 130–32.

meskanah, the broken one. Furthermore, in a society where the denial of access was the most sure sign of the exercise of power, the holy man is accessible: of Habib, John of Ephesus wrote 'he did not as being a man of high reputation refuse to go, but in order to satisfy him, would go with him at once without delay.'[20]

Above all, the holy man wielded non-coercive power. This was effective in the way which Thomas Hobbes understood so well in his *Leviathan*: 'Reputation of power is power, for it draweth to itself those who seek protection.'[21] It is in their manipulation of 'reputation of power' that the Syrian holy men were unequalled in the early Byzantine world. 'Neither yet think that the power of the saints before which these people come and groan is a void thing, lest it be roused against you and your house perish.'[22]

But such 'reputation of power' assumes a community of values. For the 'power of the saints' was shown above all in Syria by the curse of the holy man; and the curse is operative only if all parties share basic assumptions about sin and its consequences, and are prepared to link any notable misfortune with the utterance of a precise agent of the holy. The pathetic fragility of agrarian prosperity in a Near Eastern environment made certain that every town and every village had its staple diet of misfortune to interpret:[23] in this particular case—a fire, a stroke, the incompetence of a widow and the dishonesty of the servants levelled the cursed man's fam-

---

20. John of Ephesus, *Lives of the Eastern Saints*, p. 9. For the normal relations between patron and client, see the Rabbinic source most appositely quoted by Mac-Mullen, *Roman Social Relations*: 'How should the client-tenant seek a word with a "man of the arm"? . . . He does not barge in on him abruptly, but comes, stands outside his gateway and tells the servant, "So-and-So is standing at the gate of your court. Perhaps you will permit him to enter"' (p. 45).

21. Thomas Hobbes, *Leviathan* I, 10, ed. M. Oakeshott (Oxford, 1960), p. 50.

22. John of Ephesus, *Lives of the Eastern Saints*, p. 72; see above, pp. 122–23.

23. See T. Shanin, *The Awkward Class* (Oxford, 1972), pp. 114–15, for the decisive role of 'random oscillation of peasant households', arising from the overwhelming impact of unpredictable set-backs in peasant life in Russia and, by implication, elsewhere.

ily within two years—such an event was bound to be a topic 'for gossip and lamentation';[24] but it is the late Roman revolution that linked it so firmly to the idea of sin and of an offence against a living representative of the holy.

It is this transvaluation of patronage relationships, not a simple dialectic of resistance and assimilation, that dominated the ecclesiastical history of Syria at the time of the great Christological controversies. The logic of the institution of patronage moulded the course of the conflict of Chalcedonian and Monophysite. For this was not, as it has sometimes been represented, a straightforward conflict of town and village, of Greek and Syriac culture; it has the same ambiguous quality as the conflict of structures of patronage which we first observed in the works of Libanius. To a far greater extent than the standard textbooks of Church history help us to realize, the conflict was a conflict not of dogma but of holiness; and a conflict of holiness in Syria, as we have seen, was bound to be a conflict in 'reputation of power'.[25] The heads of the great Monophysite monasteries described by John of Ephesus—dominating the villages with their castle-like walls and armed with tentacular influence that stretched as far as the palace of the Empress Theodora in Constantinople—are the sixth-century avatars to the great generals whose intervention in patronage relationships were denounced by Libanius. The Chalcedonian–installed bishop of a town like Ingila or Amida would have been forced to watch with the same impotent fury as did Libanius a further splinter of the governing class digging itself firmly into the countryside technically dominated by his own city: 'But the bishops were

24. John of Ephesus, *Lives of the Eastern Saints*, p. 76.

25. For a tentative summary of this view, see Peter Brown, *The World of Late Antiquity* (London, 1971), pp. 109, 143–44. It is implied by W. H. C. Frend, *The Rise of the Monophysite Movement* (Cambridge, 1972), and by what we know of the history of areas of mixed allegiance, such as Palestine, as shown in the *Plerophoriae*, the 'Assurances', of John Rufus and the *Pratum Spirituale* of John Moschus: see H. E. Chadwick, 'Moschus and his friend Sophronius the Sophist', *Journal of Theological Studies*, n.s., XXV (1974): 41–74.

much ashamed before him and feared to send, or anyone to presume to enter his monastery . . . and thus two bishops passed away and died one after the other, . . . and none molested the holy Maro.'[26]

Thus, to sum up: I would doubt whether the theme of resistance and assimilation, as it has usually been treated, provides the historian with a canvas wide enough to depict, much less explain, the cultural and social revolution through which Syria passed in the late Roman period.

In the first place, the historian of any peasant society must satisfy himself that he is not dealing with worlds whose destinies remained so parallel as not to touch in any form of dialogue of resistance and assimilation. The basic weakness of all ancient empires—and this weakness was put to the acid test for Iran, for Byzantium and for Spain by the Arab invasions of the seventh century A.D.—may not be the resistance of a part of the population to the assimilative effort of their rulers so much as the quasi-total non-participation of the vast majority of the producers of wealth.

In the second place, the logic of the institution of rural patronage, especially in its religious form, by-passes the conventional model of conflict; indeed, the institution itself, whether wielded by generals in fourth-century Antioch or Monophysite leaders in the sixth century, derived its effectiveness largely through creating a *tertium quid* and so by-passed the problem in its conventional terms.

In the third place, we tend to forget the extent of what has been called the late Roman revolution. This was a truly profound revolution, in the sense that it closed the door on the terms in which certain problems had been posed throughout the ancient classical world. I would like to encourage classical scholars to close the door on these problems for a moment also. For to treat late Roman history merely as a problem of the survival of certain precise elements of the classical tradition, and to follow, in the course of the fourth, fifth, and sixth century the modification or rejection of these

26. John of Ephesus, *Lives*, p. 96.

elements—whether these are the classical literary tradition, the classical tradition in science, or the classical institutions of the Greco-Roman town—may have didactic value. But it is not an attitude which enables us to grasp the full evolution of late Roman society. Certainly, I have observed that the historical work that has emerged from such preoccupations is singularly *dimidiatus*.[27] It is often moulded by the poignant anxiety of a man waiting to see his favourite piece of china crack beyond repair. The historian of the Church and of the medieval culture of Europe and the Near East wants to know more than merely the fate of the classical tradition: and I would suggest that the history of late Roman Syria no longer tied to the horizons of Libanius and his modern avatars might well show where the novelty and excitement of the Late Antique period truly resides.

27. On profound changes from the "classical' system of social classification taking place in this time: Evelyne Patlagean, *Pauvreté économique et pauvreté sociale à Byzance* (Paris, 1977), pp. 9–35. On the change from the 'classical' to the 'late classical' town: Peter Brown, *The Making of Late Antiquity* (Cambridge, Mass., 1978), p. 29 with the notes on pp. 111–12. For the transformation of the classical tradition in literature, see S. G. MacCormack, 'Latin Prose Panegyrics: Tradition and Discontinuity in the Later Roman Empire', *Revue des études augustiniennes* XXII (1976): 29–77, and Averil Cameron, *Flavius Cresconius Corippus: In laudem Iustini Augusti minoris* (London, 1976). For the grave misconception involved in approaching Byzantine civilization as if it were of interest only as preserver of classical culture and as if this culture were a notable ingredient in its life, see the warnings of Cyril Mango, *Byzantine Literature as a Distorting Mirror* (Oxford, 1975), p. 18.

Eastern and Western Christendom
in Late Antiquity:
A Parting of the Ways[†]

I MUST BEGIN WITH THE WORDS OF THE CLERGYMAN:
'My short sermon for today is divided into three parts.
One: God. Two: Man. Three: The Universe.' It will be
impossible to do justice to the subject in hand in so short
a space. This is not only because of the vast range of time and
space involved in any consideration of the parting of the
ways between eastern and western Christianity in the Late
Antique period. To embark on such a theme involves holding up for scrutiny the very nature of ecclesiastical history.
For what we have to deal with is not merely *what* happened
in the relations between East and West, but *why* what happened happened as it did. Once the ecclesiastical historian
asks why, he will find himself sooner or later forced to grapple with the whole quality of men's lives in the past—that is,
with how they lived the full twenty-four hours of the day,
not only in their books, but in their churches, not only in
their churches, but in the most intimate and most monotonous rhythms of their life.

For one thing can be said with certainty. The parting of
the ways between East and West in Christianity cannot be
reduced to a few formulae. It cannot be explained in terms of
a map of the division of the Roman Empire between its
Greek and Latin-speaking halves. Still less can the later alien-

[†] *The Orthodox Churches and the West*, Studies in Church History, XIII (Oxford, 1976), pp. 1–24.

ation of the churches be blamed on the delinquencies of interpreters and the surprising inability of so many great Latin
minds to reach 'A' level in Greek. Tempting though this
course may be, it cannot be compressed into brilliant jux-
tapositions between representative early Christian authors.
Merely to contrast Tertullian and Clement of Alexandria,
Augustine and Basil of Caesarea, as if by the comparison
alone it were possible to trace the divergent trajectories of
two great Christian regions, may be a device of considerable
didactic power, and revealing when skilfully exploited, but it
has little explanatory value.

At this juncture in scholarship, a sense of perspective is
worth more than any so-called 'explanation' of the division
of East and West. So I would like to begin with a dictum of
Edward Gibbon: 'The distinction of North and South is real
and intelligible . . . But the difference between East and West
is arbitrary and shifts round the globe.'[1]

In the present state of Late Antique studies, Gibbon's point
needs to be stressed. Some of the most interesting work in late
Roman history in the past generations has been carried out in
terms of the East-West division of Greco-Roman civilization.
The tendency of the two *partes* of the Roman Empire to grow
apart in the fourth century has received very great prominence as one of the main factors of Late Antique history. The
alienation of East and West has been accepted as one of the
principal causes of the ruin of the Roman Empire in the West.
On the short time-scale, in the crisis that followed the death
of Theodosius in 395 and the first official division of the Empire between his sons, the inability of the two parts of the
Empire to collaborate against barbarian invasion has been explained in terms of a deep-seated difference in aims and outlook.[2] On a longer time-scale, the alienation of the two
partes, the emergence in each of a distinctive culture and so-

1. Edward Gibbon, *The History of the Decline and Fall of the Roman Empire*,
notes to the second edition, introduction, p. xxxvi.
2. S. Mazzarino, *Stilicone e la crisi imperiale dopo Teodosio* (Rome, 1942) and
E. Demougeot, *De l'unité à la division de l'empire romain* (Paris, 1951).

cial structure, has been fruitfully invoked to account for the
sinister ease with which western Roman society settled down
to life without an empire.[3] Instances of misunderstanding
and conflict in the history of Church and Empire tend, nowadays, to be seen as no more than symptomatic of a deeper
alienation: they are mere foam on a sea furrowed by ineluctable currents.

I would like to step outside this perspective for a moment, not necessarily to exclude it altogether, but to seek a
different vantage-point from which to take a new look at our
subject. I would like to suggest that the history of the Christian Church in Late Antiquity and in the early Middle Ages is
far more a part of the history of the Mediterranean and its
neighbours than it is part of the history of the division of the
Mediterranean itself between East and West. I would like
therefore to hark back to the perspective of Henri Pirenne, in
his *Mahomet et Charlemagne*.[4] Whatever the weaknesses of Pirenne's thesis from the point of view of the commercial and
maritime history of the Mediterranean, his intuition of the
basic homogeneity of Mediterranean civilization deep into
the early Middle Ages still holds good. The history of the
Christian Church is a history of *Romania à la Pirenne*. It is the
history of a religion which identified itself almost from its
origins with a Mediterranean-wide style of urban civilization; that penetrated the sprawling countryside of western
Europe along trade routes that linked it to the boom towns of
Asia Minor. It fed its imagination on Palestine and Syria; its
intellectual powerhouse in the Latin world was North Africa,
and in this Africa, Carthage, 'Rome in Africa', remained, like
Rome, a great Mediterranean town, moving to rhythms
strangely similar to those of Alexandria, Antioch and Constantinople.

3. M. Wes, *Das Ende des Kaisertums im Westen des römischen Reichs* (The Hague,
1967) and W. Goffart, 'Zosimus, the first historian of Rome's fall', *AHR* LXXVI
(1971): 412–41; see P. Brown, *Religion and Society in the Age of Saint Augustine*
(London, 1972), pp. 229–30.

4. See Peter Brown, 'Mohammed and Charlemagne by Henri Pirenne',
Daedalus CIII (1974): 25–33. [Above, pp. 63–79.]

It is important to stress this, the horizontal unity of the Mediterranean. Any divergence along the East-West spectrum of the Mediterranean was always dwarfed by the immensity of the gulf which separated the Mediterranean itself from the alien societies which flanked it.

Let us look East for a moment: seen from the point of view of the Near East, the most crucial parting of the ways was not between East and West in the Mediterranean, but between the Mediterranean itself and the exuberant hinterland that stretched eastwards across the Fertile Crescent. If Christ had lived in the Hellenistic rather than in the Roman period, or in the third century A.D. rather than in the first, then we could imagine a very different Christianity—a Christianity whose missionaries would not have been drawn into the unitary civilization of the Mediterranean at a time of its maximum gravitational pull, but who would have wandered in a more random manner into the great caravan cities and sprawling villages of eastern Syria and Mesopotamia. The beautiful new book of Robert Murray, *Symbols of Church and Kingdom, A Study in Early Syrian Tradition*, and the forthcoming study by Roberta Chesnut on the Monophysite Christologies of three Syriac authors are reminders of a whole third world of Christian experience, whose rich voice is too often drowned by the articulate and bustling Mediterranean.[5] Yet, as Gregory Dix wrote of the early Syrian liturgies—these allow us to penetrate 'behind the divergence of Greek and Western Christianity generally to that oriental world to which the Galilaean apostles had belonged.'[6]

It is the same when we look to the north of Europe. Once again, the divergence of East and West along the Mediterranean was dwarfed by the rise in north-western Europe of Christian societies which were seen to differ *toto caelo* from

5. Robert Murray, *Symbols of Church and Kingdom. A Study in the Early Syrian Tradition* (Cambridge, 1975) and Roberta Chesnut, *Three Monophysite Christologies: Severus of Antioch, Philoxenus of Mabbug, and Jacob of Sarug* (Oxford, 1975). See also, José Grosdidier de Matons, *Romanos le Mélode et les origines de la poésie religieuse à Byzance* (Paris, 1977).

6. Gregory Dix, *The Shape of the Liturgy* (London, 1945) p. 178.

the ancient Christianity of the Mediterranean. In the early Middle Ages we have to deal with a 'Mediterranean chauvinism' whose force is too often underrated. As Maurice Chevalier said: 'Old age is not so bad if you consider the alternative.' Nothing was better calculated to shrink the distance between Rome and Constantinople than the contemplation of the alien alternative across the Alps. Generalizations to the effect that the papacy served as a rallying point of western consciousness against the East assumes that there was a West to be conscious. As long as the Mediterranean remained the heart of *Romania*, the division that was 'real and intelligible' to every early medieval man was that between north and south. Listen to a Roman on his northern co-religionists: 'For the transalpine voices . . . roaring deep with their thunderous throats . . . cannot bring forth the proper sweetness of the melody, because the savage barbarity of their drunken throats, while endeavouring to utter this gentle strain, through its natural noisiness, proffers only unmodulated sounds, like unto farm carts clumsily creeping up a rutted hill.'[7] Listen to a northerner on a representative of *Romania*: 'There was a certain deacon who followed the habits of the Italians in that he was perpetually trying to resist nature. He used to take baths, he had his head very closely shaved, he polished his skin, he cleaned his nails, he had his hair cut short as if it had been turned on a lathe, and he wore linen underclothes . . .'[8]

I would suggest that we abandon a model of relations between East and West based on the assumption of deep alienation. It is not enough that we should pile up detailed studies of those persons, moments or milieus where the shores of the Mediterranean appear to have drawn closer together. Such studies have proved invaluable, ranging as they do from consideration of the Greek culture of the early Christian communities of Carthage,[9] from the figures of Au-

7. Johannes Diaconus, *Vita Gregorii* II, 7, *PL* 75, col 91.
8. Notker, *Life of Charlemagne* chap. 32, trans. Lewis Thorpe, *Two Lives of Charlemagne* (Harmondsworth, 1969), p. 130.
9. T. D. Barnes, *Tertullian* (Oxford, 1971), pp. 67–69.

gustine, Pelagius,[10] and John Cassian,[11] to the popes of the early Middle Ages,[12] from the missions of Constantine and Methodius[13] to that extraordinary galaxy of holy men at the court of Otto III[14] and in the monastery of St Alessio on the Aventine.[15] But these studies might be misinterpreted if they were seen as so many incidents of East-West relations, if by 'relations' we mean the interchange between two separate, free-standing worlds.

For this is precisely what may not have happened. Nothing has done more to handicap our understanding of Mediterranean history in the medieval period than the tendency of scholars to treat Byzantium as a world apart, standing aside and above the destinies of an 'underdeveloped' western Europe. Once this view is accepted, the East tends to be treated as a distinct and enclosed reservoir of superior culture, from which the occasional stream is released, to pour down hill— by some obscure law of cultural hydraulics—to water the lower reaches of the West. Relations between East and West, therefore, tend to be treated as so many 'releases' of Byzantine 'influence'; and the 'eastern' features of early medieval art and piety are ascribed to 'borrowings' from a superior

10. Peter Brown, 'The Patrons of Pelagius', *JTS* ns XXI (1970): 56–72 in *Religion and Society*, pp. 208–26.

11. Philip Rousseau, 'Cassian, Contemplation and the Coenobitic Life', *JEH* XXVI (1975): 113–26.

12. Peter Llewellyn, 'The Roman Church in the Seventh Century: the Legacy of Gregory I', *JEH* XXV (1974): 363–80 and Evelyne Patlagean, 'Les armes et la cité à Rome du viième au ixème siècle', *Mélanges de l'École française de Rome* LXXXVI (Rome, 1974): 25–62. [C. Mango, 'La culture grecque et l'Occident au viiie. siècle', *I Problemi dell'Occidente del secolo viii. Settimane di Studi del Centro Italiano di Studi sull'Alto Medio Evo* XX (Spoleto, 1973): 683–860.]

13. Imre Boba, *Moravia's History Reconsidered* (The Hague, 1971). If the author is right in placing Moravia in the region of Sirmium, then the mission of Constantine and Methodius took place not in the depths of eastern central Europe, but within the traditional orbit of *Romania*.

14. K. Leyser, 'The Tenth Century in Byzantine-Western Relations', *Relations Between East and West in the Middle Ages*, ed. Derek Baker (Edinburgh, 1973), pp. 29–63, at pp. 44–45.

15. B. Hamilton, 'The Monastery of S. Alessio and the Religious and Intellectual Renaissance in 10th century Rome', *Studies in Medieval and Renaissance History* (1965), pp. 265–310.

Byzantine model. Nothing has been more conducive to confusion in the study of art and religion in the Dark Ages than such an assumption.[16]

When seen in this way, also, undue attention is given to those obvious 'sluice-gates' that would facilitate the downhill flow of culture from East to West. To take one example: I suspect that we will soon no longer be as concerned as we have been with the question of whether or not Gregory the Great spoke Greek.[17] For a theory of cultural interchange that treats the build-up of a culture—especially of a religious culture—in terms of so many discrete acts of 'reception' tends to overlook the inarticulate familiarities of a shared landscape. Throughout Late Antiquity vital areas of culture were transmitted by a Mediterranean-wide process of osmosis. The ideology of the Byzantine state is inconceivable without generations of Byzantines who could 'think Latin' even when they could not read it.[18] Life in Late Antiquity was wider and more embracing than any knowledge of the right classical languages. The spread of the feast of kalends of January in the late Roman period is an astonishing example of this. A feast that had been limited to Rome in the high Empire suddenly becomes a Mediterranean-wide phenomenon in Late Antiquity.[19] Plainly, when the city-dwellers of Late Antiquity wanted to say something important about the way life was lived, and find ceremonial expression for it, they said the same thing all over the Mediterranean, in whatever language

16. J. Hubert, "Les relations artistiques entre les diverses parties de l'ancien empire romain pendant le haut moyen âge,' Settimane di Studi sull'Alto Medio Evo XI (Spoleto, 1964), pp. 453–77.

17. J. M. Peterson, 'Did Gregory the Great Know Greek?' Studies in Church History, XIII, ed. D. Baker (Oxford, 1976), 121–34.

18. Brown, Religion and Society, p. 230. H. G. Beck, 'Res Publica Romana. Vom Staatsdenken der Byzantinern', ABAW, PhK (1970): 7–41, in Das Byzantinische Herrscherbild, Wege der Forschung 341 (Darmstadt, 1975), pp. 379–414. E. Rosenthal, The Illumination of the Virgilius Romanus (Zurich, 1972), p. 98, assumes an East Roman origin for a Vergil manuscript of the sixth century, [but see A. Grabar, Cahiers archéologiques XXIV (1975): 192–94. See now G. Dagron, La Naissance d'une capitale: Constantinople et ses institutions de 330 à 451 (Paris, 1974).]

19. M. Meslin, La fête des kalendes de janvier dans l'empire romain, Collection Latomus 115 (Brussels, 1970).

came to hand. Christianity, which grew out of precisely that milieu, was exceptionally sensitive to the same Mediterranean-wide rhythms. Furthermore, adoption by osmosis came easily to a group in which oral methods of transmission had always played a great part in its religious culture: the Christian faith was passed on by oral catechesis. Christian spiritual direction was carried out in terms of a fund of monastic *apophthegmata*.

In this situation I would like to introduce the concept of a Mediterranean *koiné*. Let us take a few examples from the end of our period. The history of monasticism in the fifth and sixth centuries is not a history of an 'oriental' monasticism penetrating the West: in the simple phrase of P. Riché, we are dealing with *un monachisme méditerranéen*.[20] The new edition of a Latin translation of the *Apophthegmata* by Paschasius of Dumio shows this Christian Mediterranean *koiné* at work. Paschasius is unlocalizable; and the apophthegmatic literature that he handles has become as thickly matted as a bed of reeds, bridging the Mediterreanean with a single monastic folklore.[21] To take another example: often in the history of early medieval piety, where the unwary might acclaim a direct 'eastern' influence, it is possible to sense 'a breath of the warm south'. A Stylite hermit established outside Cologne—Wulfilach, a Lombard, from a north Italy heavy with the *koiné* of Romania.[22] A miracle connected with an icon, the only one in the *Libri Miraculorum* of Gregory of Tours—a story by Venantius Fortunatus, straight from Ravenna.[23]

There is therefore no shortcut to the problem of the parting of the ways between East and West. It would be a serious mistake to import into the history of the Christian Church supposed contrasts whose outlines have been sketched *grosso*

20. P. Riché, *Education et culture dans l'Occident barbare* (Paris, 1962), p. 149.

21. J. G. Freire, *A versâo latina por Pascasio de Dume dos Apophthegmata Patrum* (Coimbra, 1971), I, p. 17.

22. Gregory of Tours, *Libri Historiarum* VIII, 15, ed. B. Krusch, *MGH, SRM*, I, 2, p. 380.

23. Gregory of Tours, *de virtutibus sancti Martini* I, 15a, ed. B. Krusch, *MGH, SRM* I, I, p. 147.

modo by previous generations of late Roman historians of society and culture. The ecclesiastical historian cannot ignore the intimate dependence of the Christian Church on its social and cultural environment. But it is vital that he should offer a differentiated and up-to-date explanation of how such an environment was experienced in the Church, and precisely what the environment was. It is not enough to compound his own generalizations by importing the generalizations of others.

Alas, such remarks are only a preface to the main task. For now we come to the most delicate part of our undertaking. We cannot subsume the explanation of the parting of the ways between East and West beneath any overwhelming antithesis of two societies: the unity of a Mediterranean civilization exerts a constant, discreet pressure to blur such stark and convenient contrasts. If there is a divergence between the eastern and western Churches, we must look for it within the Churches themselves; and if we do this we must begin at the beginning—we must have a clear idea of the implications of the rise of Christianity in the Roman world.

Here it is a pleasure to pay tribute to a great tradition of English scholarship, well known in its representatives. W. H. C. Frend in his *Martyrdom and Persecution in the Early Church* [24] and R. A. Markus in a characteristically distinguished slim volume, *Christianity in the Roman World*, [25] have made clear that the parting of the ways between East and West springs from the way in which Christianity adapted itself to its Roman environment. The parting of the ways between East and West was implied at the joining of the ways of Christianity and classical culture. Christianity took up a different stance in East and West to the state, to society, to classical culture. In the West, the Church maintained its 'twice-born' attitudes. It stood to one side of the *saeculum*.

24. W. H. C. Frend, *Martyrdom and Persecution in the Early Church* (Oxford, 1965). See Peter Brown, 'Approaches to the Religious Crisis of the Third Century A.D.' *EHR* LXXXIII (1968): 542–58 in *Religion and Society*, esp. pp. 91–93.
25. R. A. Markus, *Christianity in the Roman World* (London, 1975).

West Roman society and culture, first shunned as demonic, was firmly *entzaubert* by Augustine: no mystique but the most sinister was allowed to rest upon it. Later, when this society was in the hands of barbarians, it sank to the status of a passive and potentially refractory laity dominated by a clearly defined clerical élite. The contrast with eastern Christianity, whose apologists had early acclaimed a harmony between Christianity and Greek culture, and whose emperors, from Constantine onwards, had negotiated endlessly for the unanimity of Church and state, stands out in pointed contrast to that situation.

As a result of such studies, the contrast of East and West has become firmly rooted in 'the history of Christian self-awareness in the Roman world'; and this is a history which, as we all know, has been pursued with quite exceptional insight into the social and cultural environment of the classical and Late Antique world. Such studies are the meeting point par excellence of all that is best in the full range of late Roman studies. It is in this tradition, rather than in the more pragmatic side of late Roman economic and administrative history, that it is possible to catch the full significance of the Late Antique revolution and to seize most clearly its implications for the medievalist.

I would like to end by adding to this perspective rather than by challenging it. I feel obscurely that the social and cultural historians of the relations of Christianity and the classical world have had their say and have said it very well. It is now time for the strictly religious historian to take up his cue. I would like to suggest that we trace some features of the divergence between East and West in terms of diverging attitudes to the idea of the *holy* in the two churches. Far from proposing an alternative explanation, I would like to bring this approach to bear like an ultra-violet light which enables us to see differing structures in one and the same crystal.

In Late Antiquity attitudes to culture and society were inextricably intertwined with attitudes to the holy. The religious revolution of Late Antiquity did not only see the rise of the Christian Church as a society within a society and a culture within a culture. Hence the study of the Christian Church in East and West cannot be reduced to its stances towards culture and society. The rise itself was intimately connected with a drastic redistribution and re-definition of those points at which the holy was thought to impinge on human affairs.

Unlike paganism and much of Judaism, the Christian communities were prepared to invest individual human beings with supernatural powers or with the ability to exercise power on behalf of the supernatural. It was as precisely identifiable bearers of the holy, and as the heirs of an imagined genealogy of similar bearers of the holy—apostles, martyrs, prophets—that the Christian leaders were able to form the Christian communities. The groups that took up a stance to the society and culture of their times were formed around known and revered *loci* of the holy—and these *loci* tended to be human beings. As the rabbis told Justin Martyr: 'but as for you, who have forsaken God and put your trust in a man, what salvation can await you?'[26]

The early Christians lived down to these strictures. Small details of their behaviour, revealed in passing in the acts of the martyrs, speak volumes: 'Polycarp took off all his clothing, loosed his belt and even tried to take off his sandals, although he had never had to do this before: for all the Christians were always eager to be the first to touch his flesh.'[27] In this respect, Christianity added a radical twist to a tide in Late Antique sensibility. Pagan biographies of θεῖοι ἄνδρες, 'divine men,' and later rabbinic literature show a common search for heroes who would sum up in their persons the values of the group.[28] Ideals that had been allowed to float free, available to any member of an educated or religious class but attached to

26. Justin, *Dialogus cum Tryphone* viii, 4, *PG* 6, col 493B. [On what follows, see now Peter Brown, *The Making of Late Antiquity* (Cambridge, Mass., 1978), 11–22.]

27. *Martyrium Polycarpi*, 13 ed. and trans. H. Musurillo, *The Acts of the Christian Martyrs* (Oxford, 1972), p. 13.

28. L. Bieler, ΘΕΙΟΣ ΑΝΗΡ *Das Bild des 'göttlichen Menschen' in Spätantike und Frühchristentum* (Vienna, 1935) and J. Neusner, *A History of the Jews in Babylonia*, IV

no one in particular, come to be given 'an earthly habitation and a name', and so a power that is best caught in some of the masterpieces of third- and fourth-century portrait sculpture.[29] Throughout the Mediterranean world, face and halo tend to come together in Late Antiquity.

Pagans who might have taken more kindly to divine men than did their Jewish contemporaries were appalled by what the Christians did to their heroes when dead—they brought the stench of death into the preserve of the holy. This was new. For all his intimacy with the goddess Artemis, in dying Hippolytus was cut off by the unbridgeable chasm which the fact of death itself had opened between himself and his goddess: ἐμοὶ γὰρ οὐ θέμις φθιτοὺς ὁρᾶν / οὐδ' ὄμμα χραίνειν θανασίμοισιν ἐκπνοαῖς.[30]

In Eunapius of Sardis' account of the Christianization of the great temples of Egypt we can catch the charnel horror of the rise of Christianity: 'For they collected the bones and skulls of criminals who had been put to death for numerous crimes . . . made them out to be gods, haunted their sepulchres, and thought that they became better by defiling themselves at their graves. "Martyrs" the dead men were called, and "ministers" of a sort, and "ambassadors" with the gods to carry men's prayers.'[31] Yet much of medieval history is inconceivable without the preliminary decision to allow the dead into a central position in worship:[32] 'Male fecit ergo Romanus episcopus qui super mortuorum hominum Petri et Pauli, secundum nos ossa venerabilia, secundum te vilem

---

(Leiden, 1969), pp. 297–402. See now E. Urbach, *Ḥazal: pirqe emunoth we de 'oth* [*The Sages: Their concepts and beliefs*] (Jerusalem, 1969).

29. H. P. L'Orange, *Apotheosis in Ancient Portraiture* (Oslo, 1947) and H. von Heintze, 'Vir gravis et sanctus. Bildniskopf eines spätantiken Philosphen', *JAC* VI (1963): 35–53.

30. Euripides, *Hippolytus*, lines 1437–8: 'It is not right for me to look upon the dead, And strain my eyesight with the mists of dying men.'

31. Eunapius of Sardis, *Lives of Sophists* 472, ed. and trans. W. C. Wright, Loeb Classical Library (London, 1961), p. 425.

32. T. Klauser, 'Christliche Märtyrerkult, heidnische Heroenkult und spätjüdische Heiligenverehrung', *Gesammelte Arbeiten zur Liturgiegeschichte, Kunstgeschichte und christlichen Archäologie*, ed. E. Dassmann, *JAC* Ergänzungsband III (1974), pp. 221–29.

pulvisculum, offert Domino sacrificia et tumulos eorum Christi arbitrantur altaria.'[33]

Yet it is precisely around such idealized objects that Christianity succeeded in crystallizing lasting pyramids of dependence. In the Roman world of the third and fourth centuries the old forms of power and dependence were being transformed and re-articulated with abrasive vigour: we need only think on the one hand of the elaboration of the imperial ceremonial,[34] and on the other on the tightening and the rendering more explicit of the links of patronage in town and countryside.[35] In this situation, the pyramids of idealized dependence erected by the Christian Church around men and objects thought of as 'holy' stand with uncanny congruence in a society constantly experimenting with forms of power and social influence.

It is in this region that I would like to look for a parting of the ways between East and West. Even if we cannot reach an explanation of the phenomenon, I would like to suggest that we are dealing with a phenomenon to explain.

In the West the precise *locus* of the supernatural power associated with the holy was fixed with increasing precision. Cyprian of Carthage, in his astute handling of the *confessores* and in his statements on the position of the bishop,[36] has a bafflingly 'medieval' ring about him: this may well be be-

33. Jerome, *Contra Vigilantium* 8, *PL* 23, col 346: 'So you think, therefore, that the bishop of Rome does wrong when, over the dead men Peter and Paul, venerable bones to us but to you a heap of common dust, he offers up sacrifice to the Lord, and their graves are called altars of Christ.' [Peter Brown, *The Cult of the Saints: Its Rise and Function in Latin Christianity* (Chicago, 1981).]

34. See now the important studies of Sabine G. MacCormack, 'Change and Continuity in Late Antiquity: the Ceremony of *Adventus*', *Historia* XXI (1972): 721–52; 'Latin Prose Panegyrics', *Empire and Aftermath*, Silver Latin 2, ed. T. A. Dorey (London, 1975), pp. 143–205; 'Latin Prose Panegyrics: Tradition and Discontinuity in the Later Roman Empire,' *Revue des études augustiniennes* XXII (1975): 1–49; 'Roma, Constantinopolis, the Emperor, and His Genius,' *Classical Quarterly* XXV (1975): 131–50 [and *Art and Ceremony in Late Antiquity* (Berkeley and Los Angeles, 1981).]

35. Peter Brown, 'The Rise and Function of the Holy Man', *JRS* LXI (1971): 80–101 at pp. 85–87. [Above, pp. 115–20.]

36. J. Speigl, 'Cyprian über das judicium bei der Bischofseinsetzung', *Römische Quartalschrift* LXIX (1974): 30–45.

cause no serious doubt as to the precise nature and location of spiritual power and the means by which it was exercised in ritual actions troubled his own mind or those of most of his successors.[37] At the same time, the eastern Church had entered on to what came to strike early medieval western observers as a baffling 'crisis of overproduction' of the holy. More men were accepted as bearers or agents of the supernatural on earth, and in a far greater variety of situations, than came to be tolerated in a Western Europe. As a result, the precise *locus* of spiritual power in Byzantium remained, by western standards, tantalizingly ambiguous,[38] and Byzantine attitudes to sanctity, and hence to the world in general against which the holy was placed, were shot through with paradox. By the end of Late Antiquity, this contrast was clear, and it was all the clearer for being seen not as an inevitable contrast, but rather as the cumulative result of mutations within a single *koiné*—a *koiné* which, by the end of this period had already spilled far from the shores of the Mediterranean, to the Nestorian hagiography of Sasanian Iran[39] and the Celtic holy men of Northumbria.

I think it would be best to move from two clear examples, briefly sketched, to the implications of these examples.

37. Dix, p. 116 on Cyprian and the consecration of the Eucharist: 'that sort of logical directness and unity which has always appealed to Western theologians'. For the possible influence of Roman pagan attitudes to religion, the most suggestive treatment is by A. D. Nock, 'A Feature of Roman Religion', *HTR* XXXII (1939): 96 in *Essays on Religion and the Ancient World*, ed. Zeph Stewart (Oxford, 1972), I, pp. 491–92. To go further by ascribing to classical Roman attitudes and to the study of Roman law a 'legalism' which distinguished western Christianity, is to import into our understanding of men of whose background we know little—see Barnes, pp. 22–29 ('Still less can "Tertullian the jurist" be invoked to explain the later development of Latin Christendom'), and G. W. Clarke, 'The Secular Profession of Saint Cyprian of Carthage', *Latomus* XXIV (1965): 633–38—writing in a late classical milieu of uncertain nature, a dizzy continuity with the world of Cicero. I have no head for such heights; but they must be considered, more especially on points of religious practice: for one example, see. F. Dölger, *Der Exorzismus im altchristlichen Taufritual* (Paderborn, 1906), p. 97.

38. Brown, 'Holy Man', pp. 95–96. [Above, pp. 138–41.]

39. G. Wiessner, 'Christlicher Heiligenkult im Umkreis eines sassanischen Grosskönigs', *Festgabe deutscher Iranisten zum 2500 Jahrfeier Irans*, ed. W. Eilers (Stuttgart, 1971), pp. 141–55, esp. p. 149.

The rise and function of the holy man in the sixth-century eastern Mediterranean as revealed in the work of John of Ephesus stands in marked contrast to the world of religious experience—mainly crystallized around relics—revealed in the works of John's contemporary, Gregory of Tours.[40] The contrast is all the greater for having become crystallized from a Mediterranean-wide *koiné*. For Gregory can embrace *Romania*.[41] His gaze pierces to Edessa, where a miraculous annual rainstorm washes clean the dunged-up *souk* after the great fair of St Thomas.[42] It even reaches as far as Sergiopolis (Resafa), where St Sergius is known as a stern protector of *ex-voto* offerings to his shrine: so stern, indeed, is he that chickens dedicated to him, if stolen, emerge from the cooking-pot even tougher than when they went in![43] This was a fact known also to the Shahanshah of Iran himself, none other than Khusro II Aparwez, who, in a great silver *ex-voto* dish, had proclaimed to St Sergius his gratitude for success and had reported on the exceptional favours enjoyed by his Christian wife, the beautiful Shirin.[44] (The inscription is the last great address of a Near Eastern ruler to his gods, of which the first, by Khusro's predecessor Darius, looks out from the cliffs of Bisutun, to be read only by gods and rock-climbers.) Nevertheless, with Gregory we can trace the direction of a mutation that would finally weaken the hold of the Mediterranean *koiné* on Gaul, and consequently on the emergent societies of north-western Europe, in such a way as to bring about a final confrontation of East and West.

In the eastern Mediterranean, the holy man had been

40. John of Ephesus, *Lives of the Eastern Saints* ed. and trans. E. W. Brooks, *PO* 17, pp. 1–304, 18, pp. 513–697, 19, pp. 153–273, and *HE*, trans. E. W. Brooks, *CSCO, Script. Syr.* LV (Louvain, 1936). A strictly religious commentary exists neither for Gregory nor John.

41. Gregory's isolation from the eastern Mediterranean has been exaggerated by N. H. Baynes, 'M. Pirenne and the Unity of the Mediterranean', *Byzantine Studies* (London, 1960), pp. 310–14. [Averil Cameron, 'The Byzantine Sources of Gregory of Tours', *Journal of Theological Studies* n.s. XXVI (1975), 421–26.]

42. Gregory of Tours, *de gloria martyrum*, cap. 32, pp. 57–58.

43. Ibid., cap. 96, p. 103.

44. P. Peeters, 'L'*ex voto* de Khusro Aparwez à Sergiopolis', *An. Bol.* LXV (1947): 5–56.

forced to the fore by those exuberant and abrasive developments by which new classes came to compete for control of the countryside.[45] The position of holy men in Syria is a paradigm of the need of eastern Christians to consider as 'holy' ascetic figures on whom they could place their hopes for a 'holy', that is for an idealized, patronage, in a world overshadowed by an 'unholy', that is, by an only too real, patronage. This aspect of East Roman social and spiritual life is well summed up by Thomas Hobbes in chapter ten of his *Leviathan:* 'Reputation of power is power: because it draweth with it the adherence of those that need protection.' The saints described by John of Ephesus had no doubts on that score: 'Neither yet think that this power of the saints before whom these people come and groan is a void thing, lest it be roused against you and your house perish.'[46]

All this is striking and well-known, yet let us look for a moment at the precise basis of this power. Here we must enter deeply into the materials from which East Romans framed their expectations of the holy, and how they combined these in such a way not only to facilitate the exercise of 'reputation of power' but, tacitly, to delimit this same exercise.

The Christian *koiné* was articulated in the eastern Mediterranean not to place the holy man above human society, but outside it. The holy man lived a life that was an imitation of the angels.[47] He gained his powers from retiring to the desert, that is, to the antithesis of human life, where Christ had been served by the angels,[48] and where the angels had invested John the Baptist with the first monk's cloak.[49] The holy, therefore, was at its most holy when least connected with that

45. Brown, 'Holy Man', pp. 85–91. [Above, pp. 115–29.] These views have been modified and placed in a wider context by R. M. Price, 'The Role of Military Men in Syria and Egypt from Constantine to Theodosius II', unpublished Oxford D. Phil. thesis 1974.

46. John of Ephesus, *PO* 17, p. 72.

47. P. Nagel, *Die Motivierung der Askese, Texte und Untersuchungen* 95 (Berlin 1966), pp. 34–48. [Brown, *Making of Late Antiquity*, 86–87.]

48. G. Kittel, see under ἔρημος *Theologisches Wörterbuch zum Neuen Testament*, II (Stuttgart, 1935), pp. 634–57 and Philipp Vielbauer 'Tracht und Speise Johannes des Täufers,' *Aufsätze zum Neuen Testament* (Munich, 1965), pp. 47–54.

49. This became a prominent issue in the Iconoclastic controversy: Peter

conflict of human interests which it was constantly called upon to palliate.

The East Roman holy man, as we observe him in both the fourth and fifth centuries, and in the age of Gregory and John, preserved his reputation, therefore, by an exacting ritual of de-solidarization and even of social inversion.[50] He wielded his 'idealized' power in society by adopting stances that were the exact inverse of those connected with the exercise of real power. Where the patron was inaccessible, the holy man was open to all comers: of Habib it was said, 'he did not, as a man of high reputation, refuse to go, but, in order to satisfy him, would go with him at once without delay.'[51] Where the patron flaunted his status and his immunity, the holy man was 'an afflicted one', and often carried chains, associated in the Near East not with physical discomfort so much as with the status of a political prisoner fallen from his high estate. Thus, in few societies outside the *sanyasi* culture of Hindu India, has 'reputation of power' within a society been exercised on so strict a tacit understanding that those who exercised it should be seen to stand outside this society.[52]

I feel that we touch here on something more revealing than merely the social strategies of a charismatic *ombudsman*. We are dealing with a society which accepts such strategies because they could be associated with other basic ideas about the nature of the holy and its impingement on human affairs. Here I would risk a suggestion. The holy escaped social definition—or, rather, its absence of social definition became intelligible—because it was thought of principally as a power that 'manifested' itself in a manner that was as vivid as it was discontinuous with normal human expectations. If this is so, then we are in a very ancient world indeed. It is the world of

Brown, 'A Dark-Age Crisis: Aspects of the Iconoclastic Controversy' *EHR* LXXXVIII (1973): 1–34 at p. 21. [Below, p. 281.]
50. Brown, 'The Holy Man,' pp. 91–92. [Above, pp. 130–31.]
51. John of Ephesus, *PO*, 17, p. 9.
52. L. Dumont, 'World Renunciation in Indian Religions', *Religion, Politics and History in India* (Paris and the Hague, 1970), pp. 33–60, *ASR* VII (1959): 45–69.

the *epiphaneia*, of the sudden appearances of the gods. It is not enough that the divine should exist, it must be seen to exist, in the occasional flash of clear vision.[53] Such moments of *epiphaneia* were significantly widely-distributed throughout the whole range of East Roman religious experience. They could suddenly highlight any moment of East Roman religious life and can penetrate into any corner of East Roman Christian society. *Epiphaneia* might occur in the waking dream;[54] liturgical expectations were articulated in terms of potential *epiphaneia*—trembling, in many sources, on the edge of breaking forth[55]—with the presence of the angel at the altar[56] and the *epidemia*, the *adventus*, of the divine in the Eucharist.[57] Hagiography was read as so many unpredictable manifestations in diverse times and places of men of every possible social status. At a slightly later time, icons rose to prominence as so many visions frozen in encaustic and mosaic.[58]

Such an idea of the holy, so strictly defined as all that was non-human in any situation and all that could be suddenly 'manifested' from beyond human consciousness, tended to erode rather than to reinforce those institutional structures in which it might have found a nesting place. Sanctity, for East

53. A. J. Festugière, *La révélation d'Hermès Trismégiste* (Paris, 1950), pp. 33–37 and 44–66, A. D. Nock, 'A Vision of Mandulis Aion,' *HTR* XXVII (1934): 68–74 in *Essays* I, pp. 368–74. See J. Kirchmeyr, under 'Grecque (Église)', *Dictionnaire de la spiritualité* 6 (Paris, 1965), col 848. In the sixth century a pagan at the shrine of Sts Cosmas and Damian in Constantinople knew exactly what he wanted: ἀξιῶσαι αὐτὸν ὀπτασίας τινὸς καὶ θείας ἐκλάμψεως, 'to be granted some vision or divine illumination.' A. Deubner, *Kosmas and Damian* (Leipzig, 1907), 10, 22–23, p. 118.

54. E. R. Dodds, *Pagan and Christian in an Age of Anxiety* (Cambridge, 1965), pp. 38–39. For a later period, the patriarch Germanus confesses his debt to icons for αἱ καθ' ὕπνους πολλάκις τῶν γεγραμμένων ἐπιφάνειαι, 'appearances of those painted in icons in my dreams.' Mansi, 13, col 125A.

55. John Moschus, *Pratum Spirituale*, 25, *PG* 87, cols 3, 2872.

56. Well expressed by A. Veilleux, *La liturgie dans le cénobitisme pachômien au ivème siècle* (Rome, 1968), pp. 203–4 and esp. p. 363: 'Dans la pensée orientale, il s'agit plutôt d'une descente, d'une manifestation et d'une présence de choses célestes à travers les sacrements.'

57. Dix, pp. 163, 168: for the same ideas surrounding the arrival of the Emperor, see MacCormack, 'The Ceremony of *Adventus*', pp. 727–28.

58. Peter Brown and Sabine MacCormack, 'Artifices of Eternity', *New York Review of Books*, XXII (1975): 19–32. [See above, p. 207–21.]

Romans, always bordered on the paradoxical. For what we have are men with 'reputation of power'; yet this power was thought to have been drawn from outside any apparent niche in the power-structure of society. It was gained in the desert, beyond human sight, and depended upon a freedom to speak to God, the exact extent of which lay beyond human power to gauge. A woman dreamed that her daughter would be cured at a certain monastery. The monks brought her the abbot. No, said she, this is not the man I dreamed of. Bring me the red-faced one, with warts on his knees. Byzantine monastic folk-lore toyed lovingly with the possibilities of this situation. For at any one time, the man who enjoyed most favour with God in Heaven might be, not St Antony, but a doctor in Alexandria, not St Macarius, but a farmer in an Egyptian village, and even, who knows, an imperial inspector of brothels in Alexandria.[59] There is nothing in the sixth and seventh-century West to equal the *Life* of St Symeon the Holy Fool.[60] In this seventh-century masterpiece, the paradoxes of sanctity are explored with exemplary thoroughness. Here the dogged role-inversion of those hard-worked Syrian cursers has spilled over into a delightful study of a man who, because he fulfils no overt social function, can enjoy to the full the position of the 'outsider' allotted to the bearer of the holy—*ut novellus pazzus*. In Emesa you could go to the tavern of the mad monk and watch Symeon dancing the jig with the people of the town.[61]

Paradox, after all, is a device of inclusion. The paradox of sanctity enabled the holy to scatter itself widely throughout

59. Brown, 'The Holy Man', p. 95 [above, p. 139] for this and further evidence.

60. *Vita Symeonis ASB* July 1 (Paris / Rome 1865) cols 121–51. [See now *Léontius de Néapolis: Vie de Syméon le Fou et Vie de Jean de Chypre*, ed. and comm. A. J. Festugière (Paris, 1974); J. Grosdidier de Matons, 'Les thèmes d'édification dans la vie d'André Salos', *Travaux et Mémoires du centre de recherches de civilisation et histoire byzantine* IV (1970): 277–328; N. Challis and H. W. Dewey, 'The Blessed Fools of Old Russia', *Jahrbuch für Geschichte Osteuropas* XXII (1974): 1–11; H. Petzold, 'Die Frömmigkeit des heiligen Narren', *Die Einheit der Kirche. Festgabe P. Meinhold* (Wiesbaden, 1977), pp. 140–53.]

61. *Vita Symeonis*, 33, col 136E.

Byzantine society. At the top, the touch of the hand of God gave an inexhaustible reservoir of initiative to the Byzantine Emperors.[62] At the bottom, it fell heavily on prostitutes as it never fell on the equally whore-laden towns of Italy.[63] In between, it ratified the anomalous position of the soldier, and did so to such an extent that, when, in the eleventh century, the chaplain Hugh of Avranches attempted to reassure the Norman knights with examples of warriors pleasing to God, he could only find a catalogue dominated by *Byzantine* saints.[64]

Let us now see what Gregory of Tours does *not* share with this world. I have been struck by the following features:

First: there is the obvious feature of a marked shortage of living holy men. A society which knew all about Symeon Stylites[65] somehow did not want one of its own: our Wulfilach was told in no uncertain terms to get down off his column.[66] The appearance of itinerant holy men in Tours are recounted by Gregory in tones of 'While the cat's away, the mice do play.'[67] Now this is easier said than understood. I would like to posit a climate of opinion that actively withheld enthusiasm from all but the most well-tried bearers of the holy. 'Call no man holy until he be dead' is the motto of Gregory's writings. While in Syria the hillsides on which the stylites perched their columns would be ominously ringed by brand new, empty *martyria*, waiting to receive their guaranteed holy occupants,[68] with the world of Gregory even death marks only the beginning of long and acrimonious hagiographical manoeuvres. Was Nicetius of Lyon, who died in

62. John of Nikiu, *Chronicle*, trans. R. H. Charles (London, 1916), p. 89 and the commentary of S. MacCormack, 'Roma, Constantinopolis', p. 146.

63. F. Graus, *Volk, Herrscher und Heiliger im Reich der Merowinger* (Prague, 1965), pp. 103–4.

64. Ordericus Vitalis, *HE* 6, 2, ed. and trans. M. Chibnall, *The Ecclesiastical History of Ordericus Vitalis* III (Oxford, 1972), p. 217.

65. V. H. Albern, 'HIC SCS SYMION. Eine vorkarolingische Kultstatue des Symeons Stylites in Poitiers,' *CA* XVI (1966): 23–38.

66. Gregory of Tours, *Lib. Hist.* VIII, 15, p. 381.

67. Ibid., IX, 6, p. 417.

68. See the evidence in H. Delehaye, *Sanctus* (Brussels, 1927), p. 114.

573, and whose tomb lay in the basilica of the apostle at Lyon, a saint? This was decidedly not the opinion of his successor, Priscus, nor of Priscus' wife, Susanna, nor of any of their friends and dependents. One of Priscus' deacons used the late bishop's chasuble, among other things, as a dressing-gown—'A robe from whose very hems, if one was to believe aright, healing would have come to the sick'—and, when challenged, threatened to make a pair of bedroom slippers out of it.[69] Priscus and Nicetius rest together in the same church. Maybe the inscription of Priscus contains a tacit dig at his hated neighbour.[70] But time heals even sixth-century feuds. In 1308 both tombs were examined and both occupants declared saints. Only readers of Gregory can guess from this one clear example the febrile and insecure accumulation and dispersal of reputation that went to make up what too often strikes the unwary as the marmoreal facade of western episcopal sanctity.

A governing class carried the tensions of a governing class as well as exercising its power.[71] Here we are dealing with oligarchies of bishops powerful enough to overshadow

69. Gregory of Tours, *Vitae Patrum* 8, 5, p. 246; compare *Lib. Hist.* IV, 36, p. 169.

70. In the epitaph of Priscus, *iurgia conponens more serenifero*, 'smoothing out conflicts with accustomed serenity,' (*Corpus Inscriptionum Latinarum* 13, 2399, 8) may echo the *iurgia despiciens suscipiensque Deum*, 'despising conflicts and placing his trust in God,' of Nicetius (ibid. 2400, 20).

71. There is room for a reconsideration of the structure of the sixth-century aristocracy of Gaul. Its tensions and areas of fragility have received less attention than its supposed homogeneity and continuity with the Roman past. My article, 'Sorcery, Demons and the Rise of Christianity,' *Witchcraft Confessions and Accusations, Association of Social Anthropologists Monographs*, IX (London, 1970), p. 27, in *Religion and Society*, p. 131 certainly exaggerates: 'In the West, the triumph of the great landowners ensured that senatorial blood, episcopal office and sanctity presented a formidable united front.' Such exaggeration is widespread. [It is a viewpoint continued by M. Heinzelmann, *Bischofsherrschaft in Gallien. Zur Kontinuität römischer Führungsschichten vom iv. bis vii. Jht.* (Munich, 1976), but has been effectively criticized for one example, by R. W. Mathisen, 'Hilarius, Germanus and Lupus: the Aristocratic Background to the Chelidonius Affair', *Phoenix* XXXIII (1979): 160–69; see also P. Wormald, 'The Decline of the Roman Empire and the Survival of Its Aristocracy', *Journal of Roman Studies* LXVI (1976): 217–26, esp. pp. 225–26 and below, pp. 243–49.]

any other bearers of the holy, but who were themselves locked in such bitter competition to remain equal as to deny holiness to any but the most well-tried, that is, the most safely-dead figure. The patriarchate of Constantinople in the late sixth century is the only milieu that can offer an analogy to Gregory. Here we have the remarkable *Life* of St Eutychius,[72] a 'saint' on whom John of Ephesus had his own opinions.[73] But this is nothing compared with the convergence of hagiography and propaganda that marked the *Adelsheilige* of the sub-Roman West.[74]

Second: the contact with the holy itself, in the form of the relic, is fraught with an open-ended quality lacking in the piety of the Eastern Empire. The *locus* of the holy might be ambiguous in the East; but its *epiphaneia* was an unambivalently good event. In the work of Gregory, by contrast, we come across an element which strikes me as quite remarkable. Contact with the supernatural is fraught with all the open-ended quality of an ordeal. It is a searing light, that can throw the *merita* of the recipient into high relief.[75] The theme runs through Gregory's works. At Bazas, the relic in a cross —a crystallized drop of the divine mercy that had once fallen on the altar from the vault (where, as at Ravenna, the Lamb of God may have stood among the stars of heaven)—'when it is adored, will appear crystal clear to a man free of sin; but if, as often happens, some evil is attached to the frail human nature of the beholder, appears totally obscure.'[76]

Therefore, a holy relic does not merely enhance the status of a church or a locality, giving its favours indiscriminately to all connected with the site. There is nothing in Gregory of

72. Eustathius, *Vita Eutychii*, PG 86, 2, cols. 2273–402.
73. John of Ephesus, *HE* II, 31–7, pp. 71–4 and III, 18, p. 107.
74. F. Prinz, *Frühes Mönchtum im Frankenreich* (Munich, 1965) pp. 489–502. The function of such hagiography is already clearly adumbrated in Gregory; there is therefore less discontinuity between the hagiography of the sixth and that of the seventh century than Prinz would allow.
75. Gregory of Tours, *de gloria martyrum* 1, p. 38; 5, p. 4; 27, p. 54; 31, p. 56; 54, p. 76; 85, pp. 95–96.
76. Gregory of Tours, *de gloria martyrum* 12, p. 46.

the universal franchise on the favours granted by St Thecla to all citizens of Seleucia,[77] nor to the open-handed, consular *sparsio* of protection which the inhabitants of Thessalonica saw in their St Demetrius.[78] Nor is there any of that informal access to the holy across the frontier that any man may pass when he goes to sleep. The right to dream in the presence of the holy is denied. There is no incubation in Gaul. Again when there is no incubation, the 'holy' is denied a chance to express itself at its most paradoxical. The shrine of St Martin of Tours never witnessed the *psychodrames* that were played out regularly in the *iatriké skéné*, 'the play-house of healing,' of the great incubatory shrine of Sts Cosmas and Damian in Constantinople. No paralytic was emboldened by the saint to make love to a dumb lady.[79] No hulking butcher was told to shave a touchy senator.[80]

Rather, the contact with the holy is used to mark out unambiguously those individual members of the community who enjoyed a permanent status different from the rest. We meet in Gregory's works a whole gallery of individuals clearly designated as those who enjoyed greater intimacy with the supernatural because their *merita* were declared acceptable by

77. *Miracula Sanctae Theclae* 18 PG 85, cols 597AB: ἐφ' ὑψηλοῦ τινος καὶ χρυσηλάτου καὶ ἐπηρμένου θρόνου διανέμειν δὲ ἑκάστῳ τῶν συνεληλυθότων κατὰ τήν πανήγυριν τὰ ὑπὲρ αὐτῆς τῆς πανηγύρεως δῶρα λαμπρά τε καί πολλά, καὶ αὐτῆς τῆς παρεχούσης ἄξια. 'seated on high on a raised gilded throne, distributing to each and everyone who had come to her feast splendid and numerous gifts, worthy of herself as the giver.' This power extends to 'the poor and artisans': cap 7, col 576B. [For a masterly account of the milieu associated with the shrine of Saint Thecla and the idiosyncrasies of the author of the book of miracles, see now G. Dagron, *Vie et miracles de sainte Thècle*, Subsidia Hagiographica LXII (Brussels, 1978), no. 33, p. 378 and no. 23, p. 348, for the passages cited.]

78. *Miracula Sancti Demetrii*, PG 116, col 1232A: ὡς τινα ὕπατον παρὰ βασιλέως ἐξουσίαν λαβόντα, διανεῖμαι τῷ δήμῳ τὰς χάριτας ἐρχόμενον: 'like a consul with authority delegated to him from the Emperor, coming in procession to distribute favours to the people.'

79. Deubner, *Kosmas und Damian*, 24, pp. 162–64.

80. Ibid., 34, pp. 184–87. [Now translated by A. J. Festugière, *Sainte Thècle, Saints Côme et Damien, Saints Cyr et Jean (Extraits), Saint Georges* (Paris, 1971), at pp. 158–59 and 181–85. On incubation in general in the Eastern Empire, see N. Fernandez Marcos, *Los Thaumata de Sofronio* (Madrid, 1975).]

the 'ordeal of the holy'.[81] From a Christian *koiné* that linked sin and miracle, Gregory has drawn sharper conclusions. The blessing of the relic falls most heavily on those vested protectors and agents of the relic, and that, in Gregory's case, is almost invariably the bishop. The cult of the relic reaches its annual climax in a ceremony modelled on the old-fashioned imperial *adventus* ceremony of the western provinces;[82] but it is a ceremony where the elements of heady enthusiasm and ideal concord are acted out in such a way as to re-create and so re-embellish the precarious concord of the Christian community around its bishop. Idealized *consensus* around Martin re-lives the far-from-ideal *consensus* on which every Gallic bishop depended for his own position.[83] In that way the ceremonial of the martyrs differs *toto caelo* from the *panygyreis* of East Rome. It is a ceremony of the bishop and his shrine; it is not the ceremony of a town. At a time when the Byzantine town had sucked the churches on its periphery into its traditional urban centre,[84] and the mosaics of the church at Qasr el-Lebya contain reference to the *Tyche* of the city,[85] the western towns were already being pulled out of shape around their peripheral shrines.[86] Somehow, as in the case of Nicetius of Lyon, the holy shrine carried with it the associations of the

---

81. *de gloria martyrum* 41, p. 66—on Aredius of Limoges. For the reverse, see *Lib. Hist.* VII, 31, p. 351: 'and Mummolus taking one of them [a fragment of the relic of St Sergius], departed, though not with the favour of the martyr, as the sequel shall declare.'

82. MacCormack, 'The Ceremony of *Adventus*' pp. 721–39, 'Latin Prose Panegyric' pp. 154 seq. 178 seq. and 184. [See now *Art and Ceremony*.] The *adventus* of relics is shown for Vienne: *Bulletin de la Société des amis de Vienne* 67 (1971), pl. 2 on p. 31. See Gregory of Tours, *de virt Mart* II, 25, p. 167, II, 28, p. 169, and *de gloria martyrum* 89, pp. 97–98. [Brown, *The Cult of the Saints*, p. 98–100.]

83. D. Claude, 'Die Bestellung der Bischöfe im merowingischen Reiche', *ZRG LXXX KA* XLIX (1963): 1–75, esp p. 23.

84. D. Claude, *Die byzantinische Stadt im 6. Jahrhundert*, *Byzantinisches Archiv* 13 (Munich, 1969), p. 95.

85. A. Grabar, 'La mosaique de pavement de Qasr el-Lebya,' *Comptes rendus de l'Académie d'Inscriptions et de Belles Lettres* (June, 1969), pp. 264–82.

86. J. Hubert, 'Évolution de la topographie et de l'aspect des villes de Gaule du vème aux xème siècle, *Settimane di Studio sull'Alto Medio Evo* VI (1959): 529–58.

aristocratic family grave; it was a 'fine and private place'.[87]

Third: much of this is intelligible in terms of a streak in Gregory which defines the holy very strictly in terms of individual salvation. The Christian *koiné* by which the miracle is meaningful as a deliverance from sin bears a very heavy weight in Gregory: 'O if only the blessed confessor [Martin] would have deigned to make himself known in such an act of power to me, in loosing the fetters of my sins in the same way as he smashed the vast weight of the chains that held that man.'[88]

Holiness is possible only after death, because only after death can salvation be secure. Gregory's hagiography is an illustration of the deep roots of an Augustinian doctrine of predestination. A chill breath blows through Gregory's works when he contemplates the vast anonymity of cemeteries. The silence of the Polyandrion—the place of the great majority—at Autun is broken only by a few mysterious echoes of chanted psalms, betraying the presence, among so many thousands, 'of a few tombs of faithful souls worthy of God.'[89] Gregory was oppressed by how infinitesimally small the number of such tombs must be. For these were the tombs of the predestinate; they belonged to the 'snow white number of the elect'.[90]

I must repeat that all this is easier said than explained. It would be facile to reduce it to a contrast between the exuberant and basically optimistic world of East Rome and the grim and depleted Gaul of Gregory. To do this would be to ignore the *koiné* of basic attitudes which ran from one end of the Mediterranean to the other: John and Gregory, for instance,

87. Gregory of Tours, *Vitae Patrum* 8, 5, p. 245—Nicetius had been expected to leave a legacy to the basilica in which his tomb lay. See also *Lib. Hist.* X, 12, p 495 on Ingytrudis: 'Haec vero cum filia discordiam tenens, pro eo quod res suas ei abstulerit, obtestaretque, ut neque in monasterio, quod instituit, neque super sepulchrum eius permitteretur orare': 'She now swore that Berthegund should never be allowed to offer prayers either in the nunnery which she had founded or at her tomb.'

88. Gregory of Tours, *de virt Mart* I, 23, p. 150.

89. Gregory of Tours, *de gloria confessorum* 72, p. 341.

90. Gregory of Tours, *Vitae Patrum* 1, praef. p. 213.

both write history under the shadow of the approaching end of the world.[91] In some respects, admittedly, the parting of the ways is a parting in two styles of urban life. The holy tended, in the West, to be increasingly confined to the rhythms of the great basilica-shrine and the monastery, while in the Byzantine Empire it could spill out unself-consciously to join the vast ceremoniousness of Byzantine urban life. Styles of liturgy and preaching show how easily the street flowed into the basilica; and the receding tide brought out much of the holy into the street.[92] When the straitlaced Carolingian divines attacked the Byzantine cult of icons, they thought they saw in it a disastrous 'over-production' of the holy, strictly connected with a blurring of the boundaries between basilica and street: 'Si ergo vulgus partim laetitiae bachatu effrenis, partim saecularis pompae novitate arcessitus, partim ventosi honoris inflatione cupidus, partim adolationis vitio stimulatus, partim publicae securis metu perterritus imperatorum imagines vanis et perniciosis laudibus honorat, quid ad nos . . . ?'[93]

Yet much more needs to be said, especially by an ecclesiastical historian. I would like to return to the definition of the holy in East Rome as what is *outside* human society. This is not a definition which Gregory accepts in the way in which it was meant by a Byzantine. The holy, in the West, could be defined as it was in the East, in terms of a stark discontinuity between the human and the non-human: the drop of divine mercy at Bazas caused the jewels to fall out of the frame into

91. John of Ephesus, *HE* I, 3, p. 1; Gregory of Tours, *Lib. Hist.* I, praef. p. 2.

92. G. La Piana, *Le rappresentazioni sacre nella letteratura bizantina* (Grottaferrata, 1912; Variorum Reprints, 1971); T. F. Mathews, *The Early Churches of Constantinople: Architecture and Liturgy* (Pennsylvania, 1971); and Sabine MacCormack, *EHR* CXXXVIII (1973): 366–68.

93. *Libri Carolini*, I, 19 ed. H. Bastgen, *MGH Leg.* sectio III, Concilia ii (Berlin, 1924) p. 79: 'If then the vulgar mob, partly maddened by excitement and partly swayed by the novelties of secular pomp, partly eager to puff themselves up with an empty sense of self importance, partly urged on by a weakness for adulation and partly prompted by fear of punishment by the authorities, should choose to honour the images of emperors with vain and unhealthy praise, this is no affair of ours.'

which it was first inserted—there was no *consortium caelestibus cum terrenis*.[94] And yet this discontinuous holy is deeply inserted into human society. In the most poker-faced and unparadoxical manner it makes clear who has received grace in its sight and who has not. This declaration is held to have immediate social consequences: slaves healed by St Martin are automatically emancipated.[95] Its blessing is clear and covers a narrower range: it rests heavily on bishops of predictable *merita*. And this blessing is thought of as the intrusion into human life of those dead men and women who had persevered in clear roles within the human community rather than in the desert.

I would risk the suggestion that these phenomena reveal a mentality where the holy plays a more permanent role in law and in politics than it would ever play in East Rome. Gregory's world is one in which men worry much about perjury: Claudius, riding to Tours to bring Eberulf, dead or live, from the sanctuary of St Martin, is one example among many in the pages of Gregory—'Upon his way, after the custom of the barbarians, he began to take notice of omens, and to find them unfavourable. At the same time he enquired of many whether the power of the holy martyr had of late been made manifest against breakers of oaths . . .'[96] We are touching on a world where many of the human relations basic to the working of society are made subject to sacred law.[97] The use of the holy in day to day affairs in this manner is parallelled, in East Rome, only in villages in the forbidding hinterland of Asia Minor.[98]

In Gregory's works, the Mediterranean *koiné*—which

94. Gregory of Tours, *de gloria martyrum* 12, p. 46: 'no joining is possible between heavenly and earthly objects.' See Peter Brown, 'Society and the Supernatural: A Medieval Change', *Daedalus* CIV (1975): 133–51 at p. 141. [Below, p. 319.]
95. For example Gregory of Tours, *de virt Mart* II, 4, p. 161; II, 58, p. 178; II, 59, p. 179; III, 46, p. 193: IV, 46, p. 211; *de gloria confessorum* 67, p. 338.
96. Gregory of Tours, *Lib. Hist.* VII, 29, p. 347.
97. For example Gregory of Tours, *Lib. Hist.* VII, 6, p. 329 and VII, 14, p. 336.
98. F. Steinleitner, *Die Beicht im Zusammenhang mit der sakralen Rechtspflege in*

had always linked oaths with the holy and treated the drama of exorcism as an informal law-court, in which public judgement was passed on those sins that plainly disrupted society [99]—is hardened to take the strain of permanent government. In the Mediterranean world of Late Antiquity this coalescence had never quite happened. A glance at the *Dialogues* of Gregory's namesake, Gregory the Great, shows this. We are still in the world of *le monachisme méditerranéen* which is a world of mild paradoxes. There are tame bears and salad-gardens—warm memories of a Mediterranean-wide monastic anecdotage. Nor do we have the same phenomenon even among the stern heroes of John of Ephesus. These knew how to exercise the 'power of the saints' in society. Occasionally, among the loose-knit inhabitants of the mountains, the mirage of a theocracy founded around a holy man, where excommunication from the company of the believers replaced the blood feud, flickers a good century before Islam: [100] but the Djebel Izala was no Mecca, and Simon the Mountaindweller left no *Koran*. For the 'power of the saints' in Syria was based upon a dizzy ritual of social inversion; it existed for occasional, dramatic application to a society that was normally accustomed to looking after itself. The social use of the holy was delimited to those moments when a normative legal and social structure had broken down. With Gregory, the holy is losing its function as an emergency surrogate for justice. It is securely vested in men who knew what it was to rule, and who lived in a society where few men were prepared to rule as they were. The path towards the position of the early medieval bishop, whose social and sacred functions interlocked around an invincible sense of *das Tremendum*, may be slower than some exegetes of Gregory would have us believe: [101] the relation of the bishop to his

---

der Antike (Leipzig, 1913), p. 99 and L. Robert, *Nouvelles Inscriptions de Sardes* (Paris, 1964), p. 26.

    99. Brown, 'The Holy Man', p. 89. [Above, p. 124.]

    100. John of Ephesus, *PO* 17, pp. 229–47.

    101. H. Prinz, 'Die bischöfliche Stadtherrshaft im Frankenreich', *HZ* CCXVII (1973): 1–35 exaggerates for the sixth century.

town, for instance, still has an untidiness that belongs to Late
Antique *Romania*—even in Tours, acclamation by the people
can be as deadly a political weapon as it was in Edessa or
Constantinople; and Gregory could be threatened by it.[102]
Nevertheless, Gregory's works take us to the crest of a watershed: the manner in which he assumes a linking of law and the
holy makes him look north rather than south, to the Middle
Ages rather than to Late Antiquity, and therefore, away from
the East. He is the first Auvergnat as Michelet described them:
'on dirait une race méridionale grelottante au vent du nord, et
comme reserrée, durcie sous ce ciel étranger'.[103]

A perceptive if unsympathetic western thinker put his finger on this contrast: in his *Philosophy of History* Hegel wrote—
'The history of the highly civilised Eastern Empire—where
as we might suppose, the Spirit of Christianity could be taken
up in its truth and purity—exhibits to us a millennial series
of uninterrupted crimes, weaknesses, basenesses and want of
principle . . . It is evident here how Christianity may be abstract, and how as such it is powerless, on account of its very
purity and intrinsic spirituality . . . Light shining in darkness
may perhaps give colour, but not a picture animated by Spirit.
The Byzantine Empire is a grand example of how the Christian religion may maintain an abstract character among a cultivated people, if the whole organisation of the State and of the
Laws is not reconstructed in harmony with its principle.'[104]

This contrast of East and West does exist. But it need not
be interpreted in so harsh a manner. I hope that a historical
examination of the Late Antique phase of the parting of the
ways of East and West may make plain part of the Byzantine
answer. Byzantine society could take the strain of life on its
own, frankly secular, terms.[105] Ringed, in the early Middle

102. Gregory of Tours, *Lib. Hist.* V, 18, p. 219. On the use of acclamations,
see W. Liebeschütz, *Antioch* (Oxford, 1972), pp. 209–13.

103. J. Michelet, *Tableau de la France* (Paris, 1949), p. 29.

104. G. W. F. Hegel, *Philosophy of History*, trans. J. Shibree (New York, 1944),
p. 338.

105. N. H. Baynes, 'Some Aspects of Byzantine Civilisation', *Byzantine Studies* (London, 1960), p. 75: 'The law of Islam was fashioned by the religious con-

Ages, on one side by Islam, where religion and law fused, and on the other by a Western Europe, where religion blew through gaping cracks in the structure of society, Byzantines could keep the holy where they needed it—and in so doing, they preserved a vital part of its meaning—it was an unexpected wellspring of delight in the scorching summer of Mediterranean life.

sciousness of Islam: religion and law were inextricably intertwined . . . But the Christian Church, professing a creed of altruism, accepted a code of law which, as Mitteis has shown, is logically so completely satisfying because consistently based on the presuppositions of an egoism untroubled by humanitarian scruples.' For the ordeal in Western Europe and the conditions under which sacred and profane were mingled and later disentangled, see Brown, 'Society and the Supernatural', pp. 135–43 [below, pp. 302–332.] and Rebecca V. Colman, 'Reason and Unreason in Early Medieval Law', *JIntH* IV (1974): 571–91.

The View from the Precipice†

N O FIELD OF HISTORY SHOWS MORE CLEARLY than does the history of religious art the utter indifference of the past to its own future. A visitor to the excavations beneath the Vatican can step, in a few yards, from the tasteful burial chambers of the Roman pagans to beneath a grill, where he looks up into the golden inscription around the dome of St. Peter's. The historian may wish to trace the evolution that linked the one to the other, but to the dead, who lay in their pagan tombs, the transformation was inconceivable. They had lived their lives with their backs turned on the future. Even if these vaults had contained early Christians, the unimaginable quality of the future would have been no less.

Historians of the early Church have been known to turn the dead in their graves to look into that future; but historians of early Christian art have, on the whole, avoided doing this violence to the dead and to the evidence. For this reason, the study of early Christian and Byzantine art is something more than an indulgence of scholar aesthetes, or a light fringe of illustration to the heavy realities of later Roman history. It is the best balcony from which to view the sheer drop of the precipice that separates us from our ancient past.

The six books here reviewed can, in their various ways, be consulted with profit and confidence as glimpses into an

†*New York Review of Books* XXI (1974): 3–5.

alien world.[1] Michael Gough's *The Origin of Christian Art* is a sufficiently comprehensive guide. It may be described without irony in the author's own words referring to the artistic quality of the coins of the Emperor Anastasius: like these it has a 'reassuring if gloomy solidity',[2] and it is especially enriched by the late author's deep acquaintance with the little-known and inaccessible monuments of Asia Minor.

The world surveyed briefly by Gough from the first to the eighth centuries A.D. can only be fully understood if the difficulties in understanding are squarely faced at the outset. Hence the *Handbook of the Byzantine Collection* from Dumbarton Oaks, Washington, challenges us by the surprising extent of the artifacts associated with the early Christian period—great silver dishes, exquisite little rings, cut gems, gold-leaf glass: for what were such diverse objects used? Professor Cyril Mango's admirable collection and translation of Byzantine texts—*The Art of the Byzantine Empire, 312–1453 A.D.*—encourages us to listen in to the Byzantines themselves talking about their art; but what we hear is an alien language: early Christians insist on saying very different things from what we would say when we stand before the same monuments as they had visited and commissioned.

Professor Thomas F. Mathews's *The Early Churches of Constantinople: Architecture and Liturgy* shows how we must think away the religious life of all later Christian centuries before we can even begin to imagine what a Christian service in Constantinople in the fifth and sixth centuries was really like. To have extracted from the pathetic debris of a modern Turkish city, and from a humus of accepted traditions current since the early Middle Ages in the Orthodox church a picture

1. Michael Gough, *The Origins of Christian Art* (New York, 1973); *Handbook of the Byzantine Collection*, Dumbarton Oaks, Washington, D.C. (New York, 1973); C. A. Mango, *The Art of the Byzantine Empire, 312–1453 A.D.: Sources and Documents* (Englewood Cliffs, N.J., 1972); T. F. Mathews, *The Early Churches of Constantinople: Architecture and Liturgy* (Pennsylvania State University, 1972); G. H. Forsyth and K. Weitzmann, *The Monastery of Saint Catherine at Mount Sinai: The Church and Fortress of Justinian* (Ann Arbor, Michigan, 1973); A. T. Lucas, *Treasures of Ireland: Irish Pagan and Early Christian Art* (New York, 1973).

2. Gough, *Origins*, p. 142.

of the ceremonial aspects of the early Christian liturgy, is a triumph of fruitfully applied speculation. That some of Professor Mathews's reconstruction must remain hypothetical and open to challenge on matters of detail is a tribute to the perseverance with which the author has thought his way through an unpromising debris of evidence to the distinctive flavour of the religious ceremonies in which the Christian people of Constantinople participated when their city was the capital of a world empire.

Forsyth and Weitzmann's *The Monastery of Saint Catherine* is a superb dossier of photographs (as yet without a text) on one of the great shrines and pilgrimage centres of the age of Justinian. Last of all, we have a book which, surprisingly, can serve as a model for them all, A. T. Lucas's *Treasures of Ireland: Irish Pagan and Early Christian Art*: surprisingly—because it is about the art of prehistoric and early medieval Ireland (a world originally unimaginably distant from the Mediterranean origins of Christian art, to which a Mediterranean culture came only through missionaries at the end of the early Christian period); a model—because it shows how the challenge of the exceptionally alien art of the La Tène age can be met by a trained eye, a skilled pen, and an adventurous choice of illustrations.

A review may best proceed by urging the authors of these very different books to a conversation on the present difficulties we experience on entering fully into the early Christian world. Of one thing we can be certain: premature certainty in understanding early Christian art is our common enemy. Two factors encourage such premature understanding. First, there is the obvious temptation to read back the rich later history of Christian art into its origins in an ancient world which was, by the time Christianity appeared as a cultural force, very ancient indeed, and very certain of its artistic traditions. Second, there is the over-availability of photographs. Seen in isolation on a page, so many skilful modern reproductions create a false impression. For nothing that we see in books on early Christian art ever stood alone in this way. Men once stood before them; even the most humble objects were once used for specific purposes; other monuments—some a thousand years older—stood beside the churches and carvings of the early Christian period.[3]

Premature understanding is an enemy to which each author has squared up in his own way. Michael Gough's approach is the most straightforward. He tells us briefly what elements in the art of the classical world contributed to the formation of Christian art; he tells us what the enigmatic figures in the catacombs symbolize; a warm appreciation of the monuments of Asia Minor breaks out in a discussion of the architecture of the dome in the light of the excavation which he himself had conducted in Alahan Dagh.[4] Briefly, he tells us what there is to see in early Christian art and how it got there. He tells less of what this art might have meant to early Christians. To take one example: we have a page on late Roman jewelry in general—but we have to turn to the *Handbook of the Byzantine Collection* to learn how to enjoy those gold wedding belts worn by Byzantine ladies of the sixth century—for example, no. 184, where Christ stands behind a couple joining their right hands in the old Roman manner, embraced by the inscription: 'From God, two of a single mind.'[5]

In a different way, Professor Mango's anthology of contemporary texts helps to place Christian art firmly in its context at the time when Christianity became the public religion of the empire, after A.D. 312. In these texts, we seldom find ourselves in front of an isolated artifact; we are immersed in the bustle of an ancient town. It took all sorts to make that world. Sixth-century poems catch a richness now lost forever. All the activities of a great town open up before us: we have a poem 'On an image of a professor at Pergamon set up

3. Peter Brown, 'Art and Society in Late Antiquity', *The Age of Spirituality. Metropolitan Museum Symposium*, ed. K. Weitzmann (New York, 1981).

4. Gough, *Origins*, pp. 65–68.

5. Gough, *Origins*, pp. 140–42; *Handbook of the Byzantine Collection*, no. 184, p. 52; Chiara Frugoni, 'L'iconografia del matrimonio e della coppia nel medioevo', *Il matrimonio nella società altomedioevale, Settimane di Studi del Centro Italiano di Studi sull'Alto Medio Evo* XXIV (Spoleto, 1977), 901–63.

for him on account of a civic embassy. . . .'[6] We would gladly have seen the portrait that inspired another: 'I have been a courtesan in Byzantine Rome and offered my love for sale to all comers. I am crafty Callirhoe. Smitten by passion, Thomas has set up this, my portrait, showing all the ardour he has in his breast.'[7]

In Mango's dossier we find a reason for the gulf between ourselves and contemporary witnesses of early Christian art. The great churches arose in towns already heavy with public monuments. Now it is the fate of a public monument to be taken for granted: for such monuments were dependable reminders of surviving affluence and public generosity now channeled into the Christian Church. The superb silver work of the sixth-century churches shows this affluence on a small scale.[8]

Public monuments taken for granted in this way are the despair of the historian of art; and Byzantines, in particular, inherited a long tradition in describing public monuments which encouraged them to tell either too little or too much. It is the crowd beneath the mosaics that they address. This crowd does not want to be told what they can see in any case: they want to be told what it means to them at that particular moment. We would want to know precisely what the Nativity cycle in a sixth-century church in Gaza looked like. Not so the orator Choricius—himself a native of Gaza. He did not need to be a camera. Instead, when the angel appears to the shepherds announcing the birth of Christ, Choricius articulates for his audience what it was possible for them to *feel* about the participants in the events depicted, down to the last detail: 'The sheep, because of their innate stupidity, do not turn towards the vision.'. . . The dog, however, an animal hostile to strangers, appears to be looking intently at the extraordinary apparition.'[9]

6. Mango, *Art of the Byzantine Empire*, p. 119.
7. Ibid.
8. *Handbook of the Byzantine Collection*, nos. 63–70, pp. 18–20; Brown, 'Art and Society'.
9. Mango, *Art of the Byzantine Empire*, p. 65. For a sensitive and balanced

Yet in this rococo example we have part of the secret of early Christian art in its environment. For we have moved from the mosaic itself to the capacity of the Byzantine audience to enter, by their own participation, into the events depicted on the mosaic with the same gusto as they entered into the same events as conjured up in the dramatic homilies of their bishops. In a word, the art of a church could be regarded as a backdrop to a world of ceremony and drama—as has recently been made plain in a perceptive juxtaposition of secular ceremonial and religious preaching.[10]

For without the early Christians our photographs of much of early Christian art are more than usually silent. It is an art that accompanies early Christians in their performance of actions which meant more than the art itself. Only from the mid-sixth century do we find works of art such as icons used as a direct aid to religious contemplation. Like the other monuments of an ancient town, early Christian monuments were the discreet witnesses of a noisy and tempestuous world. Professor Mathews shows this clearly. His study of the liturgy of Constantinople is the study of 'the life of the ceremonial movement which the building was created to shelter. Colorful, vibrant and fascinating. . .'—very much, that is, part of the ceremonial rhythms of an ancient town.[11]

In this, the liturgy of early Christian Constantinople differed vastly from that of later centuries. It began with a solemn procession into the church; and in the church, the bishop, the Eucharist, the preacher were exposed as never later to the full participation of the 'many-voiced' Christian populace. When we read in Paul the Silentiary how the sixth-century congregation would 'strive to touch the sacred [Gospel] book with their lips and hands, the countless waves of the surging people break around',[12] we are in a world not so

treatment of the problem, see H. Maguire, 'Truth and Convention in Byzantine Descriptions of Works of Art', *Dumbarton Oaks Papers* XXVIII (1974): 113–40.

10. S. G. MacCormack, *English Historical Review* LXXXVIII (1973): 366–68.
11. Mathews, *The Early Churches*, p. 64.
12. Mango, *Art of the Byzantine Empire*, p. 95.

far from that which Henry James once sensed in the Roman amphitheater of Arles: 'the murmurs and shudders, the thick voice of the crowd that died away some fifteen hundred years ago.'

So a final question remains. How important for the religious life of the early Christians was early Christian art? The answer that these books suggest is: far less than we think. The exception is Mount Sinai. Here we have a pilgrimage site and a monastery. Pilgrims travelled to it from all over the Mediterranean and the Near East, and hence there is no incongruity in a later Moslem mosque on the same site. Here was where God had appeared to Moses in a burning bush, and on the peak above He had given the Law to Moses. In the mosaic in the conch of the apse, Christ is shown blazing in the glory of His Transfiguration. Here we have a momentary vision of the other world caught in mosaic.[13] The pilgrim had come for this. But the evidence for the search for a vision of the other world through art, which takes on such prominence in the literature of the Iconoclast controversy of the eighth and ninth centuries, is slight for the early Christian period. When Augustine wept in the basilica of Milan, it was at the chanting of the psalms, not before the still face of an icon.

Often indeed, the holy was a focus of spiritual 'power' as faceless as a modern car battery—a silver casket in which the relics of the saint were enshrined.[14] The piety that crystallized around these was not concerned with anything as subdued as visual contemplation of a work of art. It was a piety of physical gestures and of physical contact with a holy object. The traveller who stands in some great Moslem shrine, watching the crowds surging up to the silver grill around the grave of

13. See below, p. 212, and J. Snyder, 'The Meaning of the "Maiestas Domini" in Hosios David', *Byzantion* 37 (1967), 146–147, for the later legend of a monk who came to Thessalonica as a pilgrim at the time of the Iconoclasts. He prayed that he might see Christ as He would appear at the Last Day; wherewith, the whitewashed canvas fell from the apse, to reveal the hidden mosaic!

14. Peter Brown, *The Cult of the Saints: Its Rise and Function in Latin Christianity* (Chicago, 1981), pp. 87–88.

an *imam* and rubbing their faces passionately against the hard metal, is more likely to see, on the border of Central Asia, the authentic continuation of the basic styles of early Christian piety than he will see in any church in Europe.

If early Christian art has a religious message, it is very different from that of later centuries. To find out what this might be it is not enough to ask what a specific scene 'meant' in terms of what Biblical episode it represented or what Christian rite it symbolized. Rather we have to enter into what religious attitudes were conveyed as a total visual impression on the beholder. In many ways the books under review give only a partial answer to this problem. If these authors have failed in any way it is because they have not considered the aesthetic value of the representations they have studied. Professor Mango, for instance, is abrupt with 'contemporary scholars' who have 'expressed some subtle views concerning the aesthetic value of Byzantine art.'[15] One may agree that there is no royal road to entering into the aesthetic values of the early Christians, but, difficult though it may be, it is a road along which not only the historian of religious experience but also the historian of art must be encouraged to stumble.

For Mango's judgement omits a factor of which Lucas in his fine *Treasures of Ireland* is constantly aware: human beings have eyes, and artists, we assume, have trained eyes. A work of early Christian art—and the art of Ireland may stand for the rest—has to be looked at carefully and long before we can see what it conveys: as Lucas says, 'What appears to the lazy eye as a repetitive mosaic of broken symmetry appears to the alert one a perpetual motion running in endless circles.'[16] By constant attention to the aesthetic values of otherwise opaque works of art, Lucas inserts these into their social and cultural context more convincingly than would any more strictly 'functional' explanation of their meaning, and presence. Of the 'Petrie crown' of the La Tène age he can write: 'It is this

15. Mango, *Art of the Byzantine Empire*, p. xiv.
16. Lucas, *Treasures of Ireland*, p. 63.

203

disengagement from all appeal to the sensuous life which gives the object so much of its cold and esoteric beauty.'[17] With a judgement like this in mind, we can read his pages, appreciate his illustrations, and find ourselves in the world of the early Irish poets:

> God be praised who ne'er forgets me
> In my art so high and cold
> And still sheds upon my verses
> All the magic of red gold.[18]

The difference between the 'lazy eye' and the 'alert one' has something to do with aesthetics. For this reason alone, Professor Mango's admirable collection of documents is best read in conjunction with, not instead of, the short book of an Old Master—Gervase Mathew's *Byzantine Aesthetics*; for here is an attempt to find the 'alert eye' and the intellectual universe behind the Byzantine texts published by Professor Mango.[19]

Early Christian art needs this 'alert eye' to grasp its specific religious message. For unlike that of later, medieval, art this message is alive to us precisely because it is so unobtrusively ever-present.[20] Here we have an art which expresses, with all the poignancy of centuries of Mediterranean imagery, a deep religious preoccupation with rest, with the good life, with the miracle of a sheltered garden imagined in the broiling summers of a Mediterranean city. 'Fear no more the heat of the sun.' Early Christianity was about Paradise.[21] So was Islam: hence the direct continuity that links Greco-Roman garden paintings, through Byzantium, to the first great surviving mosque at Damascus. By early Christian stan-

17. Ibid., p. 54.
18. Frank O'Connor, *The Little Monasteries* (Dublin, 1963), p. 10.
19. Gervase Mathew, *Byzantine Aesthetics* (London, 1963).
20. C. Geertz, 'Art as a Cultural System', *Modern Language Notes* XCI (1976): 1473–99 is of considerable help in understanding how a work of art can communicate to a given society by its formal quality quite as much as by its overt, 'iconographic' meaning.
21. Peter Brown, *The Cult of the Saints*, pp. 75–76.

dards, this building conveyed a deeply religious message.[22]

The early Christian paradise was not yet a court of Heaven. Human faces did not crowd out its airy landscapes. It is here that the 'alert eye' must wake up to see, behind the solemn, well-documented 'meaning' of each scene, the subtle message of the total visual impression. Any textbook will tell you which scene in the mosaics of Santa Maria Maggiore represents the blessing of Jacob by Isaac; many scholars will show the exact meaning of such a scene for a man of the fifth century A.D.:[23] but the eye pierces beyond the figures that can be explained in this way to a light green hill crowned with cypresses and a curtain floating in the breeze. The whole scene is a glimpse of rest provided in the sheltered space of an urban basilica. Around the corner, in Santa Prassede, martyrs tread on poppies as red as they still grow every spring in the Roman Campagna.

It is only because we look instinctively to the history of the Christian art of the Middle Ages—an art consisting predominantly of human faces and of statues in the round—that the quiet insistent message of mosaics such as these tends to be explained away as so many 'relics' or as so many 'influences' from a pagan, classical past. In fact, it is such mosaics that are central, and the future development of Christian medieval art that was deeply irrelevant, to the men of the early Christian world. 'Naked Erotes, embroiled in the vines, stood there smiling sweetly and making fun from on high of those who walk below.'[24] The description refers to a secular building in Constantinople. But we meet our *Erotes* in Christian churches also. Such a scene is neither secular nor religious, pagan nor Christian: it is an image of happiness and rest. Early Christian art—like some of early Christian literature—has given us some of the most enchanting of such im-

22. Annemarie Schimmel, 'The Celestial Garden in Islam', *The Islamic Garden*, ed. E. B. MacDougall and R. Ettinghausen (Washington, D.C., 1976), pp. 11–39.
23. B. Brenk, *Die frühchristlichen Mosaiken in Santa Maria Maggiore zu Rom* (Wiesbaden, 1975).
24. Mango, *Art of the Byzantine Empire*, p. 45.

ages.[25] It is only later centuries of Christian thought and art that make such human scenes so strangely inaccessible to modern men.

25. For a warm plea against the false Puritanism that treats scenes of leisure and drinking as nothing more than incongruous 'pagan survivals' in early Christian art, see P. A. Février, 'À propos du repas funéraire: culte et sociabilité', *Cahiers archéologiques* XXVI (1977): 29–45. Being concerned with joy, rest and concord, early Christianity continued this imagery with unalloyed enthusiasm: see N. Himmelmann, 'Lo bucolico en el arte antiguo', *Habis* V (1974): 141–52.

Artifices of Eternity[†]

NY VISITOR TO A MUSEUM OR ART GALLERY WILL
in due course come to realize the extent to which medieval Christianity in its varying forms fostered the
growth of visual art. The books reviewed here are
a testimony to some of its manifestations.[1] Françoise Henry
presents new reproductions of large parts of the great Gospel
Book of Kells, now preserved in the Library of Trinity College, Dublin. Icons of Byzantium and Eastern Europe, scattered in museums throughout the world, are catalogued and
ingeniously dated by David and Tamara Talbot-Rice. The
catalogue of the exhibition of 1974, 'Venice and Byzantium',
reminds us that in San Marco in Venice we have a living museum of the art of Constantinople at its peak. Sirarpie Der
Nersessian has commented on eleven of the luxuriant manuscripts of the Armenian communities scattered throughout
the Near East, now preserved in the Walters Art Gallery. Furthermore, we have guides to the very different societies that
produced such art: the masterly survey of Professor Jaroslav

[†]Written with Sabine MacCormack, *New York Review of Books*, XXII (1975):
pp. 19–22.

1. Jaroslav Pelikan, *The Spirit of Eastern Christendom (600–1700)* (Chicago,
1974); *Venezia e Bizanzio*, ed. Sergio Bettini (Venice, 1974); David and Tamara
Talbot-Rice, *Icons and Their History* (New York, 1974); Sirarpie Der Nersessian, *Ar-
menian Manuscripts in the Walters Art Gallery* (Baltimore, 1974); John T. McNeill, *The
Celtic Churches: A History, A.D. 200 to 1200* (Chicago, 1974); Françoise Henry, *The
Book of Kells* (New York, 1974).

Pelikan, *The Spirit of Eastern Christendom (600–1700)*, can be fruitfully contrasted with the northern world evoked in the enthusiastic narrative of Professor John T. McNeill, *The Celtic Churches: A History*, A.D. 200 to 1200.

With books such as these we learn to enter a world where the patronage and execution of works of art could not be taken for granted. The brittle magnificence of the monasteries of the Celtic world, as fragile and isolated as the courts of their neighbours and patrons, the Celtic chieftains, collapsed at a touch with the Viking invasions of the ninth century. The history of many of the icons dated by David and Tamara Talbot-Rice is the history of feudal families living at risk in the ravaged Balkans. The tranquil masterpieces of Russian art were produced in towns overshadowed by the Tartar horsemen: 'I painted these four pictures of the temple and those of the Evangelists which you saw when I, in fear of Yedigei, fled to Tver and found refuge with you in my grief, and showed you all the books which were left to me after my flight and ruin.'[2] Even in the few periods of peace, in early medieval Ireland and Byzantium, leisure and wealth were a volatile surplus, hurriedly placed beyond the envy of time in the form of those great works of religious art that we now admire in the solid comfort of galleries.

There is a yet greater gulf which we must leap. A majority of the works of art discussed here have a theme in common. They were considered, in their varying ways, as points where men and the supernatural could meet. Each of them asked to be judged by the degree of success they achieved in helping the mind to that high peak from which another world—a world palpable, ever present, and hidden only by the passing mist of the human body—might be viewed. A revolution in western religious sentiment stands between ourselves and this early medieval zenith of Christian art.

We in this present period expect religious art to instruct us, to stir up appropriate feelings in us, to clutter our childhood imaginations with tasteful vignettes of Near-Eastern

2. Talbot-Rice, *Icons*, p. 101.

life inserted as illustrations to our Bibles and Sunday School textbooks. We do not expect a work of art to be a direct bridge to the holy. Yet an icon, for instance, is just this: it is a clean patch in the misted pane of glass that stands between us and the invisible presences that press in around us from the other world. The Russian acquaintance of a friend, when presented with a bad copy of the icon of Our Lady of Vladimir, dismissed it instinctively: 'No,' said he, 'it is not *transparent* enough.' It is this translucence of the good icon that made it, as it were, a window opening on to the other world. Art and closeness to the supernatural converge: 'The icons which came to be most revered and admired in Russia and credited with miraculous powers, are also among the finest from the aesthetic point of view.'[3]

To understand why this should be so we may turn first to Professor Pelikan's *Spirit of Eastern Christendom*. It is a pleasure to salute this masterpiece of exposition. The foundation of this model book is to be found in its margins, where reference follows reference down the side of the page, indicating an astonishingly deep absorption of the primary evidence. Through these, Professor Pelikan enables us to hear the Eastern Christians speaking in their own language about the concerns that were built into the heart of their theology.

'We make out of the quarrel with others, rhetoric, but of the quarrel with ourselves, poetry.' Byzantines are notorious for their rhetoric. The impression given by most surveys is of a contentious world, where the streets of great classical cities were filled by clashing bands of circus factions and slogan-chanting monks. Professor Pelikan has abandoned this facile image. He has rediscovered for us the sustained poetry of the Eastern Christian argument with itself. Precisely for being so resolutely abstract, this is as true a picture of the realities of Eastern Christian society as is the more fashionable interest in the garish aspects of Byzantine factionalism. We are dealing with a society whose leaders had inherited from the classical world a yearning for retirement—where

3. Ibid., p. 90.

the cultivated intellectual would chirrup like a cicada in the long summer sunlight of scholarly leisure—and had reinforced this tendency by seeking the solemn shelter of great monasteries, in which many of the masterpieces of Eastern Christian theology came to be written.

Beneath the overt issues of each of the many controversies that raged in the Eastern Christian world is the logical development by which each problem unfolded out of the other. This is what Professor Pelikan calls the 'hidden agenda'[4] of Eastern Christian thought, and he shows rare intellectual flair in uncovering it. The book flows like a great river, slipping easily past landscapes of the utmost diversity —the great Christological controversies of the seventh century, the debate on icons in the eighth and ninth, attitudes to Jews, to Muslims, to the dualistic heresies of the high Middle Ages, to the post-Reformation churches of Western Europe. Not the least value of Professor Pelikan's treatment is his refusal to adopt a false phil-Hellenism. His book succeeds in being a study of the Eastern Christian tradition as a whole.

His evocation of the development of the Nestorian tradition—of a Christianity, that is, that developed outside the frontiers of Byzantium, in Persian and, later, Islamic, territory, and that expressed itself in Syriac not in Greek—is exceptionally illuminating. A book that can realize the stature of Babai the Great and Abdisha of Nisibis[5] alongside the well-known figures of Maximus the Confessor and St John Damascene can only help us to appreciate more fully the richness of a great Christian tradition.[6] For in the Nestorians we have a truly Eurasian Christianity. In great fortress-like monasteries in the hills of northern Mesopotamia Nestorian thinkers grappled with the problems shared by Christian intellectuals in Constantinople and Antioch, while in the wake of soldiers and traders Nestorian monks and clergymen carried their ideas to the oases of Central Asia, to Malaya and Peking. In 635 A.D. the emperor of China was presented

4. Pelikan, *Eastern Christendom*, p. 199.   5. Ibid., pp. 39–40.
6. See above, p. 169.

with a statement of their faith which, beneath its alien language, was a faithful echo of the basic concerns of Eastern Christian thought.[7]

Within his exposition of the evolution of Eastern Christian teaching in all its multiplicity, Professor Pelikan offers us the austere road to an understanding of the need for icons in the Eastern Church. As he frequently makes plain, the basic concern of Eastern theology was the manner in which the divine world is revealed to humans, frail as they are. Thus the constantly recurring apprehension that 'things divine are real'[8] was for ever in the grip of the question which asked: if they are real, how are men, alienated by the Fall and their own sins, to recapture a reality that is so close and yet so far?[9] The icon offered one such bridge to the other world. In front of an icon, the Eastern Christian felt his ever-labile mind come to rest; its grave face, 'expressive of the silence of God',[10] was a 'nest' to which the fluttering soul, its wings tired with the ill-directed flights of imagination, could return.[11]

For over a century, in the late eighth and early ninth centuries, the fate of the icons hung in a balance. Their role in the church was challenged by the Iconoclastic movement in the Byzantine Empire. This movement did not object to art as such. Professor Pelikan's and other studies have made plain that the Iconoclasts were concerned to replace icons by what they considered to be yet more effective vehicles of the holy —by the blessed Eucharist and the compact symbol of the cross.[12] They shared the Eastern Christian obsession with bridging the gulf between the human and the divine; only the vehicles they chose were different. Thus in the victory of icons what was won was not art itself; it was the role of the visual element in man's perception of the divine.

Icons gave precision and location to the immensity of the invisible world, much as a shadow, hitherto blurred, takes on

7. See above, p. 78.   8. Pelikan, *Eastern Christendom*, p. 13.
9. Ibid., pp. 117–45.   10. Ibid., p. 133.
11. *Vita Sancti Stephani Iunioris, Patrologia Graeca* 100: 1157 B.C.
12. See below, p. 258.

clear, hard lines as the sun emerges from behind a cloud. The icon took the believer to the threshold of the visionary experience which always has remained the warm heart of Eastern Christendom. For what the prophet or the holy man had seen with his own eyes, the average man could rightly imagine in the icon, its tones as clear, as sharp in outline, and as shadowless as a dream. An icon showing an event in the Gospel did not attempt to instruct the believer, or merely to mobilize his feelings: it strove 'to transfer the event from the terrestrial world in which it had occurred to the celestial, to which the persons concerned had been transported.'[13]

The icon, therefore, was a patch of clear visibility. This, of course, was vision, or perception, going in two ways. The 'red corner' in a Russian house, where the icons were hung, was also the corner from which God and his saints watched their human protégés. The icon scanned with silent gaze the crises of domestic life. In Greece, so we are told, the discreet adulterer would cover the face of the icon—for if you gazed at it, it gazed at you.[14] Throughout the Eastern Christian world, icon and vision validated each other. Some deep gathering into one focal point of the collective imagination— a subject that remains to be studied—ensured that, by the sixth century, the supernatural had taken on the precise lineaments, in dreams and in each person's imagination, in which it was commonly portrayed in art. The icon had the validity of a realized dream. Often it served as an Identikit: the dreamer, on waking, would find out by referring to his icon which invisible protector had appeared to him in the night.

What we have in Byzantium and Russia, is a religious art which cannot be prised loose from the other means by which a society strove to obtain intimacy with the divine. Together with the Scriptures and the liturgy, religious art was an indispensable component of the 'melody of theology'. Professor Pelikan demonstrates this conclusively in his third chapter,

13. Talbot-Rice, *Icons*, p. 93.
14. D. Savramis, 'Der abergläubliche Missbrauch der Ikonen in Byzanz', *Ostkirchliche Studien* IX (1960): 174–92.

and the Talbot-Rices assume it in contrast to western art: 'While the orthodox paintings were invariably closely linked to the cult, the Western paintings were not created exclusively to serve as vehicles of worship.'[15] What is more difficult to seize are the full implications of such a view for the art historian and the historian of religious sentiment. Hence the value of comparing a world where the exceptionally strict integration of art and worship is assumed, with societies where it is either subjected to strain—as in early modern Russian icon painting—or is sapped by alien civilizations—as in Armenia —or is arrived at from a totally different starting point, in a world dominated by totally different assumptions—as in Celtic Ireland.

To go to Venice and to come, in San Marco, upon a candle-lit plaque of eleventh-century marble, white and waxen as a lily, is to meet Byzantine art at its peak: there is nothing in that still figure that is left unmobilized in the attempt to catch a vision in stone. It is the Virgin, 'depicted in painting as she is in writings and visions.'[16]

The catalogue of the summer 1974 exhibition 'Venice and Byzantium' and the opening chapters of the Talbot-Rices' book bring home the tragedy of this great art. The culture of Byzantium was burned out at its heart. What survives comes less from Constantinople than from the ragged fringes of the Empire—from the Balkans, from Italy, from the Crusader kingdoms. Even to talk of 'Byzantine influence' is misleading. The exhibition has enabled us to appreciate the continued prestige of Byzantine craftsmanship throughout the Mediterranean up to the thirteenth century;[17] but such 'Byzantinizing' artifacts are mere disjointed fragments compared with what a true Byzantine wanted from the beaten gold and

15. Talbot-Rice, *Icons*, p. 92.

16. Photius, Homily 17, 6: *The Homilies of Photius, Patriarch of Constantinople*, trans. C. Mango (Cambridge, Mass., 1958), p. 295.

17. And far longer than that in Venice itself: see Rona Goffen, 'Icon and Vision: Giovanni Bellini's Half-Length Madonnas', *Art Bulletin* LVII (1975): 487–518: 'In Venice the *maniera greca* was not arcane but familiar—an alternative, native means of expression' (p. 488).

gold enamelling of the faces of angels and saints—the vision of another world.

It is to Russia that we should turn to find the search for the vision of another world continued into modern times. The 'hidden agenda' of Professor Pelikan continued to mould the art of the icon at a particularly stormy period of Russian piety. With this aspect of the Russian icon, the Talbot-Rices have not done as well for us as they might have done. Their notes show a heavy dependence on the great Russian catalogue of Antonova and Mneva of 1963. The water flows fast under that particular bridge; they could have said more, both in detail and in general.[18]

The 'sleuthing' of icons, in order to date them, in the light of recent Russian research, can now take place against a fascinating background of subtle and decisive shifts of emphasis in the theological tradition in early modern Russia. The icons of fifteenth- and sixteenth-century Russia are reminders that the Eastern tradition, though stable, was never static. We find the painters of Russia struggling to catch in their art an invisible world whose *dramatis personae* and structure change, beneath the pressure of religious sentiment.[19] At the end, with the arrival of western baroque art in the seventeenth century, the ancient, sure guides to vision were swept aside, and in the protests of the conservatives we can sense the pain of a dreamer to whom a beloved face has appeared horribly transfigured in a nightmare: '. . . the number of painters using an unseemly manner of icon-painting has increased in our land. They paint the image of the Saviour Emmanuel with bloated face, red lips, swollen fingers and large fat legs and thighs. . . .'[20]

18. Particularly in the analysis of formal elements in icons, perspective and the representation of space, in the work of L. F. Zhegin, *Iazik zhivnopisnogo proizhdeniia* (Moscow, 1970), now followed by B. V. Raushenbakh, *Prostranstvennye postroeniia v drevnerusskoi zhivopisi* (Moscow, 1975).

19. V. A. Plugin, *Mirovozzrenie Andreia Rubleva* (Moscow, 1974); O. I. Podobedova, *Moskovskaia shkola zhivopisi pri Ivane iv.* (Moscow, 1972), pp. 40–58.

20. *Zhitie Protopopa Avvakuma*, ed. N. K. Gudzii (Moscow, 1960), p. 135; John Stuart, *Ikons* (London, 1975), pp. 128–35.

With the fine plates of the Armenian manuscripts and meticulous commentary of Sirarpie Der Nersessian, we enter a corner of Eastern Christendom very different from the solemn, self-absorbed refinements of Russian icon-painting. Here are the manuscripts of Armenian communities notorious for their combination of tenacity and adaptability. We follow them to the end of the seventeenth century. A breath of the Muslim Near East blows through them: the manuscript of 1455, produced at Khizan, to the southwest of Lake Van, shows the figures of Christian story moving with gusto against a background of bright patterns and twining flowers that reminds us of Muslim tiles and metalwork. The Marriage Feast at Cana has become a very Near Eastern occasion: the men squat with their long-stemmed wine jars and shallow drinking cups in a garden without women. Later, as Armenian colonies spanned the trade routes from Venice to Isfahan, fragments of western baroque art—the same that so disconcerted the Russians—are happily integrated wherever the firm cycle of Byzantine themes had left a gap to be filled.

A Byzantine reviewer might not have liked these manuscripts: 'The restraint of an ever-present law', writes O. M. Dalton, 'may impoverish imagination, but it forbids rhetoric. . . . The mean and trivial accidents of life do not intrude into the sphere of these high abstractions.'[21] The Armenian manuscripts, where Christ, for instance, in the Harrowing of Hell is shown 'clad in a tight-fitting bodice, wide trousers and shod with high, nail-studded boots',[22] are impenitent offenders against this rule, so lovingly and finely observed in the far-distant plains of Russia. The distinctive quality of Armenian art is a reminder of the sweep of the Eastern Christian tradition. For the exuberance of Armenia, its unparalleled scattering of energies and interest, nevertheless took place from a firm base.

A second look at the manuscripts that first strike us by their departure from Byzantine reticence shows how the

21. O. M. Dalton, *Byzantine Art and Archaeology* (Oxford, 1911), p. 35.
22. Sirarpie Der Nersessian, *Armenian Miniatures*, p. 36.

drawn-out 'melody of theology' still predominates and gives each manuscript a tone of Mediterranean tranquillity. For the Evangelists remain Byzantines. Heirs, like Professor Pelikan's theologians scattered in monasteries between Constantinople and the edges of Iran, of the late classical ideal of the writer inspired by the Muses, they sit in their classical robes, in front of classical writing desks—desks strangely misconceived, at times, by Near Eastern artists more used to writing across their knees; so that the dolphin of the desk support comes to live a gay life of its own, yet recognizable.[23] The inspiration of God falls on them as they write. They are the models for centuries of Eastern Christian theologians, who, so they insisted, wrote in the same way under the same inspiration, and, with clear eyes, gazed into the same Heaven.[24]

Compared with these quiet, classical figures, the men we meet in the Celtic world of the Book of Kells are unrecognizable. The moment of inspiration is past for them; they grip closed books, their eyes see no vision, they are stamped on the holy pages like intricate talismans. The book itself, not the writer and his vision, is the palpable reminder of the other world.

To turn from Armenian manuscripts to the Book of Kells is to appreciate, from a distant viewpoint, just how close-knit and polished by age was the synthesis of art and religion which was achieved in the eastern Mediterranean, and which extended for a millennium from Persia to the Baltic, when compared with the unruly world of the Celtic illuminator. To enter this world Professor McNeill's survey is somewhat less helpful than that provided by Professor Pelikan for Eastern Christendom. Professor McNeill has, understandably, succumbed to the charm of the Celts. 'The people who have

23. H. I. Marrou, *Mousikos Anér. Étude sur les scènes de la vie intellectuelle figurant sur les monuments funéraires romains* (Grenoble, 1938).
24. As Gregory of Nazianze, described by Severus of Antioch, who was able to gaze into the Light of the Trinity, with 'wide awake and unsleeping eyes': *Homily 65, Patrologia Orientalis* 8, p. 327, cited in Roberta C. Chesnut, *Three Monophysite Christologies* (Oxford, 1976).

been our companions through these pages constitute a rare and choice company.'[25] Indeed they do. There is 'Saint Piro, Samson's predecessor at Ynys Byr, who is said to have met his death by falling into a well while inebriated';[26] St Brigid, who, when her coach overturned when attempting to cross the low wall of a boreen, remarked, 'Short cuts make broken bones';[27] St Columba, who when 'According to the verses of Dallán Forgaill, 1,200 bards entered the meeting and lauded in song the embarrassed saint, . . . covered his face with his cowl.'[28]

However, Professor McNeill's scholarly vigilance has not been lulled by this cavalcade. The relevant critical erudition on the Celtic Churches is carefully mobilized in his pages and notes. He knows the extent to which the image of the Celtic Church is a creation of its decline. The legends of the twelfth century attempt to gather the shreds of the past together in cosy tales that tell us little about the early medieval Celtic Church but much about their audience—the men who carved and patronized the little squat figures on the Irish tombs that are provincial variants of the high art of the Gothic period, in which hardly a trace survives of the electrifying subtleties of Irish art in earlier centuries.

Yet Professor McNeill has succumbed to the temptation both to write a narrative history from such intractable material, and, what is more, to write it in a tone of buoyant optimism. Continuous narrative is dangerous enough in the state of our knowledge of the *lacunae* of the evidence for the early centuries of Celtic Christianity; but optimism is doubly so. For the *lacunae* in the evidence seem to hint at vast geological faults that intermittently opened in the path of the Christian mission to this strange, northern world. A history of the Celtic Church has to do full justice to its discontinuities—to recessions, to new starts, to starting transmutations forced upon the Christian Church in an alien environ-

25. McNeill, *The Celtic Churches*, p. 225.   26. Ibid., p. 39.
27. Ibid., p. 80.   28. Ibid., p. 98.

ment. Such a history would enable us to seize the creativity of that Third World of early medieval Christendom, a world incredibly remote from the ancient Mediterranean of Rome and Byzantium.

To contrast the Book of Kells with the world of the icon is to realize how little of northern life and experience could be mobilized to form the kind of discreetly articulated vehicle of worship that Mediterranean men could take for granted. What we have in a Celtic Gospel book is the impact of a few powerful symbols of the holy on a society unprepared for their appearance, whose artistic traditions and ways of seeing the world remained recalcitrant of incorporation in a 'melody of theology'.

The Christian missionaries brought books, not faces. As the Celtic legend of St Patrick says—faced by his first convert 'He baptized him . . . and handed him the A.B.C.'[29.] When tribesmen murdered a missionary on the North Sea coast and looted his encampments: 'Rushing together around this treasure trove with whoops of joy, they smashed the chests, only to find books, not gold, parchment leaves covered with divine knowledge, not silver.'[30] It was in the pages of the Gospels that a northern Christian hoped to find his God. The contemplative did not gaze eye to eye into the face of an icon; he crouched in rapt attention over an open page:

> . . . bright candles
> over the holy white scriptures.[31]

For the northern Christian lived in a half-pagan world where his visions still escaped the unconscious moulding force of centuries of the Christianization of the imagination. Vision and icon did not coincide, as they did in the calm, classical faces that ringed the imagination of Mediterranean

29. Cited in H. I. Marrou, *A History of Education in Antiquity* (London, 1956), p. 333.

30. *Vita Bonifacii auctore Willibaldo*, ed. W. Levison, Monumenta Germaniae Historica in usum scholarum (Hanover, 1915), p. 51.

31. Cited by Beryl Smalley, *The Study of the Bible in the Middle Ages* (Oxford, 1952), p. xi.

men. If he dreamed of supernatural presences, these were as likely to take the form of those totemlike animals that summed up, far more effectively than could any human face, the realities of northern life—the raven, the dragon, the ravening wolf whose sparse shape, scratched on the rocks of southern Scotland, twisted the conventional Christian lion of St Mark into a new and strangely powerful shape in the Lindisfarne Gospel book of the seventh century.

A world of hunters drew the boundary between the human and the animal differently from a world of townsmen in Byzantium. A world of poets and exquisite jewellers knew how formal qualities of ornament could create a vision of their own, linking the strange half-human forms of the new figures of the Christian faith to the sure-footed procession of holy words across those white pages among which, as in the lines of an Irish poet, the deer, the salmon, the great hunting dog run and leap. The craftsmanship itself—a craftsmanship that still carried an aura of quasi-magical powers—and not any vision mediated in paint made the Celtic Gospel book a holy thing in an unholy world. The book of Durrow, we learn from Professor McNeill, 'did duty as a magic cure for cattle'[32] until it found its way into Trinity College, Dublin, where it now lies, in tasteful impotence, beneath glass.

With this in mind we can turn over the pages of the superb reproduction of the Book of Kells and savour to the full the wisdom of Françoise Henry's remarkable commentary, which drives home the essence of the great book and so helps us to grasp what distinguished the Celtic tradition of religious art from its Mediterranean counterpart. We have an art where not every detail is caught in the fine meshes of a long-prepared iconographic tradition. There is room for the greatest diversity, even for lack of orientation, and so for the elaboration of totally unexpected versions of ancient themes. St Mark and his lion intertwine on plate 51, 'irreverent perhaps to our stilted minds, though it must have looked simpler and commonplace to the freer imagination of the paint-

32. McNeill, *The Celtic Churches*, p. 125.

er.'[33] The unknowable Trinity plays hide and seek with us from behind a letter, on plate 12.

There are 'weight free' areas, totally unconcerned to communicate any religious message. These 'give us a glimpse of the farmyard which was no doubt attached to the monastery',[34] where we meet an old acquaintance of the Atlantic—the barnacle goose. Ultimately, the letters count for most. The majority of the pages of the Book of Kells are devoted to the text of the Gospels. This text is of greater beauty and certainty of touch than are the few great pages of virtuoso illumination which form the normal subject of reproductions of this manuscript. A superb calligraphy enshrines the religious joy of a page covered with holy words. It is a singular merit of this edition that we should be given a fair share of such pages, and the analysis of the differing scribes at work upon them is a high point in Françoise Henry's commentary.

The Evangelists gave this book to the world. Portrayed in the weird totemic shapes they had taken in the vision of the Apocalypse, they stand in serried ranks behind the Gospel Book: 'the great commotion of the fiery cloud still seems to linger about them.'[35]

So here we have two worlds of religious experience and of artistic expression. Each joins religious experience and artistic expression on different terms. Byzantium assumes a synthesis based on the total Christianization of the imagination. In the Celtic world, by contrast, we find confrontations and recalcitrant outcrops of untamed nature. When Professor McNeill writes that the Celtic saints managed 'to implant and preserve a Christian culture like a cultivated garden amid a wilderness of disorder'[36] one wonders whether this is, after all, the true measure of their success. It might lie elsewhere. A 'cultivated garden' is not always the best environment for growth and creativity. In the study of the northern world of the early Middle Ages, it is the weeds that blow in over the fence from the 'wilderness of disorder' that made the Celtic

33. Henry, *The Book of Kells*, p. 208.   34. Ibid., p. 200.
35. Ibid., p. 197.   36. McNeill, *The Celtic Churches*, p. 86.

churches so immeasurably rich and robust. The very uncertainty and recalcitrance to Christianity of much of the ornament of the Book of Kells is one such vigorous weed: the rare beauty of the book depends on Christian monks who have not lost touch with skills that reached back to prehistory. It is the same with the vernacular literature of the British Isles in the early medieval period: the rank weeds of Anglo-Saxon and Old Irish epic sprouted happily in the monastic garden.[37]

These books, therefore, raise the problem of the role of religion in very different societies. In the one, men choose to live by a tradition that is quietly and insistently mobilized toward a single, sacred goal. In another, the restless solidities of daily life find an utterly unself-conscious expression among the lines of holy texts. And in that northern society of the monks who produced the Book of Kells, sacred and profane have fought themselves to a draw—and so we find men passing quietly backward and forward from figures still glowing from the glory of the vision, to the crouched hare, the poultry in the yard, and the barnacle goose.

> A hedge of trees is all around;
> The blackbird's praise I shall not hide;
> Above my book so smoothly lined
> The birds are singing far and wide;
> In a green cloak of bushy boughs
> The cuckoo pipes his melody.
> Be good to me, God, on judgment day!—
> How well I write beneath the trees.[38]

37. Patrick Wormald, 'Bede, Beowulf and the Conversion of the Anglo-Saxon Aristocracy', *Bede and Anglo-Saxon England*, ed. R. T. Farrell (British Archaeological Reprints, 1978), pp. 32–95.

38. Frank O'Connor, *The Little Monasteries* (Dublin, 1963), p. 9.

Relics and Social Status
in the Age of Gregory of Tours[†]

I N OFFERING FOR THE STENTON LECTURE THE TITLE
of *Relics and Social Status in the Age of Gregory of Tours*,[1] I
have been moved by a sense of the urgent need for a full
religious commentary—a *religionsgeschichtliches Kommen-*
tar—on the works of Gregory of Tours. For, to the best of
my knowledge, no consistent attempt has been made to

[†] The Stenton Lecture, 1976 (University of Reading, 1977).

1. My citations are taken throughout from the editions of Bruno Krusch, *Gre-*
gorii episcopi Turonensis Miracula et Opera Minora, *Monumenta Germaniae Historica*,
Scriptores rerum Merowingicarum I, 2 (Hanover, 1885) and Bruno Krusch and Wilhelm
Levison, *Libri historiarum*, *Monumenta Germaniae Historica*, *Scriptores rerum Merowin-*
gicarum I (2nd edition, Berlin, 1937–51). The reader will appreciate that it is not out
of affectation that I call what is generally known as *The History of the Franks* by its
more revealing original title, *Libri historiarum*. [For the translations that I now in-
clude, I have followed as far as possible those of Lewis Thorpe, *Gregory of Tours: The*
History of the Franks (Harmondsworth: Penguin Classics, 1974). Parts of the *Miracula*
are being translated by John Corbett of Scarborough College, University of Toron-
to.] Out of the large modern literature on Gregory and his age, I refer only to those
studies that have been of direct help to me. I wish to encourage the reader to go
direct to Gregory's works as a whole, as he himself would have wished (*Lib. hist.*
XI, 31, 536ff.) and as his finest modern exegete has insisted, see J. M. Wallace-
Hadrill, 'The Work of Gregory of Tours in the Light of Modern Research', T.R.H.S.
5, I (1951), in *The Long-Haired Kings* (London, 1962), pp. 49–70 at p. 70. I am now
grateful to Sofia Boesch Gaetano, *Il santo nella visione storiografica di Gregorio di Tours*,
Atti del XII Convegno storico internazionale dell'Accademia Tudertina, Todi 1971,
which was unavailable to me at the time of writing. [So much of the work of this
article is incorporated and expanded in parts of my *The Cult of the Saints: Its Rise and*
Function in Latin Christianity (Chicago, 1981) that it is not necessary to refer to the
pages in that book in which the themes of this study are dealt with in greater detail.]

organize around this singularly rich text the vast erudition amassed in this century on the religious ideas and practices of Late Antiquity. Nor has any consequential attempt been made to seize the incidents and attitudes revealed in the works of Gregory of Tours in a human or social context of satisfying precision. Instead, a tradition of interpretation that is inclined to join, as in a maximum and minimum thermometer, the low ebb of Gregory's Latinity with the high tide of his credulity still rests heavily on the subject.[2]

In the course of one lecture, I can only point to the shape of this lacuna: I cannot dare to fill it. I shall proceed by asking questions and by drawing attention to paradoxes. I will begin by evoking the intrinsic content of the sixth-century belief in relics. Then I will go on to discuss the subjective attitudes which this belief crystallized, the precise nature of that *reverentia* which, in the opinion of Gregory, the relic demanded. Lastly, I shall attempt to point out how the contours of a belief in relics and the attitude and behaviour expected to follow from such a belief, played a part in the attempt of the bishops of sixth-century Gaul to define and stabilize their status.

I suggest that we begin with tombs. Gregory's world is full of tombs. They stood in the shady corners of the great basilicas, in crypts, scattered in the great dormitory suburbs of the dead outside the town, or they lay hidden in the brambles of some deserted village.[3] Take the mausoleum in the basilica of St Venerandus at Clermont: 'Where there are many tombs of carved Parian marble, in which no small number of

2. Bruno Krusch, 'Kulturbilder aus dem Frankenreiche zur Zeit Gregors von Tours. Ein Beitrag zur Geschichte des Aberglaubens', *Sitzungsberichte der Berliner Akademie der Wissenschaften. Philol.-Hist. Klasse* (1934): 785–800 at p. 789: 'Der Aberglaube erreicht bei Gregor einen Grad, der nicht mehr steigerungsfähig zu sein scheint'. [The equation becomes more confident as the author addresses a more elementary audience: for example, C. Warren Hollister, *Medieval Europe* (New York, 1978): 'Yet Gregory's *History* is written in ungrammatical Latin and is filled with outrageous and silly miracles' (p. 41).]

3. Mary Vieillard-Troiekouroff, *Les monuments religieux de la Gaule d'après les oeuvres de Grégoire de Tours* (Paris, 1976) now provides an exhaustive catalogue.

holy men and religious ladies lie. There is no doubt that they were Christians, for the images on the tombs show the miracles of the Lord and His Apostles.'[4]

On such tombs, therefore, men of the sixth century could see the primal scenes of deliverance and healing. The blind, the crippled, the possessed, even the dead spring to new life under the outstretched hand of Christ. Gregory prefaced his *De gloria martyrum* with a tense, compact sentence summing up these miracles:[5] they are the overture of Gregory's hagiographic work. Could such scenes be reenacted in his own day?[6] This is the first question.

The second comes from the inscriptions on the tombs. Like all late Roman epitaphs, these did not stint themselves in their certainty about the fate and the merits of the occupant.[7] They reiterated a dizzy paradox: the body was in the tomb, the soul was in the stars.[8]

> hoc tomolo cuius tantum nam membra quiescunt
> letatur patria mens, paradise, tua.[9]

For sixth-century men the question is not ours—did they really? But, given that some could, who precisely had? Out of all those great tombs, the epitaph of each proclaiming that

4. *De gloria martyrum*, 66, 83.　　5. *Glor. mart.*, 2, 38–39.

6. The re-enactment of miracles was mediated by the solemn readings of the miracles of the saints, as at the tomb of Saint Martin at Tours: *De virtutibus Martini* II, 43, 174: 'quotiens hic prophetarum et sublimium virorum virtutes olim gestas legimus, renovari miramur' ('As often as we read here of the miraculous works of the prophets and the great men of old, so are we amazed to see these miracles played out again in our own time'), v. inf. n. 26.

7. *De gloria confessorum*, 41, 324: 'quis qualis quantusque fuerit iuxta saeculi dignitatem sepulchrum eius hodie patefecit, quod marmore Phario sculptum renitet.' ('What sort of person he was and how much dignity he enjoyed as a man of the world is made plain today by his tomb, which is carved in shining Parian marble'.)

8. G. Sanders, *Licht en Duisternis in de christelijke Grafschriften* (Brussels, 1965), esp. pp. 502–13.

9. E. Diehl, *Inscriptiones Latinae Christianae veteres*, I (Berlin, 1924), no. 149, 9–10. 'You, whose limbs alone lie in this tomb, your soul rejoices in its homecountry, Paradise.' Compare *Corpus Inscriptionum Latinarum*, xiii, 2395 on Rusticus of Lyon (died 501): 'astra fovent animam corpus natura recepit.' ('The stars nurture the soul and nature has received the body.')

the souls of the dead rested in the stars, in which one had this really happened?

Basically this is what a tomb and its relic—its *reliquiae*, its human remains—was: a *locus* where earth and heaven met in the person of the dead, made plain by some manifestation of supernatural power—some *virtus*—of some *miraculum*, some wonderful happening: 'What sort of reward he has in heaven is shown at his grave; the power coming out of his tomb declares him to be living in paradise.'[10] This precisely is what the tomb enclosing the body of St Martin was for Gregory:

> Hic conditus est sanctae memoriae Martinus episcopus
> cuius anima in manu Dei est sed hic totus est
> praesens manifestus omni gratia virtutum.[11]

and the great tower to the east of the basilica pointed upwards, 'like a crag of gold', to the sky behind which the soul of Martin now blazed in glory.[12]

Gregory was oppressed by how infinitesimally small the number of such tombs must be.[13] For these were the tombs of the predestinate; they belonged to the 'snow-white num-

10. *Glor. conf.*, 52, 329. On the meaning of *reliquiae* now see John M. Mc-Culloh, 'The Cult of Relics in the Letters and Dialogues of Pope Gregory the Great: A Lexicographical Study', *Traditio* XXXII (1975): 145–84, at pp. 153–56. As the author points out, however, Gregory of Tours differs in his usage from Gregory the Great by speaking frequently of *pignora* for relics.

11. E. Le Blant, *Les inscriptions chrétiennes de la Gaule*, I (Paris, 1856), no. 178, 240: 'Here lies Martin the bishop, of holy memory, whose soul is in the hand of God; but he is fully here, present and made plain in miracles of every kind.' The opinion is high-lighted by the scepticism of a Jewish doctor, *Virt. Mart.*, II, 50, 194: 'Martinus enim tibi nihil proderit, quem terra obpraemens terrenum fecit . . . non enim poterit mortuus viventibus tribuere medecinam.' ('Martin will do you no good, on whom the earth now rests, turning him to earth . . . a dead man can give no healing to the living.')

12. *Sermo de combustione basilicae sancti Martini*, *P.L.* 133, 733. See M. Vieillard-Troiekouroff, *Monuments religieux*, p. 398.

13. This great sadness affected others differently. It is understandable that a priest in Tours could be uncertain as to whether the average Christian could ever rise from the dead: *Lib. hist.*, X, 13, 496: 'Quod dominus in adsumpto homine mortuus fuerit ac resurrexerit non ambigo; illud tamen, quod reliqui resurgunt mortui, non admitto.' ('I do not doubt that our Lord Himself, as incarnate man, died and rose again; but I can't accept that all the other dead will rise.')

ber of the elect'.[14] A chill breath blows through Gregory's works, as he contemplates the vast anonymity of cemeteries. The silence of the Polyandrion—the Place of the Great Majority—at Autun, is broken only by a few mysterious echoes of chanted psalms, betraying the presence, among thousands, 'of a few tombs of faithful souls worthy of God'.[15]

Standing out against this sombre background, however, the tombs of the Very Special Dead are the vehicles of a poetic imagery of surprisingly intimate power. The miracles of Gregory of Tours are poetry in action. We should not be more brutish than were the men of the sixth century in our image of the working of the saints. Like their clients, saints could be hard men, or were imagined as such: 'This Lupus will not stretch out his hands from the tomb, this day, to snatch you from my hands.'[16]

Perhaps because this strikes us as so strange, we rather tend to revel in it, and to give such incidents undue prominence. In the majority of miracles described by Gregory we are not as far as we might think from the *dulcedo* of Venantius Fortunatus. It is conventional to contrast Venantius, the sleek classical Italian, with the proto-medieval rigours of Gregory.[17] Both are Late Antique men in one vital respect: both have performed the extraordinary emotional feat of turning the *summum malum* of physical death into that into which all that is beautiful and refined in the life of their age can be condensed. In the miracles of Gregory we enter a world as

14. *Vitae Patrum*, 1 Praef., 213.   15. *Glor. conf.*, 72, 341.
16. *Glor. conf.*, 66, 337.
17. E.g., R. Vinay, *San Gregorio di Tours* (Turin, 1940), pp. 96–97 on Gregory's acceptance of the *feretas* and *strenuetas* of the Franks. F. Prinz, *Frühes Mönchtum im Frankenreich* (Munich, 1965), p. 480, speaks of the 'more primitive religiosity' of the Merovingian age as summed up by Gregory: 'So ist der grosser Turoner Bischof auch als Schriftsteller seiner frankischer Gegenwart und der Zukunft stärker zugeordnet als der spätantik-gallorömischen Vergangenheit, der er nach Bildung und Herkunft entstammte.' Such sharp antitheses between 'Late Antique' and 'early medieval' elements in the culture of the late sixth century can be misleading, as has recently been shown for Byzantium also by Averil Cameron, 'Corippus' Poem on Justin II: A Terminus of Antique Art?' *Annali della scuola normale superiore di Pisa*, ser. iii, V (1975): 129–65.

bright and as shimmering as a mosaic-laden church: sweet perfume,[18] trees that blossom like doves' down,[19] dried out lilies that spring up once a year around the tomb, as a potent image of how the dead man within 'flourishes like a palm tree in paradise.'[20] As Aredius of Limoges, a connoisseur of the *bouquet* of the holy, said: 'These are certain to be relics, which the martyr has marked out by a touch of paradise': *paradisiacis virtutibus illustravit.*[21] We get closer to the aesthetics of the sixth century in Gregory's miracles than in most other sources. Their taste is rather *art nouveau*. Take Gregory of Langres—'His blessed face was so filled with glory that it looked like a rose. It was deep rose red, and the rest of his body was glowing white like a lily.'[22] It is a warm echo of tastes which Virgil had once shared.

The aesthetic was based on the denial that the death of the Very Special Dead had anything to do with the observed effects of the death of the average Christian. When the tomb of a martyr is visited 'everyone of our party filled our nostrils with the scent of lilies and roses.'[23] When a priest at Clermont was locked up in a tomb of Parian marble by his bishop, 'the remains of the dead man, as he used afterwards to relate, gave out a mortal stench which caused a tremor not only in his external organs of sense, but in his very vitals.'[24] Late Antique people knew it: witness the pathetic little phials

18. *Lib. hist.*, II, 16, 64, on the basilica of Namatius at Clermont: 'Terror namque ibidem Dei et claritas magna conspicitur, et vere plerumque inibi odor suavissimus quasi aromatum advenire a religiosis sentitur.' ('In it one is conscious of the fear of God and of a great brightness, and those at prayer are often aware of a most sweet and aromatic odour which is being wafted towards them.') *Lib. hist.*, II, 31, 77, on the ceremonial of the baptism of Clovis: 'talemque ibi gratiam adstantibus tribuit, ut aestimarent se paradisi odoribus collocari.' ('God filled the hearts of all present with such grace that they imagined themselves to have been transported to some perfumed paradise.') *Glor. conf.*, 94, 359: 'cumque Davitici carminis laudationem clerici canere coepissent odor suavitatis in basilicam sancti advenit.' ('When the clergy began to chant David's Psalms of praise, a sweet odour came into the basilica.') For paradise as a mountain heavy with fragrance: Robert Murray, *Symbols of Church and Kingdom. A Study in Early Syriac Tradition* (Cambridge, 1975), p. 261.

19. *Glor. mart.*, 90, 98.   20. *Glor. conf.*, 50, 328.

21. *De virtutibus Juliani*, 41, 131.   22. *Vit. Patr.*, vii, 3, 238.

23. *Glor. conf.*, 40, 323.   24. *Lib. hist.*, IV, 12, 143.

of perfume placed in the graves of children in the fourth-century Christian cemetery excavated at Pécs.[25]

The thought of the physical death and dismemberment of their heroes, blocked out as irrelevant to themselves, became all the more operative on deeper layers of the imagination of the hearers. The actual imaginative content of the *Passiones*, the 'sufferings', read out at the Festivals of the Martyrs would repay close attention. Many cures coincide exactly with the reading of the *Passio*.[26] This would be a moment of high excitement. But perhaps we can be more precise: what excitement in particular? First, and foremost, triumph: the re-enactment of the martyr's power to triumph over suffering and disintegration. Second, the re-enactment and the resolution of this suffering. Of the Coptic passions of the martyrs, those that recount the most grisly details of the breaking up and the miraculous putting together of the martyr's body are those most closely associated with healing shrines.[27] Thus, many of the cures which Gregory experienced himself were connected with a precise and congruent moment of suffering in the martyr. At Brioude he was cured of a splitting headache caused by sunstroke after dousing his head in the fountain of St Julian—that is, in the water where the martyr's own head had been washed clean after the ultimate headache of decapitation.[28]

Cure, therefore, was associated with the mobilizing of the precise associations connected with a holy object. Furthermore, it was an entering into relation with a holy person. For the dead were, also, persons. Indeed the cult of the saints in sixth-century Gaul is an illustration of that ancient and poignant theme—the quest for the Ideal Companion.[29] The saints, said Ambrose (displaying his usual acumen on the workings of the Mediterranean family), were the only rela-

25. F. Fülep, 'Késörómai temetö Pécs', *Archaeologiai Értesitö* XCVI (1969): 3–42.

26. E.g., *Virt. Jul.*, 16, 121; *Virt. Mart.*, II, 14, 163; 29, 170, 49, 176.

27. T. Baumeister, *Martyr Invictus* (Munster, 1972), p. 169.

28. *Virt. Jul.*, 25, 125.

29. For the late classical background, see A. D. Nock, 'The Emperor's Divine *Comes*', *Journal of Roman Studies* XXXIX (1947): 102–16 in *Essays on Religion and the*

tives that you were free to choose.[30] Their protection had the intimacy of a surrogate kinsman. Such intimacy was needed. For the great basilicas could be grim places. A human refuse tip was piled up against their walls. These were the incurable cripples who had not even come for cures: they had just been dumped there by their families so that they could at least have a chance of begging enough to eat from the visitors.[31] A woman 'put on show' in this way by her relatives at the basilica at Brioude dreamed of St Julian: 'He was tall, he was spotlessly dressed and suave, he had a lit-up face, blonde hair greying slightly, brisk in his movements, smooth spoken and charming to talk to; his complexion was brighter than a lily, so that out of all the thousands of men she had ever seen, she had never seen the like of him.' And he gave her his arm, and led her to the tomb—and she woke up cured.[32] We should bear this in mind. A bishop like Gregory was not only the awesome official representative of St Martin.[33] His life and his sensibilities were constantly moulded by a network of intense relations with his invisible companions. Scratch a bishop, and we often find, to our surprise, the susceptible hero worshipper—the *peculiaris alumnus* of a martyr.[34]

Given these intrinsic qualities in the dead, how in fact did men relate themselves to them? Here we should be careful. It

---

Ancient World, ed. Zeph Stewart (Oxford, 1972), pp. 653–75; S. G. MacCormack, 'Roma, Constantinopolis, the Emperor and His Genius', *Classical Quarterly* XXV (1975): 68–72.

30. Ambrose, *De viduis*, XI, 54; *P.L.*, xvi, 250.

31. *Virt. Jul.*, 9, 118; 12, 119; *Virt. Mart.* I, 31, 153; 40, 154.

32. *Virt. Jul.*, 9, 118.

33. As in the incident in *Lib hist.*, VIII, 6, 374: 'Ecce a domino meo in legatione ad te directus sum.' ('Listen . . . I have been sent by my master to give you a message.') But the remark is a joke. The context shows that Guntram expected that Gregory had been 'put up' to making a petition by a human rival. He did not expect the *dominus* of Gregory to have been St Martin. 'Cui ego subridens, Beatus Martinus, inquio, misit me.' ('I answered with a smile: "It was Saint Martin who told me to come."')

34. See the will of Bertram of Le Mans, who leaves a hundred *solidi*, 'ad sepulcrum domni et peculiaris patroni sancti Martini antistitis ubi comam deposui' ('to the tomb of my lord and special protector St Martin the bishop, where I laid down my hair' [by receiving the tonsure]). Aredius of Limoges is seen in this way by

is a reflex of historians of distant periods to assume that what they themselves do not possess the men of the past had in superabundance. Credulity, carefully discouraged in themselves, is allowed to rage without limit throughout sixth-century Gaul: 'La crédulité est la caractéristique essentielle de l'époque franque, qui semble vivre dans un rêve et ignorer les lois même les plus élémentaires du monde extérieure.'[35]

This judgement puts an emphasis on a subjective capacity for religious emotion that is inappropriate to the study of ancient and of much medieval religion. Gregory, at least, was not interested in so vague a concept. He wanted something precise—*reverentia*. *Reverentia* is a key word to Gregory's religious world. It meant, as far as I can see, the focusing of belief onto precise, if invisible, objects, in such a way as to lay the participant under specific obligations, to commit him to definite rhythms in his life, to lead him to react to emergency in a specific way, and to cause him to be aware of his actions and the actions of others as being divided between good and bad fortune in direct relation to his good and bad relations with this specific, if invisible, object. *Reverentia* would vary over a wide spectrum. This spectrum could be seen as so many differing forms of etiquette towards the supernatural that gave structure to life, to experience and to remembered happenings. Its natural antithesis was *rusticitas*, which is best translated as 'boorishness', 'slipshodness'—the failure, or the positive refusal, to give life structure in terms of relations with specific supernatural landmarks.

Gregory's use of *rusticitas* points to a situation which requires great delicacy of interpretation.[36] A sharp dichotomy between 'town' and 'country,' 'Christian' and 'pagan' does

---

Gregory: *Virt. mart.*, III, 24, 188. Gregory himself is seen as the *alumnus* of St Julian (from Brioude), by Venantius Fortunatus: *carmen*, V, 3, 11: 'Martino proprium mittit Julianus alumnum'. ('Julian sends to Martin his very own protégé.') See below, p. 241, n. 74.

35. A. Marignan, *Études sur la civilisation française. Le culte des saints sous les Mérovingiens* (Paris, 1889), p. 33.

36. J. Le Goff, 'Paysans et monde rural dans la littérature du haut moyen-âge', *Settimane di Studi sull'Alto Medio Evo* XIII (1966): 723–41 and 'Culture cléricale et

not do justice to its nuances. For *rusticitas* overlapped with the habits of the rural population; but it by no means coincided exclusively with them. In the same way, patterns of life and systems of cure and of the explanation of misfortune associated with *rusticitas* were usually inherited from the past; but it is only in that diluted sense that they can be called 'pagan'. We have a world where a Catholic structuring of life and of the use of time, associated with the observance of holy days, and a Catholic system for the explanation and reversal of misfortune are assumed to embrace the whole of society, but to admit greater and lesser degrees of applicability. The grid becomes noticeably weaker as the distance increases from the controls exerted by the life of a Catholic town.[37] Most men found themselves on a slippery slope, that pointed downwards to *rusticitas*: and the fact that the career of the average man could take him either to the town or out into the countryside did heighten awareness of this slope.[38] In all strata of society, however, the Catholic grid met with forms of unwillingness to participate fully in its controls; and, in the minds of most, it had to coexist uneasily with alternative systems of explanation. Claudius riding to Tours to bring Eberulf, dead or alive, from the sanctuary of St Martin, is one example among many in the works of Gregory: 'Upon his way, after the custom of the barbarians, he began to take notice of omens and find them unfavourable. At the same time he enquired of many whether the power of the holy martyr had of late been made manifest against breakers of

---

tradition folklorique dans la civilisation mérovingienne', *Annales* XXII (1967): 780–91.

37. Caesarius of Arles, *Sermo*, 44, 7, ed. G. Morin, Corpus Christianorum 103, I (Turnholt, 1953), p. 199. The contrast is between *sapientes* who know how to avoid intercourse on Sundays and *rustici* who lack self-control.

38. *Vit. Patr.*, ix, I, 252: 'Discede longius, o rustice. Tuum est enim opus oves pascere, meum (vero) litteris exerceri; qua de re nobiliorem me ispius officii cura facit.' ('Move away, you yokel. Your job is to pasture the sheep, while mine is to learn letters, by which I have been made more noble than to do such a chore.')—said one man to his own brother. Gregory adds: 'Erant enim non quidem nobilitate sublimes, ingenui tamen.' ('For they were neither of them members of the high nobility, but were free-born men.')

oaths.'[39] Thus, large areas of Gallic society can exist as a nadir of *reverentia* without practising any form of pagan worship. Gregory's choice of enemies throws into high relief the content of his belief that life made sense in terms of a Catholic *reverentia*. For these enemies are the bearers of alternative systems of explanation—the soothsayer, the folk-doctor and (quite as important for Gregory, because also the bearer of a rival system of cure and explanation) the Christian popular prophet[40], or they are those on whom *reverentia* exerted a low gravitational pull—the perjurer[41] and those who work[42] or copulate[43] on forbidden days. They are not the rural pagan priest or the smoking country altar.

At a simple level, *reverentia* meant the use of the sign of the cross in all life's emergencies; and *rusticitas* meant, for instance, poking sly fun at people who did.[44] It meant taking one's dreams seriously even if they involved having to move out of a cottage because a relic had spent the night in its granary: 'He took no notice of the vision . . . *ut habet rusticitas.*'[45] Any gaffe in the punctilio demanded by the supernatural was *rusticitas*. So Gregory himself could commit *rusticitas* as much as anyone. A fragment of silk wrappings of the Holy Cross at Tours caused him a moment's hesitation: 'Not being in the know, we found it hard to believe': *apud rusticitatem nostram incredibile haberetur.*[46]

Rusticitas, therefore, was a refusal to see the world as intelligible; and *reverentia* was a tacit agreement that life was intelligible in terms which Gregory laid out in no uncertain manner. Put briefly: a world made intelligible in terms of *reverentia* was a world where fortune and misfortune were thought of as so many direct and palpable consequences of the remission and the retribution of sin. Gregory's work, therefore, emerges as the culmination of an attempt by gen-

39. *Lib. hist.*, VII, 29, 347.
40. *Virt. Jul.*, 45, 131; 46, 132; *Virt. mart.*, 1, 26, 151; *Vit. Patr.*, ix, 2, 254 (a prophetess emerges at a time of plague); *Lib. hist.*, VII, 44, 365, ix; 6, 417.
41. *Glor. conf.*, 28, 315.   42. *Glor. conf.*, 80, 89.
43. *Virt. mart.*, iii, 45, 89.   44. *Vit. Patr.*, x, 1, 256.
45. *Glor. mart.*, 37, 70.   46. *Glor. mart.*, 5, 41.

erations of Christian preachers to render human life as lived in Gaul explicable exclusively in terms of sin and its consequences.[47] It was an attempt which cut across all other previous schemes of explanation.[48] The distinction of barbarian and Roman, of upper and lower class, of town and country, of good Latin and the *sermo rusticus*—all these categories faded into unimportance, in the works of Gregory of Tours, compared with the comprehensive ravages of sin.

Gregory's *Libri historiarum* is a book about many things. Part of the secret of its narrative power, of its free-ranging curiosity and of the delightful lack of shame which it betrays at every turn, is that it is an attempt to make the world intelligible in terms of new organizing principle: *reverentia*, sin and misfortune. Human action is freed from the Late Antique carapace of cultural and ethnic criteria. Instead men are remembered above all for their misfortunes, and for those known breaches of *reverentia* by which they had exposed themselves to these misfortunes. Throughout the *Libri historiarum* Gregory puts two and two together. Whenever we get a catalogue of Frankish or Roman swine, we may be sure that a notable misfortune is on its way, and not only that Gregory will tell it well, but that Gregory knows exactly why it happened and will tell you so at the end, in one lapidary sentence. Guntram Boso was smoked out of the bishop's palace and died so stuck with spears that he could not even keel over and fall to the ground: 'Fuit autem hic in actu levis, avariciae rerum alienarum ultra modum cupidus, omnibus iurans et nulli promissa adimplens . . . Ariolus et sortis saepe utebatur, ex quibus futura cognoscere cupiens, remansit inlusus.'[49]

47. For this reason I am unconvinced by the contrast between Gregory and the preachers of an earlier age as drawn by F. Prinz, *Frühes Mönchtum*, pp. 479–81, and would accept the more balanced judgement of J. M. Wallace-Hadrill, 'Gregory of Tours and Bede', *Frühmittelalterliche Studien* II (1968) in *Early Medieval History* (London, 1976), p. 102: 'He comes within measurable distance, whether consciously I cannot be sure, of the teaching tradition of Caesarius of Arles.'

48. The absence of traditional classical sources and of traditional criteria also struck M. Oldoni, 'Gregorio di Tours e i *Libri Historiarum*', *Studi Medievali*, 3, XIII (1972), esp. p. 599.

49. *Lib. hist.*, IX, 10, 425. 'Guntram Boso was an unprincipled sort of man,

One might not have needed the bishop of Tours to tell you that Guntram Boso had it coming to him. Gregory is at his best, rather, when the links between sin and retribution are less visible to the naked eye. Here we have Gaul laid bare beneath the gaze of a man who believes that nothing happens by accident. Palladius Count of Javols committed suicide. Gregory knew why. He had called the bishop a pansy and had said: 'Where are your husbands, with whom you live like a slut?'[50] Now we know: 'quod non ob aliam causam nisi ob iniuriam episcopi haec ei evenisse.'

Gregory obeys the law of all hagiography. He makes the world explicable in relation to a single fixed point: it is a method summed up by Lewis Carroll in the *Hunting of the Snark*:

> There was also a Beaver who stood on the deck
> Or sat making lace in the bow
> And had often the Bellman said,
> Saved them from wreck,
> Though none of the sailors knew how.

Gregory wrote to tell how.

To connoisseurs of Gregory this is a digression. But it is necessary for our argument. The *reverentia* which was accorded to saints in the sixth century should not be seen as some luxurious undergrowth of credulity or neo-paganism:[51] it was

---

greedy and avaricious, coveting beyond measure the goods of other people, giving his word to all, keeping his promises to none . . . It was his habit to consult fortune tellers and to put his trust in sorcery, in an attempt to foresee the future, but this gave him little solace.'

50. *Lib. hist.*, IV, 39, 170. 'It is clear that this fate befell him only because he had wronged his bishop.'

51. As A. Marignan, *Le culte des saints*, pp. 28–29: 'On peut donc dire que peu de choses sont nouvelles dans la piété de l'époque mérovingienne'; and recently, J. M. Wallace-Hadrill, 'Early Medieval History', *Early Medieval History* (London, 1976), p. 3: 'We begin to see the saint for what he really was: successor to the local pagan divinity, some of whose attributes he might inherit. If anywhere, there is continuity here.' F. Graus, *Volk, Herrscher und Heiliger im Reich der Merowinger* (Prague, 1965), pp. 171–96 is rightly more cautious. There is a danger of underestimating the discontinuity in belief and practice implied in the worship of a *human* figure (the saint) as orchestrated by a living human representative (the bishop).

a highly structured matter—it involved specific rhythms of life and a conscious and relatively novel determination on the part of articulate Christian leaders to put two and two together in one particular way and no other. Just as the seemingly effortless fertility of the Mediterranean landscape easily makes us forget the back-breaking skills of terracing and dry farming involved, until we look outside the fields to the vast scrub lands beyond, so the *reverentia* of Gregory of Tours is set in a potential wilderness. A veritable *garrigue* of *rusticitas* hemmed in this carefully tended garden. It was a seemingly endless prospect. A Breton count had used a church vessel as a footbath, hoping to be cured by it: 'Stulti et inertes non cognoscentes quod sacrata Deo vasa non debeant ad usus humanos aptari.' It did him no good: 'Sed et Langobardorum ducem fecisse similiter comperi.'[52] Arians, for instance, had no *reverentia*. This meant not only that they looted Catholic churches and broke Catholic sanctuary (Visigothic treasures could contain 60 chalices, 50 patens, 20 gospel cases).[53] But when they had done it, they cheerfully refused to relate life's misfortunes to what had happened. 'Have you ever heard such a thing! Just listen to what the Romans would say. They say I am down with fever because I took away their property. A fever is just one of those things that happen to a body [iuxta consuetudinem humani corporis accidit]. They won't have it back while I am alive.'[54]

The maintenance of *reverentia*, at first sight so seemingly spontaneous, was a plant that needed careful pruning. Without it, relics would have enjoyed no status, and so the tombs of the dead might have lain unnoticed forever in their places. For Gregory was acutely aware that the tombs of the holy dead might lack the reverence to which they were entitled. His own age had seen an improvement in the standard of *reverentia*.[55] The integration of the idealized holy figures and

52. *Glor. mart.*, 84, 95. 'Stupid and limited in mind, not knowing that vessels consecrated to God should not be applied to human uses. But I have heard that a Lombard duke has done the same thing.'
53. *Lib. hist.*, III, 10, 107.   54. *Glor. mart.*, 78, 91.
55. *Glor. conf.*, 29, 316, on the tomb of Stremonius at Issoire: 'ad quod cruda

objects we have described depended, therefore, on a large measure of hard work on the part of the human community. It is to this that we must now turn.

Relics needed status. By and large, Gregory is no Pausanias and no Agnellus: he is not the loving describer of immemorial cult sites. The festal atmosphere of St Julian's shrine at Brioude or happy messing about in the tombs in Tours are rarities in his account. The dominant note of his hagiographical work is of the sudden discovery of long lost saints, dramatic arrivals of relics from distant regions, the discovery of *passiones* that gave face and drama to the long forgotten dead, the miracles which ratify the establishment of new cults. It is a world of movement. We are often on the roads of Gaul and Italy. New things are always happening. New forms of *gloria* are 'revealed,' 'shine forth'. These are ratified in festivals, in dramatic readings of the *passiones*, in churches with shimmering mosaics and with verse inscriptions.[56] We have a febrile sensibility, closer to the world of Counter-Reformation Baroque than to any image of a timeless cult site. The *De gloria martyrum* is a book about the tapping of new resources. It is written to make plain the miracles which up to now had lain undiscovered, and which God was deigning to increase every day.[57] In his own times, Gregory thought, the earth was giving up rich treasures of ideal beauty and healing. It was even a world of dogged prospectors. Ebergisil of Cologne had heard that St Mallosus was at Birten, where an oratory was dedicated to him. So the bishop built a basilica

---

(priorum) rusticitas, licet sciens quo quiesceret, nullum tamen ibi exhibebat honoris cultum.' ('At this grave, the men of old, in their raw boorishness, did not offer the honours of worship, although they knew where he lay.') *Glor. conf.*, 79, 347, on Ursinus of Bourges: 'non enim adhuc populus ille intellegebat sacerdotes domini venerare eisque reverentiam debitam exhibere.' ('This people had not yet understood that priests of the Lord should be venerated and that they were to show due reverence to them.') On the movement of such tombs from burial crypts up to the main basilica, see M. Vieillard-Troiekouroff, *Monuments religieux*, pp. 395–96.

56. Hence a competitive element in Gregory's fostering of the cult of St Martin, well seen by J. M. Wallace-Hadrill, *The Long-Haired Kings*, p. 70.

57. *Glor. mart.*, praef., 37–38.

and waited: 'So that, when he had received some revelation about the martyr, he could place the blessed limbs in that basilica.' A deacon of Metz had the dream. Seven feet down in the apse, they struck 'an incredibly beautiful smell'—St Mallosus. 'And they say that the martyr Victor is buried there too—but we do not know yet if he has been revealed.'[58]

This atmosphere is shown most clearly by one facet of the movement—the role of the possessed.[59] As in Late Antique society as a whole, these were the infallible seismographs of sanctity.[60] Their uninhibited and vivid cries gave:

> '. . . to airy nothing
> An earthly habitation and a name'[61]

It is the possessed who provide the high drama surrounding the arrival of the relics in new regions. So sensitive a register were the possessed, that it was they who get the date of a festival right, sensing as they did the invisible *adventus*, the approach of the saint: 'Run along, citizens; out of the village with you. Go out to greet St Vincent. Behold his coming to attend our vigils.'[62]

The possessed, however, were lucky. For the demons in

58. *Glor. mart.*, 62, 80.

59. On the shreds of the night-cap of Nicetius of Lyon (whose sanctity was far from unchallenged—see below, p. 245) see *Vit. Patr.*, viii, 7, 248: 'Posui, fateor, de his pignoribus et in aliis basilicarum altaribus in quibus inergumeni sanctum confitentur.' ('As I say, I placed some of these relics in the altars of other churches, where the possessed confess to the power of the saint.')

60. We should not think of the *inergumeni* as stray, disturbed individuals. They were a recognized group, permanently attached to the shrine, where they would be blessed daily, given food . . . and set to scrub the floors: *Statuta ecclesiae antiqua*, 62, 64, ed. G. Morin, *S. Caesarii Arelatensis Opera Varia*, II (Maredsous, 1942), pp. 94–95. Along with the beggars, they could take up stones and sticks to defend the shrine of St Martin: *Lib. hist.*, VIII, 29, 349. Some could be hired to abuse a bishop and praise his rival: *Lib. hist.*, IV, 11, 142. Others, having praised a bishop and abused a king, discreetly vanished: *Vit. patr.*, xvii, 2, 279.

61. *Virt. Jul.*, 30, 127: 'ita sanctos Dei humanis mentibus repraesentant, ut nulli sit dubium eos inibi commorari.' ('In this manner they bring the saints of God before our human minds, that there should be no doubt that they are present at their shrines.')

62. *Glor. mart.*, 89, 97.

---

them knew a good relic when they saw one. They are so important in sixth-century Gaul precisely because mere human beings did not know. As a German critic of archaeology once said, 'Töpfen haben keine Seelen'—'Pots have no souls'; and relics had no tongues. A relic that is not acclaimed is, candidly, not a relic. Even a tomb can be faceless; and, once outside the tomb, the relic and the blessed object associated with the holy is caught in a spiral of ambiguity. Indeed a whole psychology of vesting the opaque, the fragile, even the downright unpalatable with ideal qualities is at work in this: fragments of bone, such as the thumb of St John the Baptist;[63] shreds from silk hangings connected with the funeral of a holy figure or with his tomb;[64] a proliferation of candles and little flasks of oil from a shrine; the damp handkerchief with which a charwoman, locked up for the night in a crypt at Bordeaux, had wiped up the seawater which St Stephen had dropped onto the floor (for he had kept the other saints waiting for their evensong because he was rescuing a shipwreck far out at sea) and given to the bishop Bertram, 'who received it with great joy and wonder . . . and from this handkerchief many ill people received cures, and the bishop often would take scraps from it and place them in the churches which he consecrated, as relics.'[65]

Here we come, more bluntly than in most cases, to the element of purely human strategy at work on the holy. For, faced with an *embarras de richesse* of apparently indistinguishable holy objects, the local group wielded a tacit right to withhold recognition. The arrival of a relic or the establishment of a festival was an acid test of the alignments of a community. In the quaint but precise language of the anthropologist describing the *Mulid* (the birthday festival) of Sufi saints in North Africa: 'here the range of persons attending and their social relations with each other are critical and often of local level political importance. Such occasions give an op-

63. *Glor. mart.*, 13, 47.   64. E.g., *Virt. Jul.*, 34, 128.
65. *Glor. mart.*, 33, 59.

portunity for establishing, renewing, realigning or even severing social ties before an audience of significant others.'[66]

The relic of the Holy Cross arrived at St Radegund's
monastery at Poitiers, but the bishop Maroveus would not
play: 'The queen requested the bishop himself to deposit
them in the convent with chanting of psalms and all due honour.[67] But he disregarded her proposal, mounting his horse,
and going off to a country estate. The queen sent a fresh
message to King Sigibert, begging him to command one of
the bishops to place the relics in the convent with all the
honour due to them, and in compliance with her vow. The
king then enjoined the blessed Eufronius, Bishop of Tours,
to perform this task; who, coming with his clergy to Poitiers, in the absence of the bishop of their city, brought the
holy relics to the monastery with much chanting of psalms,
with pomp of gleaming tapers and incense.'[68] The relic of the
True Cross, with its clear Christian associations, its imperial
connection and its splendid Byzantine casing was about the
least ambiguous fragment of the holy available in sixth-century Gaul.[69] Yet Gregory's account is one of the slow and
canny creation and nursing of a reputation.[70] Whatever the
modern historian may have done, if confronted with a relic,
sixth-century men can be trusted to have looked their gift
horse firmly in the mouth.

'Credulity', therefore, is too flimsy a key to unlock for us
the motives of those involved in the cult of relics. Nor are we

66. Michael Gilsenan, *Saint and Sufi in Modern Egypt* (Oxford, 1973), p. 48.

67. Cf. *Concil. Epaon.* (517 A.D.), can. 25, ed. C. de Clercq, *Concilia Gal-
licana*, Corpus Christianorum 148 A (Turnholt, 1963), p. 30: 'Sanctorum reliquiae
in oratoriis villarebus non ponantur. nisi forsitan clericus cuiuscumque paroechiae
vicinus esse contingit qui sacris cineribus psallendi frequentia famuletur.' ('The relics
of the saints shall not be placed in the oratories of country-houses unless it happens
that the cleric whose diocese the estate adjoins should escort these holy ashes with a
procession and chanting of the Psalms.')

68. *Lib. hist.*, IX, 40, 464.

69. See Averil Cameron, 'The Early Religious Policies of Justin II', *Studies in
Church History* XIII (1976): 51–68.

70. *Glor. mart.*, 5, 40.

dealing with something as massive and as seemingly self-explanatory as the rallying of a whole community to some *avatar* of the protecting gods of the city. The evidence of Gregory cannot be read in so simple a manner. His works enable us to sense a more delicate and volatile element in the incorporation of a holy object in the community. For we frequently stumble upon a situation more personalized than any simple mobilization of a group for or against the relic. The arrival of the relic was an occasion to highlight the personal merits of its recipient.[71] The tenacious grip of the Gallic bishops on the reception and the distribution of relics in this period is a fact almost too big to be seen.[72] Yet the bishop never became merely transparent to the relic. The arrival of a relic was an occasion for a skilfully enacted dialogue between relic and bishop, in which the secure holiness of the one high-lighted and orchestrated the personal and, so, fragile holiness of the other. The relics of Agricola and Vitalis were fetched by Namatius to Clermont. The bishop led the procession to welcome them. The meeting was a moment for highlighting the personal quality of Namatius himself: he would not look at the relics; 'For the Lord himself judged to be blessed those who had believed what they had not seen.' A torrential rainstorm narrowly missed the ceremony; for 'with the faith of the bishop so clear for all to see, the Lord revealed the glory of his saints in that act of power'—Namatius had backed into the limelight of Agricola and Vitalis.[73]

We return, by a roundabout route, to a theme which I emphasized at the beginning. The relic may be an opaque fragment, but the saint is an Ideal Companion. We are in a

71. See Peter Brown, 'Eastern and Western Christendom in Late Antiquity: A Parting of the Ways', *Studies in Church History* XIII (1976): 18. [Above, p. 188.] The relic could declare in no uncertain manner whether it approved of its owner: Mummolus, having in a most extraordinary incident commandeered and chopped up a relic of St Sergius, took it with him, *Lib. hist.*, VII, 31, 351: 'Sed non, ut credo, cum gratia martyris, sicut in sequenti declaratum est.' ('But not with the approval of the martyr, as the remainder of the story has made clear.') Compare *Glor. mart.*, 54, 76: a woman who is given a fragment finds that she cannot ride away with it.

72. E.g., *Lib. hist.*, IX, 6, 418–19.   73. *Glor. mart.*, 43, 67.

world of men whose personal status, whose *merita*, depend on a highly personalized and intense dialogue with such Ideal Companions.[74] This streak enables us to paint an inner portrait of Gregory of Tours, for instance, quite as vivid as that of Aelius Aristides; for we can trace the rhythms of life of a sixth-century man with the same sharpness associated with the *Sacred Tales* of that florid second-century hypochondriac. It is in the hagiographical works that we meet Gregory as a little boy, having dreams as to how to cure his father of the gout:[75] sitting with his mother in front of the high-piled fire on a winter's evening, solemnly discussing the supernatural merits of St Eusebius of Vercelli[76]: Gregory living life convinced that he had too much blood in him—but avoiding blood-letting out of respect for St Martin, despite that superabundant blood that showed itself in the throb of headaches, in his mouth ulcers and in his raging toothaches;[77] Gregory gingerly, after six days of constipation, pressing the silk cloth above the tomb of St Martin to his stomach.[78]

As is so often the case in Late Antiquity, there is more to an intimate relationship with Ideal Companions than a sheltered piety. For the saints were a very special type of human being—they were those whose *merita* now stood secure in the other world.[79] The physical remains—the relics—through

74. See above, n. 29. Compare Sidonius Apollinaris, Ep., VII, 17, on abbot Abraham: 'Abraham sanctis merito sociante patronis quos tibi collegas dicere non trepidem.' ('Abraham worthy to stand beside the celestial patrons whom I shall not fear to call thy colleagues.') Supernatural guardians remained necessary in the sixth century: e.g., bishop Praetextatus on his protégé Merovech, *Lib. hist.*, V, 18, 222: 'Petii, fateor, amicitias eorum habere cum eo, et non solum hominem, sed si fas fuisset, angelum de caelo evocaveram qui esset adiutor eius.' ('I confess that I sought their friendship for him . . . Had it been right to do so, I would have asked not only mortal man, but even an angel from Heaven to come to his assistance.') The idea that merit was shown by closeness to the saints underlay the practice of *depositio ad sanctos*: e.g., Le Blant, *Inscriptions chrétiennes*, i, no. 293, p. 396: 'qui meruit sanctorum sociari sepulcris' ('whose worth ensured that he should be joined to the tombs of saints').

75. *Glor. conf.*, 39, 322.   76. *Glor. conf.*, 3, 300.

77. *Virt. mart.*, II, 60, 179; III, 60, 197; IV, 1, 199 and 2, 200.

78. *Virt. mart.*, IV, 1, 200.

79. *Virt. patr.*, xiv, 2, 268: 'Denique et aeternus Dominus, qui iugiter glorificat sanctos suos, coepit coelestem famuli meritum terrigenis declarare.' ('Then the

which this security was made manifest to human onlookers in the form of miracles, did not merely heal and bless: they answered the question of the precise *merita* of those who stood, with far less unambiguous security, at the head of the Christian communities of the Gallic towns. For the quest for *merita* was, plainly, a vexed question in the sixth century.[80] 'Merit' was a volatile substance that had to be handled with the greatest care. One man's merit might be another man's vainglory. Vainglory is a constant concern for Gregory. Some had it bad—witness the career at Clermont of the priest Cato: 'But he, all swollen and vainglorious as he was, made this answer: "Ye know by general report that from my earliest years I have ever lived according to religion; that I have fasted, and had delight in almsgiving; that many a time I have prolonged my vigils; that often I have stood the whole night through firmly chanting the psalms. Nor shall the Lord my God suffer me now to be deprived of this consecration, since I have shown so great a zeal in his service. . . ." When they heard this, the bishops departed, expressing their disgust at his vanity.'[81] Unlike Cato, Gregory learned young. He was travelling with his mother from Burgundy to Clermont and the party was hit by a storm. His mother raised her relics towards the thunderclouds, and the storm parted on either side of them. Gregory thought that this had happened because he was such a good little boy—'quia innocentiae meae Deus praestiterit, ut haec merear'; wherewith his horse slipped, and our budding saint ended up very sore indeed.[82]

What we have, therefore, is a distinctive system of re-

Everlasting God, who instantly glorifies his saints, began to make manifest to us men on earth the standing in Heaven of His servant.')

80. Viventiolus of Lyon could be described on his tomb as 'vir potens meritis nosterque sacerdos' ('a man powerful in his standing in Heaven, our own bishop'); CIL, xiii, 2396. [Compare similar usage in Venantius Fortunatus, *Carm.* III, xi, 4; xv, 2; IV, i, 7 and 31; x, 9, where *honor* is what a bishop inherits and *merita* are what he achieves by his own piety.]

81. *Lib. hist.*, IV, 6, 139.

82. *Glor. mart.*, 83, 95: 'that God might have granted it to my innocence, that I should gain a miracle'.

ligious beliefs, often expressed with great power and beauty, which hung together in such a way as to leave considerable play for precise forms of social manoeuvring. Concern with the personal merits established by contact with the supernatural is the most revealing aspect of this problem. We have seen how the relic itself and the nature of its contact with human beings was fraught with ambiguity. It is an ambiguity congruent with precisely those uncertainties of status which affected Gregory and his colleagues. It points to a zone of shadow in their public life.

For we tend to exaggerate the certainty of touch with which the bishops established their position in the Gaul of the sixth century. We assume that, for men of senatorial family, outright dominance came easily and without challenge: 'In the West, the triumph of the great landowners ensured that senatorial blood, episcopal office and sanctity presented a formidable united front.'[83] These are the words of one whose judgement was green in matters Merovingian. It has wilted considerably in the course of the years. The exact opposite may be closer to the truth. Any bishop who wished to establish himself had to draw on a wide range of frequently conflicting criteria of status. In the creation of status, public opinion counted for as much as family wealth, genealogy and an entry in Karl Stroheker's *Senatorischer Adel in Spätantiken Gallien*.

The hoarding of reputation and its rapid dispersal by others was an earnest occupation in Gregory's world. In the *Libri historiarum* we have a classic example of what every bishop, and indeed every member of the governing class of Gaul, was doing most of the time: storing up facts deeply detrimental to human nature. Gregory was the John Aubrey of the sixth century. He must have been wonderful company. Siggo the *referendarius*, seated beside him at a banquet, suddenly found that although the bishop of Tours was on his bad ear, he could hear him quite clearly; and I do not think it was

83. Peter Brown, *Religion and Society in the Age of Saint Augustine* (London, 1972), p. 131.

only the relics of St Martin hung around Gregory's neck that had made Siggo sit up and take notice.[84] Others were at it. A history of the Gallic Church by King Chilperic would have made good reading: 'In his private hours no men were more often the butt of his ridicule and his jests than the bishops. To one he imputed levity, to a second arrogance, to a third excess, to a fourth loose living; one bishop he would call a vain fool, another pompous'[85]—all of which epithets are used by Gregory of one or other of his colleagues. So would have been the account of Gregory's own family as written by Felix of Nantes: of how Gregory's brother, Peter, had killed the bishop-elect of Langres by sorcery; how he was, predictably, exonerated by his maternal uncle, Nicetius of Lyon; but was at last, rightfully, run through on the road by the son of his victim.[86] There were many such stories to be got right in sixth-century Gaul. Bishops had the awkward habit of setting to at state banquets: Bertram and Palladius, for instance; 'commoti in invicem multa sibi de adulteriis ac fornicatione exprobaverunt, nonnulla etiam de periuriis. Quibis de rebus multi ridebant.'[87] Think of Bishop Droctigisel of Soissons: 'Et licet erat vorax cibi et putator vini extra modum quam sacerdotalem cautelam decuit, tamen nullum de eo adulterium quispiam est locutus'[88]—plainly not for lack of trying. Gossip is a constant factor in the life of the sixth-century Church. It is a factor which we should take very seriously in the attempts of the bishops to establish their status in society. A century later, we are told, the bishops of Gaul wielded an impregnable sense of *das Tremendum*.[89] It is not a quality which they had learned to ascribe to each other by 590.

84. *Virt. mart.*, III, 17, 187.   85. *Lib. hist.*, VI, 46, 320.
86. *Lib. hist.*, V, 5, 200.
87. *Lib. hist.*, VIII, 7, 376: 'But they began to quarrel, accusing each other in turn of adultery and fornication, and even made accusations of perjury. Many present thought this a great joke.'
88. *Lib. hist.*, IX, 37, 457: 'Everyone agreed that he ate and drank far more than was seemly for a bishop, but no word was ever breathed against him on the score of adultery.'
89. E. Ewig, 'Milo et eiusmodi similes', *Sankt Bonifatius Gedenkgabe* (Fulda, 1954), pp. 432–33.

Hence, perhaps, the importance for such men of the cult of the saints. They, at least, were secure. They had passed the test of time. 'Call no man holy until he be dead' is the motto of Gregory's writings; and even that was 'a dam' close-run thing'. While in Syria the hillsides on which the Stylites perched on their columns would be ominously ringed by brand new, empty *martyria*, waiting to receive their guaranteed holy occupants,[90] in the world of Gregory death can mark only the beginning of long and acrimonious hagiographical manoeuvres. Was Nicetius of Lyon, who died in 573, and whose tomb lay in the basilica of the Apostles at Lyon, a saint? This was decidedly not the opinion of his successor, Priscus, nor of Priscus' wife, Susanna, nor of any of their friends and dependents. One deacon of Priscus' used the late bishop's chasuble, among other things, as a dressing gown—'A robe from whose very hems, if one was to believe aright, healing would have come to the sick'—and, when challenged, threatened to make a pair of bedroom slippers out of it.[91] Priscus and Nicetius rest together in the same church. Maybe the inscription of Priscus contains a tacit dig at his hated neighbour.[92] But time heals even sixth-century feuds. In 1308 both tombs were examined and both occupants declared saints.[93] Only readers of Gregory can guess from this one clear example the febrile and insecure accumulation and dispersal of reputation that went to make up what too often strikes the unwary as the marmoreal facade of Gallo-Roman episcopal sanctity. We are far closer than we might think, in the pages of Gregory, to the outright political propaganda associated with the lives of the *Adelsheilige* of later centuries.[94]

With these insecurities in mind, let us end by turning to

90. H. Delehaye, *Sanctus* (Brussels, 1927), p. 114.

91. *Vit. patr.*, viii, 5, 246; cf. *Lib. hist.*, IV, 36, 169.

92. *CIL*, xiii, 2399, 8: *iurgia conponens more serenifero* of Priscus may echo the *iurgia despiciens suscipiensque Deum* of Nicetius, see 2400, 20. [Above, p. 186, n. 70.]

93. G. Guige, 'Procès-verbal du xivème siècle', *Bulletin de la Societe des Antiquaires de France* (1876), pp. 145–59.

94. F. Prinz, *Frühes Mönchtum*, pp. 489–502.

the meaning of the great feasts of the saints over which the bishops of Gaul presided. We must begin by reminding ourselves that the position of any bishop in the age of Gregory of Tours depended on the magnificently open-ended formula of his election: *consensum facere*.[95] The neighbourhood had 'reached a consensus' that he should preside over them. How this *consensus* was arrived at, and in what dosage the various groups of interested participants had made their desires felt, were a matter of high politics, and so were kept decently impenetrable—even to the sharp eyes of those who write in the *Kanonistische Abteilung* of the *Savigny Stiftung*.[96]

What we should note is how very delicate and fissile the *consensus* surrounding a sixth-century bishop had remained.[97] I find it difficult to envisage for most Gallo-Roman towns what F. Prinz has recently characterized as a 'quasi innenpolitischen "translatio imperii"'.[98] I do not think that this

95. D. Claude, 'Die Bestellung der Bischöfe im merowingischen Reiche', *Zeitschrift der Savigny Stiftung für Rechtsgeschichte. Kanonistische Abteilung* XLIX (1963): 1–77, esp. p. 23: 'Der Erlangung des *consensus civium* wurde grosse Bedeutung beigemessen' and p. 25: 'Die Konzilien kennen überhaupt keinen anderen Weg zum Bistum als den über einen consensus.'

96. Thus the elements in the support claimed for Gregory of Tours escape neat categories: Venantius Fortunatus, *carmen*, V, 13, 11–15:

> Martino proprium mittit Julianus alumnum
> et fratre praebet quod sibi dulce fuit.
> quem pastoris Aegidii domino manus alma sacravit
> ut populum recreet, quem Radegundis amet.
> huic Sigibercthus ovans favet et Brunechildis honori.

('Julian sends to Martin his very own protégé, and passes on to his brother one who was his own sweet friend. A man whom the dear hand of bishop Aegidius has consecrated, so that he may bring new life to the people. A man whom Princess Radegundis loves; to his honour Sigibert gave the acclaim of his favour, along with Queen Brunhilda.')

97. The circumstances of an episcopal election did not help: *Sermo de vita Honorati*, 28, *PL*, 50, 1264–65: 'prima ei concordiae fuit et praecipuus labor fraternitatem calentibus adhuc de assumendo episcopi studiis dissidentem mutuo amore connectare.' ('His first task of bringing concord was to knit together again the brethren, among whom the dissensions caused by canvassing for who should take the post of bishop were still hot.')

98. F. Prinz., 'Die bischöfliche Stadtherrschaft im Frankreich', *Historische Zeitschrift* CCXVII (1973): 1–35 at p. 3. I would prefer Henry C. J. Beck, *The Pastoral Care of Souls in South-East France During the Sixth Century* (Analecta Gre-

happened in the smooth and ineluctable manner that he posits. Sixth-century Gallic towns were still late Roman towns; that is, they were bear-gardens. The history of the town, as we read it in the *Libri historiarum* is a history of urban rioting, of public insult, and of deeds of *contumacia* among the clergy which frequently exceed in sheer narrative horror the better-publicized *feretas* of the Franks. Acclamation, for instance, had remained, as it remained in eastern cities, a deadly political weapon: 'I will call together the people of Tours, and I will say to them: "Cry loud against Gregory, that he is unjust and accordeth justice to no man." And when they shout, I shall make answer to them: "I myself, the King, can find no justice at his hands, and how shall ye lesser folk find it?" '[99] The *consensus* on which the status of a bishop like Gregory depended, even with St Martin behind him, could be as thin as ice.

The fragility of the *consensus* surrounding the bishop brings us to our last question: apart from general excitement, what is the specific message of the ceremonial of the saint's festival in sixth-century Gaul? I think we can be clear—it is a ceremony of *adventus* and *consensus*. The saint arrives at a shrine, and this arrival is the occasion for the community to show itself as a united whole, embracing its otherwise conflicting parts, in welcoming him.[100] The same ceremonial is as

---

goriana 51) (Rome, 1950), p. 317: 'Properly to understand the public activities undertaken by prelates of our period, the historian must bear in mind that neither in the fifth century under the Emperors nor in the sixth under barbarian kings did Gallic bishops ever come to hold true public office in their municipalities.'

99. *Lib. hist.*, V, 18, 219. On the political use of acclamations in eastern cities, see W. Liebeschütz, *Antioch* (Oxford, 1972), pp. 209–13 and Alan Cameron, *Circus Factions* (Oxford, 1976), pp. 237–44.

100. See Victricius of Rouen, *De laude sanctorum*, 2, PL, 20, 445A: 'Ecce omnis aetas in vestrum funditur famulatum.' 446B: 'hinc denique totius populi circa maiestatem vestram unus affectus.' ('Behold, every age-group pours out to do you service.' 'Hence, now, the unity of feeling of the whole people around your Majesty.') 454D/455A, a reference to *secular adventus*: 'matres tecta complerent, portae undam populi moverent, omnis aetas in studium divisa.' ('The mothers of families would crowd on to the roof-tops, the gates would unleash a wave of people, every age-group would show its distinctive enthusiasm.') The *adventus* of a bishop is an occa-

valid for the great regular festivals as for the arrival of a new
relic. An element of suspense is built into the cult. On one
gloomy occasion, a possessed man had even shouted out that
St Martin was not going to come—he had gone away to
Rome. Gregory urged the congregation to fall to praying,
'that we should deserve the presence of the saint'. A sudden
outburst from the possessed relieved all doubts; St Martin
would come; 'We could await with certainty the arrival of the
blessed figure.' It was a notable moment. Gregory, his eyes
wet with tears, spoke out: 'Let fear depart from your hearts,
for the blessed confessor is here among us.'[101] As the study of
the ceremony of *adventus* and of related aspects of late Roman
ceremonial has shown, these ceremonies were more precise
than meets the eye—they were rituals of *consensus*.[102] Everyone, therefore, ratified the event by his participation. The
terror of illness, of prison, of blindness, resided in the fear
that, at this great moment of solidarity, the sinner would be
placed by his suffering outside the community.[103] Hence the
miracles that were remembered are precisely those in which

---

sion for the same solidarity: see Venantius Fortunatus on the *adventus* of Gregory of
Tours: *carmen*, V, 3, 3:

> hoc puer exertus celebrat, hoc curva senectus,
> hoc commune bonum praedicet omnis homo.

('This is an event the upstanding youth turns out to proclaim, and curved old-age;
let each man acclaim the common good.') The Late Roman ceremonial survived in
Gallic towns: *Lib. hist.*, VI, 11, 281: 'dux scilicet et episcopus, cum signis et laudibus
diversisque honorum vexillis.' ('The duke and the bishop entered [Marseilles] with
banners flying, with acclamations of praise and the standards of the town's leading
groups on display.') The *adventus* of a relic is shown on a sixth-century carving at
Vienne: *Bulletin de la société des amis de Vienne* LXVII (1971): 31, fig. 2.

    101. *Virt. mart.*, II, 25, 167.

    102. This has been pointed out by S. G. MacCormack, 'Change and Con-
tinuity in Late Antiquity: The Ceremony of *Adventus*', Historia XXI (1972):
721–52, and the element of *consensus* in this, and similar, ceremonies will be made
plain in her book *Art and Ceremony in Late Antiquity* (Berkeley and Los Angeles,
1981).

    103. *Vit. mart.*, II, 28, 169: 'vae mihi, quae caecata peccatis non mereor hanc
festivitatem cum reliquo populo spectare.' ('Woe is me who, blinded by my sins,
have not gained the favour of being able to view the festival with the rest of the
people.')

248

the barriers holding the individual back from the *consensus universorum* were dissolved. The blind can suddenly see the ceremony; the cripple can walk up to receive the Eucharist;[104] the prisoners in the lockhouse roar in chorus to be free to take part;[105] and, at that high moment, the demons loose the chains in which they had held back the crippled and the possessed.[106] A great moment of ideal *consensus*—such was the ceremonial associated with the festival of the saints. As such, it re-enacted with gusto and with unambiguous positive feeling, the precise ceremony of *consensus* on which the position of every bishop had depended. The *adventus* of the saint to his shrine, therefore, gave an annual reassurance for which the average Gallic bishop was only too grateful.

To sum up: we have followed a body of beliefs and ceremonies that are intelligible as part of the rich humus of early Christian piety. They have come to be orchestrated in such a way as to achieve a profile that would remain stable for much of the early Middle Ages. Yet their Late Antique roots are plain: for the orchestration of the cult of relics in Gaul took the form that it did, I would suggest, partly in order to add the 'fixative' of the holy to a delicate and volatile perfume of status, such as preoccupied men who still moved, in a full-blooded manner, amidst the ambiguities of a Late Antique urban society.

To link 'relics' and 'social status' in this way must remain a tentative juxtaposition. It will be of value only if it urges us to look beyond the immediate Late Antique context. More is at stake than the imposition of an 'explanation' on the exuberant and intractable religious information contained in the works of Gregory. Speculation on the connecting links between the social and the religious phenomena of the age must form part of a wider, more groping search for the human community behind the Dark Age evidence. It must end, as it began, with a respect for the wordless cunning with which men in Late Antique and early medieval societies drew on

104. *Virt. mart.*, II, 14, 163.   105. *Virt. mart.*, I, 11, 145.
106. *Virt. Jul.*, 9, 119; *Glor. conf.*, 86, 354; 93, 357.

invisible objects of love and loyalty to cope with the delicate business of living. For only when he has attempted to un-cover the alien cunning of small, face-to-face societies in a distant past,[107] through detailed consideration of the religious content of a well-known body of texts, can the historian move on to set his insights to work in the study of the *realia* of medieval life—a study in which the University of Reading has played such a leading role in modern English scholarship, through its connection with Sir Frank Stenton. In so doing, he will have travelled a road that Sir Frank Stenton saw so clearly in a distant model. In a memorable page of that *enta geweorc*, his *Anglo-Saxon England*, Sir Frank has traced, with an evident thrill of self-recognition, the evolution of the Ven-erable Bede. It was an evolution by which a sheltered man, the loyal guardian of a traditional definition of scholarship, had come to write a new kind of history: he had emerged 'at last', as Sir Frank writes, 'from the atmosphere of ancient science and exegesis to prove himself the master of a living art'.[108]

107. We have been forcibly reminded of the small scale of the communities of early medieval Europe by J. M. Wallace-Hadrill, *Early Medieval History*, p. 3.
108. Sir Frank Stenton, *Anglo-Saxon England* (Oxford, 3rd edition 1971), p. 186.

A Dark Age Crisis:
Aspects of the Iconoclastic Controversy[†]

IKE THE RELIGIOUS REFORM OF THE PHARAOH AKH-
naton (Amenhotep IV, 1385–58 B.C.), to which it has
been likened, the Iconoclast controversy in the eighth-
century Byzantine Empire has long tantalized the historian: for he seems to be confronted with a rare phenomenon —with a sudden break in the even flow of a society
with a reputation for unswerving traditionalism.[1] This view
of the Iconoclast controversy dates back to the attitude of the
Iconodules in the Council of Nicaea of 787 and the triumph
of Orthodoxy of 843.[2] On these occasions it was stated that
the icons had been preserved in the Church since the days of
the Apostles, and so that their removal, between 730 and 787,
had been an abrupt hiatus in the continuum of the Christian
religion. Iconodule historians were quick to present the Iconoclast movement as a thoroughly un-Byzantine interlude.
The Emperors Leo III and Constantine V and their advisers
were said to have acted under the influence of persons and of
ideas alien to the core of Byzantine civilization.[3] Modern re-

---

[†]*English Historical Review* LXXXVIII (1973): 1–34.

1. By Eduard Meyer, *Geschichte des Altertums*, II, 2 (1953), 414.

2. See the masterly study of J. Gouillard, 'Le Synodikon de l'Orthodoxie:
édition et commentaire', *Travaux et Mémoires du Centre de Recherche d'histoire et civilisation byzantines*, II (1967), 1–316.

3. P. J. Alexander, *The Patriarch Nicephorus of Constantinople. Ecclesiastical Policy
and Image Worship in the Byzantine Empire* (1958), pp. 6–22, discusses the evidence
customarily advanced for such views.

search has removed the more spectacular examples of non-Byzantine scapegoats. Renegade Muslims and Jewish sorcerers have been definitively ousted: in the period between 726 and 730, Leo III took his decisions through the advice of sober provincial bishops, in a thoroughly Byzantine attempt to placate God, whose anger with the Christian people had been shown by Arab invasions and by volcanic eruptions.[4] Careful study of Byzantine-Arab relations in the eighth century;[5] a re-examination of the Muslim attitude to images in the same century;[6] re-assessment of the position of the Jews in the Byzantine empire[7]—these converging studies have led to the greatest caution in invoking the influence of any non-Christian culture in the genesis of the Iconoclast movement. A consideration of the attitude of the early Church to images[8]

4. G. Ostrogorsky, *History of the Byzantine State* (trans. J. M. Hussey, 1968), pp. 160 ff. [S. Gero, *Byzantine Iconoclasm During the Reign of Leo III, with Particular Attention to the Oriental Sources*, Corpus Scriptorum Christianorum Orientalium CCCXLVI, Subsidia XLI (Louvain, 1973).]

5. A. Grabar, *L'iconoclasme byzantin. Dossier archéologique* (1957), pp. 101–10, and P. Lemerle, *Le premier humanisme byzantin* (1971), pp. 31–33.

6. K. A. C. Cresswell, 'The Lawfulness of Painting in Early Islam', *Ars Islamica* XI–XII (1946): 159–66, and U. Monneret de Villard, *Introduzione allo Studio dell' Archeologia islamica* (1966), pp. 249–75. [R. Paret, 'Die Entstehungszeit des islamischen Bilderverbots', *Kunst des Orients* XI (1976–77): 158–81; O. Grabar, *The Formation of Islamic Art* (New Haven, Conn., 1973), pp. 75–103, and 'Islam and Iconoclasm', *Iconoclasm. Papers Given at the Ninth Spring Symposium of Byzantine Studies at the University of Birmingham*, ed. A. Bryer and J. Herrin (Centre of Byzantine Studies, University of Birmingham, 1977), pp. 45–52; A. Welch, 'Epigraphy as Icon: The Role of the Written Word in Islamic Art', *The Image and the Word: Confrontation in Judaism, Christianity and Islam*, ed. J. Gutman (Missoula, Mont.: Scholars Press, 1977), pp. 63–74.]

7. A. Sharf, *Byzantine Jewry. From Julian to the Fourth Crusade* (1971), pp. 61–81.

8. N. H. Baynes, 'Idolatry and the Early Church', *Byzantine Studies and Other Essays* (1960), pp. 116–43, and 'The Icons Before Iconoclasm', *Harvard Theological Review* XLIV (1951): 93–106 and in *Byzantine Studies*, pp. 226–39. [But see the most important criticism of these views in Sister Charles Murray, 'Art and the Early Church', *Journal of Theological Studies*, n.s., XXVIII (1977): 303–45. There was no latent hostility to art in the early Church that could surface in the eighth century: though not necessarily explicable in non-Christian terms, the concern with icons in the eighth century does represent a new departure in the attitude of the early Church to the status and function of art.]

and the discovery of an Iconoclast movement in the totally Christian environment of seventh-century Armenia[9] have led almost all scholars to regard Iconoclasm as endogenic: it was a crisis within Byzantine Christianity itself.

Nevertheless, the perspective of the triumph of Orthodoxy lingers tenaciously in its central tenet. Iconoclasm is still treated in most accounts as representing the momentary emergence of elements in Byzantine culture that were, if not totally alien, at least provincial or non-Hellenic, and the triumph of Orthodoxy is presented as the assertion of the mainstream of the Byzantine tradition over a deviant tributary. Somewhat nostalgically, the re-instatement of the icons is hailed as a victory of the representational traditions of Greece over the non-representational piety of the oriental provinces of the Empire.[10] Two recent interpretations have been taken to support this impression. In the first place, Ostrogorsky was able to isolate a strong Monophysite streak in the iconoclastic theology of Constantine V. This discovery has been held sufficient, in itself, to lay the Iconoclast movement under the *praeiudicium* of having originated among an oriental population that was either hostile or indifferent to the Chalcedonian synthesis of the divine and the human in Christ and, consequently, to the showing of Christ in human form.[11] In the second place, it is assumed that the social changes of the late seventh and eighth centuries shifted the

9. S. Der Nersessian, 'Une Apologie des Images au septième siècle', *Byzantion* XVII (1945): 58–87, and P. J. Alexander, 'An Ascetic Sect of Iconoclasts in Seventh Century Armenia', *Late Classical and Medieval Studies in Honor of Albert Matthias Friend, Jr.* (1955), pp. 151–160. [Now in *Religious and Political History and Thought in the Byzantine Empire* (London: Variorum Reprints, 1978).]

10. Karl Schwarzlose, *Der Bilderstreit. Ein Kampf der griechischen Kirche um ihre Eigenart und um ihre Freiheit* (1890). Note the subtitle.

11. G. Ostrogorsky, *Studien zur Geschichte des byzantinischen Bilderstreites* (1929: photographic reprint 1964), pp. 5, 25–28, 40. This thesis is examined with further elaborations by Alexander, *Patriarch Nicephorus*, pp. 44 ff. Baynes (*Byzantine Studies*, p. 136) was unconvinced: 'there is little if anything to be said for the view and there is no need for us to accept their contention.' [Sebastian Brock, 'Iconoclasm and the Monophysites', *Iconoclasm*, pp. 53–57, and Marlia Mundell, 'Monophysite Church Decoration', *Iconoclasm*, pp. 59–74.]

centre of gravity of the Byzantine state towards the oriental populations of the countryside of Anatolia, at the expense of the traditional urban culture of the Aegean. These changes were sharpened by the military reforms of the same time. It has been assumed that the armies of the newly-instituted Themes were recruited locally; and, so, in supporting the Iconoclast emperors who had originated from the same provinces, the eastern armies are held to have been expressing the sullen hostility of a whole provincial culture towards the alien, Iconodule piety of its capital.[12]

Altogether, the Iconoclast controversy is in the grip of a crisis of over-explanation. It is necessary to raise some *prima facie* objections to the views just stated, if only to free the subject for further investigation along different lines. First: the Christological background of Iconoclasm is far from certain. The *Queries* of Constantine V were alarmingly intelligent;[13] but, on the whole, the discussion of the Christological issues involved in the worship or rejection of icons was remarkably desultory throughout the eighth century. Far away, across the Arab frontier, John of Damascus had seen and stated clearly the Christological background to the controversy. But John's *On Images* was written at a safe distance from the world, in the *wadis* of the convent of St Sabas. There is little evidence that the Byzantine clergy knew of it at the Council of Nicaea in 787. The proceedings at Nicaea show none of that certainty of touch, the smooth mobilization of *catenae* of authorities, with which Byzantine prelates had resolved those Christological controversies to which

12. H. Ahrweiler, 'L'Asie Mineure et les invasions arabes', *Revue historique* CCXXVII (1962): 1–32 at p. 23, and *Byzance et la Mer* (1966), pp. 40–41; Lemerle, *Le premier humanisme*, pp. 34–36. [H. Ahrweiler, 'The Geography of the Iconoclast World', *Iconoclasm*, pp. 21–27, now appears to reject this.]

13. Ostrogorsky, *Studien*, p. 226, and Alexander, *Patriarch Nicephorus*, pp. 47–49: 'an act of genius' (p. 48). [The intelligence and idiosyncrasy of Constantine V has now received its full due in the fine study of S. Gero, *Byzantine Iconoclasm During the Reign of Constantine V*, Corpus Scriptorum Christianorum Orientalium CCCLXXXIV (Louvain, 1977), esp. pp. 37–52 and 143–51.]

they had become only too well accustomed.[14] As we read about it in eighth-century sources, there is nothing *déjà vu* about Iconoclasm.

Second: in the early eighth-century Byzantine Empire, how far east is 'east'? The Iconoclast bishops came from Phrygia. In the sixth century, Phrygia had been thought of as 'a province that naturally loved culture and had a great taste for the study of letters'.[15] Professor Louis Robert has this to say of the countryside around Nacoleia, the see of a leading Iconoclast bishop: 'C'est une épigraphie de la campagne, et elle est grecque autant qu'abondante . . . Les dédicaces si nombreuses et intéressantes et les épitaphes n'ont pas été re-digées pour une mince couche de citoyens riches des villes, mais, du haut en bas, pour les paysans, aisés ou pauvres, des villages et des hameaux.'[16] Thus the idea that Asia Minor was a vast, undifferentiated backlands and a seed-bed of 'oriental' religiosity[17] is contradicted by most of what we know of the immediate late Roman past of those provinces in which the leading Iconoclast bishops had their sees.

Third: most current explanations of the Iconoclast con-troversy implicitly ignore the role of Constantinople as the hub of the eighth-century Byzantine world. Whatever his eastern origins, the career of Leo before he became emperor radiated from Constantinople; wherever their sees may have lain, the Iconoclast bishops probably got all their culture at Constantinople, conducted most of their business at Con-stantinople,[18] and regarded their duties as local bishops as

14. P. Van den Ven, "La patristique et l'hagiographie du Concile de Nicée de 787", *Byzantion* XXV–XXVII (1955–57): 325–62 at pp. 332–38.

15. Callinicus, *Vita Hypatii*, c. 1 (Teubner, 1895), p. 58.

16. L. Robert, *Hellenica*, XIII (1965): 54. [This does not exclude the possibility that the region, though Hellenized, might possess a sharply defined profile, as was the case in Late Antiquity: Elsa Gibson, *The 'Christians for Christians' Inscriptions of Phrygia*. Harvard Theological Studies XXXII (Missoula, Mont.: Scholars Press, 1978), and L. Robert, *Comptes Rendus de l'Academie d'Inscriptions et Belles Lettres 1978*, pp. 267–69.]

17. As Schwarzlose, *Der Bilderstreit*, pp. 44 ff.

18. J. D. Mansi, *Sacrorum conciliorum nova et amplissima collectio* (hereafter

taking them from Constantinople 'into the country'.[19] The whole unforgettable 'style' of Constantine V—the tone of an Ivan the Terrible *à la* Eisenstein—is inconceivable against any other backdrop than the crowded Hippodrome of the capital.[20]

Fourth: it has now been shown conclusively that the role of the Byzantine Theme armies in the Iconoclast controversy was far from simple. Their behaviour in the eighth century was not determined by any sense of local loyalties among the troops; least of all did the eastern Themes consistently support the Iconoclast party.[21]

Generally, the study of the Iconoclast controversy has tended to become a study of the origin of Iconoclast ideas, and this study has, in turn, been encapsulated in a search for a local, provincial setting for such ideas. As a result, attempts to assess the significance of the Iconoclast controversy show a strange mixture of the melodramatic and the parochial. Melodramatic, for it is neither certain that the victory of the Iconoclasts would have led to the triumph of a nonrepresentational art in the Eastern Empire, nor that their momentary success was a victory of the eastern over the European provinces of the Empire. The heady alternative *Orient oder Rom?* was not for a moment at stake in the course of the eighth century.[22] Parochial, because it is assumed that the crisis, seen in the terms just outlined, concerned only the Byzantine Empire. As a result, the Carolingian contribution to this debate—the *Libri Carolini*—is treated as an ill-tempered and irrelevant intervention.[23] It is one of the secondary aims of

Mansi), 1759 ff., xiii. 33CD (the bishop of Myrai); 108D (Thomas, Iconoclast bishop of Claudiopolis); 430CD and 434CD (canons 10 and 15 of Nicaea).

19. Mansi, xii. 115E.
20. E.g., *Vita Stephani Iunioris, Patrologia Graeca*, c. 1136B.
21. W. Kaegi, 'The Byzantine Armies and Iconoclasm', *Byzantinoslavica* XXVII (1966): 48–70.
22. Lemerle, *Le premier humanisme*, exaggerates: 'Les iconodules sont dans la ligne du christianisme "humaniste", infléchi par la tradition gréco-romaine; les iconoclastes (comme avant eux les monophysites), dans celle du christianisme sémite et asiatique. Ce fut le dernier grand choix que les chrétiens eurent à faire' (p. 107).
23. G. Haendler, *Epochen karolingischer Theologie. Eine Untersuchung über die*

this paper to show that the other great Christian state, the Frankish Empire, had also been challenged to take up an attitude to its own religious traditions in a way that synchronized with the Iconoclast movement in Byzantium. For the alternative between East and West within the Byzantine Empire was trivial compared with the burning problem shared by all Christian states in the eighth century—how to adjust to the crevasse that had opened between their rich Late Antique past and an anxious present overshadowed by the armies of Islam. The first part of this paper, therefore, must concentrate on the problem of why icons were considered so vulnerable in the eighth century, the second, why they had achieved sufficient prominence in the Late Antique period to have drawn attack upon themselves; the third part will suggest some possible implications for an understanding of the changes in eighth-century Byzantine society.

I

We should begin again with the considerable and explicit body of evidence for the religious views of the Iconoclasts[24] —most notably the *Queries* of Constantine V[25] and the *Horos*

---

karolingische Gutachten zum byzantinischen Bilderstreit (1958) is no more than a beginning. [S. Gero, 'The Libri Carolini and the Image Controversy', *Greek Orthodox Theological Review* XVIII (1973): 7–34. We can expect an edition to supersede that of Bastgen in the *Monumenta Germaniae Historica* series from Professor Ann Freeman, together with an English translation and commentary. The Carolingians were prepared to accept the canons of the Council of Nicaea: J. H. A. Lynch, 'A Carolingian Borrowing from Second Nicaea (787)', *Medievalia et Humanistica* V (1974): 127–38. That they should have attempted to apply to the totally different economic conditions of the Church in Western Europe the decrees of this Council against simony betrays a touching faith in the continued unity of Christendom. See also P. Henry, 'Images of the Church in the Second Nicene Council and the *Libri Carolini*', *Law, Church and Society: Essays In Honor of Stephan Kuttner*, ed. K. Pennington and R. Somerville (Philadelphia, 1977), pp. 237–52.]

24. Now available in *Textus byzantinos ad Iconomachiam pertinentes in usum academicum*, ed. Herman Hennephof (1969) (hereafter Hennephof). A few of these have been translated in C. Mango, *The Art of the Byzantine Empire, 312–1453 A.D.: Sources and Documents* (Englewood Cliffs, New Jersey, 1972), pp. 123–77, and *Iconoclasm*, pp. 180–86.

25. Hennephof, nos. 141–87, pp. 52–57, extracted from Nicephorus, *Anti-*

of the Iconoclast Council of 754[26]—and for the repercussion of these views among the Iconodules at the Council of Nicaea in 787. Let us propose a definition of the Iconoclast controversy in the light of this evidence: the Iconoclast controversy was a debate on the position of the holy in Byzantine society. On the issue of what was holy and what was not the Iconoclasts were firm and unambiguous. Certain material objects were holy because they had been solemnly blessed by ordained priests. This blessing had raised them from the material to the supernatural: such was the Eucharistic bread—ὁ διὰ τῆς ἱερατικῆς τελετῆς ἀναφερόμενος ἐκ τοῦ χειροποιήτου πρὸς τὸ ἀχειροποίητον.[27] Only objects so raised were entitled to the attitudes demanded by the presence of the holy; they could be objects of worship in the full sense. For the Iconoclasts, there were only three such objects: the Eucharist, which was both given by Christ and consecrated by the clergy;[28] the church building, which was consecrated by the bishop;[29] the sign of the cross.[30] This last was not only a traditional sacramental gesture, whose power was shown in the rite of exorcism; for an eighth-century Byzantine, it was a sign given directly by God to men, when it first appeared in the sky to the Emperor Constantine. On this view, no other object could claim to be holy. It appeared to the Iconoclasts that icons had, at a comparatively recent time, sidled over the firmly-demarcated frontier separating the holy from the pro-

rhetici, P. G. c. 205–553, also edited with commentary by Ostrogorsky, Bilderstreit, pp. 11–45.

26. Hennephof, nos. 200–64, pp. 61–78, extracted from Mansi, xiii. 205–364. [Gero, Constantine V, esp. pp. 68–94, for a careful translation.]

27. Hennephof, no. 168, p. 55 (Niceph. 337C): 'which is raised by rites performed by a priest from being a material object to become a vehicle of the supernatural.' [Compare Gero, Constantine V, 77: 'the offering of the priest mediating the passage from the (sphere of the) common to (that of) the holy', and his remarks on pp. 101–103 and article, 'The Eucharistic Doctrine of the Byzantine Iconoclasts and Its Sources', Byzantinische Zeitschrift LXVIII (1975): 4–22.]

28. Hennephof, no. 226, pp. 67–68 (Mansi, xiii. 261DE).

29. Hennephof, no. 184, p. 57 (Niceph. 477C).

30. G. Millet, 'Les Iconoclastes et la Croix. À propos d'une inscription de Cappadoce', Bulletin de correspondance hellénique XXXIV (1910): 96–109.

fane. The Iconoclast bishops of 754 meant to put them firmly back in their place: οὔτε εὐχὴν ἱερὰν ἁγιάζουσαν αὐτήν [Ἡ τῶν ψευδωνύμων ἐικόνων κακωνυμία], ἵν' ἐκ τούτου πρὸς τὸ ἅγιον ἐκ τοῦ κοινοῦ μετενεχθῇ, ἀλλὰ μένει κοινὴ καὶ ἄτιμος, ὡς ἀπήρτισεν αὐτὴν ὁ ξωγράφος.[31]

Icons could not be holy because they had received no consecration from above. They had received only an illegitimate consecration from below. They were merely thought to be holy, and this for the same deeply sinister reason as pagan cult images were thought to be holy: the devil had taken advantage of the simplicity of the masses to reintroduce into the Christian people the error of idolatry.[32] Icons, therefore, could suffer the same fate as any pagan cult objects: they could be burnt.[33]

It is on this central issue of the holy that the author of the Carolingian *Libri Carolini* can be seen, over a generation later, to be moving along exactly the same orbit as Constantine V and his bishops. For this author knows exactly where the holy lies, and that it has little to do with icons. For the people of Israel, for instance, it lay in the awesome Ark of the Covenant—'siquidem illa condita est Domino imperante, istae [the icons] conduntur artis industria iuvante; illa a sancto viro Moyse, istae a quolibet opifice; illa a Legislatore, istae a pictore; illa redundat mysteriis, istae colorum tantummodo fucis'.[34] For the Christians of the present, it tended to lie in the great consecrated basilica. The succession of miracle stories ascribed to icons by the Iconodule bishops at Nicaea leave this author cold; but Gregory the Great had described how

31. Hennephof, no. 227, p. 68 (Mansi, xiii. 268BC, 269CD): 'For the ill-omened name of "holy" for the icons is misplaced. No prayer of any priest has blessed the icon, so that, through such consecration, it passes beyond ordinary matter to become a holy thing; but it remains common and without honour, just as it leaves the hands of the painter.' (This free translation attempts to render the argument of the whole passage from which the citation is taken.)

32. Hennephof, no. 207, pp. 62 ff. (Mansi, xiii. 221CD).

33. *V. Steph. Iun., P.G.* c. 1085.

34. *Libri Carolini*, ed. H. Bastgen, *Monumenta Germaniae Historica*, Legum sectio III, Concilia, ii (1924), ii, 26, p. 85.

the oil lamps of a great basilica had remained unquenched in a torrential flood—that, he concludes, is a *real* miracle![35] Even the Iconodules were unable to wrench themselves free from the gravitational pull of this central problem. Their attitude to icons is incoherent precisely because they accept the terms of their opponents. Iconoclasts and Iconodules of the eighth century are closer to each other, in their obsession with a common problem of the holy, than are the Iconodules of that century to their more refined and cautious successors in the ninth century.

The Iconodules wanted to have their cake and eat it. They had inherited from Late Antiquity a solution of their difficulties that was both impressive (as part of the imagined unalterable tradition of the Church) and clear. If pictures can move the beholder, can record, can narrate, can bring faces and deeds to his memory, then they can communicate the Christian message. Standing on the cool walls of the churches, pictures were more permanent reminders to the passer-by than were the liturgy and reading of the gospels of the story of Jesus and the passions of the saints.[36] Because we regard this view as so eminently reasonable we assume that the Iconodules regarded it as eminently natural. For all that, the Iconodules were not deeply concerned to present icons as merely useful. They presented them consistently as holy.[37] An icon, or a wall painting, might be known to have made St Gregory of Nyssa weep[38], it had reminded St Anastasius, at a crucial moment, of the courage of the martyrs[39], it might lead the mystical devotee, in a more subtle way, 'by the hand' to contemplate the incarnation of Christ[40]; but it could do more than this. The icon was a hole in the dyke separating

35. *Lib. Carol.* iv, 12, p. 192.

36. Mansi, xiii. 361A. [G. Lamp, *Bild und Wort. Die katheketische Funktion des Bildes in der griechischen Theologie des sechsten bis zum neunten Jahrhundert* (Würzburg, 1969).]

37. Mansi, xiii. 39A: 'the venerable icons have the same spiritual status, the same power—ἰσοδυναμοῦσιν—as the Gospel-book and the venerable Cross.'

38. Ibid., 9DE.   39. Ibid., 21A.   40. Ibid., 116A.

the visible world from the divine, and through this hole there oozed precious driblets from the great sea of God's mercy: icons were active, πόσαι, εἰπέ μοι, ἐπισκιάσεις, πόσαι ἀναβλύσεις, πολλάκις δὲ καὶ αἱμάτων ῥύσεις, ἐξ εἰκόνων καί λειψάνων μαρτύρων γεγόνασι;[41]

The Iconodules wandered even deeper into the gravitational field of the Iconoclasts. They plainly accepted without question the major criterion of the holy laid down by the Iconoclasts—the criterion of consecration. Their roundabout solutions on this issue betray how important a concern it was for them. For the Iconodules could not claim that an icon produced by an artisan was holy because it had been blessed in the same solemn manner as had the Eucharistic bread or the basilica.[42] Though frequently accused by modern scholars of magical habits of mind, the Iconodule, in fact, had omitted the one element which any self-respecting magician of the time knew to be obligatory—the occult consecration of the image.[43] (For this reason alone, the term 'magical', so lavishly applied by modern scholars to the use of icons, lacks any real meaning, when dealing with the habits of men who lived in an age that knew what real, professional magic was like.) Yet they could not break out of the gravitational field of the problem by denying the relevance of the need for consecration. Some icons, the Iconodules insisted, were of immediate divine origin. They were 'not made with human

41. Ibid., 48C. 'Tell me, how many times have icons been overshadowed by the presence of God, how many times have they oozed with myrrh, how many times has blood flowed freely from icons and from the relics of the saints?' [But see the acute remarks of H. G. Beck, *Von der Fragwürdigkeit der Ikonen*, Sitzungsberichte der bayerischen Akademie der Wissenschaften, Hist. K1. VII (Munich, 1976), esp. pp. 15–16 and 26–27: the miraculous nature of icons was not stressed in the final *horos* of the Council.]

42. *Lib. Carol.* i, 27, p. 87: 'Imagines vero nullius manus impositionis vel consecrationis mysterio indigentes. . . .' ('Images, indeed, which lack the laying on of hands or any form of rite or consecration.') [The consecration of icons is a later development: I. Passarelli, 'Ancora sulla preghiera di benedizione delle icone', *Bolletino della Badia Greca di Grottaferrata*, n.s., XXXI (1977): 81–91.]

43. M. P. Nilsson, *Geschichte der griechischen Religion*, II (1950), 502–505, and T. Pekáry, 'Der römische Bilderstreit', *Frühmittelalterliche Studien*, III (1969), 18.

hands'.[44] They stood above mere art.[45] They were given by God to men in a manner that fulfilled the criteria laid down for the holy by the Iconoclasts. Other icons that did not enjoy the awesome privileges of a direct other-worldly origin nevertheless enjoyed a consecration from the past. They were thought to have originated in the immediate environment of the holy person that they represented, or to have been miraculously produced by physical contact with such a person.[46] The *Mandylion* of Edessa, on which Christ impressed His face on a handkerchief, was the prototype of such an icon.[47] We should take this idea of consecration by the past very seriously. Eighth-century Iconodules believed that the icon and the gospel were strictly contemporaneous: St Luke had sent to Theophilus not only his gospel, but his portrait of the Virgin, painted from the life, and copious illustrations of scenes from the life of Christ, as they had happened.[48] Icons of the Virgin, therefore, could well be thought of as continuations of St Luke's original, much as the clear-cut gargoyles on an Oxford college are fondly imagined to be medieval, when they are, in fact, the work of an unbroken chain of cutters who, ever since the fifteenth century, have renewed the original in soft Cotswold stone.[49] Nothing else would do. What the icons so palpably lacked in consecration from above, they made up for by consecration from the past. Taken altogether, Iconoclast, Carolingian, Iconodule were asking the same question throughout the eighth century: where is the

44. E. von Dobschütz, *Christusbilder*, Texte und Untersuchungen, XVIII (1899) is fundamental.

45. E. Kitzinger, 'The Cult of Images in the Age before Iconoclasm', *Dumbarton Oaks Papers* VIII (1954): 83–149, at p. 143, n. 257 sees this clearly.

46. Dobschütz, *Christusbilder*, p. 269.

47. Evidence collected in Dobschütz, *Christusbilder*, pp. 158*–289*.

48. *The Admonition of the Old Man*, ed. B. Melioransky, *Georgii Kiprianin i Ioann Ierusalimlianin, dva maloizviestnych bortsa za pravoslavie v VIII viekie*, Zapiski Istor.-Filolog. Fakulteta Imp. S. Peterburgskago Universiteta, LIX (1901), pp. xxviii–xxx, cf. pp. xxvi–xxvii: see Gouillard, 'Synodikon, *Travaux et Mémoires*, II, 178.

49. Dobschütz, *Christusbilder*, p. 271.

holy? what belongs to it and what does not? The Iconoclasts and the author of the *Libri Carolini* could offer a group of holy objects that were neither unduly spiritualized nor devoid of strong visual potency: they could offer the great liturgy of the Eucharist; the basilica with its solemn association with the Temple of Jerusalem and with the heavenly city;[50] the age-old focus of the figure of the cross; and—for the Carolingians—the fearsome compactness of the Ark of the Covenant, 'welling over with mystic meaning'.[51] For them Iconodule superstition was simply a haemorrhage of the holy from these great symbols into a hundred little paintings.[52] Iconoclasm, therefore, is a centripetal reaction: it asserts the unique value of a few central symbols of the Christian community that enjoyed consecration from above against the centrifugal tendencies of the piety that had spread the charge of the holy on to a multiplicity of unconsecrated objects. Seeing that what a society considers holy and what profane is very much a precipitate of that society's needs and structure, it may perhaps prove fruitful to examine what a centripetal reaction of this kind could mean in the social and religious life of eighth-century Byzantium, and so what the centrifugal tendencies of the previous centuries had implied.

We can at least set aside certain problems: a debate on the holy need have nothing whatsoever to do with art. Indeed, the only two men in the Dark Ages whom we know to have been deeply interested in art—the Emperor Theophilus[53] and Bishop Theodulf of Orléans (if Theodulf is the author of

50. Grabar, *Iconoclasme*, pp. 153–54.
51. V. H. Elbern, 'Liturgisches Gerät in edlen Materiellen zur Zeit Karls des Grossen', *Karl der Grosse* (1965), III, 115–67; Peter Bloch, 'Das Apsismosaik von Germigny-des-Prés. Karl der Grosse und das Alte Bund', ibid., pp. 234–61; M. Vieillard-Troiekouroff, 'Nouvelles études sur les mosaiques de S. Germigny-des-Près', *Cahiers archéologiques* XVII (1967): 103 ff. [See the fine observations in P. Meyvaert, 'The Authorship of the *Libri Carolini*', *Revue bénédictine* LXXXIX (1979): 29–57, esp. pp. 54–56.]
52. Hennephof, no. 102, pp. 38 ff. (Mansi, xiv. 417–22.) Letter of Michael II and Theophilus to Louis of 824.
53. Grabar, *Iconoclasme*, pp. 143 ff.

the *Libri Carolini*, as is very likely)[54]—were Iconoclast or, at least, anti-Iconodule. To love art meant knowing artists; and every ancient man knew what artists were like; they slept with their models[55]; they designed theatre posters[56]; in 692 they had been caught still painting classical pornographic scenes.[57] To the author of the *Libri Carolini*, indeed, the artist was free to do what he liked (for this reason he has been acclaimed as one of the first exponents of Art for Art's sake),[58] but provided that he remained irremediably profane.[59] For a cultivated man of the eighth century, whether he was a Western European, a Byzantine or a Muslim, art was part of a man's comfort; Byzantine and Ummayad baths and pleasure palaces show this clearly.[60] Furthermore, in Byzantium and in the West, art had also become a branch of classics. The works of art most appreciated in Carolingian and Byzantine court circles at this time were those manuscripts and ivories that faithfully preserved the art of the classical world with a heavy *décor* of pagan deities and personified natural forces.[61] The works of the artist, therefore, that were most sought at the time of the Iconoclast controversy were precisely those which had least to do with the idea of the holy in the minds of any Western European, Byzantine or Muslim.

II

It is the identification of the icon with the holy and the rejection of this claim by the Iconoclasts, and not the status of the arts in Byzantine society, that was at stake in the eighth century. Two masterly treatments by Professor André Gra-

54. Ann Freeman, 'Theodulf of Orleans', *Speculum* XXXII (1957): 663–705, esp. pp. 695–703.
55. Justin, *Apologia*, I, ix, 4. 56. Mansi, xiii. 241B.
57. *Concilium Quinisextum*, canon 100.
58. Freeman, 'Theodulf', p. 695.
59. *Lib. Carol.* i, 16, p. 39; III, 22, p. 149; III, 23, pp. 151–52.
60. F. Rosenthal, *Das Fortleben der Antike im Islam* (1965), p. 357 on paintings in bath-houses. [Trans. *The Classical Heritage in Islam* (Berkeley and Los Angeles, 1976), pp. 265–66.]
61. E. Panofsky, *Renaissance and Renascences in Western Art* (Paladin, 1970), pp. 49–52.

bar and Professor Erwin Kitzinger[62] have drawn attention to the comparatively rapid, and piecemeal, nature of the rise of the icon to holiness: Grabar begins with one of those irrefutable surprises such as only the archaeologist and the art historian can hold in store for us: some of the greatest shrines of the Byzantine period, most notably the Hagia Sophia itself, would have struck any eighth-century worshipper as almost entirely an-iconic.[63] Even if we accept the Iconodule argument, that icons had come to stay, we must think of their presence in the churches as more atomized, as less integrated in the overall decoration and meaning of the building than in later centuries.[64] The rise of the cult of icons, therefore, in the sixth and seventh centuries, and not the origins of Iconoclasm—this is the central problem of the Iconoclast controversy. It is the singular merit of Kitzinger to have made this clear, and to have suggested an explanation. At the risk of simplifying a study of great richness and differentiation, the explanation of the rise of the worship of icons that he proposes is as follows.

A tendency to worship the individual icon had always existed among Mediterranean people. Up to the late sixth century, however, the élite of the Christian Church had offered a constant resistance to 'the naive, animistic ideas of the masses'.[65] In the late sixth century, 'the resistance to such pressure on the part of the authorities decreased . . . and this relaxation of counter pressure from above was at least a major factor in the development'.[66] It was the imperial court rather

62. Grabar, *Iconoclasme*; Kitzinger, 'Cult of Images'.

63. A. Grabar, *Martyrium. Recherches sur le culte des reliques et l'art chrétien antique*, II (1946), 284, and *Iconoclasme*, pp. 153 and 166.

64. But Nicole Thierry, 'Un décor pré-iconoclaste de Cappadoce: Açikel ağa Kilisı', *Cahiers archéologiques* XVIII (1968): 33–65, is a warning against generalizing from the apparent absence of such decoration. [But see her article, 'La basilique Saint-Jean-Baptiste de Cavusin, Cappadoce', *Bulletin de la Société nationale des Antiquaires de France 1972*, pp. 198–312.] E. Kitzinger, 'Byzantine Art in the Period Between Justinian and Iconoclasm', *Berichte zum XI. internationalen Byzantinistenkongress* (1958), pp. 41–50 is the best treatment of a delicate matter [in *The Art of Byzantium*; see also his *Byzantine Art in the Making* (Cambridge, Mass., 1977), pp. 99–122.]

65. Kitzinger, 'Cult of Images', p. 146.   66. Ibid., pp. 119–20.

than the bishops who were responsible for this change. For Kitzinger emphasizes that one privileged oasis of religious feeling for an image had survived intact since pagan times— the veneration of the imperial images.[67] Religious images began to receive marks of veneration analogous to the imperial images in the sixth century or even earlier; but, at the end of the sixth century, the emperors, in Kitzinger's opinion, took the final conscious step in fostering these practices. They allowed icons of Christ and of the Virgin to stand in the place of the imperial images, and so to receive the same frankly pagan worship as their own images had always received.[68] By the seventh century, such icons were firmly established as part of the public cultus of the Byzantine Empire.[69] This study would disagree through pointing away from analogies to the cult of the imperial icons to other, sizeable areas of the social life of the Late Antique world. The taking up of the icon into the public ceremonial of the Empire is one pillar only, on which the edifice of Iconodule piety came to rest. This study would suggest that it was neither the most profoundly rooted nor the most enduring. Put bluntly: Byzantines of the sixth, seventh and eighth centuries were getting from the icons what they never expected to get from an imperial image— they got the miracle of healing and the greater miracle of a flood of tears of repentance for their sins.[70]

Imperial images could be surrounded by impressive ceremonies, that stressed the Emperor's presence and his symbolic 'arrival' in town.[71] Again, disrespect for the imperial image released a very real charge of feeling. (Did not the good soldier Schweik share his first prison cell with an unfortunate who had allowed a photograph of the Emperor

67. Ibid., p. 91.   68. Ibid., pp. 125–26.
69. Grabar, *Iconoclasme*, pp. 45 and 70–77.
70. Mansi, xiii. 12A: 'for spiritual profit and an outflowing of tears'.
71. S. G. MacCormack, 'Change and Continuity in Late Antiquity: The Ceremony of *Adventus*', *Historia* XXI (1972): 721–52 [and *Art and Ceremony in Late Antiquity* (Berkeley and Los Angeles, 1981); H. G. Thümmel, 'Kaiserbild und Christusikone. Zur Bestimmung der fünfteiligen Elfenbeindiptychen', *Byzantinoslavica* XXXIX (1978): 196–206].

Franz Josef to become flyblown?) Iconodule texts should be interpreted in the light of this release of feeling. When they appealed to the respect due to the imperial images the centre of gravity is usually negative: they argue, *a fortiori*, from the dire consequences of *dis*respect for the imperial image to the impiety of *dis*respect for the image of Christ the Emperor.[72] What they envisage is less the psychology of worship than the psychological mechanisms of contempt for a figure of authority, and the very real mixture of horror and delight which an attack on his picture does indeed stir up. The 'psychodrama' of attacks on the images of Emperor and bishops was very common in the great towns of the Eastern Empire.[73] Yet it would be wrong to conclude that, when the Emperor's images were not being either welcomed or pelted, they were being worshipped. Far from it. They were being taken absolutely for granted. They were in constant danger of being obscured, in the public places, by great portraits of more exciting figures —by portraits of great pantomime actors, charioteers and wild beast fighters.[74] To the best of my knowledge, no man, on catching the eye of the Emperor in his portrait, burst into tears 'like a cloud-burst from a rain-laden sky'[75]: and this is what a man of the eighth century was supposed to do when faced by an icon. We should look more closely, therefore, at another area of the religious life of the Late Antique world in order to find the remainder of that charge of feeling that had come, by the eighth century, to make an icon appear holy.

I would suggest that we look more closely at the holy

72. Mansi, xii. 1067 and xiii. 161AB; *V. Steph. Iun.*, *P. G.* c. 1157D; Severianus of Gabala, *de mundi creatione*, *P. G.* liv. 489. For a Near Eastern example: G. Strohmaier, 'Hunain ibn Ishaq und die Bilder', *Klio* XLIII (1965): 527.

73. See evidence collected in R. Browning, 'The Riot of 387 in Antioch', *Journal of Roman Studies* XIII (1952): 13–20 at p. 20. Also Kazimierz Majewski, 'Bezobrozowość oraz burzenie świątyń, posągów bogów i pomników władców w świecie greckorzymskim', *Archeologia* XVI (1965): 63–82, at p. 69.

74. *Codex Theodosianus*, XV, xvii, 12 (394) = *Codex Justinianus*, XI, xli, 4.

75. The supposed letter of Gregory II to Leo III, ed. J. Gouillard, 'Aux origines de l'iconoclasme: le témoignage de Grégoire II', *Travaux et Mémoires du Centre de Recherche d'histoire et civilisation byzantines*, III (1968): 285, line 114.

man. From the fourth century onwards, the holy man was a living icon. To the theologian he was man at its height, man as first made 'in the image of God'.[76] One of three hermits who used to visit St Anthony came every year and sat there while the others talked, without saying a word: 'It is sufficient for me, Father', he explained, 'just to look at you'.[77] Merely to see a holy man could be enough for a visitor.[78] At his death, he instantly became an icon: 'for by the archbishop's orders the plank was stood upright—the body [of Daniel the Stylite, died 493] had been fixed to it so that it could not fall—and thus, like an icon, the holy man was displayed to all from every side; and for many hours the people all looked at him and also with cries and tears besought him to be an advocate with God on behalf of them all'.[79] The holy man was a clearly-defined *locus* of the holy on earth. The 'presence of the Lord' overshadowed him.[80] A long social and religious history lies behind the position of the holy man in the Late Antique period.[81] What is relevant to our purpose are those psychological needs which the holy men had long met, that might find satisfaction, also, in the icon.

The holy man's position in the collective mentality of the Byzantine world of the sixth and seventh centuries rested on a deeply-embedded mechanism: one might call it a focusing mechanism. Put briefly: it was possible to bring to bear on a single object (in this case, on the silent figure of the hermit)

76. Leontius of Neapolis, *P. G.* CXIII, 1064CD: 'An image of God is man, man created after His image and especially that man who is worthy to be the dwellingplace of the Holy Spirit': Mansi, xiii. 49B. He cites Leviticus 26, 12 in the LXX: Ἐνοικήσω ἐν αὐτοῖς καὶ ἐμπεριπατήσω in the literal meaning: 'I (God) will dwell in them (the individual holy men) and will walk around in them.'

77. *Apophthegmata Patrum*, Antonios 27, *P. G.* lxv. 84D.

78. E.g., Cassian, *Collationes*, xi. 2 (*C.S.E.L.* xiii. 315).

79. *Vita Danielis Stylitae*, c. 99, ed. H. Delehaye, *Les saints Stylites*, Subsidia Hagiographica, XIV (1923), 92. It is not even certain that the original manuscript contained the comment 'like an icon'.

80. On ἐπισκίασις, see *Vita Symeonis Iunioris*, c. 118, ed. P. van den Ven, *La vie ancienne de S. Symeon le Jeune* (pp. 521–92), Subsidia Hagiographica, XXXII (1962): 97–98, and *A Patristic Greek Lexicon*, ed. G. W. H. Lampe (1961), *s.v.*, p. 531.

81. Peter Brown, 'The Rise and Function of the Holy Man in Late Antiquity', *Journal of Roman Studies* LXXI (1971): 80–101. [Above, pp. 103–52.]

hopes and fears that would otherwise have been scattered and lost on the distant vault of heaven. For the holy man could be approached directly; he could receive unflinchingly a heavy charge of entreaty, cajolery, even threats; and the prayers that he sent up to heaven were thought capable of rendering precise and relevant to his individual petitioner the inscrutable workings of God's providence.[82] Thus the core of the holy man's power in Late Antique society was the belief that he was there to act as an intercessor with God. Whether living or dead he was a favoured courtier in the distant empire of heaven: he had gained a 'boldness' to speak up successfully for his protégés before the throne of Christ.[83]

If Byzantines had not believed that it was possible for created beings to sway the will of God by their intercessions, then the rise of the holy man and the rise of the icon would not have happened. For the icon merely filled a gap left by the physical absence of the holy man, whether this was due to distance or to death. The same mechanisms that had focused on the figure of the holy man (who was often as silent or as far removed above the beholder, as would have been the case with St Symeon Stylites, as was any icon[84]) could be brought to bear on the icon: they could even be heightened by the capacity of the silent portrait of the dead to take an even heavier charge of urgency and idealization without answering back. The figures of the saints at Saqqara, in Egypt, standing with outstretched arms in the traditional pose of the praying holy man, actually have scratched upon

---

82. Ibid., pp. 96–97. [Above, pp. 143–44.]

83. The idea is central to the letters of the Patriarch Germanus in the opening phase of the Iconoclast controversy: to John of Synnada (Mansi, xiii. 104A) and to the Iconoclast Thomas of Claudiopolis (Mansi, xiii. 132C); compare *Adversus Constantinum Caballinum, P. G.* xcv. 340C. See Brown, 'Holy Man', p. 94 [above, pp. 136–37] on the late Roman background.

84. One should remember that the ideal holy man was thought of as immobile as a statue: Gregory Nazianzenos, *Eulogy on Basil of Caesarea*, 52, 2. *P. G.* xxxvi. 569A—at a moment of crisis, Basil had stood in church 'his body, his gaze, his whole attention fixed rigid, like a statue set up in honour of God and His altar'. See Brown, 'Holy Man', p. 93, n. 163 and p. 97, n. 206 [above, p. 135, n. 163, and p. 143, n. 206].

them the prayers which the believer wished them to address, on his behalf, to God.[85]

As a religious system, early Islam consciously rejected these preoccupations. Unlike the Byzantine Christ, Allah was an absolute monarch whose will was untrammelled by the pressures of his heavenly bureaucracy. To admit angelic powers as intercessors with Allah had been the last temptation of Mohammad. He had resisted it.[86] At the time of the Iconoclast controversy, the idea that any created being—angel or dead saint—could intercede with Allah was out of the question: 'cry ever again, "There is no power nor might but through Allah"; for this comes from the very treasure that is hidden beneath the throne of God.'[87] At a stroke, the icon became unnecessary. The whole drama of focusing on a particular figure was pointless if this figure had no power to move the will of God on your behalf. The Muslim rejected icons, just as he rejected the building of churches over the tombs of Christian saints[88] and the offering of incense in their names,[89] not because he disliked the human face (which we know not to have been the case in many of the monuments of the eighth century), but because his heaven was without human intercessors.

The belief in intercession, and the consequent psychological need to focus one's attention and hopes on the face of the intercessor, was the lever that shifted the religious art of the early Byzantine world. The earliest icons are those that make plain the mechanism of intercession: from the late fifth century, *ex-voto* icons published scenes from the court-life of heaven—the Virgin and Child enthroned, flanked by angels,

85. David Howell, 'Saint George as Intercessor', *Byzantion* XXXIX (1969): 133.

86. Tor Andrae, *Mohammed. The Man and His Faith* (1936), p. 28.

87. I. Goldziher, *Vorlesungen über den Islam* (1910), p. 45. Compare A. J. Wensinck, *The Muslim Creed* (1932), p. 61.

88. Monneret de Villard, *Introduzione*, p. 272.

89. Grabar, *Martyrium*, II, 83, notes 2 and 3, and S. M. Stern, ''Abd al-Jabbār's Account of How Christ's Religion Was Falsified by the Adoption of Roman Customs', *Journal of Theological Studies* XIX (1968): 128–85, at p. 147.

with little donors supported by towering saintly patrons.[90] Angels appear early, despite genuine theological scruples about giving them a human form.[91] They appear not because they were faded relics of winged victories. They had been men's guardian spirits from time immemorial, and they were those courtiers whose rank placed them nearest to the ear of God.[92] The Virgin is of crucial importance, for she represented the acme of a mortal's intercession in heaven. She was invariably portrayed with Christ sitting on her lap. For her intercessions had the infallible efficacy of a blood-relative. This is what the icon of the Virgin meant that was set up on the gate of Constantinople at the time of the Avar attack of 626: let 'the brood of darkness' beware: 'for she is indeed the mother of Him who drowned Pharaoh and all his hosts in the depths of the Red Sea.'[93] Icons also showed the saints interceding with Christ placed on the lap of the Virgin[94] or being acknowledged, in the familiar yet solemn gesture of the arm placed over the shoulder that we can see on statues of Diocletian and his colleagues, as the intimates of Christ in the government of the universe.[95]

The holy man, therefore, was the impresario of the piety that focused on the icon, as it had focused on himself, as the

90. See Grabar, *Martyrium*, II, 81: some of the earliest religious icons of public importance were in the form of *ex-votos* set up by members of the imperial family. Now see R. Cormack, 'The Mosaic Decoration of S. Demetrios of Thessaloniki', *Annual of the British School at Athens* LXIV (1969): 17–52, a most important study.

91. Raised by John, bishop of Thessalonica (610–649): Mansi, xiii. 164D.

92. Averil Cameron, *Agathias* (1970), p. 5 and n. 3; *Anthologia Palatina*, I 35 and 36: poems on *ex-voto* icons of angels marking successes in the career of lawyers. [Peter Brown, *The Making of Late Antiquity* (Cambridge, Mass., 1978), pp. 68–72 and *The Cult of the Saints: Its Rise and Function in Latin Christianity* (Chicago, 1981).]

93. A. Mai, *Patrum Nova Bibliotheca*, vi, 2 (1853), 427. Compare *Adversus Constantinum Caballinum*, P. G. xcv. 340A.

94. Mansi, xiii. 57E and 64D. Of the Byzantine signet-rings and pectoral crosses on show in the British Museum, all those of the fifth to seventh centuries show either the human protégé with his supernatural protectors or these protectors interceding with Christ. See E. Kantorowicz, 'Ivories and Litanies', *Journal of the Warburg and Courtauld Institutes* V (1942): 70–72.

95. Icon of St Menas, Bawit, illustrated, with comment, in Peter Brown, *The World of Late Antiquity* (1971), p. 102, pl. 72.

tangible presence of an intercessor before God. He had been the impresario, also, of a parallel development: the tendency to regard a material object as the vehicle of cures. Objects blessed by the holy man had been the vehicles of cures since the fourth century. These *placebos* (often no more than drinking a cup of blessed cold water) had made divine protection for the sufferer tangible and so efficacious.[96] By the end of the sixth century, icons associated with holy men, or blessed by them, had joined the more impersonal blessed objects.[97] A woman cured by St Symeon the Younger carried his portrait back home with her. But the very mechanism of focusing, which had made possible the first cure in the face-to-face encounter with the living holy man, could be brought to bear equally efficaciously around the silent portrait. Another woman came to the icon, confident that 'if I can only see his face, I shall be saved'.[98] Altogether, the role of the holy man in Late Antique society—whether speaking, blessing or just being seen to be standing in prayer—had been to translate the awesomely distant loving-kindness of God into the reassuring precision of a human face.[99]

The momentum of the search for a face made itself felt throughout the sixth century in changes in the traditional type of relics. Icons came to join the relics. In relation to the relic they played a psychological role strictly analogous to the holy man. They were human figures filling the gap between awesome holy things and the frail believer. In Rome, a saint's sarcophagus could kill the workmen who had dislodged it.[100] In Thessalonica, the deep-buried grave of St Demetrius could flash out tongues of fire with an unearthly smell.[101] Under-

96. Brown, 'Holy Man', p. 96. [Above, p. 142.]
97. Mansi, xiii. 81B, with the commentary of Kitzinger, 'Cult of Images', pp. 108 ff.
98. *V. Symeon. Iun.* c. 118, ed. P. van den Ven, 98: cited in Mansi, xiii. 76C. The passage makes plain that the power of God that 'overshadows' the living holy man 'overshadowed' the icon.
99. Brown, 'Holy Man', p. 97. [Above, p. 144.]
100. Gregory I, Ep. IV, 30.
101. *Miracula Sancti Demetrii*, ii, P. G. cxvi., 1241C.

standably, the sufferer preferred to press his face against the handsome, idealized face on the casing of the relics of St Demetrius;[102] and the inscrutable, deep-buried power of the martyr became bearable, in dreams, by appearing to the believer 'as he appears on ancient icons'.[103] The icon was the go-between. St Mary the Egyptian, a prostitute, was pushed away from the Holy Sepulchre by an invisible force surging up against her in the vast impersonal throng of the congregation; but she was able to turn to an icon of the Mother of God that hung near the door, to promise that she would repent. Faced by too crushing a sense of the holy, late Roman men had turned to the homely figure of the holy man in the same way as St Mary had turned to the icon. The holy man was prepared to act as a guarantor with God for the forgiveness of their sins. So, having prayed, gazing unflinchingly into the face of the Virgin, Mary went back into the crush.[104] She had gained from the icon precisely what the Byzantine layman gained from an interview with the holy man—confidence in approaching the Holy of Holies.

Altogether it is as well to linger on the psychological needs that sought resolution through investing the icon with that same charge of holiness as had previously surrounded the living holy man. For until these needs are stated with precision, the historian cannot go forward with a historical explanation. The idea that the rise of icons can be explained as a resurgence of the animistic beliefs of the masses[105] seems to lack just this element of precision, both psychological and, so, historical. Animism is a concept that was first put into circulation among historians of religion by the anthropological theorists of the nineteenth century. Few modern anthropologists would now treat it as valid currency. Nor is it wise to label in an easy—and dismissive—manner mechanisms of

102. *Mirac. S. Dem.* 1217D; see Grabar, *Martyrium*, II, 25–26.
103. *Mirac. S. Dem.* 1317BC.
104. Mansi, xiii. 88A; compare Brown, 'Holy Man', p. 98. [Above, pp. 145–46.]
105. Kitzinger, 'Cult of Images': 'the naive animistic ideas of the masses' (p. 146), 'a last minute withdrawal from the abyss of sheer animism' (p. 147).

focusing on a single 'vested' object which have been observed still to play an essential role in the healing processes of patients in the most modern of modern hospitals.[106] We may safely leave to any surviving Byzantines the delicate task of deciding whether their beliefs were superstitious, animistic or backward. Yet it is necessary for the historian to question this attitude to the religious beliefs of the Byzantine world. Just such an attitude has provided the *deus ex machina* that underlies Kitzinger's account of the rise and establishment of icons in the late sixth and seventh centuries. For his explanation of the public 'reception' of icons in terms of changes in official circles in the late sixth and seventh centuries can carry full conviction only if we are prepared to accept his presupposition that these changes must have been a concession to an ineluctable, and ill-defined, popular pressure.[107] It can be clearly shown that the holy man did not rise to influence in late Roman society in so simple a way.[108] No more did icons. Rather than assume that the worship of icons rose like a damp stain from the masses, we should look into the needs which the piety of Late Antique men sought to satisfy in looking at them. These needs were 'human', not 'popular'. They have no very precise location in any one stratum of Byzantine society, nor do they affect only those of a low level of education. The two-tiered model of ancient society, by which any notable change in belief can be ascribed to the upward pressure of popular superstition on a Greco-Roman élite fits few cases—and least of all this one. If anything, it was the élite of the Byzantine world whose needs were more effectively satisfied by the cult of icons than were those of the

106. E.g., C. Binger, *The Doctor's Job* (1946), p. 48.

107. Kitzinger, 'Cult of Images', pp. 119–20: 'to try to identify with any precision the forces which seem to have pressed from below could only be guesswork. What can be suggested is that the resistance to such pressure on the part of authorities decreased in that period. . . .'

108. Brown, 'Holy Man', pp. 81–82 [above, pp. 107–108]. For an acute and instructive criticism of similar views held by scholars of Western hagiography, see František Graus, *Volk, Herrscher und Heiliger im Reich der Merowinger. Studien zur Hagiographie der Merowingerzeit*, Česká akademie věd (1965), esp. pp. 31–36.

supposed masses of the population.[109] The great prominence given to the icon in the late sixth and seventh centuries does not represent a final, ineluctable triumph of popular feeling; still less does the Iconoclastic reaction represent an ineffective attempt to control the superstition of the emotional lower classes—as has been frequently suggested, with the unpleasant rider that Byzantine women are, automatically, to be treated by the historian as a 'lower class'.[110] The concluding words of a lecture by a great connoisseur of the ancient world could well serve as a warning to the religious historian of this period also: 'Thus my inquest into popular religious beliefs in the late Roman historians ends in reporting that there were no such beliefs. In the fourth and fifth centuries there were of course plenty of beliefs which we historians of the twentieth century would gladly call popular, but the historians of the fourth and fifth centuries never treated any belief as characteristic of the masses and consequently discredited among the élite. Lectures on popular religious beliefs and the Late Roman historians should be severely discouraged.'[111]

We should look for changes in a different direction.

The most influential single feature of the religious life of the sixth century was the new effervescence of civic patriotism in the Eastern Empire.[112] It was in this century that the

109. See Cameron, *Agathias*, p. 5: 'Agathias either had money to spare or was desperate enough about his examination chances to dedicate to the Archangel an *ex voto* mosaic . . .' [See the outstanding articles of Averil Cameron, 'Corippus' Poem on Justin II: A Terminus of Antique Art?', *Annali della Scuola Normale Superiore di Pisa, classe di lettere e filologia*, ser. 3, V (1975): 129–65; 'The Theotokos in Sixth-Century Constantinople: A City Finds Its Symbol', *Journal of Theological Studies*, n.s., XXIX (1978): 79–108; and 'Images of Authority: Elites and Icons in Late Sixth-Century Byzantium', *Past and Present* LXXXIV (1979): 3–35.]

110. D. Savramis, 'Der abergläubliche Missbrauch der Bilder in Byzanz', *Ostkirchliche Studien* IX (1960): 174–92 at p. 180: 'Die Rolle die die Frauen in der Bilderverhrung spielten, spricht auch für das Eindringen dieser Gewohnheit von unten her, aus den Massen.' [See above, pp. 11–12.]

111. A. D. Momigliano, 'Popular Religious Beliefs and the Late Roman Historians', *Studies in Church History* VIII (1971): 18.

112. Dietrich Claude, *Die byzantinische Stadt im 6. Jahrhundert*, Byzantinisches Archiv, XIII (1969). [In the light of recent work I would speak more of a 'readjust-

Christian Church was finally established as the focus of collective feeling.[113] The alarms of warfare alone heightened the need for common symbols of loyalty and protection.[114] The cult of the civic saints of the Empire provided such symbols. At least St Demetrius (and the clergy who fostered his cult and recorded his interventions in long sermons) was interested in maintaining the ancient civic ideals of harmony in the demoralized city of Thessalonica.[115] The icon became the visible expression of the invisible bond that linked the community with the intercessions of its patron saint. In this way, icons come to appear on the walls of a Syrian town,[116] and the *Mandylion* of Edessa, its great Christ icon, was said to have destroyed the siege-works of Khusro I in 544.[117] The shift to the icon is most revealing in this case. Two centuries previously, it was believed that Nisibis had been saved from Shapur II through the curse of the local holy man.[118] Now, in Edessa, it was the direct pledge of Christ, given to King Abgar in the form of a miraculous impression of His face, that reassured the citizens that their town, at least, would never fall: and even in Edessa, His face was thought a more suitable pledge than His letter to Abgar, which had satisfied

ment' of the life of the urban communities to changed conditions, rather than of an 'effervescence'. That is, it is possible to exaggerate the overall prosperity of the cities of the Eastern Empire, without denying the energy which the leaders of these towns, most especially the Christian clergy, put into building and religious ceremonial designed to assert a new, Christianized definition of the city: Evelyne Patlagean, *Pauvreté économique et pauvreté sociale à Byzance: 4e.–7e. siècle* (Paris, 1977), pp. 17–35 and 181–96; G. Dagron, 'Le christianisme dans la ville byzantine', *Dumbarton Oaks Papers* XXXI (1977): 11–19; and the articles of Averil Cameron cited in note 109 above.]

113. Claude, *Byzantinische Stadt*, p. 95, and A. Grabar, 'La mosaique de pavement de Qasr el-Lebya', *Comptes Rendus de l'Académie des Inscriptions et Belles Lettres*, June 1969, p. 264–82.

114. Claude, *Byzantinische Stadt*, pp. 139 ff.

115. *Mirac. S. Dem.* 1225B, 1232A, 1252C, 1268A, 1301A, 1324B, 1341BC.

116. Claude, *Byzantinische Stadt*, pp. 140 ff.

117. Evagrius, *Historia Ecclesiastica*, IV, 27, cited in Mansi, xiii. 192A, speaks of the *Mandylion* Christ-Icon; Procopius, *Bella*, II, xii, 26, still of the letter of Christ to Abgar, not of an icon.

118. Theodoret of Cyrrhus, *Historia Religiosa*, P. G. lxxxii, 1304D.

earlier centuries. In exactly the same way, the icon of the Virgin, placed on the gate of Constantinople in 626, was a tangible reminder of the manner in which the absent Emperor Heraclius had pledged the city to her protection.[119]

The need to express collective feeling went beyond the occasional emergency. The prosperous and potentially fissile villages of Asia Minor also found a similar focus in great intercessory processions and solemn junketing, among which icons began to play a part.[120] In the western Mediterranean, the plague replaced the Slav and the Persian as the catalyst of the same development.[121] When the monks of St Augustine entered Canterbury in 598 'carrying a holy cross and the image of a great King, the Lord Jesus Christ'[122] they were bringing to heathen Kent a method of supernatural prophylaxis that had been developed, comparatively rapidly, from one end of the Mediterranean to the other. In the late sixth century, therefore, the icon was not only a successor of the imperial image. It was a new dialect for the ancient language—for good or ill, the Roman Empire had remained a 'commonwealth of cities': and the icon was there to show that, in this commonwealth, the civic saints did their job.[123]

The diffusion of the icon in the sixth century demonstrates this. Many Byzantines travelled widely throughout the cities of the Mediterranean, as had their Greek forebears in the age of the Antonines.[124] They felt quite as homesick. For them, the icon was a reminder of the saint of their home-

119. Mai, *Bibliotheca Nova Patrum*, vi. w, 426.

120. The icon 'not made with human hands', in the possession of the village of Diboulion, was carried in procession through the other villages of the province in order to raise funds: Dobschütz, *Christusbilder*, pp. 5**–7**. On the general evolution see Brown, 'Holy Man', p. 90 [above, p. 127].

121. S. N. Biraben and J. Le Goff, 'La peste du haut moyen-âge', *Annales* XXIV (1969): 1498. [On the cult of the saints as a means of expressing and consolidating the *consensus* of Western towns, see above, pp. 246–49, and Brown, *The Cult of the Saints*, pp. 96–100.]

122. Bede, *Historia Ecclesiastica Gentis Anglorum*, I, 25.

123. *Adversus Constantinum Caballinum, P. G.* xcv. 340D.

124. See L. Robert, *Hellenica*, XIII (1965), 120–24 on copies of the statues of the home town in the second century A.D.

land.[125] Furthermore, the sense of living in a world with frequent interchange pushed to the fore the standardized images of universal figures—icons of Christ and the Virgin.[126] Yet local associations remained very strong. There is no more touching story than that of the citizen of Thessalonica who went blind in Constantinople. Pious reminders that God was everywhere meant little to him. His cure came only when a voice told him in which church he could find a portrait of Demetrius. He stumbled in, crying, 'where is the great Demetrius?'—and looked up to see on the wall the beloved well-known face of Demetrius—*his* saint.[127]

Though the renewed civic sense of the sixth century made icons public and put them into rapid circulation in the Mediterranean, it was the holy man who kept them beloved and gave them a more intimate and permanent religious status. The icons of the city avoided some problems. They faced the profane world from the arcades of churches, on town gates.[128] It was the monks who helped to bring them into the church, the preserve of the holy. In the cult of icons, scholars have surely been right to see the monks as the *Ton-*

125. Compare A. Deubner, *Kosmas und Damian* (1907), 13, pp. 132 ff., cited in Mansi, xiii. 65C, where the icon consoles a lady whose husband had been transferred from Constantinople, that the saints of this quintessentially Constantinopolitan shrine would still be able to 'visit' her even at Laodicea. The icon enables a ship's captain to recognize that it was St Demetrius who spoke to him in a dream: *Mirac. S. Dem.* 1253B. Two Galatians, stranded in the desert, recognize 'Plato, the martyr of their home-town', who had led them in a vision, by comparing his face with their icon: Mansi, xiii. 32E. In the shrine of St Cyrus and John (Aboukir, Egypt), an inhabitant of Damascus is not fully cured until he dreams that the patron-saint of Damascus had shared in the cure administered by the two Egyptian saints: *Miracula Sanctorum Cyri et Johannis, P. G.* lxxxvii, 3664B ff. at 3672C.

126. Grabar, *Iconoclasme*, pp. 90 ff. Compare L. Robert, *Hellenica*, XIII (1965), 124: 'De plus en plus, au cours de l'époque hellénistique et de l'époque romaine, il y a des transferts de culte, des transferts de copies de statues divines. En face des cultes locaux s'établit le grand dieu, aux pouvoirs éprouvés, sous la forme canonique de son idole'.

127. *Mirac. S. Dem.* 1384C–1385A.

128. *Mirac. S. Dem.* 1220B; Th. Nissen, 'Unbekannte Erzählungen aus dem Pratum Spirituale', *Byzantinische Zeitschrift* XXXVIII (1938): 367, on the Christ Icon at Antioch.

angebende. For the secret of the holy man's popularity was precisely that he had remained, for all his awesome sanctity, very much an average Byzantine. Monastic piety was the piety of the Byzantine layman writ large—hence its enormous appeal. The desperate need of the lonely hermit to focus his attention on some enduring and resilient figure had, also, found a resolution in the icon hanging in his monastic cell. There is a deep psychological authenticity in the account of the monk who felt tempted to rid himself of the 'spirit of fornication' that tormented him, by trampling on the beautiful idealized portrait of the Virgin with which he lived.[129] There was more to this, perhaps, than the reactions of individual monks. The mystical theology of the monks articulated a more sophisticated, psychological theory of the function of the image as an aid to contemplation.[130] The monastic church may well have been the first milieu in which this contemplative theory was put into practice. In such a church, the icon gained meaning through being part of the liturgy, and became a chosen vehicle for expressing the majestic rhythms of the divine plan of salvation.[131] The fundamental presupposition of a theory of the contemplative function of the icon—which is, quite crudely, that the worshipper should be able to spend long hours at his ease before the visible images of invisible presences,[132] was best met in the precincts of a monastery, just as pagan apologists of images had, also, en-

129. John Moschus, *Pratum Spirituale*, cited in Mansi, xiii. 193A-D. The Iconoclasts apparently cut out these passages in the *Pratum Spirituale*: Mansi, xiii. 192D.

130. Kitzinger, 'Cult of Images', pp. 139 ff. on the arguments.

131. See, for example, the role of the mosaic of the Transfiguration, in the church in the Monastery of St. Catherine at Mount Sinai: 'The Church and Fortress of Justinian', *Dumbarton Oaks Papers* XXII (1968): 14: 'To the ordinary pilgrim the Burning Bush [where the monastery was supposed to stand] was a numinous object which he viewed with awe and wonder. . . . For the monks in their nave, however, the Burning Bush was evidently just a local memento, a reminder of the unfolding of God's plan of salvation, so subtly and profoundly set forth in the mosaic [of the Transfiguration] over their main altar. Between the relic and the mosaic is only a wall, the wall of the main apse, but in idea they are very far apart.' (G. H. Forsyth)

132. Mansi, xiii. 304E.

visaged the continued lingering of a devotee among the statues of the gods in a cherished holy spot.[133] Furthermore,
monastic craftsmanship in producing icons would raise the
icon above the suspicions that, as we have seen, still clung so
heavily to the artist in any urban secular context.[134]

Perhaps the monks contributed more to the cult of icons
than through the example of individual religious habits. For
the holy man had become the arbiter of Christian discipline
in the community. It was to the holy man, and not to the
bishop, that the early Byzantine layman instinctively turned
to find out how he should behave.[135] When visiting Constantinople, Theodore of Sykeon laid down the law about the
propriety of going to the baths after church; the ruling
caused quite a stir; the clergy of the Hagia Sophia sent a delegation to him—had the holy man derived his ruling from the
Scriptures?[136] The propriety of icons belonged to the same
penumbra of Christian behaviour as having a bath. In the
early fifth century, a courtier would approach the holy man
Neilos, to ask where in his new church he should place the
cross, and where the delightful foliage and hunting scenes of
fashionable mosaics.[137] The holy man retained this role up to
the eighth century. When the Iconoclast bishop appeared in a
provincial town, the locals promptly trooped off to their local holy man to ask what they should think. 'With tears', the
old man proceeded to tell them (for the next 34 pages of
Melioransky's printed text!), to the great annoyance of the
Iconoclast bishop.[138]

Holy men and icons were implicated on an even deeper
level. For both were, technically, unconsecrated objects. Not

133. Porphyry, *Against the Christians*, cited in Alexander, *Patriarch Nicephorus*,
p. 27.

134. Theodore of Stoudion, Ep. I, 15, *P. G.* xcix. 957C.

135. Brown, 'Holy Man', p. 98 [above, p. 147].

136. *Vita Theodori Syceotae*, c. 137, ed. Festugière, Subsidia Hagiographica,
XLVIII (1970), p. 109.

137. Nilus, *Ep. ad Olympiodorum, P. G.* lxxix. 577D. [See above, p. 147,
n. 230.]

138. *The Admonition of the Old Man*, ed. Melioransky, p. v.

only was the holy man not ordained as a priest or a bishop: his appeal was precisely that he stood outside the vested hierarchy of the Byzantine Church.[139] He was holy because he was held to be holy by his clientèle, not because any bishop had conferred holy orders on him. By the end of the sixth century, the exceptional position of the holy man was made explicit in formal gesture: a mystique of its own surrounded the monastic dress, the *schema*.[140] It was the *schema*, and not consecration by the bishop, that conferred spiritual powers on the holy man. Like the icon, therefore, the monastic *schema* could only claim indirect consecration from the past: it was said to have derived its holiness from being the same garment as that which angels had conferred on St John the Baptist in the wilderness.[141]

Icons were invested with holiness in the late sixth and seventh centuries because they still expressed the continuing needs of the ancient city; they were backed up by continued loyalty to particular cult-sites, which still boasted the physical remains of supernatural protectors; they entered circulation, also, as part of the relationship between the holy man and his largely urban clientèle. They had inherited, therefore, both the strength and weakness of the religion of the ancient city. These weaknesses proved their undoing.

First: the public use of icons depended on a close association with intense feelings of local patriotism. In the seventh century these feelings had become dangerously centrifugal. Byzantium did have to face a crisis of 'regionalism and independence' in the face of the first Slav and the first Arab attacks.[142] In Thessalonica, for instance, St Demetrius tended

139. Brown, 'Holy Man', pp. 91–92 and 95. [Above, pp. 131–32 and 139.]

140. See K. Holl, *Enthusiasmus und Bussgewalt beim griechischen Mönchtum* (1898), p. 205 f.

141. See, especially, the long and passionate digression on the holiness of the monastic *schema*, in a text concerned, ostensibly, with the holiness of icons: P. Peeters, 'Saint Romain le néomartyr (†1. mai 780) d'après un document géorgien', *Analecta Bollandiana* XXX (1911): 417.

142. See now A. Guillou, *Régionalisme et indépendance dans l'empire byzantin au viième siècle* (1969), pp. 248–52.

to eclipse the Emperor and his officials. In the *Miracles of St Demetrius* we see local opinion viewing imperial governors of the seventh century with the same misgivings as had the town council of Antioch in the fourth century, as we see it through the writings of Libanius. Like Libanius, St Demetrius knew a difficult governor when he saw one. Like Libanius, St Demetrius (and the clergy who reported his actions) could make or break a foreign official's reputation in the city.[143] Some never learnt. When the town council swore on the grave of St Demetrius that they were innocent of cooking their tax accounts this was too much for the governor: 'He said that the most glorious martyr was hand in glove with the townsmen.' The council trooped out, covering their ears lest they hear further blasphemies. In two days the governor was down with a stroke.[144] The essentially Late Antique friction was suddenly magnified in the crisis of the seventh century. When there was a rumour that the town would have to be evacuated, a citizen dreamt that St Demetrius had refused the imperial mandate of God to leave his city: he would not desert his 'fellow citizens' for any emperor.[145] Similar feelings had crystallized in the smaller towns of Asia Minor and Syria. They could either be disruptive to the unity of the Empire or they would have their bluff called in any really serious crisis.[146]

Second: while the icon focused strong collective feelings, it also bore the brunt of that urge for privacy, for a special relationship with the divine, for advice and blessing in competitive situations, that had existed in the great Mediterranean cities since Roman times.[147] Hence the growing popularity of the icon among the upper classes of the Byzantine world. The courtiers and the educated clergy of the sixth and seventh centuries are the direct descendants of Aelius Aris-

---

143. *Mirac. S. Dem.* 1204A—for a 'good testimonial' on a governor, couched entirely in traditional terms.

144. Ibid., 1272BC.   145. Ibid., 1352A.

146. Claude, *Byzantinische Stadt*, pp. 127–44.

147. E. R. Dodds, *Pagan and Christian in an Age of Anxiety* (1965), p. 45.

tides. Like him, they needed the constant special attentions of private protectors in a competitive world.[148] Some of the first references to icons come from just such men, facing such difficulties.[149] In every class, the icon overcame the great loneliness of men and women in an urban setting. Its well-known face, rather than the crowded, frighteningly impersonal shrines, ministered to the day-to-day needs of the *quartier*.[150]

Hence an important shift in the religious topography of the Late Antique city. The great Christian basilicas of the previous centuries tended to stand empty, except for great occasions. In these, the solemn liturgy of the Eucharist was celebrated. But this liturgy had become awesome and distant. In it, Christ was withdrawn from the masses in a deliberate attempt to surround the Eucharist with the trappings of an imperial ceremonial.[151] Personal piety, therefore, leaked away towards the icons. For the icons were the way to the intercessions of the saints who formed the back-stairs government of that awesome throne.[152] Even when the basilica remained the focus of attention, as in Thessalonica, its collective meaning

148. St Demetrius is represented as the 'intimate friend' (with all the political overtones of such designation—'a friend at court') of the bishop and of individual leading figures of Thessalonica: *Mirac. S. Dem.* 1212A; 1213A; 1336A. [Brown, *Making of Late Antiquity*, pp. 63–64.]

149. The Patriarch Germanus appealed to his own experiences of cures, of the resolution of difficulties, of dreams, all connected with icons: Mansi, xiii. 125A.

150. On the role of the icon of the Virgin at Blachernae in the conception and childhood of St Stephen: *V. Steph. Iun., P. G.* c. 1176B–1080A. [For a similar tendency of holy images and neighborhood shrines to escape the controls of civic religious ceremonial, see the brilliant study of R. C. Trexler, 'Ritual Behavior in Renaissance Florence: The Setting', *Medievalia et Humanistica*, n.s., IV (1973): 125–44, esp. pp. 131–32.]

151. K. Holl, 'Die Entstehung der Bilderwand in der griechischen Kirche', *Gesammelte Aufsätze*, II (1928), 225–37, if he exaggerates the speed with which the monumental chancel became the fully-fledged iconostasis, separating the faithful from the altar, is nevertheless right on the growing solemnity of the ceremonies surrounding the Eucharist in the late sixth century (at pp. 231–32). [T. F. Mathews, *The Early Churches of Constantinople: Architecture and Liturgy* (Pennsylvania State, 1971), pp. 138–79.]

152. *V. Steph. Iun., P. G.* c. 1080A—the icon of the Virgin is, for the mother of Stephen, 'my surety, my patron, my helper'.

was increasingly blurred by the encroachment of *ex-voto* icons. Plainly to have St Demetrius as one's personal protector, by making him the godfather of one's children and by recording the transaction in a votive icon, meant more to individuals than did the imposing collective liturgy of the Eucharist. 'Released from the serried ranks of a narrative cycle or of a pictorial litany or calendar and no longer part of a universal scheme, an objective, supra-personal order, the sacred representation may become the object of a more intimate rapport, a more personal relationship.'[153] Not every age can afford such luxury. The untidinesss implicit in the need for 'a more intimate rapport' might strike a more orderly and militant age as superstition.

III

The Arab raids of the late seventh century fell like a hammer-blow on the rich and loosely-knit world that we have described. They created a deep demoralization. Only one city, Nicaea, felt that it could convincingly ascribe its deliverance to its local icons.[154] Pergamon, by contrast, fell after a resort to the most grisly form of pagan sorcery.[155] Incidents such as this show that the problem of morale was too big to handle by traditional methods.[156] Loss of confidence is not a feeling that we can expect to find on the surface of the official historiography of the Byzantine Empire; but in the course of the seventh century, this human fact can be felt pressing in on every facet of the Byzantine world.

Yet demoralization, in itself, cannot explain why any particular society chooses a particular scapegoat. This is true of Byzantine society in the eighth century. Byzantines had faced enough crises to know what to do. They knew that God was frequently angry with them for their sins. They knew what

153. Kitzinger, 'Byzantine Art', *Sitzungsberichte* (1957), p. 44. Compare Grabar, *Martyrium*, II, 87 f.; *Iconoclasme*, pp. 84–88 and 203.

154. Theophanes, *Chronographia*, A. M. 6217, ed. de Boor, pp. 404–406: Hennephof, no. 3, p. 3.

155. Theophanes, *Chronographia*, A. M. 6208, ed. de Boor, pp. 390.

156. E.g., Theophanes, *Chronographia*, A. M. 6201, ed. de Boor, p. 377.

these sins were: homosexuality, blasphemy, tolerance of pagans, Jews and heretics.[157] They had frequently punished such sins. Even Leo III had done his best in a tradition inherited directly from Justinian. He had ordered the forcible baptism of all Jews within the Empire.[158] Plainly, however, this time it was not thought enough. What the Iconoclasts were intent on removing and punishing was not particular sins but something more serious: the root sin of the human race, the deep stain of the error of idolatry.[159] Only a change in the mental climate of the age can account for such a drastic shift of emphasis.

Muslim propaganda can be discounted. Even if the Arab armies contained a high proportion of Syrian and Egyptian adventurers who might have been renegades and so could have provided Greek-speaking propagandists of Islam, it is unlikely that the Muslims used such methods and, in any case, that they would have been listened to by those at the receiving end.[160] If we wish to find debates about icons between Christians and Muslims, we must go to the humdrum life of the Syrian coast, where Cypriot merchants still frequented Gabala and passed the time of day by arguing with the customs officers.[161] Islamic propaganda was unnecessary. The influence of the Old Testament upon the public image of the Byzantine Empire had grown steadily since the reign of Heraclius: the Byzantines were the 'true Israel'.[162] The post-Justinianic law was presented, by Leo III in the preface to his *Ecloga*, as no more than an elaborate implementation of the law of Moses.[163] This evolution gave the Byzantine clergy

157. Theodosius II, *Novella*, iii, 8 (438)—Jews, Samaritans, pagans, and heretics; Justinian, *Novella*, cxli (549)—homosexuals.

158. Sharf, *Byzantine Jewry*, p. 61.

159. Horos of 754: Hennephof, no. 205, p. 62.

160. P. G. xcii. 1365D—an Arab insulted the inhabitants in the siege of 717: 'calling the city "Constantia" and the Great Church merely "Sofia"'.

161. Mansi, xiii. 80A.

162. E.g., George of Pisidia, *In restitutionem S. Crucis*, line 25 f., ed. A. Pertusi, *Giorgio di Pisidia, Panegirici epici*, Studia Patristica et Byzantina, VII (1960), 226.

163. Ecloga, *Proemion*, trans. E. H. Freshfield, *A Manual of Roman Law* (1926), pp. 66–70. [One should add the thorough-going and self-conscious programme for

what they sorely needed in a time of crisis. It provided them with a body of ideas that, to quote an anthropologist, 'allows the verbalisation of anxiety in a framework that is understandable and that implies the possibility of doing something about it'.[164]

The savage and raw mood of the Iconoclasts, and the determination with which they attacked images as idolatrous, owes most to their ability to verbalize their anxiety. It is our first impression of them. When, in the 720s, the Patriarch Germanos wrote to Thomas of Claudiopolis, the worship of icons was an issue on which he was quite prepared to compromise. It was a practice which, like the taking of wine among the sages of the Book of Proverbs, should be treated 'μετὰ βουλῆς'.[165] What shocked Germanus was that, as a provincial bishop, Thomas was formulating the public mood in unusually stark terms.[166] Thomas had been saying that 'the Christian people have gone astray'.[167] It was the presupposition that 'the Christian people' could err so seriously as to lapse back into idolatry, and not the attack on icons themselves, that shocked the patriarch.[168] It was a presup-

---

the suppression of pagan survivals and liturgical divergences enunciated, if not enforced, in the *Quinisext Council in Trullo*: F. Trombley, 'The Council in Trullo (691–692): A Study of the Canons Relating to Paganism, Heresy and Invasions', *Comitatus* IX (1978): 1–18, and Ilse Rochow, 'Zu "heidnische" Bräuche bei der Bevölkerung des byzantinischen Reiches im 7. Jahrhundert', *Klio* L (1978): 483–98.]

164. Clyde Kluckhohn, cited in G. Lienhardt, *Social Anthropology* (1966), p. 125.

165. Mansi, xiii. 109B.

166. Ibid., 105A. Thomas of Claudiopolis is told that he would be better occupied praying that the empire should have peace.

167. Mansi, xiii. 124D. Thomas preached this 'as if it was a matter of common and irrefutable doctrine', ibid., 109E. [The extent to which such a mentality was specific to the region in which Thomas preached remains an open question, despite Nicole Thierry, 'Mentalité et formation iconoclaste en Anatolie', *Journal des Savants* 1976, pp. 81–119; for whether a tendency to abstract church decoration is a positive symptom of local iconoclast tendencies or merely the continuation of a common trend towards abstraction in art is far from certain: see R. M. Cormack, 'The Arts During the Age of Iconoclasm', *Iconoclasm*, p. 41.]

168. Mansi, xiii. 109B-D; 121D—'that the accusation of the Scriptures on the fate of idolaters is not applicable to us'; 128D—the critics are 'accusers of the Christians'.

position which the Iconoclasts found writ large in the Bible.
In the Old Testament, Israel had apostasized on many occasions; according to St Paul, the 'wrath of God' was 'poured
out' over the human race for its idolatrous tendencies.[169] Such
a perspective stated nothing less than the truth. The Arab
invasions had come to assume proportions of 'a great aboriginal catastrophe'; only national apostasy, and no amount of
individual laxity, could explain them. The apostasy of Israel
had always taken the form of a return to idols,[170] and the slow
decline of mankind into the mire of sin had taken the form of
a steady increase in idolatry.[171] Thus Iconoclasts could appeal
to a fact which even the most elementary historical awareness
could discover about their immediate past—there had been
an apparent increase in the use and prominence accorded to
images. Last, like all melodramatic verbalizations of anxiety,
its appeal lay in an implicit optimism. Blasphemy and homosexuality were likely to be always with the people of God;
but it had been known that the pious kings in Judah[172] and
pious Christian emperors after Constantine had effectively
extirpated idolatry.[173] A quite unmistakable streak of reforming zeal, a frank admission that institutions can get worse and
a confidence that they can be made better, is one of the most
tantalizing features of the Iconoclast movement.[174] But it is
perhaps not as isolated as we had thought. All over Europe,
Christians were drawing concrete historical and political
conclusions from the Old Testament. In Northumbria, Bede

169. Ibid., 121D and *Admonition of the Old Man*, ed. Melioransky, p. xviii: the
Iconoclast bishop, 'raising his voice, asked the people directly: "What do you think
of the Wisdom of God?"' and pp. xxiii–xxiv.

170. *The Admonition of the Old Man*, ed. Melioransky, p. xxiv. Cf. *Adversus
Constantinum Caballinum*, P. G. xcv. 320C.

171. Mansi, xiii. 121D and *The Admonition of the Old Man*, p. xvi quoting
Wisdom, xiv.

172. Gouillard, 'Synodikon', p. 287, lines 138–40, also in Hennephof, no. 79,
p. 34.

173. Letter of Epiphanius of Salamis to Theodosius II: Hennephof, no. 111,
p. 45.

174. Mansi, xiii. 228B. Compare *Adversus Constantinum Caballinum*, P. G. xcv.
341B.

was meditating on the account of Gildas of how the Britons had once lost their promised land to the Saxons, with an anxious sense that perhaps the turn of the Saxons might come round.[175] His exact contemporary, Thomas of Claudiopolis, was drawing equally bleak conclusions 'from too straightforward a rumination on the Holy Scriptures'.[176] The elemental and stark theme of the apostasy, dereliction and repentance of the people of Israel had become contemporary to men who were beginning to feel the cold chill of the advance of Islam.

The Iconoclasts could not, perhaps, have gone so far if they had not been able to state their case with such irrefutable clarity. The anxieties they mobilized were less tidy. Savage disillusionment and contempt for failed gods are important factors in the Iconoclast movement. They are neither surprising nor peripheral. Faced by real distress, the Byzantine Age of Faith was as skin-deep as any other. An old man who had failed to receive a cure from the shrines of Sts Cosmas and Damian stormed out: ἐπίθετας ἀποκαλῶν τοὺς ἁγίους καὶ μηδεμίαν ἐνέργειαν εὐεργεσίας κεκτημένους, ἀλλὰ μάτην καὶ ἔκ τινος προλήψεως τὴν δόξαν τοῦ δύνασθαι παρὰ θεῷ ἔχοντας.[177]

The Iconoclast controversy has a blustering inconclusive character. The Arab invasions of the late seventh century account for this. For these invasions marked the end of the ancient world in Asia Minor: 'in the days of old cities were numerous in Rūm (Anatolia) but now they have become few.'[178] At a stroke, therefore, the icons lost half their back-

175. J. M. Wallace-Hadrill, *Early Germanic Kingship in England and on the Continent* (1971), p. 74.

176. Germanus, *de haeresibus*, c. 40, P. G. xcviii. 77A.

177. Deubner, *Kosmas und Damian*, p. 145, 32: 'calling the saints impostors, who possessed no real power to do anybody any good, but who enjoyed an imagined reputation for power to move God, due to prejudice.'

178. *Hudūd al ʿĀlam: The Regions of the World*, trans. V. Minorsky (1937), p. 157. H. Ahrweiler, 'L'Asie Mineure', pp. 28–32. [But see now the cogent arguments of Clive Foss, 'The Persians in Asia Minor and the End of Antiquity', *English Historical Review* XC (1975): 721–47, supplemented by his 'The Fall of Sardis in 616 and the Nature of Evidence', *Jahrbuch der österreichischen Byzantinistik* XXIV (1975): 11–22; *Byzantine and Turkish Sardis* (Cambridge, Mass., 1976), pp. 1–66; 'Late Antique and Byzantine Ankara', *Dumbarton Oaks Papers* XXXI (1977): 27–87; 'Archae-

ing. We have seen to what an extent the icons of the immediately previous age had owed their charge of holiness to acting as a focus of very real civic patriotism. By the eighth century, this had vanished. The morale of the towns was broken. The pilgrimage-sites that had dotted Asia Minor were deserted.[179] The relics of the saints were abandoned or hurriedly transferred.[180] The icon had circulated largely on the security of these firm local associations. Now icons were in danger of a giddy inflation. Refugees were bringing, from all corners of the Empire, icons that lacked local approval.[181] Craftsmen were turning out increasingly standardized images of Christ and of the Virgin that had none of the homely familiarity of the image of one's local martyr.[182] It is not surprising that the crisis was first felt in the western provinces of Asia Minor. This was not because Iconoclasm had strong local roots in these areas. Far from it: it was Iconodulism which had the local roots;[183] but these roots had been shaken by the Muslim invasions.

Icons suffered, in part, because they were the symbols of a style of political life that was out of date. The Byzantine Empire could no longer afford the luxury of remaining a 'commonwealth of cities'. Self-help had proved to be either

ology and the "Twenty Cities" of Byzantine Asia', *American Journal of Archaeology* LXXXI (1977): 469–86; also Nicole Thierry, 'Un problème de continuité et de rupture: la Cappadoce entre Rome, Byzance et les Arabes', *Comptes Rendus de l'Académie d'Inscriptions et Belles Lettres 1977*, pp. 98–144. Plainly it affects one's interpretation of the immediate psychological effect of the Arab invasions if they were not, as I had assumed, an entirely novel experience. But the discontinuity between the urban life of the late sixth and early eighth centuries would, apart from the issue of morale, have rendered the religious 'style' of the first age of icons untenable: see the acute study of J. F. Haldon, 'Some Remarks on the Background of the Iconoclast Controversy', *Byzantinoslavica* XXXVIII (1977): 161–84.]

179. Mansi, xiii. 125AB, recognizes the decline in the powers of the icon of the Virgin at Sozopolis. See H. Ahrweiler, 'L'Asie Mineure', p. 3, n. 4, on how numerous such cult-sites had been.

180. Grabar, *Martyrium*, II, 351, 354–55.

181. E.g., Mansi, xiii. 21D, on the resistance of a woman of Caesarea to the relic and icon of a new saint.

182. Grabar, *Iconoclasme*, pp. 90 ff.

183. As seen by Dobschütz, *Christusbilder*, p. 265, n. 3.

treasonable or ineffective. The Emperor had to be omnicompetent, and be seen to be omnicompetent.[184] For the collapse
of the city left a void in men's view of the Empire. A new
patriotism had to be created. The void was filled by more
concrete emphasis than ever previously on the Byzantines as
a people of God, whose political imagery was borrowed
from the Old Testament. We have already seen the repercussion of this grave awareness on the ideology of the Iconoclasts. This was decisive. What was at stake was not only that
images had been forbidden in the second Commandment
(this everyone knew, and the Patriarch's copy of the Old Testament even had a marginal note at the place),[185] but that the
Byzantines were the people of God to whom this holy law
had been delivered. Therefore, the idea of the Church as the
core of Byzantine identity hardened. From the seventh century onwards, Byzantines thought of themselves as the 'baptized people'.[186] It was an attitude that had spasmodic reper-
cussions in forcible attempts to baptize Jewish communities
on Byzantine territory.[187] They found that they were not only
all baptized, but, also, far more united than previously. The
Christological rancours of the sixth century had diffracted
the religious life of the towns.[188] Now this religious life could
fall into place: and it fell into place around the basilica and the
liturgy of the Eucharist.[189] The Eucharist, as we have seen,
was one of the potent symbols of the holy which the Iconoclasts presented as the correct alternative to icons. How very

184. Thus the Emperors Leo III and Constantine V took over the building of
local town walls: Theophanes, *Chronographia*, A. M. 6232, ed. de Boor, p. 412.
These were marked only by traditional prophylactic signs of the Cross: A. Frolow,
'IC XC NIKA', *Byzantinoslavica* XVII (1956): 106.

185. Mansi, xiii. 188B.

186. The Jews are juxtaposed with 'the baptized people': *Mirac. S. Dem.*
1332B.

187. Sharf, *Byzantine Jewry*, pp. 53 and 61.

188. E.g., John Moschus, *Pratum Spirituale*, P. G. lxxxvii 2877C, where the
Eucharistic elements pass between a wife and her Chalcedonian woman neighbour,
to the predictable annoyance of the Monophysite husband.

189. *Mirac. S. Dem.* 1349A—it is assumed that in Thessalonica everyone is
present at the Eucharist.

potent it was to men of the early eighth century can be appreciated in a sculpture of a colleague and contemporary of the Iconoclast bishops—the cross of Bishop Acca of Hexham of 740. 'Acca's cross and its decorations are distinguished by an almost iconoclastic dismissal of figural panel . . . . The vine scroll, the symbol of the church in union with Christ, or Christ's sacramental presence in the Eucharist, covers the whole surface.'[190] Such a symbol had not been shared by the urban population of the great towns of the sixth century. In the Little Byzantium left over by the Arabs, it could regain its position.[191]

The emperors had to win in battle if they were to survive at all. For this purpose the sign of the cross, with its unbroken association with victory over four centuries, was a more ancient and compact symbol than any Christ-icon could be.[192] When it came to winning battles, the cross was stronger medicine: Heraclius,[193] Oswald of Northumbria,[194] the Armenians[195] all realized this; and the Arabs repaid the compliment—for them, Christians were not icon-worshippers, they were 'worshippers of the wood' (of the cross).[196] In a word: by asserting that only a limited number of symbols were in-

190. Rosemary Cramp, *Early Northumbrian Sculpture*, Jarrow Lecture 1956, p. 7. [Silvana Casartelli Novelli, 'La cattedrale di marmi carolingi di Torino nelle date dell'episcopato di Claudio l'iconoclasta', *Cahiers archéologiques* XXV (1976): 93–100. On the attitude to icons of the Venerable Bede, see now the important new article of P. Meyvaert, 'Bede and the Church Paintings at Wearmouth-Jarrow', *Anglo-Saxon England* VIII (1979): 63–77.]

191. Mansi, xiii. 124B. Germanus appeals to the solidarity of the solemn celebration of the Eucharist, which he has in common with the Iconoclasts.

192. Grabar, *Iconoclasme*, p. 153: 'Sainte-Sophie n'offrait primitivement aucune figuration chrétienne en dehors de la croix repétée maintes fois, et cet exemple illustre rappelle la tradition à laquelle se rattachaient les iconoclastes.'

193. Grabar, *Iconoclasme*, pp. 29 and 155, and 'La précieuse Croix de la Lavra de S. Athanase au Mont Athos', *Cahiers archéologiques* XIX (1969): 113, on the revival of the use of the simple cross at the time of the Byzantine military successes of the tenth century. See also Frolow, 'IC XC NIKA', pp. 98–110.

194. R. Cramp, *Early Northumbrian Sculpture*, p. 5.

195. B. Arakelian, *Armenian Reliefs of the IVth to VIIth Centuries* (1949), pp. 60–61, fig. 49, in Armenian.

196. Mansi, xiii. 357D.

vested with the idea of the holy, the Iconoclasts were choosing just those symbols that best suited a more collective and more highly centralized society. Norman Baynes has talked of the 'steel framework' of the Byzantine state.[197] Leo III and Constantine V attempted to ensure that this 'steel framework' stood out with a streamlined austerity, after generations of cluttering-up by the traditions of a more affluent and easy-going age. Let us examine how the Iconoclast controversy reflects this change.

In the first place, it may explain the inconclusive quality of the Iconoclastic controversy. Iconoclast persecutions of Iconodules amount to very little. One might easily dismiss them as a 'chopping at twigs.'[198] But this is just the point. The Iconoclasts were only faced with twigs. Their policy had a firm, traditional basis, very much in tune with the average sentiments of the Byzantine secular clergy. It amounted to strengthening the backbone of the Byzantine Church at the expense of pockets of centrifugal and illegitimate spiritual power. Their measures, therefore, though histrionic and brutal, were more like the clearing away of undergrowth in a well-established forest. The symbols to which the Iconoclasts appealed as the true repository of the holy carried implications that summed up a system of strong centralized government. It was Iconodulism rather than Iconoclasm that polarized strong local feelings. This is suggested by the fact that it was only after the reversal of Iconoclasm that some provincial cities regained, from the Empress Irene, a shadow of those lavish exemptions and privileges, which, in the seventh century, had been granted on the pretext of honouring the patron saints of these cities.[199] There was indeed a radical

197. N. H. Baynes, 'The Decline of the Roman Power in Western Europe', *Byzantine Studies*, p. 94.

198. Examined by Melioransky, in his preface to *The Admonition of the Old Man*, pp. 25–29.

199. A. A. Vasiliev, 'An Edict of the Emperor Justinian II', *Speculum* XVIII (1943): 1–13. See G. I. Bratianu, *Privilèges et franchises municipales dans l'Empire byzantin* (1936), pp. 88–98, and H. Ahrweiler, 'L'Asie Mineure', p. 25, n. 4.

wing in Iconoclasm that denied the intercession of the saints, and so denied their role as the special protectors of individuals and localities.[200] There could have been no more drastic rebuttal of the ideology of the civic saints than such a categorical denial. There was an Iconoclast Jacobinism that ruthlessly sacked local cult-sites.[201] In Constantinople itself pockets of 'illegitimate' power were, spasmodically, mopped up.[202]

It would be misleading to regard the Iconoclasts as anti-urban.[203] Rather, Constantine V acted as the midwife of a new style of urban life, by which the cities, from being pockets of local autonomy, became centres for the operation of the central government.[204] The success of Constantine V in Constantinople was spectacular. He did nothing less than recreate a city and its morale when it had been emptied by plague.[205] The immigration caused by the aftermath of this plague was an opportunity which Constantine V grasped with both hands. And he did so in the ancient, resolutely secular manner of an emperor such as Anastasius I. The images of the six Oecumenical Councils disappeared from the Milion, the hub

200. G. Ostrogorsky, *Studien*, pp. 29–40, for a differentiated account of this evidence. [Gero, *Constantine V*, pp. 152–68.]

201. The Iconoclast bishops in 754 feared extensive looting: Mansi, xiii. 332DE; Hennephof, no. 247, p. 73. See also Germanus, *de haeresibus*, c. 41, P. G. xcviii. 80AC.

202. On the fate of the relics of S. Euphemia see the material in R. Janin, *La géographie ecclésiastique de l'empire byzantin: Le siège de Constantinople* (1953), pp. 126–36, and F. Halkin, *Euphémie de Chalcédoine*, Subsidia Hagiographica XLI (1965), 81–106. The shrine in question was near the Hippodrome, of comparatively recent origin (the relics were translated from Chalcedon at the time of the Persian invasion in 615), and credited with miraculous powers. It was eminently vulnerable according to the criteria we have discussed: it had only popular recognition. By contrast, Constantine V appears to have used the more securely 'vested' relic of the Cross for formal occasions, such as the swearing of oaths: Theophanes, A. M. 6257, ed. de Boor, p. 437, 13 f. [Gero, *Constantine V*, pp. 155–65.]

203. As H. Ahrweiler, 'L'Asie Mineure', p. 24, implies.

204. M. J. Sjusjumov, 'Vizantijskij gorod (seredina vii–seredina ix. vv.)', *Vizantijskij Vremennik* XXVII (1967): 38–70 is the most recent treatment of this aspect of town life.

205. P. J. Alexander, *Patriarch Nicephorus*, pp. 123–24: 'It does seem that Constantine V made the city population prosperous at the expense of the peasants.'

of the city.[206] They were replaced by portraits of the Emperor's favourite charioteer.[207] In so doing, Constantine V revived the full-blooded and concrete mystique of the Hippodrome, with its associations of the victory of the good luck of the city and of its Emperor.[208] This was, perhaps, a welcome change from anxious dependence on the invisible Virgin.[209] It contrasts with Heraclius, who was prepared to leave the city in pledge to an icon of the Virgin. Constantine, by contrast, stayed put. And he reaped a reward of almost mystical popularity.[210] In making Constantinople the unchallenged hub of the Empire, Constantine V, rather than Heraclius, deserves the title of the founder of medieval Byzantium.

In this obscure and rancorous debate on the fate of the Byzantine town, the bishops almost invariably sided with the centralized hierarchy of the Empire. Their tastes had kept them within the firm horizon of the town. In their consecrated basilicas they celebrated the Eucharistic liturgy that was the symbol of the unity of the Christian city. In their palaces (which, frequently, were no more than a wing of the governor's palace)[211] they imposed the stern disciplinary norms of the ancient Christian penitential system on the townsfolk. They had their jails for recalcitrant country clergymen.[212] They were so used to participating with the governor in the secular ceremonial of the city life that a bishop of seventh-century Thessalonica found it only too easy to

206. *V. Steph. Iun.*, *P. G.* c. 1113A.

207. Ibid., c. 1169B, on the celebration of the Brumalia.

208. Grabar, *Iconoclasme*, pp. 156–60. Now see Alan Cameron, *Porphyrius the Charioteer* (1972).

209. Grabar, *Iconoclasme*, p. 35.

210. See the remarkable incident in the tense mood before the defeat of the Byzantine army by the Bulgars: Theophanes, *Chronographia*, A. M. 6304, ed. de Boor, p. 501. The crowd surged round the tomb of Constantine V calling on him to arise and save the Roman state. [Gero, *Constantine V*, esp. p. 108, gives the full measure of the 'charismatic' personality of Constantine.]

211. Claude, *Byzantinische Stadt*, p. 82. [F. Winkelmann, 'Kirche und Gesellschaft in Byzanz vom Ende des 6. bis zum Beginn des 8. Jahrhunderts', *Klio* XLIX (1977): 477–90.]

212. John Moschus, *Pratum Spirituale*, *P. G.* lxxxvii. 2969D.

dream that he was sitting in the theatre watching a tragedy.[213] When in the fifth century monks had protested to the bishop of Chalcedon that the governor was staging pagan games in the Hippodrome, the bishop told these zealots to mind their own business.[214] The situation plainly continued, and was reactivated in the course of the eighth century.[215] It is very significant that we should see the urban reforms of Constantine V in high relief, by the oblique light of monastic disapproval. For bishop and governor stood together, in the Iconoclast period, against the holy man of monastic background. *Cherchez le moine*: this remains the key to most Iconoclast policy, to all Iconoclast persecution, and to the overwhelming bulk of the contemporary Iconodule evidence from which we draw our impression of the period. Iconomachy in action is monachomachy. What was at stake, however, was not the dissolution of the Byzantine monasteries. It was, rather, a singularly consequential, if spasmodic, determination to break the power of the holy man in Byzantine society, both as a principal bulwark of the power of the icon and, so one might suggest, as a force in itself.

The holy man, of course, was a monk. He wore the badge of the monastic *schema* and, often, he practised from the shelter of a great monastery or great traditional grouping of hermits in single place.[216] But the Iconoclast attacks on monasteries are incidental to their main purpose. This was

213. *Mirac. S. Dem.* 1296B.   214. *Vita Hypatii*, c. 33, p. 108.

215. *V. Steph. Iun.*, P. G. c. 1120A; Peeters, 'Vie de S. Romain', *Analecta Bollandiana* XXX (1911): 413.

216. E.g., Theophanes, *Chronographia*, A. M. 6256, ed. de Boor, p. 442: Hennephof, no. 12, p. 9. *V. Steph. Iun.*, P. G. c. 1092D—the mountain of St Auxentios, a notorious lair of holy men, was turned into an imperial hunting reserve. [This interpretation has been subjected to careful criticism by S. Gero, 'Byzantine Iconoclasm and Monomachy', *Journal of Ecclesiastical History* XXVIII (1977): 241–48, who states his own position most succinctly in 'Byzantine Iconoclasm and the Failure of a Medieval Revolution', *The Image and the World* (1977) pp. 49–62. The *Life* of St Stephen the Younger has been studied, to its detriment, by G. Huxley, 'On the *Vita* of Saint Stephen the Younger', *Greek, Roman and Byzantine Studies* XVIII (1977): 97–108. The reader should bear these two studies in mind. Though I accept many of

the severing of the links between the individual holy man and his clientèle. The attack is a final illustration of the variety of the issues at stake in the eighth century. The evidence allows us to appreciate the situation very fully. We are faced with a situation strictly analogous to the notorious sorcery purges of the fourth century. These purges had happened at a time when two structures of power were sensed to conflict: the explicit, articulated vested power of the imperial servants conflicting with the inarticulate power of the traditional classes of the Roman world—with the *je ne sais quoi* of their prestige and education, and the labyrinthine tentacles of their actual political and social influence. The sorcery accusations of that period were a way of ferreting out and destroying hard nuclei of such inarticulate, unvested power. It is the same with the holy men of the reigns of Leo III and especially of Constantine V.[217] We have already seen the extent to which the Iconoclast clergy were committed to a structure of vested power. It was implicit in their contention that only objects that had been properly blessed by the appropriate authority could be treated as holy. We have seen how a whole set of social and administrative developments in the eighth century clustered behind this statement. We have seen, also, how, up to that century, holy man and icon had developed concomitantly. They were the foci of a totally different form of unvested inarticulate power. They were not blessed by anybody.[218] Both met needs that were private and not collective.

their precisions, I remain less certain than Gero that the attacks on monks, though inconclusive, did not condense an important aspect of the issues at stake in the controversy; the *Life* of St Stephen the Younger, though written later, appears to me to retain accurate knowledge of these issues as seen from the Iconodule side. The radical personality of Constantine V, though admirably presented by Gero, may not be sufficient in itself to explain the passions aroused and the strategies employed in the course of the eighth-century conflict of Iconoclasts and Iconodules.]

217. *V. Steph. Iun.*, *P. G.* c. 1129B: 'that sorcerer' is Constantine V's view of Stephen the Younger. See P. Brown, 'Sorcery, Demons and the Rise of Christianity', *Witchcraft Confessions and Accusations* (A. S. A. Monographs 9) (1970), pp. 20–25, also in *Religion and Society in the Age of St. Augustine* (1972), pp. 123–31.

218. Hence the constant pairing of arguments on the holiness and supernatural

Both very often lay outside the very horizon of the city—in suburban monasteries or on the tops of the nearest mountains. Both icon and holy man were consecrated from below. This meant, in practice, that both stood at the centre of a whole world of needs and relationships that were not included in the vested structure of the church and its collective rites.

The conflict latent in this situation was brought into the open by the events of the late seventh century. The equilibrium between collective overtones of the civic cult of the icon and the private ministrations of the holy man and of the miraculous icon, which had been perfectly maintained in a previous age, was brutally upset by the depletion of the cities. This meant that the centrifugal, the ascetic, and the non-collective and potentially non-urban elements in the worship of icons were suddenly exaggerated. It became brutally plain for the first time that either the bishop or the holy man must be the moral arbiter of Byzantium.[219] The holy man had tended to bless and foster the growth of the icon; the bishop, as the famous *Admonition of the Old Man* showed clearly, now found that this was against the law of God as he and his emperor interpreted it.[220] The holy man had played a large role in lightening the load of the early Christian penitential system; the bishop felt more strongly than ever previously that if the Byzantine Empire was a new Israel living under a single divine law, then it was he who should be its leader and the administrator of its laws for the believer.[221] The holy man had drawn his prestige largely from having opted out of urban society for the desert, while remaining within comfortable travelling distance for his urban clientèle;[222] bishop and gov-

---

origin of the monastic *schema* with arguments for the similar position of the holy icons.

219. *Adversus Constantinum Caballinum*, P. G. xcv. 329D and 332A.

220. *The Admonition of the Old Man*, ed. Melioransky, p. xviii: 'We should believe what has been said by God (in the Scriptures) and commanded by our holy Emperor.'

221. *Adversus Constantinum Caballinum*, P. G. xcv. 329D.

222. As with *V. Steph. Iun.* 1088A f.

ernor were committed to ensuring that many a small town did not sink back into the surrounding countryside.[223] The holy man, like the icon, was holy without having had this holiness delegated to him by the bishop. All this was no purely symbolic debate in eighth-century Byzantium: for, in Byzantium, as in other early medieval societies, holiness was power; and the symbol of the holy could cover a very real nexus of social influence. Hence the concern of Constantine V. We can follow it in the fully documented account of the life and martyrdom of St Stephen the Younger. Once established on the mountain of Auxentios on the Chalcedon side of the Bosphorus, Stephen became the focus of a large clientèle from Constantinople.[224] He was approached to handle large sums of money.[225] Aristocratic ladies were attached to him as their spiritual father. Later, his clientèle included army officers, and his consultations involved the worship of two private icons.[226] The presence of these icons in Stephen's cell was rather less important than Stephen himself. Like the supposed sorcerer of the fourth century, Stephen was the nucleus of inarticulate power: 'Sitting on top of his mountain', wrote the imperial spies, 'he is digging pits for you'.[227] Constantine V and his agents were right to be suspicious. The Byzantine upper class had remained, for all its new emphasis on centralized power, a singularly fluid and competitive body of men. The holy man as spiritual father (joined in the seventh and eighth centuries by the private collection of icons and by the icon of the patron saint as protector and godfather) was but one figure in a tangled skein of alternative and conflict-

223. On the profoundly non-urban quality of the position of the holy man, see E. Patlagean, 'À Byzance: ancienne hagiographie et histoire sociale', *Annales* XXIII (1968): 120–23.
224. *V. Steph. Iun.*, P. G. c 1088A; 1104.   225. Ibid., 1105B.
226. Ibid., 1153A–1156C. The degree to which Stephen continued an older tradition of the ministrations of the holy men, or was seen in that light, is shown by the use made by his biographer of the *Vita Euthymii* of Cyril of Scythopolis: J. Gill, 'The Life of Stephen the Younger by Stephen the Deacon: Debts and Loans', *Orientalia Christiana Periodica*, VI (1940): 115.
227. *V. Steph. Iun.*, P. G. c. 1164A and 1169A.

ing power structures. A politician's success depended on his ability to manipulate these alternative power structures.[228] Put crudely, success needed constant personal blessing: there is hardly a single emperor from the fifth century onwards whose career to the throne did not involve an interview with either a holy man or, for his opponents, with a sorcerer.[229] The circumstantial attention which Iconodule writers lavished on the séances of Iconoclast emperors with sorcerers, and on the influence on the careers of these emperors of the engagements entered into at such séances, is only the obverse of the readiness with which Iconodule holy men blessed would-be emperors.

Political prophecies by holy men are particularly rife in the literature of the eighth and ninth centuries. Whether these prophecies were made in answer to direct consultations with the holy man conceived of as an oracle, or whether (as is much more likely) the remark of the holy man in the course of a conversation was seized upon as significant in the light of what later happened, or was interpreted as tacit permission to act on the intentions of the group, politics were being talked on the top of the mountains around Constantinople.[230]

Nothing illustrates more vividly the determination of Constantine V and his agents to avoid a confusion of authority than the way in which he handled these insidious links between the holy man and the society around the imperial court.[231] Those holy men who are executed are those whose clientèle had become the most tenacious.[232] Execution was the fate of the spiritual father of the courtier who had heard

228. H. G. Beck, 'Byzantinische Gefolgschaftswesen', *Sitzungsberichte der bayerischen Akademie der Wissenschaften* V (1965) shows this very clearly.

229. Brown, 'Holy Man', p. 98, for late Roman evidence. See Theophanes, *Chronographia*, A. M. 6198, ed. de Boor, p. 375, 14 and A. M. 6203, ed. de Boor, p. 381, 6 for two vivid examples.

230. *Vita Iohannicii*, c. 15, 25, 28, 30, 33, *Acta Sanctorum*, 4 Nov., II, 1 (1894), 346B–347B; 355C; 357C–358A; 361C.

231. On the fate of the settlements on the Mountain of St Auxentios: *V. Steph. Iun.*, *P. G.* c. 1092D.

232. Theophanes, *Chronographia*, A. M. 6257, ed. de Boor, p. 438: 'on the

all the details of the courtier's homosexual love affair with the Emperor.[233] Nothing if not consequential and histrionic, Constantine V deconsecrated the potential holy man quite as thoroughly as he deconsecrated the icons.[234] His measures were designed to cut the links between the monastic spiritual adviser and the laity. The books of *Sayings of the Fathers*, from which monks drew on a huge reservoir of ascetic anecdotes to guide their charges through life's great casuistry, were burnt.[235] It was forbidden to visit an *Abba*. It was forbidden to take communion from him (which process might have involved the sort of embarrassing revelations to which we have just referred).[236] With an unfailing eye for the symbolic significance of great public gestures, Constantine V attacked the monastic *schema*. He performed a solemn deconsecration ceremony in the Hippodrome of Constantinople.[237] His intimate agent at Ephesus, Michael Lachonodracon, understood his master's theatrical gifts only too well. He made the monks in his province parade in the robe of a bridegroom.[238] The *schema* that had symbolized the holy man's position as standing outside normal human relations, as had been the case when the *schema* had first been conferred by angels on St John the Baptist in the Judaean desert, was replaced by the garment which a man wore when he was finally and irrevocably committed by marriage to the world of human kin-relationships. This clear and witty comment by an Iconoclast governor reinforces the impression with which we began, that the Iconoclast controversy was a debate on the holy in Byzantine

---

charge that they had been in the habit of visiting the above-mentioned recluse' (Stephen).

233. Theophanes, *Chronographia*, A. M. 6259, ed. de Boor, p. 442.

234. *V. Steph. Iun.*, *P. G.* c. 1112A sq.; 1136A f.; 1140A; 1148B.

235. Theophanes, *Chronographia*, A. M. 6263, ed. de Boor, pp. 445–46: Hennephof, no. 13, p. 10.

236. *V. Steph. Iun.*, *P. G.* c. 1109B–1112B.

237. Ibid., 1137BD; 1164B; Theophanes, *Chronographia*, A. M. 6257, ed. de Boor, p. 438: Hennephof, no. 10, p. 8.

238. Theophanes, *Chronographia*, A.M. 6263, ed. de Boor, p. 446.

society. But only the historian of the social evolution of the Late Antique and early Byzantine worlds can appreciate what a variety of factors lie behind such a debate. The scene in the Hippodrome of Ephesus, quite as much as the destruction of the icons, is no less than an attempt by a group of Byzantines to challenge three centuries of unofficial leadership in the Christian community.

Society and the Supernatural:
A Medieval Change[†]

I N THIS GENERATION, THE STUDY OF THE ELEVENTH
and twelfth centuries A.D. has been the forcing ground
for some of the best evocations of the processes of social
and intellectual change available to the student of any
pre-industrial society. To read Marc Bloch's *Feudal Society*,
Richard Southern's *The Making of the Middle Ages*, M. D.
Chenu's *La théologie au XII*[ème] *siècle*, and Colin Morris's *The
Discovery of the Individual* is to pluck with both hands a wealth
of material, brilliantly marshalled, on the kinds of intimate,
irreversible, and delicately interrelated changes of which any
pre-industrial society may be capable.[1]

The small emergent world of northwestern Europe in the

[†] *Daedalus* CIV (1975): 133–51. While my first debt is to *Daedalus*, in offering to
me the unparallelled opportunity of learning from a wider range of scholars of wider
views than I had thought possible, I owe no small protection from my own capacity
for error to my friends in Oxford—to Dr. Paul Hyams, to Patrick Wormald, to
Benedicta Ward, and to the careful criticism of Dr. Sabine MacCormack. In these
footnotes, I have on every occasion cited only those works to which I was directly
indebted.

1. Marc Bloch, *Feudal Society*, trans. L. A. Manyon (London, 1961); R. W.
Southern, *The Making of the Middle Ages* (London, 1953); M. D. Chenu, *La théologie
au XII*[ème] *siècle* (Paris, 1957), and Colin Morris, *The Discovery of the Individual*
(London, 1972). [See now J. LeGoff, *Pour un autre Moyen-âge* (Paris, 1977), p. 301: 'le
grand bouleversement du xiie. siècle, où se manifeste aussi, au sein de la permanence
de structures profondes et résistantes, un *take off* culturel et mental.' Compare C. M.
Radding, 'Evolution of Medieval Mentalities: A Cognitive–Structural Approach',
American Historical Review LXXXIII (1978): 577–97, for an even more dramatic
contrast of the cognitive processes of pre- and post-twelfth century men.]

eleventh and twelfth centuries, on which this study must concentrate, often strikes the student of the classical ancient world—and especially the student of classical Greece and ancient Israel—as strangely germane to his own concerns. Here also we find a stocktaking and revaluation of traditional religion by a newly formed intellectual élite, associated above all with the Schools of Paris and with such great names as Peter Abelard (c. 1079–1142).[2] We find a sharpening and a redistribution of roles in society, dramatically pinpointed in the sudden emergence of a new relationship between clergy and laity in the time of the Investiture Contest (a contest connected with the name of one great pope—Gregory VII [1073–1085]—but in reality a process as widespread and ineluctable as a change in the tide of western society).[3] In the course of the eleventh century the feudal knightly class emerges as a distinct group,[4] while, in the twelfth century, the facts of urban life and of a new-style mercantile professionalism had come to stay, and were slowly but surely incorporated in the medieval image of society.[5] We find novel departures in forms of law and organization: the emergence of written codes after centuries of customary, oral law, the reception of Roman law at the Schools of Bologna, and the codification of the canon law and theology of the Christian Church (in the *Decretum* of Gratian, c. 1140, and the *Sentences* of Peter the Lombard, c. 1150).[6] We have a singularly consequential attempt to found a new religious order on the basis

2. R. W. Southern, *Making of the Middle Ages*, pp. 170–218.

3. Chenu, *Théologie*, pp. 252–273, and R. W. Southern, *Western Society and the Church in the Middle Ages* (London, 1970), pp. 34–44.

4. G. Duby, "Les origines de la chevalerie," *Settimane di Studio sull'Alto Medio Evo*, XV: 2 (Spoleto, 1968), 739–761, and *I laici nella "societas Christiana" dei secoli xi. e xii.* [*Miscellanea del Centro di Studi Medioevali,* 5] (Milan, 1968), pp. 453–54. [C. Duby, *Les trois ordres ou l'imaginaire du féodalisme* (Paris, 1978).]

5. Chenu, *Théologie*, pp. 225–51, esp. p. 241. John W. Baldwin, *Masters, Princes and Merchants: The Social Views of Peter the Chanter and His Circle* (2 vols., Princeton, 1970), and Lester K. Little, "Pride Goes Before Avarice: Social Change and the Vices in Latin Christendom," *American Historical Review* LXXVI: 1 (1971): 16–49. [Alexander Murray, *Reason and Society in the Middle Ages* (Oxford, 1978).]

6. Charles H. Haskins, *The Renaissance of the Twelfth Century* (Cambridge,

of a written rationalized legislation, in the case of the Cistercians (first founded in 1098).[7] Innumerable novel ventures in administration and constant experimentation in new forms of social organization cover the face of Europe of the twelfth century.[8] Finally, and most revealing of all for our purposes, we find a probing of modes of self-expression which vary from a revival of the tradition of religious autobiography associated with St Augustine to the totally novel departure of courtly love poetry (Bernard de Ventadour was writing around 1145).[9]

Like the foundations of a great cathedral, these achievements are largely invisible to us because they are so continuous with all subsequent masonry. Compared with so solid and intimate a link between ourselves and our own twelfth-century past, the revolutions of the first millennium B.C. have the exhilarating but remote air of a mountain range seen on the edge of a far distant horizon.

The claims of the period covered by the eleventh and twelfth centuries A.D. are both more modest and more cogent: we happen to know more about them. The state of culture and society that preceded the various revolutions of

Mass., 1927; New York: Meridan Books, 1957), pp. 193–223, and Marc Bloch, *Feudal Society*, pp. 109–120. [M. T. Clanchy, 'Remembering the Past and the Good Old Law', *History* LV (1980): 165–76; and *From Memory to Written Record: England 1066–1307* (London, 1980); F. L. Cheyette, 'The Invention of the State', *Essays on Medieval Civilization*, The Walter Prescott Webb Memorial Lectures, ed. B. K. Lackner and K. R. Philip (Austin, Texas, 1978), pp. 143–78, esp. p. 160: 'The invention of the state is the story of how this small minority of literate men imposed upon the non-literate their official ways of thinking about politics and law'—he refers to the period after 1050 A.D.]

7. R. W. Southern, *Western Society and the Church*, pp. 255–259.

8. Henri Pirenne, *Medieval Cities* (Princeton, 1919). [See the excellent article of C. W. Bynum, 'Did the Twelfth Century Discover the Individual?', *Journal of Ecclesiastical History* XXXI (1980): 1–17, which, by emphasizing the 'self-conscious interest in the process of belonging to groups and filling roles' (p. 3) as a feature of the twelfth century, provides a necessary corrective to the one-sided views of the authors on whom I drew for my picture of the emergent 'individualism' of the twelfth century, and, hence, to many of the views stated in this article, esp. on pp. 328–29.]

9. C. Morris, *Discovery*, pp. 64–120. [R. Hanning, *The Individual in Twelfth-Century Romance* (New York, 1977).]

the first millennium B.C. is shadowy in the extreme compared with what we can know of the mentality and circumstances of the men of the period from A.D. 800 to 1000. It is,
therefore, possible not merely to juxtapose two static studies—a painfully reconstructed 'Before' and an exuberant
'After'—but to know this 'Before,' the state of Europe in the
Dark Ages, with sufficient certainty to hope to touch, or to
point the way for others to touch, those levers that made
possible the emergence of the one state from the other. For a
scholar possessed with insatiable curiosity, not only for what
changes have happened in the distant past but how change
happens at all, the opportunity to study the eleventh and
twelfth centuries after Christ is too good to be missed.

Let us first describe the kinds of changes which, for the
non-medievalist at least, may be the most significant. They
cluster around a redrawing of the boundaries between the
sacred and the profane. We begin in A.D. 1000, 'in a world
where hitherto the sacred and profane had been almost inextricably mixed.'[10] One cannot resist the impression that a release of energy and creativity analogous to a process of nu-
clear fission stemmed from the disengagement of the two
spheres of the sacred and the profane in the succeeding two
centuries. Take the best known example: the new demarcation of the roles of the clergy and of the laity associated with
the Investiture Contest acted to the eventual benefit of both
parties. The clergy, theoretically placed superior to the laity,
were made in reality more self-contained. A vast rise in their
cultural standards and interests was made possible by the
acute sense of being able to 'go it alone' as a professional
group with their own high professional standards. In the earlier centuries of the Middle Ages, by contrast, a gifted man
might have found himself either encapsulated in a monastery
to one side of the human group, tied as a monk to the life of
an honorary angel, or, if he were to take his place within the
group, immobilized by a network of obligations ranging

10. Bloch, *Feudal Society*, p. 107.

305

over the whole sphere of the sacred and the profane. The biographies of great bishops in tenth-century Germany, for instance, reveal men who, though impressive as pillars of the community, were forced to be jacks-of-all-trades and masters of none.

The situation of the twelfth century, by contrast, is a world where gifted men could find leisure, incentive, and personal resources to tackle more strictly delimited tasks. The laity also, though technically made inferior to the clergy, came to enjoy the freedom that came from a vast unpretentiousness. Political power was increasingly wielded without religious trappings. Government was what government did: rulers, who could no longer claim to stand for an undifferentiated, archetypal image of power, settled down to exercise what real power they actually possessed in a more rational, a more literate, and a more effective manner.[11] The age that began with the penance of the Emperor Henry IV before Gregory VII at Canossa in 1077 ends in the late twelfth and early thirteenth centuries with a brittle but unanswerable assertion of purely secular values surrounding a newly formed mystique of chivalry and a code of courtly love. Throughout society, the disengagement of the sacred from the profane opened up a whole middle distance of conflicting opportunities for the deployment of human talent compared with which the society of the early Middle Ages appears as singularly monochromatic.

These are the changes that characterize the eleventh and twelfth centuries. We will not touch on all of them. Instead, we must now take a narrow doorway into this great hall and first examine one well-documented paradigm case of the disengagement of the sacred from the profane as it took place in this period—the case of the ordeal.[12] In so doing, we will

11. R. W. Southern, *Western Society and the Church*, pp. 38–42, and *Medieval Humanism* (Oxford, 1970), pp. 51–58.
12. H. Nottarp, *Gottesurteilstudien* (Munich, 1956); P. Browe, *De ordaliis . . .* (2 vols.: Rome, 1932–33) is a good collection of texts. See also M. Szeftel, 'Le jugement de Dieu dans le droit russe ancien', *Archives d'histoire du droit oriental*, IV (1948),

attempt to seize the wider implications marshalled behind the phenomenon that we are examining. For if ever there was an area where the sacred penetrated into the chinks of the profane and vice versa, it was in the ordeal. In and around A.D. 1050, for instance, in the baptistry of Canterbury cathedral, it was possible, in the same great pool of water, both to be baptized as a Christian by the priest and, as a fully grown litigant, to undergo the ordeal of immersion in water to discover the truth about issues in a purely secular law suit: 'And it could be converted from its sacramental to its judicial function with the minimum of disturbance.' 'In all this confusion,' writes Professor Southern with an eye to the twelfth-century future, 'there is something barbaric.'[13] The withering of the ordeal in the course of the twelfth century has, therefore, been consistently viewed in terms of the clearing up of a 'barbaric confusion'.

Let us look at the process of the withering of the ordeal. Ordeals had depended on an easy passage between the sacred and the profane. A case begun among laymen in a trial in a lawcourt might find itself transferred to the solemn *mise en scène* of a great church. The upshot of dramatic and often desperately cruel actions—the effect of a hot iron on the hand that could hold it for nine paces, of boiling water on the arm that had snatched an object from a cauldron, of whether a man sank (if innocent) or floated (if guilty) in a pool of water, the result of a duel—if all these were surrounded by solemn prayers of blessing by the priest, they would be held as the final decision of God on the rights and wrongs of the case. The ordeal was a 'controlled miracle' brought to bear on the

---

263–99. [See now Colin Morris, 'Judicium Dei', *Church, Society and Politics*, Studies in Church History XII, ed. D. Baker (Oxford, 1975), pp. 95–111; R. V. Coleman, 'Reason and Unreason in Early Medieval Law', *Journal of Interdisciplinary History* IV (1974): 571–91, esp. pp. 582–91; and, for modifications and substantial disagreement with the interpretation of the ordeal proposed in this article, see C. M. Radding, 'Superstition to Science: Nature, Fortune and the Passing of the Medieval Ordeal', *American Historical Review* LXXXIV (1979): 945–69.]

13. R. W. Southern, *Saint Anselm and His Biographer* (Cambridge, 1963), p. 265.

day-to-day needs of the community:[14] small issues such as debts, money, and the ownership of cattle jostled side by side with accusations of witchcraft, poisoning, murder, and assault in the register of ordeals performed in the late twelfth century in the Hungarian town of Varad, and a similar situation prevailed over much of northwestern Europe.[15]

This is the profile of the ordeal as it was attacked in the course of the twelfth century. By 1215, the Lateran Council forbade clerics to pronounce the liturgical blessing on which the whole structure of the ordeal was held to depend. The clerical critics of the late twelfth century had created a picture of the ordeal and of its untenability of which modern scholars are still the direct heirs.[16] To invoke a controlled miracle by the ordeal in the course of a secular law suit was to 'tempt God'. This was not only because the issues decided by the ordeal were often trivial and almost invariably worldly: to 'tempt God' was also to abandon prematurely the processes of human proof and reason and to seek a certainty to which mere human beings were not entitled in such basically trivial affairs. The presence of the ordeal in the life of their age was explained away in terms that continue to be reiterated up to the present day. The ordeal, they said, was an ancient custom, vulgar, lower class, tolerated in earlier times merely as a concession by the Church to the hard hearts of the Germanic barbarians.[17] The withering of the ordeal, therefore, is hailed

14. P. Rousset, 'La croyance en la justice immanente à l'epoque féodale', *Le Moyen Age* LIV (1948): 241: 'L'ordalie suppose le miracle, l'exige comme la seule preuve capable d'ouvrir les yeux sur le bon droit.'

15. *Registrum Varadiense: Az idörenbe szedatt Váradi Füzesvaspróba Lajstrom*, ed. J. Kakácsonyi and S. Borovszky (Budapest, 1903): see I. Zajtay, 'Le Registre de Varad. Un monument iudiciare du debut du XIIIème siècle', *Nouvelle revue historique de droit français et étranger* XXXII (1954): 527–62.

16. John W. Baldwin, 'The Intellectual Preparation for the Canon of 1215 Against Ordeals', *Speculum* XXXVI (1961): 613–36. I have excluded from consideration the writings of ninth-century critics of the ordeal, as these appear to me to reflect a totally different social and intellectual climate.

17. Stephen of Tournai, *Summa*, ed. F. V. Schulte, ed. C II 5.7, 23 and 25, pp. 170 and 172; and Stephen of Blois, *Speculum iuris canonici*, ed. T. A. Reimanus (1837), p. 140; also in Browe, *De Ordaliis. . . .* vol. II, no. 99, p. 77, and no. 104, pp. 79–80 resp.

as one feature of the emergence of western civilization from the 'tunnel' of the Germanic Dark Ages and of the progress of rationality. 'The essential steps had been taken in making human justice and government an affair subject to human rules and dependent on the efficacy of human agents.'[18] A different description of the nature of the ceremonies and strategies of the ordeal, therefore, will help us to look also for different causes for its abandonment, and so to emerge with some tentative new conclusions as to the preconditions for a disengagement of the sacred from the profane in the eleventh and twelfth centuries and, perhaps, in analogous situations in other societies.

First, a remark about the evidence, and about our means of reconstructing the mentalities and social situations behind the evidence. We may know what everybody wants and has always wanted—the crowning mercy of truth in human affairs. The solemn blessings with which the ordeal begins make impressive reading: 'O God, lover and author of peace: Thou who lookest on the earth and causest it to tremble, look down we pray Thee on the faith and prayers of Thy supplicants, who have brought the causes of their complaint to Thy judgment. Send forth Thy blessing on this iron glowing with the fire to dissolve their contentions . . . that by its agency, justice should shine abroad and evil-dealing be conquered.'[19]

When the wicked sons of Fulk de Morrillon took the oath on holy relics before trial by battle, they began to stumble over one another and to walk round in circles—now *that* was a good ordeal![20] Sherlock Holmes also solved insoluble mysteries. Yet a detective novel would be a fragile basis from which to reconstruct the mentality and strategies of a modern crime squad. Unlike the detective novels, unlike the activities of Sherlock Holmes, of course, the ordeal happened. It was a dramatic and often a desperately cruel moment. An unsuc-

18. R. W. Southern, *The Making of the Middle Ages*, p. 97.

19. *Reg. Varad.*, p. 150.

20. A. J. Dickman, *Le rôle du surnaturel dans les chansons de geste* (Paris, 1926), pp. 126–28, and further examples on p. 191. [R. Howard Bloch, *Medieval French Literature and Law* (Berkeley and Los Angeles, 1977), pp. 18–25 and 46–53.]

cessful protagonist in an ordeal by boiling water could not see his way to the cauldron and, when he plunged in his arm, felt the pain as if his very heart was burning.[21] Bracton comments grimly that a man's front teeth are a valuable asset to him, 'they greatly help in winning trials by battle.'[22] There were moments of heady triumph.[23]

There were also moments of wild hope. A knight surrounded by suspicions of adultery had rushed 'prematurely' to the ordeal by hot iron and was well and truly burned.[24] As Marcel Proust said: 'Quand on se voit au bord de l'abîme et qu'il semble que Dieu nous ait abandonné, on n'hésite plus à attendre de lui un miracle.' The register of Varad in Hungary records two hundred and seventeen cases between 1208 and 1235 with a lapidary faith in the literal truth of the ceremony: 'portato ferro combusti sunt et suspensi'; 'portato ferro pro terra ista justificatus est.'[25]

The diversity and complexity of the evidence for the ordeal do not permit any simple explanation, much less any explaining away. Yet it is, I think, legitimate to look more closely into the ceremony itself in order to decide, not what men hoped for from ordeals but, more modestly, what had continued to satisfy them about ordeals—what needs led them to maintain the ceremony as a satisfactory solution to some difficulties, and then to abandon it in the course of the twelfth century for other means of proof.

We must begin with a clear idea of who is being satisfied. Up to the twelfth century these are small face-to-face groups. We are in a Europe of low overall population where human beings were still cramped into long-inhabited settlements. These settlements could be populous enough in themselves,

21. P. Marchegay, *Archives d'Anjou* I (1843), 477.

22. In A. L. Poole, *The Obligations of Society in the XII and XIII Centuries* (Oxford, 1946), p. 48, n. 1.

23. Cf. a modern African example in E. Warner, *Ordeal by Sasswood* (London, 1955), pp. 244–47.

24. Ivo of Chartres, *Ep.* 205, Migne, *PL*, CLXII, 210, also in Browe, *De Ordaliis* . . . . vol. II, no. 91.

25. *Reg. Varad.*, no. 62, p. 176; no. 182, p. 219 resp.

but they were isolated from the others by stretches of woods and poor communications.[26] The extended kin group is the primary unit of society, a fact studiously maintained and defined by the blood feud. Safety and protection still rested on coagulations of kinsmen and dependents in small, intense groups.[27] The coercive power of the state up to A.D. 1100 is weak. Literacy is severely limited. The greatest explicit ideal of the early Middle Ages is a minimal one of peace and, above all, concord: this amounted to the maintenance of a minimal consensus in a face-to-face society built up of evenly balanced family groupings. In such a society the ordeal takes on its meaning as an instrument of consensus and as a theatrical device by which to contain disruptive conflict.

The ordeal was mercifully slow. It allowed room for manoeuvre and for the evolution of a situation. To call it a controlled miracle and to dismiss it as tempting God, as late twelfth-century thinkers came to do, was to import into the ceremony a singularly brisk expectation of the miracle. God might be believed to speak in an ordeal, but the human group took an unconscionably long time letting Him get a word in edgewise. For God is revealing 'truth', not any specific fact. He was judging the status of a person or of a group, whether they and their claims were 'pure' and 'just'.[28] He was not deciding whether a piece of land really belonged to a certain claimant. What was at stake was the status in the community of the groups that had been brought into conflict. Exoneration in the ordeal was not just the revelation of the true facts, it was victory: 'Having come together in that place and duly celebrated all the rituals in the manner of the church, by the merits of St Peter that the justice of the cause

26. G. Duby, *L'Économie et la vie des campagnes dans l'occident médiéval* (Paris, 1962), pp. 66–71, and Robert Fossier, *La Terre et les hommes en Picardie*, I (Paris-Louvain, 1968), 206–207. [J. M. Wallace-Hadrill, *Early Medieval History* (Oxford, 1976), p. 3.]
27. Bloch, *Feudal Society*, pp. 123–42.
28. See *Reg. Varad.*, p. 151, for the final questions of the priest to the participant of the ordeal: *Frater, es justus ab hoc crimine de quo accusaris? Iustus sum. Mundus? Mundus sum.*

of St Martin should be shown forth, the man of this church was untouched, without a spot of red from the iron.'[29] Yet, with the ordeal, it was a victory carefully contained. For the spilling out of conflict was the curse of every early medieval society. To take one example only: 'In March, 1134, after the assassination of the sub-Dean of Orleans, all the relatives of the dead man assembled to receive the homage, not only of one of the murderers, of his accomplices and of his vassals, but also of the "best of his kin"—in all two hundred and forty persons. In every way a man's action was propagated throughout the circle of his kinsfolk in successive waves.'[30]

The ordeal placed a contraceptive barrier between what was a dramatic and violent action and its 'successive waves'. In the *Chanson de Roland*, when the traitor Ganelon is defeated in trial by battle, he is killed and the thirty kinsmen who mobilized behind him are hanged in the Accursèd Wood. That, for the writer of the poem at least, was the last of it. A real life vendetta, if unresolved through trial by battle, could drag on for years.[31] Because of this, the battle of Fontenay, fought in 841, had to be declared a *iudicium Dei* retrospectively. For this battle had been so messy an affair, and the consequences of the half-resolved confrontation involved in it were so laden with rancour and the possibility of vendetta for the Frankish nobility, that the bishops declared God had spoken, and that was to be the end to it.[32]

The very course of the ritual of the ordeal helped to contain conflict and to bring about a resolution. The ceremony

---

29. G. Fejer, *Codex Diplomaticus Hungariae*, III:1 (Buda, 1826), p. 105. Cf. J. Vansina, 'The Bushong Poison Oracle', *Man in Africa*, ed. M. Douglas and P. M. Kaberry (London, 1969), pp. 245–60, at p. 249: 'for the public ritual is as much a validation as a trial'.

30. Bloch, *Feudal Society*, p. 130.

31. Cf. Widukind, *Rerum Gestarum Saxonicarum*, II, 10 (*MGH in usum Schol.*), p. 73 and 74. Otto I ordered a trial by combat at Steel in 938 in order to avoid a public debate among the nobles over a property dispute. [K. J. Leyser, *Rule and Conflict in an Early Medieval Society: Ottonian Saxony* (London, 1979).]

32. K.-G. Cram, *Iudicium Belli. Zum Rechtscharakter des Krieges im deutschen Mittelalter. Beiheft des Archiv für Kulturegeschichte*, V (1955), pp. 37, 42, and 46. [Bloch, *Medieval French Literature*, p. 63.]

applied a discreet massage to the ruffled feelings of the group.
The most marked feature of the ordeal is the slow and solemn
processes by which human conflict is taken out of its immediate context. The representative of the conflict—the man
who undertakes the ordeal, who can be accuser or accused—
is publicly shorn of all contact with the normal world.[33]
Shaved, dressed in a shirt, for three days his diet and his
whole rhythm of life is that of a priest not of a layman. He is
solemnly blessed, stripped of talismans and amulets (the normal adjuncts of purely human conflict); he is liberally doused
with holy water and transformed by long prayers of benedic-
tion into a prototype of the ancient righteous man delivered
in times of tribulation.[34] He is no longer part of a human
lawsuit. He is the spearhead of justice, but it is a spearhead
carefully detached by long rituals from its haft, from the
pressures of the groups ranged behind a disputed issue. The
ordeal is entered into under conditions where the human
group has usually reached deadlock. An ordeal is a tacit 'de-
fusing' of the issue. It is not a judgement *by* God; it is a re-
mitting of a case *ad iudicium Dei, 'to* the judgement of God.'
This is an action tantamount to removing the keystone of the
arch on which, hitherto, all pressures had converged. Once
removed, a decision can be reached quickly and without loss
of face by either side. For by being brought to the judgement
of God, the case already stepped outside the pressures of
human interest, and so its resolution can be devoid of much
of the odium of human responsibility.

Seen from the outside, the ordeal was a *spectaculum* to
which everyone flocked.[35] Quite apart from explicit beliefs
on the nature and source of the final verdict, the ritual itself
was reassuring and peace-creating. It also had the role of a
demonstrative ceremony in a largely non-literate society. The
ordeal was only one of a series of crucial legal transactions

33. Cf. Vansina, 'Bushong Poison Oracle', p. 249.
34. Well described in Marchegay, *Archives*, pp. 452–62, for the ordeal in
Angers.
35. Ibid., p. 457.

whose validity was derived exclusively, in the early Middle Ages, from a declaratory ritual.[36] It was, like similar rituals, a fixative. It attempted by dramatic and memorable gestures—such as scars, stand-up fights, floating in water—to make a lasting impression on the public memory of a small community, where the public memory was known to be notoriously given to manipulation and to acts of selective oblivion.[37] *Verba volant, ordalia manent* could be the motto of part of the function of this great ceremony.

The verdict of the ordeal, therefore, should not be seen in isolation. It is better seen as the final precipitation of a long-drawn-out attempt to maximize certainty. In this, the ordeal was merely a particular case of a general rule: 'A decent [law] suit ended in an agreement, brought about after long discussions, in which many people had taken part. With their lack of clear lines and sharp legal distinctions and the absence of hard-cut issues, they remind us of the *palavers*, the favourite technique of settling legal disputes among the natives of Africa.'[38] Hence the flexibility surrounding the actual role of the participants of an ordeal. Like a suit of plate armour, the ordeal may seem from the outside a single impregnable whole; but each piece of the suit is so jointed as to allow an exceptional degree of free movement. Participants had time to climb down: one hundred and twenty did so at Varad.[39] Others 'chickened out' at different stages along the long ritual. Three days, for instance, had to elapse between the moment of holding the hot iron and the opening of a sealed bandage

36. A. Gurevič, 'La Notion de la propriété pendant le haut moyen-âge', *Annales*, XXVII:3 (1972), pp. 523–47, esp. pp. 532–36. [Cheyette, 'Invention of the State', pp. 156–62; J. LeGoff, 'Le rituel symbolique de la vassalité', *Simboli e simbologia nell'Alto Medio Evo, Settimane di Studi del Centro Italiano di Studi sull'Alto Medio Evo* XXIII (Spoleto, 1976): 579–688 in *Pour un autre Moyen-âge*, pp. 349–420.]

37. Marc Bloch, *French Rural History*, trans. J. Sondeheimer (London, 1966), pp. 70–71.

38. R. C. van Caenegem, *Royal Writs in England from the Conquest to Glanvill* (London, 1959), p. 42. [S. White, '*Pactum . . . Legem vincit et Amor Judicium*. The Settlement of Disputes by Compromise in Eleventh-Century Western France', *The American Journal of Legal History* XXII (1978): 281–308.]

39. Zajtay, 'Le Registre de Varad', pp. 541 and 546.

surrounding the hand. This was too much for twelve subjects of the ordeal in Varad: *sentiens se combustum confugit ad
ecclesiam.*[40] Fiction could toy delightfully with the paradoxes
involved in this freedom of manœuvre. In Gottfried of
Strassburg's romance, *Tristan*, the queen escapes unscathed
from holding the hot iron, for she had framed a specious
oath. The manoeuvring of the parties behind the form of the
oath is laid bare in the account: 'Thus a wrangle from side to
side as to what her oath should be. One man wished her ill,
another well, as people do in such matters.' The queen got
her oath, and 'she was saved by her guile, and by the doc-
tored oath that went flying up to God. . . . Thus it was made
manifest and confirmed to all the world that Christ in his
great virtue is pliant as a wind-blown sleeve. He falls into
place and clings, whichever way you try him on, closely and
smoothly.'[41] Gottfried's blasé comment, though coming at a
slightly later period, has its parallels in the real life of the
eleventh century. It is a tiny outcrop of the vast bedrock of
cunning with which medieval men actually faced and manipulated the supernatural in their affairs.[42]

There was a built-in flexibility in the ordeal that enabled
the group, which had the main interest in reaching certainty,
to maintain a degree of initiative quite contrary to the explicit
ideology of the ordeal. For an ambiguity lies at the heart of
every ceremony of ordeal. The hand that has held the hot
iron, the hand that had been plunged into boiling water are
solemnly sealed and reopened again before witnesses three
days later. If the wound heals 'normally', then the case is ad-
judged decided: God has spoken in the most elemental way,
by an assertion of the integrity of a man's rights symbolized
by the surviving integrity of his physical body in contact

40. Ibid., p. 547.
41. Gottfried von Strassburg, *Tristan* (London: Pelican Books, 1960), pp.
247–48. [Gottfried von Strassburg, *Tristan*, ed. Peter Granz, Deutsche Klassiker des
Mittelalters, Neue Folge IV (Wiesbaden, 1978), pp. xiii–xiv.]
42. E.g., the rivals of the Monks of Angers had kept their opponents talking
until the cauldron boiled to a higher temperature! Marchegay, *Archives d'Anjou*,
p. 474.

with extreme heat. But, after three days, the normal healing
of such a burn is still ambiguous.[43] The phenomenon on
which the group concentrated is, in fact, still as open-ended
as a Rorschach test. Yet, paradoxically, it is around precisely
this ambiguous experience that unanimity is crystallized.

The efficacy of the ordeal, therefore, remains a function
of the strength of feeling in the group.[44] A heretic in Soissons
'floated like a stick' when put in the blessed pool of water.
The blessed water had well and truly rejected him. 'At this
sight the whole church was filled with unbounded joy. Their
notoriety had brought together such an assembly of both
sexes that no one present could remember seeing one like it
before.'[45] It is in this excited way that the group of interested
parties could stand behind the ordeal. In a case involving
their Norman king, in the very early twelfth century, a group
of down-at-the-heels Saxon landowners in Kent had the ordeal of the hot iron inflicted on them in a matter of theft, 'so
that it was a piteous thing to see it done.' The tender-hearted
local group insisted, however, that they had emerged from
this in better condition than before. The comment of the
king, William Rufus (1087–1100), is a tribute to this strange
process of decision-making: 'What is that? Is God a just
judge? Damn whoever thinks it! He will answer for this by
my good judgement and not by God's—which can be folded
this way and that as anyone wants it.'[46]

Certain general conclusions might follow from this examination of the ordeal. What we have found in the ordeal is
not a body of men acting on specific beliefs about the supernatural; we have found instead specific beliefs held in such a

43. Petrus Cantor, *Verbum abbreviatum*, chap. 78, Migne, *PL*, CCV, 239A.
44. Ibid., 233 AB, for diverging opinions on the extent to which a man was
held to sink or float in the ordeal by water.
45. Guibert of Nogent, *De Vita Sua*, III, 17, Migne, *PL*, CLVI, 952; trans. by
C. C. S. Bland in J. F. Benton, ed., *Self and Society in Medieval France* (New York,
1970), p. 214. Cf. the case at Halberstadt in 1214: Gustav Schmidt, *Urkundenbuch des
Hochstifts Halberstadt*, I, 1883, no. 260: *quo viso omnis praesentium multitudo acclamabat,
laudes Deo concinens.* For acclamation as a form of group-consensus, see E. Peterson,
Εἷς Θεός, 1926, pp. 181–95.
46. Eadmer, *Historia Novorum*, Migne, *PL*, CLIX, 412.

SOCIETY AND THE SUPERNATURAL

way as to enable a body of men to act. The type of community that was prevalent in pre-twelfth-century Europe found in this particular form of the mingling of sacred and profane an elegant and appropriate solution to some of its problems. When the type of community survives intact, the ordeal or avatars of the ordeal survive with it. The growth of rationalism and clerical condemnation of the ordeal are largely irrelevant to this process. In the thirteenth century, for instance, in Navarre, the ordeal of the boiling cauldron continued unchanged but under lay supervision.[47] In Varad, ordeals continue long after 1215.[48] In the factious Italian towns, though these were forcing grounds of rationalism and of written law, avatars of the ordeal survived as a remedy for the ills of an evenly balanced and fissile community.[49] So we are dealing not with a strange custom inherited from a more 'barbaric' past or practiced among the more 'barbaric' members of the European world. We are dealing with a total situation to which this and analogous solutions were applied. The role of the supernatural in society—the intermingling of the sacred and the profane that so strikes scholars of the pre-twelfth-century world—is part of a style of life.

Let us examine the role of the supernatural in other areas of life in terms of this style. The need for consensus and the pressure brought by consensus in relatively small groups are the *leitmotivs* of much early medieval religion. We see this in the cult of the relics.[50] For to vest what was intrinsically ambiguous with final authority was part of a whole style of decision-making in the early centuries of the Middle Ages. Nothing could be more nondescript than a relic. It was a

47. *Fuero general de Navarra*, 5, 3, c. 18.
48. Zajtay, 'Le Registre de Varad', p. 560.
49. Robert Davidsohn, *Forschungen zur Geschichte von Florenz* (Berlin, 1900), p. 315, on trial by battle in San Gimignano.
50. H. Fichtenau, 'Zum Reliquienwesen im früheren Mittelalter', *Institut für Österreichische Geschichtsforschung, Mitteilungen* LX (1952): 60–89. [See Peter Brown, *The Cult of the Saints: Its Rise and Function in Latin Christianity* (Chicago, 1981), where I take up this line of thought in detail, but modify the extreme emphasis placed in this article on the purely instrumental role of the relic.]

nameless bone, carrying with it cold undertones of death and the earth. Yet it is precisely such bones that are the focus of early medieval devotion, especially as this devotion affected the public life of men. As with the ordeal, their very ambiguity was the secret of their power. They could be saturated with the values projected onto them by the group. Even in the reception of a relic the human group holds the initiative. For among the many newly discovered or newly arrived pieces of dust only the group can make up its mind which is the holy dust.[51] The rest would follow. It would be a churlish poor man indeed who resisted the healing powers of a relic whose authenticity had been decided by the fasting of the whole cathedral chapter and bishop of his town for three days on end.

Once vested in this way, the supernatural becomes the depository of the objectified values of the group. The miracles of the saints are, in slower rhythm, as much the hard judgement of the community that recorded and remembered them as was any ordeal. The group explained notable misfortunes in terms of the vengeance of the saints, and the threads linking any misfortune with the judgement of the saint passed through the moral accountancy of the community. Hence the notoriously matter-of-fact nature of so many of the miracles associated with local cult sites in the early medieval period. The miracles of St Foye, to take one example only, from the early eleventh century in southern France, are like a stalagmite, formed from the deposit of innumerable little drops of the gossip and value judgements of a region.[52]

The sacred, therefore, was intimately connected with the life of the group on every level. At the same time, however, it was operative because it was thought of as radically different from the human world into which it penetrated. It was all

51. Peter Brown, 'Relics and Social Status in the Age of Gregory of Tours', [above, pp. 222–50, and P. J. Geary, *Furta Sacra. Thefts of Relics in the Central Middle Ages* (Princeton, 1978), pp. 5–9].

52. *Liber Miraculorum Sancte Fidis*, ed. A. Bouillet, *Collection de Textes pour servir à l'étude et l'enseignement de l'histoire*, vol. 21 (Paris, 1897). [See above, pp. 233–35.]

that the human community was not. The ritual of an ordeal made it a place where 'there is sanctity, chastity, truth, and victory, upright behaviour, humility, goodness, leniency, the fullness of the law, and of the truth and obedience of God.'[53] Very much, that is, a place not fraught with the ambiguity of a mere human law court. A king, at certain moments of his career, takes on a stance that defines him as not the normal layman. The ideal of this society for centuries is the monk who is not technically human: he lives the life of angels.[54] The tremendous sense of the intimacy and adjacency of the holy is one of the main characteristics of the early medieval period. Priests serving at the altar must, if they spit, spit to one side or behind them; for at the altar the angels are standing.[55] This non-human in the midst of a society is available to all, for all purposes. Though the non-human is sharply and dramatically defined against the human, its application is deeply unspecialized. It penetrates the human community in any variety of circumstances.

We are dealing with the holy as an enabling device carefully (if unconsciously) ground into a tool to resolve otherwise unbearable human conflicts. Hence attitudes to the holy in person-to-person relations are strictly analogous to the ordeal. Early medieval society coped with the problem of the sinner in its midst according to exactly the same rhythms as we have observed elsewhere.[56] Penance had to maintain a strong declaratory element. A man made his peace with the community quite as much as with God, and the idea of the holy enabled him to do so without losing face. The penitent could step out of the human community by becoming a monk—that is, by becoming an honorary non-human, liv-

53. *Monumenta Germaniae Historica, Formulae,* ed. Zeumer, p. 639.

54. J. W. F. Pollock and F. W. Maitland, *The History of English Law* (re-issue, Cambridge, 1968), p. 443: 'It is not as a specially holy person, but as a propertyless and specially obedient person that the law knows the monk.' [See above, pp. 181–82.]

55. *Regula Magistri,* 48 Migne, *PL,* LXXXVIII, 1009.

56. C. Vogel, *Le pécheur et la pénitence au moyen-âge* (Paris, 1969) is a most illuminating collection of texts.

ing the angelic life. If he did not step out forever, as a monk, he could at least mark himself off, either by penitential exile or by ceremonies as elaborate, as prolonged, and as histrionic as was any ordeal.[57] The penance of a mighty man in tenth-century England was a sight to be seen: '. . . and let the powerful man try earnestly to shed tears from his eyes and bewail his sins; and let a man then feed those three days as many of God's poor as he possibly can.'[58]

The holy, being invisible, was sensed to be kinder than man. Reparation could be made to the saint for any insult. This was far from the case with visible human beings. Having struck Bernier with a chess board, Raoul de Cambrai offered to make amends to him by going fourteen leagues on his knees with Bernier's saddle on his head. Bernier would not accept even so crushing a self-abasement, hence a deadly vendetta.[59] The saints, unlike Bernier, did not have this reputation of refusing reparation. Injustice to a fellow human being could be made good without losing face through offering dramatic reparation to the angry saint rather than to the victim. On a capital at St Benoît-sur-Loire, a knight lies full length at the feet of St Benedict; the man whom he had unjustly bound is standing with arms upraised behind him, his chains having fallen from him. But it is not at the feet of his wronged captive that the knight has chosen to fall to ask forgiveness.[60]

If we are to enter into the type of change that was finally precipitated with great rapidity in the twelfth century, though it had been prepared in the eleventh century and in areas of religious devotion, for instance, had harbingers as far back as

57. E.g., Letter of Paulinus of Aquileia (d. 802) to Haistulph, Migne, *PL*, XCIX, 181–86. [See Rosamond Pierce, 'The "Frankish Penitentials"', *Studies in Church History* XI, ed. D. Baker (Oxford, 1975): 31–39, on the anxiety caused in Carolingian society by penitential practices that were considered to be not sufficiently public.]

58. Vogel, *Le pécheur*, p. 126.

59. J.-C. Payen, *Le motif du repentir dans la littérature française médiévale* (Geneva, 1967), pp. 199–200.

60. Yvonne Labaude-Mailfort, 'L'iconographie des laïcs dans la société religieuse des xiᵉ et xiiᵉ siècles', *I laici nella 'societas christiana'*, pl. V, illustr. 13.

the tenth, we should look along the demarcation line between the sacred and the profane, defined in terms of the
objectified non-human against the subjective human. This
somehow changed subtly in these centuries of transition. For
the situation we have seen in the early centuries of the Middle
Ages is one where the sacred and the profane can be inter-
mingled because the borderline between the objective and the
subjective in human experience is deliberately blurred at
every turn. To take up these examples in the cult of the
saints: the squat gold and bejewelled figure of St Foye has all
the impregnable majesty of an objective force, acting in its
own initiative, in the midst of a community riven by subjective human doubt and discord. The statue, which can still be
visited in Conques, was called the *Maiestas* of the saint.[61]
Throughout Europe similar relics had similar impregnable
qualities: 'The deficiencies in human resources were supplied
by the power of the saints. They were great power houses in
the fight against evil; they filled the gaps left in the structure
of human justice.'[62]

Yet it was a strangely subjective objectivity. For relics
were chosen because they were the remains of people. The
supernatural world was built up of a model of intense person-
to-person relationships.[63] Like any weak lord, the relic could
be rebuked by its vassals if it failed to give protection. When
St Benedict allowed his shrine to be robbed, the custodian of
St Benoît-sur-Loire beat the shrine with a stick, shouting
'You sleepy head! If you don't care enough to protect your
own bracelets, I won't care if people come in and steal the
trousers off you next time.'[64] Like any rival lord, the relic
could be insulted by its opponents. Heaven punished 'the

61. *Mirac. S. Fidis*, I, 16, p. 52.
62. R. W. Southern, *The Making of the Middle Ages*, p. 137.
63. [P. A. Ségal, 'Un aspect du culte des saints: le châtiment divin au xiie. et au
xiiie. siècle dans la littérature hagiographique du Midi de la France', *La Religion
Populaire en Languedoc du xiie. à la première moitié du xive. siècle*, Cahiers Fanjeaux XI
(Toulouse, 1976), pp. 39–59.]
64. *De miraculis S. Benedicti*, 26, Migne, *PL*, CXXIV, 929–30. [P. J. Geary,
'L'humiliation des saints', *Annales* XXXIV (1979): 27–42 offers a more differentiated
view.]

knight who, when confronted with the image of St Foye placed on a plot of land to defend her rights, threatened to kick her—but threatened he had.[65] The objectivity of the supernatural was skin deep. It was not impersonal. It was the projection of the needs of a group, and was thus sucked into the subjective values of the group. The vengeance of the saints was the visceral reaction of a small community, a reaction placed beyond the frailty and discontinuity of human subjectivity by being identified with the saint; it was, in that sense, subjectivity objectified beyond recall.[66]

What happened in northern Europe as a precondition of the shift to a different relationship between the subjective and the objective can be quickly told.

Two great changes stand out in modifying the situation we have described. The first is the more obscure. The group itself changes consistency. It would be wrong to think of pre-eleventh-century northern Europe as uniformly underpopulated. The reverse may be true: patches of uncomfortably dense population were hemmed in by intractable wasteland. Quite apart from purely physical overcrowding due to the limited space available for farming, the 'technology of human relations' placed a premium on the ability to mobilize and to retain the consensus of as large a body of kinsmen, of allies, and of dependents as possible. The twelfth century saw

65. *Mirac. S. Fidis*, I, 11, pp. 40–41.

66. [I would now formulate this somewhat differently. The reader should remember that this article was a contribution to the Daedalus conference that addressed itself to the problem of 'Transcendence' in the first millennium B.C. I was taking as my guideline the felicitous definition of S. C. Humphreys, ' "Transcendence" and Intellectual Roles: The Ancient Greek Case,' *Daedalus* CIV (1975): 91–118, esp. p. 92: ' "Transcendence", whether it takes the form of divine revelation or of theoretical cosmology, implies a search for authority outside the institutionalized offices and structures of the seeker's society. Even its most concrete form, the law code, implies a transfer of authority from the holder of office to the written rule.' My point was that in a form of authority seen as so personalized in its nature and manifestation as the power of the saints, the 'transfer of authority' to a more impersonal or even (in the case of the laws of nature) an indifferent code of rules did not occur. I would now disagree with myself on this manner of posing the question: see *The Cult of the Saints*, pp. 62–63.]

the relaxing of this claustrophobic inward pressure. Population that had built up in long-cultivated areas became more free to spill out into reclaimed land. The compact human groups in towns and villages were dissolved by a leavening of horizontal mobility; the immediate family no longer needed to blend for safety into the wider mass of the kin.[67] Such changes were slow and far from uniform, but in large parts of northern Europe they subtly removed the social pressure for envisaging the role of the supernatural in the human group in the terms we have described. The growing impersonality of a larger, more fluid group made less necessary the theatricality of an ordeal or of a public renunciation; it dissolved the sharp memories of local breaches of the accepted code of conduct on which the previous genre of miracles of the saints had depended. Men who needed to care just that little bit less about their neighbours no longer had to go through the more difficult manœuvres of their life in a limelight of supernatural rituals.

Second—and blatantly—a ceremony such as the ordeal was a theatrical bid for consensus in a society still so balanced as to make any other form of human agreement on insoluble issues seem to involve all participants in a loss of face. The lay state of the twelfth century was fast moving away from such a consensual image of its role. The ruler was no longer a peacemaker in this old-fashioned manner; he was the imposer of law and order. Wherever faced by superior coercive power, elaborate devices for maximizing the consent of all interested parties around difficult or explosive issues just withered away. In late twelfth-century England, for instance, law may not have been notably more rational than was the ordeal; but it was trenchant and it was authoritative. The gallows could speak for itself, without mystification.[68]

67. Fossier, *La Terre et les hommes* . . . , I, pp. 272–73, 290–91, cf. Mary Douglas, *Natural Symbols* (London, 1970) for most illuminating suggestions on the social preconditions for the abandonment of ritual.

68. A. L. Poole, *Obligations of Society*, p. 79: 'The system of ordeals was concerned with the proletariat' in the late twelfth century. [Murray, *Reason and Society*,

The shift from consensus to authority is one of the most subtle shifts of all in the twelfth century. It is, perhaps, the greatest single precondition for the growth of rationality. In the late twelfth century, for instance, ecclesiastical bodies throughout Europe decided that they could be expected to obey leaders elected by a simple majority of their members.[69] They acted in the faith that a decision reached in this highly artificial manner could yet carry an authority such as was inconceivable in earlier ages. Previously, nothing but a divinely inspired miracle of unanimity could cover up the all-too-naked scrimmage of interests in any hotly contested election to a bishopric or to a monastery.[70]

In a sense, the exercise of reason, as fostered by the intellectuals and the reformers of the late eleventh and twelfth-centuries, was the most blatant exercise of authority of all. For appeal to reason in clerical controversy invariably implied, at that time, that men could be expected to obey rapid and trenchant decisions—the outcome of syllogisms, the production of an authoritative written text. Previously their consent had had to be wooed and qualified by the slow, discreet molding force of appeals to ancient custom. The intuition of Professor Vernant has laid bare the substratum of an agreement to abide by the rules of the city, which lies behind the faith of the early Greek philosophers that men could be expected to abide by the laws of rational discourse.[71] In

p. 63, adds the important consideration that, in a more sophisticated society, where money circulated in greater amounts, theft occurred more frequently and had to be suppressed in a more summary manner: certainly, the crimes tested by ordeal at Varad do seem to reveal a more 'sleepy' economy than that of those areas of Europe where the ordeal came to be abandoned.]

69. L. Moulin, 'Sanior et maior pars', Nouvelle revue historique de droit français et étranger XXXI (1953): 368–94, 490–517.

70. E.g., A. Nitschke, 'Die Einstimmigkeit in den Wahlen im Reiche Ottos des Grossen', Institut für Österreichische Geschichtsforschung, Mitteilungen LXX (1962): 29–59, esp. 39 ff.

71. J.-P. Vernant, Mythe et Pensée chez les Grecs (Paris, 1966), pp. 303–304. [Murray, Reason and Society, pp. 237–44, on the emergence of the antithesis between the rational (that is, the trained) man and the unreasoning rusticus.]

the twelfth century, by contrast, in a society where coercive force had come to bear with greater hope of immediate success than in previous centuries, the shrill note of claims for the authority of reason is no discreet substratum: it sticks out like a crag in every controversy.

The concomitant of these changes in the structure and expectations of twelfth-century society was a dramatic shift in the borderline between the subjective and the objective. Briefly, the supernatural, which had tended to be treated as the main source of the objectified values of the group, came to be regarded as the preserve *par excellence* of the exact opposite; it became the preserve of intensely personal feeling. At the same time purely human actions—reasoning, law, the exploitation of nature—take on an opacity, an impersonal objectivity, and a value of their own which had been lacking in previous centuries. The capacity to juxtapose intensely subjective feeling with a growing respect for the impersonal nature of much of the world and of human relations marks the emotional and intellectual climate of many of the thinkers of the twelfth century. For example, the same age which has been acclaimed for the suddenness of its discovery of the individual also salvaged whole systems of written law from the quicksands of a legal system, which, by contrast to the impersonal maxims of Roman jurisprudence, had been a cat's cradle of human relationships. The same age saw the emergence of significantly new attitudes to the universe. Though very different from any modern view, it was 'modern' in being no longer shot through with human reference. Previously, a thunderstorm had shown either the anger of God or the envy of demons, both directed at human beings. Twelfth-century cosmological speculations gave back to the universe a certain opacity to human states of guilt, of anger, and of exultation: its greatest and most profound achievements were those that rendered to the cosmos a life of its own. For the speculations of the twelfth-century Platonists on issues such as the Soul of the World, reinforced at a slightly later period

325

by the translation of Arabic scientific treatises, pointed the
way to a natural world which no longer was a mirror-image
of the tensions of the human community.[72]

Modification of the role of the supernatural itself might
be suggested as the *leitmotiv* of the new sensibility that developed in the course of the twelfth century. As long as the supernatural was strenuously defined as that which was totally
discontinuous with the human group, the individual could
not but regard it as either irrelevant to most occasions of his
normal existence or as positively crushing. Hence the paradox of the development of Christian society in the West in
the eleventh and twelfth centuries.

From one point of view here we have a society that came
to accept a far more clearly defined hierarchy, explicitly designated in terms of the varying degrees of contact with the
supernatural. The priest was superior to the layman because
he handled the holy and the layman did not. Yet, in order for
this claim to be made with conviction, the holy itself came to
be far more strictly delimited. The cliff face of an ill-defined
notion of the holy is cut down to size, in order to become the
mounting block from which the clerical élite (in theory at
least) climbed into the saddle of western society. A whole
century of sacramental theology and of constant speculation
on the nature of the Eucharist lies behind this development.[73]
The majesty of the sacraments is heightened; but it is a majesty delimited and focused by closer definition of the nature
of sacrament. The same Lateran Council of 1215 that forbade
clerical participation in the ordeal sanctioned the doctrine of
transubstantiation. The two decrees sum up a shift in mentality. Laymen were no longer allowed to expect that the untold majesty of God might any day shine out for their benefit
in a law suit: but if they went to church, the transmutation of

72. Chenu, *La théologie*, pp. 19–51, esp. p. 30: 'la notion de la nature se charge
d'une densité inouïe'. [Radding, 'Superstition to Science', pp. 963–66, sees this
clearly. Compare LeGoff, *Pour un autre Moyen-âge*, p. 305, on the changing role of
the dream in this period: 'surtout se dilate le champ du rêve neutre, du somnium,
plus étroitement lié à la physiologie humaine.']
73. E.g., C. J. de Montclos, *Lanfranc et Bérénger* (Louvain, 1971).

bread and wine into Christ's body was certain to happen. As Braque has said: 'We lower our aims—and call it progress.' For an out-and-out rationalist would find it hard to square accounts of a century acclaimed for its advances in 'rationality' with the miracle literature that sprouted around the doctrine of transubstantiation.[74]

While it may be easier to follow the way in which the public definition of the relation of the sacred to the profane changed, it is difficult to resist the impression that this modification had an important equivalent in changing views of the individual's own capacity for experience. The early medieval definition of the supernatural had hinged on a need to maintain as strict a disjuncture as possible between the *I* and the *not-I*. The sort of ritual behaviour that we have examined throughout this study reflects the extreme difficulty that early medieval men experienced in changing their minds and communicating this fact to their fellows. In every aspect of life, from litigation to penance, the consequences of disruption in the community and of humiliation and of loss of face for the individual were almost too crushing to admit any but the most melodramatic changes of tack. Reparations for wrongs done had to be decently screened behind a supernatural décor.

A character moulded and strengthened by less dramatic but more frequent doses of regret is very much a discovery of the confessional literature of the late eleventh and twelfth centuries.[75] The period dominated by a penitential theory labelled *Contritionism* is a period of experiment on the topic of how much an individual can make good by himself, without constantly looking over his shoulder at a group to placate, whether in a face-to-face ritual of penance or by similar melodramatic acts of reparation to the invisible majesty of the local saint. The development of confessional literature is one of the spearheads of self-awareness in the twelfth century. The intimate shame of self-revelation came to be con-

74. P. Browe, *Die eucharistischen Wunder des Mittelalters* (Breslau, 1938).
75. Payen, *Le motif du repentir*, passim.

sidered expiation enough. The role of shame was all the more relevant to an age whose sense of professional achievement had created a particularly brittle façade of self-regard in knights and clerics alike.[76] One need only think of the lurking horror of hidden illness in so many Romances of the late twelfth century in order to appreciate this.[77] The man who confessed more often to more father-confessors experienced more shame in so doing, and was therefore more certain of expiation.[78] Now it was possible to canalize these bitter feelings of shame into an intimate, non-communal relationship to a father-confessor. In the course of his lifetime a man could live through stages of conflicting emotion without being subject to so drastic a pressure as to opt heavily for the one or the other. A flood of tears in a knight became an incongruity that could be tolerated; it need no longer be a breach with his past behaviour so sharp and so humiliating as to be acted out only in the decent shelter of a monastery, or in regions far removed from the group that knew him.

Regret for sin, of course, was what concerned clerics; but love concerned knights. And love was an equally incongruous mixture of states.[79] For love made brave men tremble; love made them weep like women or like monks. Love led the lover to actions and to states of feeling that bore no obvious relation to his immediate duties to his fellow men. Love took him into a strange country, where relief of obligation and the gaining of a sense of happiness had nothing

76. Wolfgang Hempel, *Übermuot diu alte. Der Superbia-Gedanke und seine Rolle in der deutschen Literatur des Mittelalters* (Bonn, 1970), pp. 104–14, on a growing positive evaluation of pride.

77. See *Mirac. S. Fidis*, III, 7, p. 139, for an earlier example.

78. Vogel, *Le pécheur*, p. 169.

79. L. Pollmann, *Die Liebe in der hochmittelalterlichen Literatur Frankreichs* (Frankfurt, 1966); and H. Heger, *Die Melancholie bei den französischen Lyrikern des Spätmittelalters* (Bonn, 1967), pp. 93–134, on the positive role of melancholy in courtly literature. [I would now be tempted to add the capacity of twelfth-century monastic writers, many of whom came from the knightly class, to think of authority and its exercise in terms that broke with the usual stereotypes of male dominance: C. W. Bynum, 'Jesus as Mother and Abbott as Mother in Twelfth-Century Cistercian Writing', *Harvard Theological Review* LXX (1977): 257–84.]

whatever to do with scrupulous attention to the reciprocities of the life of the group:

> Ses peccat pris penedensa,
> E ses tort fait quir perdo,
> E trais de rien gen do
> E ai d'ira benvolensa.
> E gaug entier de plorar.
> E d'amor doussa sabor.
> E sui arditz per paor
>
> (Piere Vidal. XXVIII)

Twelfth-century poets, as we know, explored the permissible incongruities of love with all the glee of children who have discovered a new toy. Yet sober father-confessors were not above toying with the paradoxes of regret in the same almost euphoric way: Could a man make his act of contrition into the ear of his horse?[80]

Last of all, we come to the hallmark of a sensibility of transcendence as it affected medieval culture. The supernatural itself comes to be defined gradually and tentatively, but with a growing conviction all the more strong for being largely unwitting, as an upward extension of the individual. The supernatural becomes an awareness of the individual's own potentiality, salvaged by being raised above the ambiguities and illusions of the natural world. Angels wither away in the mind and in the art of the twelfth century[81]—ancient symbols of the non-human, they are rapidly replaced by symbols of the idealized human. They are replaced by the figure of the Virgin. In the growth of the legends of the Virgin, for instance, we have entered a world where the individual seeks from the supernatural invisible companionship with all that is most tender, most pure, most unambivalently good in his own imagination. The Virgin, for instance, has no relics. There is nothing as ambivalent about her as dead flesh and bone: what she leaves to men are pure, celestial tokens

---

80. Vogel, *Le pécheur*, pp. 28–31.

81. Chenu, *La théologie*, pp. 52–61; cf. E. Delaruelle, 'La Culture religieuse des laïcs en France', *I laici nella 'societas christiana'*, p. 551.

—drops of her milk, her shawl, memories of her presence. She is owned by no locality. Compared with the Virgin of twelfth-century devotion, a saint like St Foye, with her glittering image placed menacingly on the borders of a disputed plot of land[82] or carried 'at the charge' in order to quell a brawl in the cloister at the monastery at Conques, could not be said to represent so tender a portion of the soul.[83]

St Foye, whose miracles were first written by an outsider from Chartres, then by a local, a monk of Conques, in 1020, has the interest of being a transitional figure. Like Mary, she is a beautiful virgin.[84] The many miracles of deliverance from prison—reminders of the truly Gothic horror of a feudal dungeon—are not so dramatic as those of previous centuries. Chains do not slip from the prisoner 'like broken glass'. She is, rather, a figure of inspiration. She prompts the knight, in dreams, to make use of his purely human ingenuity and luck.[85] She enters into the high adventures of the local aristocracy without melodrama, as a source of good dreams, brainwaves, and a point of reference in moments of good fortune. Yet St Foye remained a concentrate of those unmodified feelings of anger and of vengeance that go with a community's sense of justice. She still had more to do in life than be perfect. She was the heavy voice of the group.[86]

The Virgin, in a rising flood of miracles associated with her from the first decade of the twelfth century, was on the other side of a watershed.[87] She had come to stand for the inner resources of the individual. Occasionally these inner resources are explicitly pitted against the group. Whole cycles of miracles dwell lovingly on the hiatus between outer

82. *Mirac. S. Fidis*, III, 14, p. 153.   83. Ibid., IV, 16, p. 203.
84. Ibid., I, 1, p. 10 and IV, 8, p. 190.   85. E.g., ibid., III, 4, p. 133.
86. E.g., ibid., III, 17, p. 156.

87. I am particularly indebted to 'William of Malmesbury, Miracles of the Virgin Mary', edited and translated by P. N. Carter, Merton College, Oxford, unpublished Oxford Doctoral Thesis, 1959. [See LeGoff, *Pour un autre Moyen-âge*, p. 341, on the relation between 'la foudroyante percée de la Vierge au xiie. siècle' and the greater—albeit temporary—acceptance of anomaly in twelfth-century society.]

appearances and inner dispositions. Society might bury a fornicating monk in unhallowed ground; but a lily growing from the mouth of a corpse showed that, on his way to his *innamorata*, the monk had always said his *Ave Maria*.[88] The miracles of the Virgin are miracles of divine justice suspended and of unmodified human rigour exposed as mistaken. They introduce an air of ambiguity into human affairs, such as the hard certainties of the group had not previously been able to permit. Miracles of justice give way to miracles of inspiration, of individual guidance, visions of sweetness, and snatches of heavenly music: 'Let others think what they like,' wrote William of Malmesbury, 'I would prefer a single vision of her to all the world, or to any miracle whatever.'[89]

The supernatural has become what Renan said it was: 'The way in which the ideal makes its appearance in human affairs.' The definition comes with all the certainty of a post twelfth-century European. It has been the purpose of this paper to show how this sharpening and delimitation of the role of the supernatural took place, and how many of the well-tried devices of living in small groups had to be weakened, overruled, or neglected before so finely whittled a concept could emerge. Increased impersonality and a tendency to delimit what is above man to a fragile extension of his own good intentions are not necessarily the recipe for human happiness. Not everybody wished to move so fast into the modern age. A twelfth-century knight, crippled by a stroke, first thought that it was just his bad luck—not a reassuring thought for one facing the numb horror of partial paralysis. Then he dreamt that he was slapped in the face by the Virgin and reminded that he had poached on the fishing rights of the local monastery. The knight was able to make reparation in the ancient manner, having experienced the Virgin in the ancient manner.[90] Here we have a man who drew back, in dreams at least, from a world where both suffering and guilt—two main

88. 'William of Malmesbury', p. 418.   89. Ibid., p. 348.
90. Guibert of Nogent, III, 18, Migne, *PL*, CLVI, 954A.

331

themes of human history—threatened to break the mercifully precise bounds of a face-to-face world. Perhaps the later history of the Middle Ages and of the Reformation (as seen by some scholars) might provide a sober epilogue entitled 'Risks of Transcendence'; but then, it is in the form set by the twelfth century, if in a very different idiom, that we still run these particular risks.

INDEX

333

Savramis, D., 212n, 275n
Sawyer, P. H., 70n
Saxons, 74, 221, 288, 316
Sayings of the Fathers, 300
Scandinavia, 39–40, 84
Schema, 281, 296n–297n, 300
Schiît, 139
Schimmel, Annemarie, 205n
Schirò, G., 139n
Schmidt, Gustav, 316n
Schulte, F. V., 308n
Schwartz, Eduard, 103n
Schwarzlose, Karl, 253n, 255n
Schweik, 266
Scienza Nuova, 4
Scotland, 29, 219
Ségal, P. A., 321n
Seleucia, 188
Senatorischer Adel in Spätantiken Gallien, 243
Sentences, 303
Sergiopolis, 180
Sergius, 180, 189n, 240n
Severianus of Gabala, 267n
Severinus of Noricum, 132n
Severus of Antioch, 156, 216n
Sexuality, 35
Shakespeare, W., 16n
Shanin, T., 162n
Shapur II, 102n, 276
Sharf, A., 252n, 285n, 290n
Shibree, J., 194n
Shirin, 180
Shirokogoroff, S. M., 124n
Shrines, 6–7, 8, 17–19, 189–190, 223–228, 235–236, 238, 265
Sidonius Apollinaris, 241n
Siggo, 243–244
Sigibert, 239
Simon, M., 152n
Simon the Mountaindweller, 193
Sin, 232–234
Sinai, Mount, 202, 279n
Sinbad the Sailor, 69
Sjusjumov, M. J., 293n
Smalley, Beryl, 218n
Smith, A., 96n
Snyder, J., 202n
Soissons, 316
Soldier and Civilian in the Later Roman Empire, 51
Soldiers, 113–114, 119n, 159, 160, 163, 164

Somerville, R., 257n
Sondeheimer, J., 314n
Sorcery purges, 296
Southern, Richard W., 140n, 152n, 302–309n *passim*, 321n
Sozopolis, 289n
Spain, 45, 84, 164
Speigl, J., 178n
Spinoza, Benedict, 21
Spirit of Eastern Christendom, 207–208, 209–210
Sproemling, H., 71n
Status, social, 187–189, 222–250
Steel, 312n
Steinleitner, F., 107n, 192n
Stenton, Frank, 250
Stenton Lecture, 222
Stephen (St), 238, 283n
Stephen of Blois, 308n
Stephen of Tournai, 308n
Stephen the Younger, 295n, 296n, 298
Stern, S. M., 270n
Stewart, Zeph, 179n, 229n
Strabo, 12
Stranger, holy man as, 130–137, 161
Stratoniceia, 99n
Stremonius tomb, 235n–236n
Stroheker, Karl, 243
Strohmaier, G., 267n
Strube, Christine, 159n
Stuart, John, 214n
Styger, P., 14n
Stylites, 112–148 *passim*, 153, 157, 173, 185, 245, 268, 269
Subjectivity, 321–322, 325
Sufis, 238
Sulpicius Severus, 15, 125n, 137n
Susanna, 186, 245
Symbols of Church and Kingdom, 50, 53–54, 58, 169
Symeon Stylites, 112–136n *passim*, 144, 153, 157, 185, 269
Symeon the Holy Fool, 184
Symeon the Younger, 272
Synesius of Cyrene, 13–14
Syria, 53–54, 69, 75, 77–78, 168, 169, 210, 285; holy men of, 53, 109–137, 139, 146, 148, 153–165, 181, 185, 193, 245; icons in, 276, 282
Szeftel, M., 306n
Szücs, J., 84n

Designer: Sandy Drooker
Compositor: G&S Typesetters
Printer: Vail-Ballou Press
Binder: Vail-Ballou Press
Text: Bembo